LOEB CLASSICAL LIBRARY
FOUNDED BY JAMES LOEB 1911

EDITED BY
JEFFREY HENDERSON

# CICERO
# XXI

LCL 30

# CICERO

## DE OFFICIIS

WITH AN ENGLISH TRANSLATION BY

WALTER MILLER

HARVARD UNIVERSITY PRESS
CAMBRIDGE, MASSACHUSETTS
LONDON, ENGLAND

*First published* 1913



ISBN 978-0-674-99033-3

*Printed on acid-free paper and bound by
The Maple-Vail Book Manufacturing Group*

# CONTENTS

# LIST OF CICERO'S WORKS SHOWING ARRANGEMENT IN THIS EDITION

## RHETORICAL TREATISES. 5 VOLUMES

VOLUME

I. [Cicero], Rhetorica ad Herennium

II. De Inventione. De Optimo Genere Oratorum. Topica

III. De Oratore, Books I–II

IV. De Oratore, Book III. De Fato. Paradoxa Stoicorum. De Partitione Oratoria

V. Brutus. Orator

## ORATIONS. 10 VOLUMES

VI. Pro Quinctio. Pro Roscio Amerino. Pro Roscio Comoedo. De Lege Agraria Contra Rullum

VII. The Verrine Orations I: In Q. Caecilium. In C. Verrem Actio I. In C. Verrem Actio II, Books I–II

VIII. The Verrine Orations II: In C. Verrem Actio II, Books III–V

PHILOSOPHICAL TREATISES. 6 VOLUMES

LIST OF CICERO'S WORKS

LETTERS. 8 VOLUMES

XXII. Letters to Atticus, Letters 1–89

XXIII. Letters to Atticus, Letters 90–165A

XXIV. Letters to Atticus, Letters 166–281

XXIX. Letters to Atticus, Letters 282–426

XXV. Letters to Friends, Letters 1–113

XXVI. Letters to Friends, Letters 114–280

XXVII. Letters to Friends, Letters 281–435

XXVIII. Letters to Quintus and Brutus. Letter Fragments. Letter to Octavian. Invectives. Handbook of Electioneering

# INTRODUCTION

In the *de Officiis* we have, save for the latter Philippics, the great orator's last contribution to literature. The last, sad, troubled years of his busy life could not be given to his profession; and he turned his never-resting thoughts to the second love of his student days and made Greek philosophy a possibility for Roman readers. The senate had been abolished; the courts had been closed. His occupation was gone; but Cicero could not surrender himself to idleness. In those days of distraction (46–43 B.C.) he produced for publication almost as much as in all his years of active life.

The liberators had been able to remove the tyrant, but they could not restore the republic. Cicero's own life was in danger from the fury of mad Antony and he left Rome about the end of March, 44 B.C. He dared not even stop permanently in any one of his various country estates, but, wretched, wandered from one of his villas to another nearly all the summer and autumn through. He would not suffer himself to become a prey to his overwhelming sorrow at the death of the republic and the final crushing of the hopes that had risen with Caesar's downfall, but worked at the highest tension on his philosophical studies.

The Romans were not philosophical. In 161 B.C. the senate passed a decree excluding all philosophers

and teachers of rhetoric from the city. They had no taste for philosophical speculation, in which the Greeks were the world's masters. They were intensely, narrowly practical. And Cicero was thoroughly Roman. As a student in a Greek university he had had to study philosophy. His mind was broad enough and his soul great enough to give him a joy in following after the mighty masters, Socrates, Plato, Zeno, Cleanthes, Aristotle, Theophrastus, and the rest. But he pursued his study of it, like a Roman, from a "practical" motive—to promote thereby his power as an orator and to augment his success and happiness in life. To him the goal of philosophy was not primarily to know but to do. Its end was to point out the course of conduct that would lead to success and happiness. The only side of philosophy, therefore, that could make much appeal to the Roman mind was ethics; pure science could have little meaning for the practical Roman; metaphysics might supplement ethics and religion, without which true happiness was felt to be impossible.

Philosophical study had its place, therefore, and the most important department of philosophy was ethics. The treatise on Moral Duties has the very practical purpose of giving a practical discussion of the basic principles of Moral Duty and practical rules for personal conduct.

As a philosopher, if we may so stretch the term as to include him, Cicero avows himself an adherent of the New Academy and a disciple of Carneades. He had tried Epicureanism under Phaedrus and Zeno, Stoicism under Diodotus and Posidonius; but Philo of Larissa converted him to the New Academy.

Scepticism declared the attainment of absolute

knowledge impossible. But there is the easily obtainable golden mean of the probable; and that appealed to the practical Roman. It appealed especially to Cicero; and the same indecision that had been his bane in political life naturally led him first to scepticism, then to eclecticism, where his choice is dictated by his bias for the practical and his scepticism itself disappears from view. And while Antiochus, the eclectic Academician of Athens, and Posidonius, the eclectic Stoic of Rhodes, seem to have had the strongest influence upon him, he draws at his own discretion from the founts of Stoics, Peripatetics, and Academicians alike; he has only contempt for the Epicureans, Cynics, and Cyrenaics. But the more he studied and lived, the more of a Stoic in ethics he became.

The cap-sheaf of Cicero's ethical studies is the treatise on the Moral Duties. It takes the form of a letter addressed to his son Marcus (see Index), at this time a youth of twenty-one, pursuing his university studies in the Peripatetic school of Cratippus in Athens, and sowing for what promised to be an abundant crop of wild oats. This situation gives force and definiteness to the practical tendencies of the father's ethical teachings. And yet, be it observed, that same father is not without censure for contributing to his son's extravagant and riotous living by giving him an allowance of nearly £870 a year.

Our Roman makes no pretensions to originality in philosophic thinking. He is a follower—an expositor—of the Greeks. As the basis of his discussion of the Moral Duties he takes the Stoic Panaetius of Rhodes (see Index), Περὶ Καθήκοντος, drawing also

from many other sources, but following him more or less closely in Books I and II; Book III is more independent and much inferior. He is usually superficial and not always clear. He translates and paraphrases Greek philosophy, weaving in illustrations from Roman history and suggestions of Roman mould in a form intended to make it, if not popular, at least comprehensible, to the Roman mind. How well he succeeded is evidenced by the comparative receptivity of Roman soil prepared by Stoic doctrine for the teachings of Christianity. Indeed, Anthony Trollope labels our author the "Pagan Christian." "You would fancy sometimes," says Petrarch, "it is not a Pagan philosopher but a Christian apostle who is speaking." No less an authority than Frederick the Great has called our book "the best work on morals that has been or can be written." Cicero himself looked upon it as his masterpiece.

It has its strength and its weakness—its sane common sense and noble patriotism, its self-conceit and partisan politics; it has the master's brilliant style, but it is full of repetitions and rhetorical flourishes, and it fails often in logical order and power; it rings true in its moral tone, but it shows in what haste and distraction it was composed; for it was not written as a contribution to close scientific thinking; it was written as a means of occupation and diversion.

# BIBLIOGRAPHY

The following works are quoted in the critical notes:—

*MSS.* A = *codex Ambrosianus*. Milan. 10th century.
B = *codex Bambergensis*. Hamburg. 10th century.
H = *codex Herbipolitanus*. Würzburg. 10th century.
L = *codex Harleianus*. London. 9th century.
a b = *codices Bernenses*. Bern. 10th century.
c = *codex Bernensis*. Bern. 13th century.
p = *codex Palatinus*. Rome. 12th century.

*Editio Princeps*: The first edition of the *de Officiis* was from the press of Sweynheim and Pannartz at the Monastery of Subiaco; possibly the edition published by Fust and Schöffer at Mainz is a little older. Both appeared in 1465. The latter was the first to print the Greek words in Greek type. The *de Officiis* is, therefore, the first classical book to be issued from a printing press, with the possible exception of Lactantius and Cicero's *de Oratore* which bear the more exact date of October 30, 1465, and were likewise issued from the Monastery press at Subiaco.

*Baiter & Kayser*: M. Tullii Ciceronis opera quae supersunt omnia. Lipsiae, 1860–69.

# BIBLIOGRAPHY

*Beier*: M. Tullii Ciceronis de Officiis libri tres . . . cum commentariis editi a Carolo Beiero. Lipsiae, 1820.

*Erasmus*: *Melanchthon*: M. Tullii Ciceronis Officia, diligenter restituta. Ejusdem de Amicitia et Senectute dialogi . . .: cum annotationibus Erasmi et P. Melanchthonis. Parisiis, 1533.

*Ed.*: M. Tullii Ciceronis Scripta quae manserunt omnia recognovit C. F. W. Müller. Teubner: Lipsiae, 1879. This edition is the basis of the text of the present volume.

*Ernesti*: M. Tullii Ciceronis opera ex recensione novissima. J. A. Ernesti; cum eiusdem notis, et clave Ciceroniana. Editio prima Americana. Bostoniae, 1815–16.

*Facciolati*: M. Tullii Ciceronis de Officiis libri tres, de Senectute, de Amicitia, de Somnio Scipionis, et Paradoxa. Accedit Q. fratris commentariolum petitionis. Ex recensione J. Facciolati. Venetiis, 1747.

*Fleckeisen, Alf.*: Kritische Miscellen. Dresden, 1864.

*Gernhard*: M. Tullii Ciceronis de Officiis libri tres. Rec. et scholiis Iac. Facciolati suisque animadversionibus instruxit Aug. G. Gernhard. Lipsiae, 1811.

*Graevius*: M. Tullii Ciceronis de Officiis libri tres; . . . de Senectute; . . . de Amicitia; Paradoxa; Somnium Scipionis; ex recensione J. G. Graevii. Amstelodami, 1689.

*Gulielmus*: *Gruter*: M. Tullii Ciceronis opera omnia quae extant . . . emendata studio . . . J. Gulielmi et J. Gruteri. Hamburgi, 1618–19.

*Heine, Otto*: M. Tullii Ciceronis de Officiis ad

Marcum Filium Libri tres. 6te Aufl. Berlin, 1885.

*Heusinger:* M. Tullii Ciceronis de Officiis libri tres . . . recensuit adjectisque J. M. Heusingeri et suis annotationibus . . . editurus erat J. F. Heusinger. (Edited by C. Heusinger.) Brunsvigae, 1783.

*Holden:* M. Tullii Ciceronis de Officiis libri tres, with Introduction, Analysis and Commentary by Herbert Ashton Holden. 7th Edition. Cambridge, 1891. To his full notes the translator is indebted for many a word and phrase.

*Klotz:* M. Tullii Ciceronis Scripta quae manserunt omnia. Recognovit Reinholdus Klotz. Lipsiae, 1850–57, 1869–74.

*Lambinus:* M. Tullii Ciceronis opera omnia quae extant, a D. Lambino . . . ex codicibus manuscriptis emendata et aucta . . . Lutetiae, 1566–84.

*Lange:* M. Tullii Ciceronis de Officiis lib. III. Cato Major vel de Senectute . . . Laelius vel de Amicitia . . . Paradoxa Stoicorum sex, Somnium Scipionis . . . opera C. Langii recogniti . . . ejusdem in hosce . . . libros annotationes. Cum annotationibus P. Manutii, etc. Antverpiae, 1568.

*Lund:* De emendandis Ciceronis libris de Officiis observationes criticae. Scripsit G. F. G. Lund. Kopenhagen, 1848.

*Manutius:* M. Tullii Ciceronis Officiorum libri tres: Cato Maior, vel de Senectute: Laelius, vel de Amicitia: Paradoxa Stoicorum sex . . . additae sunt . . . variae lectiones. (Edited by P. Manuzio.) P. Manutius; Venetiis, 1541.

*Müller, C. F. W.:* M. Tullii Ciceronis de Officiis libri III. Für den Schulgebrauch erklärt. Leipzig, 1882.

*Muretus :* M. Antoni Mureti Scholia in Cic. officia. Mureti opera ed. Ruhnken. Lugd. Bat., 1879.

*Orelli :* / *Baiter :* / *Halm :* M. Tullii Ciceronis opera quae supersunt omnia, ac deperditorum fragmenta . . . Edidit J. C. Orellius (M. Tullii Ciceronis Scholiastae. C. M. Victorinus, Rufinus, C. Julius Victor, Boethius, Favonius Eulogius, Asconius Pedianus, Scholia Bobiensia, Scholiasta Gronovianus, Ediderunt J. C. Orellius et J. G Baiter. Turici, 1826–38). Ed. 2. Opus morte Orellii interruptum contin. J. G. Baiterus et C. Halmius, 1845–62.

*Pearce :* M. Ciceronis de Officiis ad Marcum filium libri tres. Notis illustravit et . . . emendavit Z. Pearce. Londini, 1745.

*Stuerenburg :* M. Tullii Ciceronis de Officiis libri III. Recensuit R. Stuerenburg. Accedit Commentarius. Lipsiae, 1843.

*Unger :* M. Tullii Ciceronis de Officiis libri III. Erklärt v. G. F Unger. Leipzig, 1852.

*Victorius, P.* · M. Tullii Ciceronis opera, omnium quae hactenus excusa sunt castigatissima, nunc primum in lucem edita. 4 tom. Venetiis, 1532–34–36.

*Zumpt :* M. Tullii Ciceronis de Officiis libri tres cum selectis J. M. et J. F. Heusingerorum suisque notis. Scholarum in usum iterum edidit Car. Tim. Zumptius. Brunsvigae, 1849.

# BIBLIOGRAPHICAL ADDENDUM


## Editions

C. Atzert (*Teubner*), Leipzig 1963
M. Testard (*Budé*, Paris), 2 vols: I (Book 1), 1965; II (Books 2, 3), 1970
M. Winterbottom (*Oxford Classical Texts*), Oxford 1994

## Translation

John Higginbotham, *Cicero on Moral Obligation* (intr., trans., notes), Berkeley and Los Angeles 1967

## Study

H. A. K. Hunt, *The Humanism of Cicero*, Melbourne 1954

## Surveys

A. E. Douglas (*Greece & Rome Surveys* No. 2), *Cicero*, Oxford 1968
S. E. Smethurst (*Cicero: Philosophical Works*), *CW* 51 (1957) 1–4, 32–41; 58 (1964–5) 36–44; 61 (1967) 125–33


G. P. G.

# CICERO DE OFFICIIS

## BOOK I

### MORAL GOODNESS

# LIBER PRIMUS

1 I. Quamquam te, Marce fili, annum iam audientem Cratippum, idque Athenis, abundare oportet praeceptis institutisque philosophiae propter summam et doctoris auctoritatem et urbis, quorum alter te scientia augere potest, altera exemplis, tamen, ut ipse ad meam utilitatem semper cum Graecis Latina coniunxi neque id in philosophia solum, sed etiam in dicendi exercitatione feci, idem tibi censeo faciendum, ut par sis in utriusque orationis facultate. Quam quidem ad rem nos, ut videmur, magnum attulimus adiumentum hominibus nostris, ut non modo Graecarum litterarum rudes, sed etiam docti aliquantum se arbitrentur adeptos et ad dicendum [1] et ad iudicandum.

2 Quam ob rem disces tu quidem a principe huius aetatis philosophorum, et disces, quam diu voles ; tam diu autem velle debebis, quoad te, quantum proficias, non paenitebit ; sed tamen nostra legens non multum a Peripateticis dissidentia, quoniam utrique Socratici et Platonici volumus esse, de rebus ipsis utere tuo iudicio (nihil enim impedio), orationem autem Lati-

[1] *dicendum* Edd.; *discendum* MSS. (i.e. acquisition of learning).

# BOOK I

1 I. My dear son Marcus, you have now been studying a full year under Cratippus, and that too in Athens, and you should be fully equipped with the practical precepts and the principles of philosophy; so much at least one might expect from the pre-eminence not only of your teacher but also of the city; the former is able to enrich you with learning, the latter to supply you with models. Nevertheless, just as I for my own improvement have always combined Greek and Latin studies—and I have done this not only in the study of philosophy but also in the practice of oratory—so I recommend that you should do the same, so that you may have equal command of both languages. And it is in this very direction that I have, if I mistake not, rendered a great service to our countrymen, so that not only those who are unacquainted with Greek literature but even the cultured consider that they have gained much both in oratorical power and in mental training.

Introduction: the importance of combining Greek and Latin studies.

2 You will, therefore, learn from the foremost of present-day philosophers, and you will go on learning as long as you wish; and your wish ought to continue as long as you are not dissatisfied with the progress you are making. For all that, if you will read my philosophical books, you will be helped; my philosophy is not very different from that of the Peripatetics (for both they and I claim to be followers of Socrates and Plato). As to the conclusions you may reach, I leave that to your own judgment (for I would put no hindrance in your way), but by reading my philosophical

Greek Philosophy and Cicero's own.

nam efficies profecto legendis nostris pleniorem. Nec vero hoc arroganter dictum existimari velim. Nam philosophandi scientiam concedens multis, quod est oratoris proprium, apte, distincte, ornate dicere, quoniam in eo studio aetatem consumpsi, si id mihi assumo, videor id meo iure quodam modo vindicare.

3 Quam ob rem magnopere te hortor, mi Cicero, ut non solum orationes meas, sed hos etiam de philosophia libros, qui iam illis fere se [1] aequarunt, studiose legas; vis enim maior in illis dicendi, sed hoc quoque colendum est aequabile et temperatum orationis genus. Et id quidem nemini video Graecorum adhuc contigisse, ut idem utroque in genere elaboraret [2] sequereturque et illud forense dicendi et hoc quietum disputandi genus, nisi forte Demetrius Phalereus in hoc numero haberi potest, disputator subtilis, orator parum vehemens, dulcis tamen, ut Theophrasti discipulum possis agnoscere. Nos autem quantum in utroque profecerimus, aliorum sit iudicium, utrumque certe secuti sumus.

4 Equidem et Platonem existimo, si genus forense dicendi tractare voluisset, gravissime et copiosissime potuisse dicere, et Demosthenem, si illa, quae a Platone didicerat, tenuisset et pronuntiare voluisset, ornate splendideque facere potuisse; eodemque modo de Aristotele et Isocrate iudico, quorum uterque suo studio delectatus contempsit alterum.

[1] *se* A c, Edd.; not in B H a b p.
[2] *elaboraret* Lambin., Edd.; *laboraret* MSS.

---

[a] Cicero is alluding to his Republic, Tusculan Disputations, Theories of the Supreme Good and Evil, The Nature of the Gods, Academics, Hortensius, his essays on Friendship (Laelius), Old Age (Cato), Fate, Divination, etc. (15 in all).

writings you will be sure to render your mastery of the Latin language more complete. But I would by no means have you think that this is said boastfully. For there are many to whom I yield precedence in knowledge of philosophy; but if I lay claim to the orator's peculiar ability to speak with propriety, clearness, elegance, I think my claim is in a measure justified, for I have spent my life in that profession.

**Philosophy and oratory.**

3 And therefore, my dear Cicero, I cordially recommend you to read carefully not only my orations but also these[a] books of mine on philosophy, which are now about as extensive. For while the orations exhibit a more vigorous style, yet the unimpassioned, restrained style of my philosophical productions is also worth cultivating. Moreover, for the same man to succeed in both departments, both in the forensic style and in that of calm philosophic discussion has not, I observe, been the good fortune of any one of the Greeks so far, unless, perhaps, Demetrius of Phalerum can be reckoned in that number—a clever reasoner, indeed, and, though rather a spiritless orator, he is yet charming, so that you can recognize in him the disciple of Theophrastus. But let others judge how much I have accomplished in each pursuit; I have at least attempted both.

4 I believe, of course, that if Plato had been willing to devote himself to forensic oratory, he could have spoken with the greatest eloquence and power; and that if Demosthenes had continued the studies he pursued with Plato and had wished to expound his views, he could have done so with elegance and brilliancy. I feel the same way about Aristotle and Isocrates, each of whom, engrossed in his own profession, undervalued that of the other.

II. Sed cum statuissem scribere ad te aliquid hoc tempore, multa posthac, ab eo ordiri maxime volui, quod et aetati tuae esset aptissimum et auctoritati meae. Nam cum multa sint in philosophia et gravia et utilia accurate copioseque a philosophis disputata, latissime patere videntur ea, quae de officiis tradita ab illis et praecepta sunt. Nulla enim vitae pars neque publicis neque privatis neque forensibus neque domesticis in rebus, neque si tecum agas quid, neque si cum altero contrahas, vacare officio potest, in eoque et colendo sita vitae est honestas omnis et neglegendo[1] turpitudo.

5 Atque haec quidem quaestio communis est omnium philosophorum; quis est enim, qui nullis officii praeceptis tradendis philosophum se audeat dicere? Sed sunt non nullae disciplinae, quae propositis bonorum et malorum finibus officium omne pervertant. Nam qui summum bonum sic instituit, ut nihil habeat cum virtute coniunctum, idque suis commodis, non honestate metitur, hic, si sibi ipse consentiat et non interdum naturae bonitate vincatur neque amicitiam colere possit nec iustitiam nec liberalitatem; fortis vero dolorem summum malum iudicans aut temperans voluptatem summum bonum statuens esse certe nullo modo potest.

6 Quae quamquam ita sunt in promptu, ut res disputatione non egeat, tamen sunt a nobis alio loco disputata. Hae disciplinae igitur si sibi consentaneae

de Fin. II, 12 ff.; Tusc. Disp. IV-V; de Off. III, 117

[1] *et neglegendo* A H a b, Edd.; *et in neglegendo* B c.

**Statement of subject.**

II. But since I have decided to write you a little now (and a great deal by and by), I wish, if possible, to begin with a matter most suited at once to your years and to my position. Although philosophy offers many problems, both important and useful, that have been fully and carefully discussed by philosophers, those teachings which have been handed down on the subject of moral duties seem to have the widest practical application. For no phase of life, whether public or private, whether in business or in the home, whether one is working on what concerns oneself alone or dealing with another, can be without its moral duty; on the discharge of such duties depends all that is morally right, and on their neglect all that is morally wrong in life.

**The philosophic schools and ethical teaching.**

5 Moreover, the subject of this inquiry is the common property of all philosophers; for who would presume to call himself a philosopher, if he did not inculcate any lessons of duty? But there are some schools that distort all notions of duty by the theories they propose touching the supreme good and the supreme evil. For he who posits the supreme good as having no connection with virtue and measures it not by a moral standard but by his own interests—if he should be consistent and not rather at times over-ruled by his better nature, he could value neither friendship nor justice nor generosity; and brave he surely cannot possibly be that counts pain the supreme evil, nor temperate he that holds pleasure to be the supreme good.

**Reasons for choice of subject and authorities.**

6 Although these truths are so self-evident that the subject does not call for discussion, still I have discussed it in another connection. If, therefore, these

velint esse, de officio nihil queant dicere, neque ulla officii praecepta firma, stabilia, coniuncta naturae tradi possunt nisi aut ab iis, qui solam, aut ab iis, qui maxime honestatem propter se dicant expetendam. Ita propria est ea praeceptio Stoicorum, Academicorum, Peripateticorum, quoniam Aristonis, Pyrrhonis, Erilli iam pridem explosa sententia est; qui tamen haberent ius suum disputandi de officio, si rerum aliquem dilectum [1] reliquissent, ut ad officii inventionem aditus esset. Sequemur [2] igitur hoc quidem tempore et hac in quaestione potissimum Stoicos non ut interpretes, sed, ut solemus, e fontibus eorum iudicio arbitrioque nostro, quantum quoque modo videbitur, hauriemus.

7 Placet igitur, quoniam omnis disputatio de officio futura est, ante definire, quid sit officium; quod a Panaetio praetermissum esse miror. Omnis enim, quae [a] ratione [3] suscipitur de aliqua re institutio, debet a definitione proficisci, ut intellegatur, quid sit id, de quo disputetur. . . .[4]

III. Omnis de officio duplex est quaestio: unum genus est, quod pertinet ad finem bonorum, alterum, quod positum est in praeceptis, quibus in omnis partis usus vitae conformari [5] possit. Superioris generis huius modi sunt exempla: omniane officia perfecta sint, num quod officium aliud alio maius sit, et quae sunt generis eiusdem. Quorum autem officiorum praecepta traduntur, ea quamquam pertinent ad finem bonorum, tamen minus id apparet, quia magis ad institutionem vitae communis spectare videntur;

[1] *dilectum* B H a b, Edd.; *delectum* A c.
[2] *sequemur* Graevius, Edd.; *sequimur* MSS.
[3] [*a*] *ratione* Ed.; *a ratione* MSS.; *ratione* Müller.
[4] Cicero's definition must have followed here, something like *Omne igitur, quod ratione actum est officium appellamus* Unger. [5] *conformari* Edd.; *confirmari* MSS. (i.e. fortified).

schools should claim to be consistent, they could not say anything about duty; and no fixed, invariable, natural rules of duty can be posited except by those who say that moral goodness is worth seeking solely or chiefly for its own sake. Accordingly, the teaching of ethics is the peculiar right of the Stoics, the Academicians, and the Peripatetics; for the theories of Aristo, Pyrrho, and Erillus have been long since rejected; and yet they would have the right to discuss duty if they had left us any power of choosing between things, so that there might be a way of finding out what duty is. I shall, therefore, at this time and in this investigation follow chiefly the Stoics, not as a translator, but, as is my custom, I shall at my own option and discretion draw from those sources in such measure and in such manner as shall suit my purpose.

7 Since, therefore, the whole discussion is to be on the subject of duty, I should like at the outset to define what duty is, as, to my surprise, Panaetius has failed to do. For every systematic development of any subject ought to begin with a definition, so that everyone may understand what the discussion is about.

III. Every treatise on duty has two parts: one, dealing with the doctrine of the supreme good; the other, with the practical rules by which daily life in all its bearings may be regulated. The following questions are illustrative of the first part: whether all duties are absolute; whether one duty is more important than another; and so on. But as regards special duties for which positive rules are laid down, though they are affected by the doctrine of the supreme good, still the fact is not so obvious, because they seem rather to look to the regulation of every-

**Classification of duties.**

de quibus est nobis his libris explicandum. Atque etiam alia divisio est officii.

8 Nam et medium quoddam officium dicitur et perfectum. Perfectum officium rectum, opinor, vocemus, quoniam Graeci κατόρθωμα, hoc autem commune officium καθῆκον vocant.[1] Atque ea sic definiunt, ut, rectum quod sit, id officium perfectum esse definiant; medium autem officium id esse dicunt, quod cur factum sit, ratio probabilis reddi possit.

9 Triplex igitur est, ut Panaetio videtur, consilii capiendi deliberatio. Nam aut honestumne factu sit an turpe dubitant id, quod in deliberationem cadit; in quo considerando saepe animi in contrarias sententias distrahuntur. Tum autem aut anquirunt[2] aut consultant, ad vitae commoditatem iucunditatemque, ad facultates rerum atque copias, ad opes, ad potentiam, quibus et se possint iuvare et suos, conducat id necne, de quo deliberant; quae deliberatio omnis in rationem utilitatis cadit. Tertium dubitandi genus est, cum pugnare videtur cum honesto id, quod videtur esse utile; cum enim utilitas ad se rapere, honestas contra revocare ad se videtur, fit ut distrahatur in deliberando animus afferatque ancipitem curam cogitandi.

10 Hac divisione, cum praeterire aliquid maximum vitium in dividendo sit, duo praetermissa sunt; nec

[1] *officium καθῆκον vocant* Pearce, Ed., Heine; *officium vocant* MSS., Bt. [2] *anquirunt* A B H b; *inquirunt* a c.

---

[a] Cicero's technical terms are difficult because he has to invent them to translate Greek that is perfectly simple:

*rectum* is 'right,' i.e. perfect, absolute. Its opposite is *medium*, 'mean,' i.e. intermediate, falling short of the 'absolute' and occupying a middle ground; common; ordinary.

*honestum* is 'morally right'; as a noun, 'moral goodness' (= *honestas*); its opposite is *turpe*, 'morally wrong.'

*honestas* is 'moral rectitude,'—'moral goodness'; 'morality'; its opposite *turpitudo*, 'moral wrong,' 'immorality.'

day life; and it is these special duties that I propose to treat at length in the following books.

8 And yet there is still another classification of duties: we distinguish between "mean"[a] duty, so-called, and "absolute" duty. Absolute duty we may, I presume, call "right," for the Greeks call it κατόρθωμα, while the ordinary duty they call καθῆκον. And the meaning of those terms they fix thus: whatever is right they define as "absolute" duty, but "mean" duty, they say, is duty for the performance of which an adequate reason may be rendered.

9 The consideration necessary to determine conduct is, therefore, as Panaetius thinks, a threefold one: first, people question whether the contemplated act is morally right or morally wrong; and in such deliberation their minds are often led to widely divergent conclusions. And then they examine and consider the question whether the action contemplated is or is not conducive to comfort and happiness in life, to the command of means and wealth, to influence, and to power, by which they may be able to help themselves and their friends; this whole matter turns upon a question of expediency. The third type of question arises when that which seems to be expedient seems to conflict with that which is morally right; for when expediency seems to be pulling one way, while moral right seems to be calling back in the opposite direction, the result is that the mind is distracted in its inquiry and brings to it the irresolution that is born of deliberation.

**The threefold classification of Panaetius.**

10 Although omission is a most serious defect in classification, two points have been overlooked in

**The question is fivefold.**

*honestus*, on the other hand, is always 'honourable'; and *honores* are always 'offices of honour.'

enim solum utrum honestum an turpe sit, deliberari solet, sed etiam duobus propositis honestis utrum honestius, itemque duobus propositis utilibus utrum utilius. Ita, quam ille triplicem putavit esse rationem, in quinque partes distribui debere reperitur. Primum igitur est de honesto, sed dupliciter, tum pari ratione de utili, post de comparatione eorum disserendum.

11 IV. Principio generi animantium omni est a natura tributum, ut se, vitam corpusque tueatur, declinet ea, quae nocitura videantur, omniaque, quae sint ad vivendum necessaria, anquirat et paret, ut pastum, ut latibula, ut alia generis eiusdem. Commune item [1] animantium omnium est coniunctionis adpetitus procreandi causa et cura quaedam eorum, quae procreata sint; [2] sed inter hominem et beluam hoc maxime interest, quod haec tantum, quantum sensu movetur, ad id solum, quod adest quodque praesens est, se accommodat paulum admodum sentiens praeteritum aut futurum; homo autem, quod rationis est particeps, per quam consequentia cernit, causas rerum videt earumque praegressus [3] et quasi antecessiones non ignorat, similitudines comparat rebusque praesentibus adiungit atque annectit futuras, facile totius vitae cursum videt ad eamque degendam praeparat res necessarias.

12 Eademque natura vi rationis hominem conciliat homini et ad orationis et ad vitae societatem inge-

[1] *item* Manutius, Edd.; *autem* MSS.
[2] *procreata sint* B H a b; *procreata sunt* A (?), Bt.; *procreantur* c. [3] *praegressus* A H a b, Edd.; *progressus* B c.

---

[a] For Panaetius was a Stoic, and the Stoics did not admit that there were any degrees of right or wrong.

the foregoing:[a] for we usually consider not only whether an action is morally right or morally wrong, but also, when a choice of two morally right courses is offered, which one is morally better; and likewise, when a choice of two expedients is offered, which one is more expedient. Thus the question which Panaetius thought threefold ought, we find, to be divided into five parts. First, therefore, we must discuss the moral—and that, under two sub-heads; secondly, in the same manner, the expedient; and finally, the cases where they must be weighed against each other.

11 IV. First of all, Nature has endowed every species of living creature with the instinct of self-preservation, of avoiding what seems likely to cause injury to life or limb, and of procuring and providing everything needful for life—food, shelter, and the like. A common property of all creatures is also the reproductive instinct (the purpose of which is the propagation of the species) and also a certain amount of concern for their offspring. But the most marked difference between man and beast is this: the beast, just as far as it is moved by the senses and with very little perception of past or future, adapts itself to that alone which is present at the moment; while man—because he is endowed with reason, by which he comprehends the chain of consequences, perceives the causes of things, understands the relation of cause to effect and of effect to cause, draws analogies, and connects and associates the present and the future—easily surveys the course of his whole life and makes the necessary preparations for its conduct.

**The essential differences between man and the lower animals.**

**Instinct and Reason.**

12 Nature likewise by the power of reason associates man with man in the common bonds of speech and life; she implants in him above all, I may say, a

**Family ties.**

neratque in primis praecipuum quendam amorem in eos, qui procreati sunt, impellitque, ut hominum coetus et celebrationes et esse et a se obiri velit ob easque causas studeat parare ea, quae suppeditent ad cultum et ad victum, nec sibi soli, sed coniugi, liberis ceterisque, quos caros habeat tuerique debeat; quae cura exsuscitat etiam animos et maiores ad rem gerendam facit.

13 In primisque hominis est propria veri inquisitio atque investigatio. Itaque cum sumus necessariis negotiis curisque vacui, tum avemus aliquid videre, audire, addiscere cognitionemque rerum aut occultarum aut admirabilium ad beate vivendum necessariam ducimus. Ex quo intellegitur, quod verum, simplex sincerumque sit, id esse naturae hominis aptissimum. Huic veri videndi cupiditati adiuncta est appetitio quaedam principatus, ut nemini parere animus bene informatus a natura velit nisi praecipienti aut docenti aut utilitatis causa iuste et legitime imperanti; ex quo magnitudo animi exsistit humanarumque rerum contemptio.

14 Nec vero illa parva vis naturae est rationisque, quod unum hoc animal sentit, quid sit ordo, quid sit, quod deceat, in factis dictisque qui modus. Itaque eorum ipsorum, quae aspectu sentiuntur, nullum aliud animal pulchritudinem, venustatem, convenientiam partium sentit; quam similitudinem natura ratioque ab oculis ad animum transferens

strangely tender love for his offspring. She also prompts men to meet in companies, to form public assemblies and to take part in them themselves; and she further dictates, as a consequence of this, the effort on man's part to provide a store of things that minister to his comforts and wants—and not for himself alone, but for his wife and children and the others whom he holds dear and for whom he ought to provide; and this responsibility also stimulates his courage and makes it stronger for the active duties of life.

13 Above all, the search after truth and its eager pursuit are peculiar to man. And so, when we have leisure from the demands of business cares, we are eager to see, to hear, to learn something new, and we esteem a desire to know the secrets or wonders of creation as indispensable to a happy life. Thus we come to understand that what is true, simple, and genuine appeals most strongly to a man's nature. To this passion for discovering truth there is added a hungering, as it were, for independence, so that a mind well-moulded by Nature is unwilling to be subject to anybody save one who gives rules of conduct or is a teacher of truth or who, for the general good, rules according to justice and law. From this attitude come greatness of soul and a sense of superiority to worldly conditions. Search after truth.

14 And it is no mean manifestation of Nature and Reason that man is the only animal that has a feeling for order, for propriety, for moderation in word and deed. And so no other animal has a sense of beauty, loveliness, harmony in the visible world; and Nature and Reason, extending the analogy of this from the world of sense to the world of spirit, find that Moral sensibility.

multo etiam magis pulchritudinem, constantiam, ordinem in consiliis factisque conservandam [1] putat cavetque, ne quid indecore effeminateve faciat, tum in omnibus et opinionibus et factis ne quid libidinose aut faciat aut cogitet.

Quibus ex rebus conflatur et efficitur id, quod quaerimus, honestum, quod etiamsi nobilitatum non sit, tamen honestum sit, quodque vere dicimus, etiamsi a nullo laudetur, natura esse laudabile.

15 V. Formam quidem ipsam, Marce fili, et tamquam faciem honesti vides,
Phaedr., 250 D mirabiles amores," ut ait Plato, "excitaret sapientiae." Sed omne, quod est honestum, id quattuor partium oritur ex aliqua: aut enim in perspicientia veri sollertiaque versatur aut in hominum societate tuenda tribuendoque suum cuique et rerum contractarum fide aut in animi excelsi atque invicti magnitudine ac robore aut in omnium, quae fiunt quaeque dicuntur, ordine et modo, in quo inest modestia et temperantia.

(15) Quae quattuor quamquam inter se colligata atque implicata sunt, tamen ex singulis certa officiorum genera nascuntur, velut ex ea parte, quae prima discripta [2] est, in qua sapientiam et prudentiam ponimus, inest indagatio atque inventio veri, eiusque
16 virtutis hoc munus est proprium. Ut enim quisque maxime perspicit, quid in re quaque verissimum sit,

[1] *conservandam* MSS.; *conservanda* codd. aliquot recentiores, Bt.

[2] *discripta* Heine; *descripta* MSS., Bt.

[a] Cicero plays on the double meaning of *honestum*: (1) 'moral goodness,' and (2) 'honourable,' 'distinguished,' etc.

beauty, consistency, order are far more to be maintained in thought and deed, and the same Nature and Reason are careful to do nothing in an improper or unmanly fashion, and in every thought and deed to do or think nothing capriciously.

It is from these elements that is forged and fashioned that moral goodness which is the subject of this inquiry—something that, even though it be not generally ennobled, is still worthy of all honour;[a] and by its own nature, we correctly maintain, it merits praise, even though it be praised by none.

15 V. You see here, Marcus, my son, the very form and as it were the face of Moral Goodness; "and if," as Plato says, "it could be seen with the physical eye, it would awaken a marvellous love of wisdom." But all that is morally right rises from some one of four sources: it is concerned either (1) with the full perception and intelligent development of the true; or (2) with the conservation of organized society, with rendering to every man his due, and with the faithful discharge of obligations assumed; or (3) with the greatness and strength of a noble and invincible spirit; or (4) with the orderliness and moderation of everything that is said and done, wherein consist temperance and self-control.

The four Cardinal Virtues.

(15) Although these four are connected and interwoven, still it is in each one considered singly that certain definite kinds of moral duties have their origin: in that category, for instance, which was designated first in our division and in which we place wisdom and prudence, belong the search after truth and its discovery; and this is the peculiar

Their several provinces.

16 province of that virtue. For the more clearly anyone observes the most essential truth in any given

quique acutissime et celerrime potest et videre et explicare rationem, is prudentissimus et sapientissimus rite haberi solet. Quocirca huic quasi materia, quam tractet et in qua versetur, subiecta est veritas.

17 Reliquis autem tribus virtutibus necessitates propositae sunt ad eas res parandas tuendasque, quibus actio vitae continetur, ut et societas hominum coniunctioque servetur et animi excellentia magnitudoque cum in augendis opibus utilitatibusque et sibi et suis comparandis, tum multo magis in his ipsis despiciendis eluceat. Ordo autem [1] et constantia et moderatio et ea, quae sunt his similia, versantur in eo genere, ad quod est adhibenda actio quaedam, non solum mentis agitatio. Iis enim rebus, quae tractantur in vita, modum quendam et ordinem adhibentes honestatem et decus conservabimus.

18 VI. Ex quattuor autem locis, in quos honesti naturam vimque divisimus, primus ille, qui in veri cognitione consistit, maxime naturam attingit humanam. Omnes enim trahimur et ducimur ad cognitionis et scientiae cupiditatem, in qua excellere pulchrum putamus, labi autem, errare, nescire, decipi et malum et turpe ducimus.[2] In hoc genere et naturali et honesto duo vitia vitanda sunt, unum, ne incognita pro cognitis habeamus iisque temere assentiamur; quod vitium effugere qui volet (omnes autem

[1] *autem* MSS., Müller, Heine; *item* Pearce, Ed., Bt.
[2] *ducimus* c, Edd.; *dicimus* A B H a b.

case and the more quickly and accurately he can see and explain the reasons for it, the more understanding and wise he is generally esteemed, and justly so. So, then, it is truth that is, as it were, the stuff with which this virtue has to deal and on which it employs itself.

17 Before the three remaining virtues, on the other hand, is set the task of providing and maintaining those things on which the practical business of life depends, so that the relations of man to man in human society may be conserved, and that largeness and nobility of soul may be revealed not only in increasing one's resources and acquiring advantages for one's self and one's family but far more in rising superior to these very things. But orderly behaviour and consistency of demeanour and self-control and the like have their sphere in that department of things in which a certain amount of physical exertion, and not mental activity merely, is required. For if we bring a certain amount of propriety and order into the transactions of daily life, we shall be conserving moral rectitude and moral dignity.

18 VI. Now, of the four divisions which we have made of the essential idea of moral goodness, the first, consisting in the knowledge of truth, touches human nature most closely. For we are all attracted and drawn to a zeal for learning and knowing; and we think it glorious to excel therein, while we count it base and immoral to fall into error, to wander from the truth, to be ignorant, to be led astray. In this pursuit, which is both natural and morally right, two errors are to be avoided: first, we must not treat the unknown as known and too readily accept it; and he who wishes to avoid this error (as A. Wisdom.

velle debent), adhibebit ad considerandas res et
19 tempus et diligentiam. Alterum est vitium, quod quidam nimis magnum studium multamque operam in res obscuras atque difficiles conferunt easdemque non necessarias.

Quibus vitiis declinatis quod in rebus honestis et cognitione dignis operae curaeque ponetur, id iure laudabitur, ut in astrologia C. Sulpicium audivimus, in geometria Sex. Pompeium ipsi cognovimus, multos in dialecticis, plures in iure civili, quae omnes artes in veri investigatione versantur; cuius studio a rebus gerendis abduci contra officium est. Virtutis enim laus omnis in actione consistit; a qua tamen fit intermissio saepe multique dantur ad studia reditus; tum agitatio mentis, quae numquam acquiescit, potest nos in studiis cognitionis[1] etiam sine opera nostra continere. Omnis autem cogitatio motusque animi aut in consiliis capiendis de rebus honestis et pertinentibus ad bene beateque vivendum aut in studiis scientiae cognitionisque versabitur.

Ac de primo quidem officii fonte diximus.

20 VII. De tribus autem reliquis latissime patet ea ratio, qua societas hominum inter ipsos et vitae quasi communitas continetur; cuius partes duae,[2] iustitia, in qua virtutis est splendor maximus, ex qua viri boni nominantur, et huic coniuncta beneficentia,

[1] *cognitionis* A, Bt., Müller, Heine; *cogitationis* B H a b c (error caused by *cogitatio* in next line).

[2] *partes duae* B H b; *partes duae sunt* c, Bt., Heine.

all should do) will devote both time and attention
19 to the weighing of evidence. The other error is that some people devote too much industry and too deep study to matters that are obscure and difficult and useless as well.

If these errors are successfully avoided, all the labour and pains expended upon problems that are morally right and worth the solving will be fully rewarded. Such a worker in the field of astronomy, for example, was Gaius Sulpicius, of whom we have heard; in mathematics, Sextus Pompey, whom I have known personally; in dialectics, many; in civil law, still more. All these professions are occupied with the search after truth; but to be drawn by study away from active life is contrary to moral duty. For the whole glory of virtue is in activity; activity, however, may often be interrupted, and many opportunities for returning to study are opened. Besides, the working of the mind, which is never at rest, can keep us busy in the pursuit of knowledge even without conscious effort on our part. Moreover, all our thought and mental activity will be devoted either to planning for things that are morally right and that conduce to a good and happy life, or to the pursuits of science and learning.

With this we close the discussion of the first source of duty.

20 VII. Of the three remaining divisions, the most B. Justice
extensive in its application is the principle by which society and what we may call its "common bonds" are maintained. Of this again there are two divisions—justice, in which is the crowning glory of the virtues and on the basis of which men are called "good men"; and, close akin to justice,

quam eandem vel benignitatem vel liberalitatem appellari licet.

Sed iustitiae primum munus est, ut ne cui quis noceat nisi lacessitus iniuria, deinde ut communibus pro communibus utatur, privatis ut suis.

21 Sunt autem privata nulla natura, sed aut vetere occupatione, ut qui quondam in vacua venerunt, aut victoria, ut qui bello potiti sunt, aut lege, pactione, condicione, sorte; ex quo fit, ut ager Arpinas Arpinatium dicatur, Tusculanus Tusculanorum; similisque est privatarum possessionum discriptio.[1] Ex quo, quia suum cuiusque fit eorum, quae natura fuerant communia, quod cuique obtigit, id quisque teneat; e quo [2] si quis sibi appetet, violabit ius humanae societatis.

22 Sed quoniam, ut praeclare scriptum est a Platone, non nobis solum nati sumus ortusque nostri partem patria vindicat, partem amici, atque, ut placet Stoicis, quae in terris gignantur, ad usum hominum omnia creari, homines autem hominum causa esse generatos, ut ipsi inter se aliis alii prodesse possent, in hoc naturam debemus ducem sequi, communes utilitates in medium afferre mutatione officiorum, dando acci-

Ep. IX, ad Archytam, 358 A

[1] *discriptio* B, Edd.; *descriptio* A H a b c.
[2] *e quo* A H a b c, Müller; *eo* B, *de quo* Bt. (suppl.), Heine.

charity, which may also be called kindness or generosity.

The first office of justice is to keep one man from doing harm to another, unless provoked by wrong; and the next is to lead men to use common possessions for the common interests, private property for their own.

21 There is, however, no such thing as private ownership established by nature, but property becomes private either through long occupancy (as in the case of those who long ago settled in unoccupied territory) or through conquest (as in the case of those who took it in war) or by due process of law, bargain, or purchase, or by allotment. On this principle the lands of Arpinum are said to belong to the Arpinates, the Tusculan lands to the Tusculans; and similar is the assignment of private property. Therefore, inasmuch as in each case some of those things which by nature had been common property became the property of individuals, each one should retain possession of that which has fallen to his lot; and if anyone appropriates to himself anything beyond that, he will be violating the laws of human society. Public *vs.* private interests.

22 But since, as Plato has admirably expressed it, we are not born for ourselves alone, but our country claims a share of our being, and our friends a share; and since, as the Stoics hold, everything that the earth produces is created for man's use; and as men, too, are born for the sake of men, that they may be able mutually to help one another; in this direction we ought to follow Nature as our guide, to contribute to the general good by an interchange of acts of kindness, by giving and receiving, and thus by

piendo, tum artibus, tum opera, tum facultatibus devincire hominum inter homines societatem.

23 Fundamentum autem est iustitiae fides, id est dictorum conventorumque constantia et veritas. Ex quo, quamquam hoc videbitur fortasse cuipiam durius, tamen audeamus imitari Stoicos, qui studiose exquirunt, unde verba sint ducta, credamusque, quia fiat, quod dictum est, appellatam fidem.

Sed iniustitiae genera duo sunt, unum eorum, qui inferunt, alterum eorum, qui ab iis, quibus infertur, si possunt, non propulsant iniuriam. Nam qui iniuste impetum in quempiam facit aut ira aut aliqua perturbatione incitatus, is quasi manus afferre videtur socio; qui autem non defendit nec obsistit, si potest, iniuriae, tam est in vitio, quam si parentes aut amicos aut
24 patriam deserat. Atque illae quidem iniuriae, quae nocendi causa de industria inferuntur, saepe a metu proficiscuntur, cum is, qui nocere alteri cogitat, timet ne, nisi id fecerit, ipse aliquo afficiatur incommodo. Maximam autem partem ad iniuriam faciendam aggrediuntur, ut adipiscantur ea, quae concupiverunt; in quo vitio latissime patet avaritia.

25 VIII. Expetuntur autem divitiae cum ad usus vitae necessarios, tum ad perfruendas voluptates. In quibus autem maior est animus, in iis pecuniae cupiditas spectat ad opes et ad gratificandi facultatem, ut nuper M. Crassus negabat ullam satis

---

[a] Of course, "good faith" "and made good" have just as little etymological connection as *fiat* and *fidem*.

our skill, our industry, and our talents to cement human society more closely together, man to man.

23 The foundation of justice, moreover, is good faith—that is, truth and fidelity to promises and agreements. And therefore we may follow the Stoics, who diligently investigate the etymology of words; and we may accept their statement that "good faith" is so called because what is promised is "made good," although some may find this derivation [a] rather far-fetched. Good faith

There are, on the other hand, two kinds of injustice—the one, on the part of those who inflict wrong, the other on the part of those who, when they can, do not shield from wrong those upon whom it is being inflicted. For he who, under the influence of anger or some other passion, wrongfully assaults another seems, as it were, to be laying violent hands upon a comrade; but he who does not prevent or oppose wrong, if he can, is just as guilty of wrong as if he deserted his parents or his friends or his country. Injustice; active and passive.

24 Then, too, those very wrongs which people try to inflict on purpose to injure are often the result of fear: that is, he who premeditates injuring another is afraid that, if he does not do so, he may himself be made to suffer some hurt. But, for the most part, people are led to wrong-doing in order to secure some personal end; in this vice, avarice is generally the controlling motive.

25 VIII. Again, men seek riches partly to supply the needs of life, partly to secure the enjoyment of pleasure. With those who cherish higher ambitions, the desire for wealth is entertained with a view to power and influence and the means of bestowing favours; Marcus Crassus, for example, not long since The dangers of ambition.

magnam pecuniam esse ei, qui in re publica princeps vellet esse, cuius fructibus exercitum alere non posset. Delectant etiam magnifici apparatus vitaeque cultus cum elegantia et copia; quibus rebus effectum est, ut infinita pecuniae cupiditas esset. Nec vero rei familiaris amplificatio nemini nocens vituperanda est, sed fugienda semper iniuria est.

26 Maxime autem adducuntur plerique, ut eos iustitiae capiat oblivio, cum in imperiorum, honorum, gloriae cupiditatem inciderunt.[1] Quod enim est apud Ennium:

Fab. inc. (Thyestes?) Vahlen², 404

Núlla sancta sócietas
Néc fides regni ést,

id latius patet. Nam quicquid eius modi est, in quo non possint plures excellere, in eo fit plerumque tanta contentio, ut difficillimum sit servare "sanctam societatem." Declaravit id modo temeritas C. Caesaris, qui omnia iura divina et humana pervertit propter eum, quem sibi ipse opinionis errore finxerat, principatum. Est autem in hoc genere molestum, quod in maximis animis splendidissimisque ingeniis plerumque exsistunt honoris, imperii, potentiae, gloriae cupiditates. Quo magis cavendum est, ne quid in eo genere peccetur.

27 Sed in omni iniustitia permultum interest, utrum

[1] *inciderunt* A B H L a b; *inciderint* c.

declared that no amount of wealth was enough for the man who aspired to be the foremost citizen of the state, unless with the income from it he could maintain an army. Fine establishments and the comforts of life in elegance and abundance also afford pleasure, and the desire to secure it gives rise to the insatiable thirst for wealth. Still, I do not mean to find fault with the accumulation of property, provided it hurts nobody, but unjust acquisition of it is always to be avoided.

26 The great majority of people, however, when they fall a prey to ambition for either military or civil authority, are carried away by it so completely that they quite lose sight of the claims of justice. For Ennius says:

"There is no fellowship inviolate,
No faith is kept, when kingship is concerned;"

and the truth of his words has an uncommonly wide application. For whenever a situation is of such a nature that not more than one can hold pre-eminence in it, competition for it usually becomes so keen that it is an extremely difficult matter to maintain a "fellowship inviolate." We saw this Caesar. proved but now in the effrontery of Gaius Caesar, who, to gain that sovereign power which by a depraved imagination he had conceived in his fancy, trod underfoot all laws of gods and men. But the trouble about this matter is that it is in the greatest souls and in the most brilliant geniuses that we usually find ambitions for civil and military authority, for power, and for glory, springing up; and therefore we must be the more heedful not to go wrong in that direction.

27 But in any case of injustice it makes a vast deal The motives to wrong.

perturbatione aliqua animi, quae plerumque brevis est et ad tempus, an consulto et cogitata [1] fiat iniuria. Leviora enim sunt ea, quae repentino aliquo motu accidunt, quam ea, quae meditata et praeparata inferuntur.

Ac de inferenda quidem iniuria satis dictum est.

28 IX. Praetermittendae autem defensionis deserendique officii plures solent esse causae; nam aut inimicitias aut laborem aut sumptus suscipere nolunt aut etiam neglegentia, pigritia, inertia aut suis studiis quibusdam occupationibusve sic impediuntur, ut eos, quos tutari debeant, desertos esse patiantur. Itaque
Rep. VI, 485 ff.; VII, 520 D videndum est, ne non satis sit id, quod apud Platonem est in philosophos dictum, quod in veri investigatione versentur quodque ea, quae plerique vehementer expetant,[2] de quibus inter se digladiari soleant, contemnant et pro nihilo putent, propterea iustos esse. Nam alterum [iustitiae genus] assequuntur,[3] ut [4] inferenda ne cui noceant iniuria, in alterum incidunt; [5] discendi enim studio impediti,
Rep. I, 347 C quos tueri debent, deserunt. Itaque eos ne ad rem publicam quidem accessuros putat nisi coactos. Aequius autem erat id voluntate fieri; nam hoc ipsum ita iustum est, quod recte fit, si est voluntarium.

29 Sunt etiam, qui aut studio rei familiaris tuendae aut odio quodam hominum suum se negotium agere

[1] *cogitata* A B H a b p, Edd.; *cogitatu* c, *cogitato* alii, Madvig (ad De Fin. p. 696).

[2] *expetant* A B a b; *expectant* H; *exspectant* c.

[3] *alterum iustitiae genus assequuntur* MSS.; *alterum assequuntur* Pearce, J. M. Heusinger, et al.; *alterum genus assequuntur* Beier.

[4] *ut* Halm; *in* MSS.; om. Bt.

[5] *in alterum incidunt* A B H a b; *in altero delinqunt* c, Bt. (*delinquunt*, i.e. they offend in the other direction).

of difference whether the wrong is done as a result of some impulse of passion, which is usually brief and transient, or whether it is committed wilfully and with premeditation; for offences that come through some sudden impulse are less culpable than those committed designedly and with malice aforethought.

But enough has been said on the subject of inflicting injury.

28 IX. The motives for failure to prevent injury and so for slighting duty are likely to be various: people either are reluctant to incur enmity or trouble or expense; or through indifference, indolence, or incompetence, or through some preoccupation or self-interest they are so absorbed that they suffer those to be neglected whom it is their duty to protect. And so there is reason to fear that what Plato declares of the philosophers may be inadequate, when he says that they are just because they are busied with the pursuit of truth and because they despise and count as naught that which most men eagerly seek and for which they are prone to do battle against each other to the death. For they secure one sort of justice, to be sure, in that they do no positive wrong to anyone, but they fall into the opposite injustice; for hampered by their pursuit of learning they leave to their fate those whom they ought to defend. And so, Plato thinks, they will not even assume their civic duties except under compulsion. But in fact it were better that they should assume them of their own accord; for an action intrinsically right is just only on condition that it is voluntary.

**Motives to passive injustice;**

**a. Preoccupation.**

29 There are some also who, either from zeal in attending to their own business or through some

**b. Self-interest.**

dicant nec facere cuiquam videantur iniuriam. Qui altero genere iniustitiae vacant, in alterum incurrunt; deserunt enim vitae societatem, quia nihil conferunt in eam studii, nihil operae, nihil facultatum.

Quando igitur duobus generibus iniustitiae propositis adiunximus causas utriusque generis easque res ante constituimus, quibus iustitia contineretur, facile, quod cuiusque temporis officium sit, poterimus, nisi
30 nosmet ipsos valde amabimus, iudicare; est enim
Heaut. Tim. 77. difficilis cura rerum alienarum. Quamquam Terentianus ille Chremes "humani nihil a se alienum putat"; sed tamen, quia magis ea percipimus atque sentimus, quae nobis ipsis aut prospera aut adversa eveniunt, quam illa, quae ceteris, quae quasi longo intervallo interiecto videmus, aliter de illis ac de nobis iudicamus. Quocirca bene praecipiunt, qui vetant quicquam agere, quod dubites aequum sit an iniquum. Aequitas enim lucet ipsa per se, dubitatio cogitationem significat iniuriae.

31 X. Sed incidunt saepe tempora, cum ea, quae maxime videntur digna esse iusto homine eoque, quem virum bonum dicimus, commutantur fiuntque contraria, ut reddere depositum, facere promissum quaeque pertinent ad veritatem et ad fidem, ea mi-

sort of aversion to their fellow-men, claim that they are occupied solely with their own affairs, without seeming to themselves to be doing anyone any injury. But while they steer clear of the one kind of injustice, they fall into the other: they are traitors to social life, for they contribute to it none of their interest, none of their effort, none of their means.

**Rules of duty required by Justice.**

Now since we have set forth the two kinds of injustice and assigned the motives that lead to each, and since we have previously established the principles by which justice is constituted, we shall be in a position easily to decide what our duty on each occasion is, unless we are extremely self-centred; for
30 indeed it is not an easy matter to be really concerned with other people's affairs; and yet in Terence's play, we know, Chremes "thinks that nothing that concerns man is foreign to him." Nevertheless, when things turn out for our own good or ill, we realize it more fully and feel it more deeply than when the same things happen to others and we see them only, as it were, in the far distance; and for this reason we judge their case differently from our own. It is, therefore, an excellent rule that they give who bid us not to do a thing, when there is a doubt whether it be right or wrong; for righteousness shines with a brilliance of its own, but doubt is a sign that we are thinking of a possible wrong.

**Change of duty in change of circumstances.**

31 X. But occasions often arise, when those duties which seem most becoming to the just man and to the "good man," as we call him, undergo a change and take on a contrary aspect. It may, for example, not be a duty to restore a trust or to fulfil a promise, and it may become right and proper sometimes to evade and not to observe what truth and honour

grare interdum et non servare fit iustum. Referri
Ch. VII enim decet ad ea, quae posui principio, fundamenta iustitiae, primum ut ne cui noceatur, deinde ut communi utilitati serviatur. Ea cum tempore commutantur, commutatur officium et non semper est
32 idem. Potest enim accidere promissum aliquod et conventum, ut id effici sit inutile vel ei, cui promissum sit, vel ei, qui promiserit. Nam si, ut in
e.g. Eur. Hipp. 1315-1319 fabulis est, Neptunus, quod Theseo promiserat, non fecisset, Theseus Hippolyto filio non esset orbatus; ex tribus enim optatis, ut scribitur, hoc erat tertium, quod de Hippolyti interitu iratus optavit; quo impetrato in maximos luctus incidit. Nec promissa igitur servanda sunt ea, quae sint iis, quibus promiseris, inutilia, nec, si plus tibi ea noceant quam illi prosint, cui[1] promiseris, contra officium est maius anteponi minori; ut, si constitueris cuipiam te advocatum in rem praesentem esse venturum atque interim graviter aegrotare filius coeperit, non sit contra officium non facere, quod dixeris, magisque ille, cui promissum sit, ab officio discedat, si se destitutum queratur. Iam illis promissis standum non esse quis non videt, quae coactus quis metu,

[1] *cui* B a, Edd.; *cui quod* H b; *cui quid* A c.

---

[a] The three wishes were: (1) safe return from Hades; (2) escape from the Labyrinth; (3) the death of Hippolytus.

would usually demand. For we may well be guided by those fundamental principles of justice which I laid down at the outset: first, that no harm be done to anyone; second, that the common interests be conserved. When these are modified under changed circumstances, moral duty also undergoes a change,
32 and it does not always remain the same. For a given promise or agreement may turn out in such a way that its performance will prove detrimental either to the one to whom the promise has been made or to the one who has made it. If, for example, Neptune, in the drama, had not carried out his promise to Theseus, Theseus would not have lost his son Hippolytus; for, as the story runs, of the three wishes [a] that Neptune had promised to grant him the third was this: in a fit of anger he prayed for the death of Hippolytus, and the granting of this prayer plunged him into unspeakable grief. Promises are, therefore, not to be kept, if the keeping of them is to prove harmful to those to whom you have made them; and, if the fulfilment of a promise should do more harm to you than good to him to whom you have made it, it is no violation of moral duty to give the greater good precedence over the lesser good. For example, if you have made an appointment with anyone to appear as his advocate in court, and if in the meantime your son should fall dangerously ill, it would be no breach of your moral duty to fail in what you agreed to do; nay, rather, he to whom your promise was given would have a false conception of duty, if he should complain that he had been deserted in his time of need. Further than this, who fails to see that those promises are not binding which are extorted by intimidation or which we make when

**Non-fulfilment of promises.**

quae deceptus dolo promiserit? quae quidem pleraque iure praetorio liberantur, non nulla legibus.

33 Exsistunt etiam saepe iniuriae calumnia quadam et nimis callida, sed malitiosa iuris interpretatione. Ex quo illud "Summum ius summa iniuria" factum est iam tritum sermone proverbium. Quo in genere etiam in re publica multa peccantur, ut ille, qui, cum triginta dierum essent cum hoste indutiae factae, noctu populabatur agros, quod dierum essent pactae, non noctium indutiae. Ne noster quidem probandus, si verum est Q. Fabium Labeonem seu quem alium (nihil enim habeo praeter auditum) arbitrum Nolanis et Neapolitanis de finibus a senatu datum, cum ad locum venisset, cum utrisque separatim locutum, ne cupide quid agerent, ne appetenter, atque ut regredi quam progredi mallent. Id cum utrique fecissent, aliquantum agri in medio relictum est. Itaque illorum finis sic, ut ipsi dixerant, terminavit; in medio relictum quod erat, populo Romano adiudicavit. Decipere hoc quidem est, non iudicare. Quocirca in omni est re fugienda talis sollertia.

XI. Sunt autem quaedam officia etiam adversus eos servanda, a quibus iniuriam acceperis. Est enim ulciscendi et puniendi modus; atque haud scio an satis sit eum, qui lacessierit, iniuriae suae paenitere,

---

[a] Each praetor, at his inauguration, announced publicly the principles and policies that should guide him in the administration of his office. These were the source of the *Ius Praetorium*, which explained and supplemented the common law (*Ius Civile*) and even modified its ancient rigour so as to conform with a more advanced public sentiment, and form a most valuable part of the body of Roman Law.

[b] This story is told of Cleomenes, King of Sparta (520–491 B.C.), in the war with Argos. (Plutarch, Apophth. Lacon. 223 A.)

misled by false pretences? Such obligations are annulled in most cases by the praetor's edict in equity,[a] in some cases by the laws.

33 Injustice often arises also through chicanery, that is, through an over-subtle and even fraudulent construction of the law. This it is that gave rise to the now familiar saw, "More law, less justice." Through such interpretation also a great deal of wrong is committed in transactions between state and state; thus, when a truce had been made with the enemy for thirty days, a famous general [b] went to ravaging their fields by night, because, he said, the truce stipulated "days," not nights. Not even our own countryman's action is to be commended, if what is told of Quintus Fabius Labeo is true—or whoever it was (for I have no authority but hearsay): appointed by the Senate to arbitrate a boundary dispute between Nola and Naples, he took up the case and interviewed both parties separately, asking them not to proceed in a covetous or grasping spirit, but to make some concession rather than claim some accession. When each party had agreed to this, there was a considerable strip of territory left between them. And so he set the boundary of each city as each had severally agreed; and the tract in between he awarded to the Roman People. Now that is swindling, not arbitration. And therefore such sharp practice is under all circumstances to be avoided.

Chicanery.

XI. Again, there are certain duties that we owe even to those who have wronged us. For there is a limit to retribution and to punishment; or rather, I am inclined to think, it is sufficient that the aggressor should be brought to repent of his wrong-doing, in

Our duty to those who have wronged us.

ut et ipse ne quid tale posthac et ceteri sint ad iniuriam tardiores.

34 Atque in re publica maxime conservanda sunt iura belli. Nam cum sint duo genera decertandi, unum per disceptationem, alterum per vim, cumque illud proprium sit hominis, hoc beluarum, confugiendum est ad posterius, si uti non licet superiore.
35 Quare suscipienda quidem bella sunt ob eam causam, ut sine iniuria in pace vivatur, parta autem victoria conservandi ii, qui non crudeles in bello, non immanes fuerunt, ut maiores nostri Tusculanos, Aequos, Volscos, Sabinos, Hernicos in civitatem etiam acceperunt, at Carthaginem et Numantiam funditus sustulerunt; nollem Corinthum, sed credo aliquid secutos, opportunitatem loci maxime, ne posset aliquando ad bellum faciendum locus ipse adhortari. Mea quidem sententia paci, quae nihil habitura sit insidiarum, semper est consulendum. In quo si mihi esset optemperatum, si non optimam, at aliquam rem publicam, quae nunc nulla est, haberemus.

Et cum iis, quos vi deviceris, consulendum est, tum ii, qui armis positis ad imperatorum fidem confugient, quamvis murum aries percusserit, recipiendi. In quo tantopere apud nostros iustitia culta est, ut ii, qui

order that he may not repeat the offence and that others may be deterred from doing wrong.

34 Then, too, in the case of a state in its external relations, the rights of war must be strictly observed. For since there are two ways of settling a dispute: first, by discussion; second, by physical force; and since the former is characteristic of man, the latter of the brute, we must resort to force only in case
35 we may not avail ourselves of discussion. The only **Excuse for war.** excuse, therefore, for going to war is that we may live in peace unharmed; and when the victory is won, we should spare those who have not been blood-thirsty and barbarous in their warfare. For **Justice toward the vanquished.** instance, our forefathers actually admitted to full rights of citizenship the Tusculans, Aequians, Volscians, Sabines, and Hernicians, but they razed Carthage and Numantia to the ground. I wish they had not destroyed Corinth; but I believe they had some special reason for what they did—its convenient situation, probably—and feared that its very location might some day furnish a temptation to renew the war. In my opinion, at least, we should always strive to secure a peace that shall not admit of guile. And if my advice had been heeded on this point, we should still have at least some sort of constitutional government, if not the best in the world, whereas, as it is, we have none at all.

Not only must we show consideration for those whom we have conquered by force of arms but we must also ensure protection to those who lay down their arms and throw themselves upon the mercy of our generals, even though the battering-ram has hammered at their walls. And among our countrymen justice has been observed so conscientiously in

civitates aut nationes devictas bello in fidem recepissent, earum patroni essent more maiorum.

36 Ac belli quidem aequitas sanctissime fetiali populi Romani iure perscripta est. Ex quo intellegi potest nullum bellum esse iustum, nisi quod aut rebus repetitis geratur aut denuntiatum ante sit et indictum. [Popilius imperator tenebat provinciam, in cuius exercitu Catonis filius tiro militabat. Cum autem Popilio videretur unam dimittere legionem, Catonis quoque filium, qui in eadem legione militabat, dimisit. Sed cum amore pugnandi in exercitu remansisset, Cato ad Popilium scripsit, ut, si eum patitur[1] in exercitu remanere, secundo eum obliget militiae sacramento, quia priore amisso iure cum hostibus

37 pugnare non poterat. Adeo summa erat observatio in bello movendo.][2] M. quidem Catonis senis est epistula ad M. filium, in qua scribit se audisse eum missum factum esse a consule, cum in Macedonia bello Persico miles esset. Monet igitur, ut caveat, ne proelium ineat; negat enim ius esse, qui miles non sit, cum hoste pugnare.

XII. Equidem etiam illud animadverto, quod, qui proprio nomine perduellis esset, is hostis vocaretur, lenitate verbi rei tristitiam mitigatam. Hostis enim apud maiores nostros is dicebatur, quem nunc pere-

[1] *patitur* A B H a b; *patiatur* c.
[2] *Popilius . . . movendo* bracketed by Madvig, Edd.; *Popilius . . . poterat* bracketed by Unger.

---

[a] Lucius Aemilius Paulus (B.C. 168).

this direction, that those who have given promise of protection to states or nations subdued in war become, after the custom of our forefathers, the patrons of those states.

36 As for war, humane laws touching it are drawn up in the fetial code of the Roman People under all the guarantees of religion; and from this it may be gathered that no war is just, unless it is entered upon after an official demand for satisfaction has been submitted or warning has been given and a formal declaration made. Popilius was general in command of a province. In his army Cato's son was serving on his first campaign. When Popilius decided to disband one of his legions, he discharged also young Cato, who was serving in that same legion. But when the young man out of love for the service stayed on in the field, his father wrote to Popilius to say that if he let him stay in the army, he should swear him into service with a new oath of allegiance, for in view of the voidance of his former oath he could not legally fight the foe. So extremely scrupulous was the observance of the laws in regard to the

37 conduct of war. There is extant, too, a letter of the elder Marcus Cato to his son Marcus, in which he writes that he has heard that the youth has been discharged by the consul,[a] when he was serving in Macedonia in the war with Perseus. He warns him, therefore, to be careful not to go into battle; for, he says, the man who is not legally a soldier has no right to be fighting the foe.

The humanity of Rome's laws of war.

XII. This also I observe—that he who would properly have been called "a fighting enemy" (*perduellis*) was called "a guest" (*hostis*), thus relieving the ugliness of the fact by a softened expression; for "enemy" (*hostis*) meant to our an-

grinum dicimus. Indicant duodecim tabulae: AUT STATUS DIES CUM HOSTE, itemque: ADVERSUS HOSTEM AETERNA AUCTORITAS. Quid ad hanc mansuetudinem addi potest, eum, quicum bellum geras, tam molli nomine appellare? Quamquam id nomen durius effecit [1] iam vetustas; a peregrino enim recessit et proprie in eo, qui arma contra ferret, remansit.

38 Cum vero de imperio decertatur belloque quaeritur gloria, causas omnino subesse tamen oportet easdem, quas dixi paulo ante iustas causas esse bellorum. Sed ea bella, quibus imperii proposita gloria est, minus acerbe gerenda sunt. Ut enim cum civi aliter contendimus, si [2] est inimicus, aliter, si competitor (cum altero certamen honoris et dignitatis est, cum altero capitis et famae), sic cum Celtiberis, cum Cimbris bellum ut cum inimicis gerebatur, uter esset, non uter imperaret, cum Latinis, Sabinis, Samnitibus, Poenis, Pyrrho de imperio dimicabatur. Poeni foedifragi, crudelis Hannibal, reliqui iustiores. Pyrrhi quidem de captivis reddendis illa praeclara:

Ennius, Ann. VI, Vahlen², xii, 194-201

Nec mi aurum posco nec mi pretium dederitis,
Nec [3] cauponantes bellum, sed belligerantes
Ferro, non auro vitam cernamus utrique.

[1] *effecit* Edd.; *efficit* MSS.
[2] *cum cive* [Edd.: *civi*] *aliter contendimus si* L, Anemoecius, Edd.; *cum civiliter contendimus aliter si* A B H a b c.
[3] *Nec* A B H b c; *Non* L p, Bt., Heine.

cestors what we now call "stranger" (*peregrinus*). This is proved by the usage in the Twelve Tables: "Or a day fixed for trial with a stranger" (*hostis*). And again: "Right of ownership is inalienable for ever in dealings with a stranger" (*hostis*). What can exceed such charity, when he with whom one is at war is called by so gentle a name? And yet long lapse of time has given that word a harsher meaning: for it has lost its signification of "stranger" and has taken on the technical connotation of "an enemy under arms."

**Justice in war.**

38 But when a war is fought out for supremacy and when glory is the object of war, it must still not fail to start from the same motives which I said a moment ago were the only righteous grounds for going to war. But those wars which have glory for their end must be carried on with less bitterness. For we contend, for example, with a fellow-citizen in one way, if he is a personal enemy, in another, if he is a rival: with the rival it is a struggle for office and position, with the enemy for life and honour. So with the Celtiberians and the Cimbrians we fought as with deadly enemies, not to determine which should be supreme, but which should survive; but with the Latins, Sabines, Samnites, Carthaginians, and Pyrrhus we fought for supremacy. The Carthaginians violated treaties; Hannibal was cruel; the others were more merciful. From Pyrrhus we have this famous speech on the exchange of prisoners:

"Gold will I none, nor price shall ye give; for I ask none;
Come, let us not be chaff'rers of war, but warriors embattled.
Nay; let us venture our lives, and the sword, not gold, weigh the outcome.

Vosne velit an me regnare era, quidve ferat Fors,
Virtute experiamur. Et hoc simul accipe dictum:
Quorum virtuti [1] belli fortuna pepercit,
Eorundem libertati me parcere certum est.
Dono, ducite, doque volentibus cum magnis dis.

Regalis sane et digna Aeacidarum genere sententia.

39 XIII. Atque etiam si quid singuli temporibus adducti hosti promiserunt, est in eo ipso fides conservanda, ut primo Punico bello Regulus captus a Poenis cum de captivis commutandis Romam missus esset iurassetque se rediturum, primum, ut venit, captivos reddendos in senatu non censuit, deinde, cum retineretur a propinquis et ab amicis, ad supplicium redire maluit quam fidem hosti datam fallere.

40 [Secundo autem Punico bello post Cannensem pugnam quos decem Hannibal Romam astrictos misit iure iurando se redituros esse, nisi de redimendis iis, qui capti erant, impetrassent, eos omnes

[1] *virtuti* A B² L c, Edd.; *virtute* B¹ H b; *virtutei* Vahlen.

Make we the trial by valour in arms and see if Dame Fortune
Wills it that ye shall prevail or I, or what be her judgment.
Hear thou, too, this word, good Fabricius: whose valour soever
Spared hath been by the fortune of war—their freedom I grant them.
Such my resolve. I give and present them to you, my brave Romans;
Take them back to their homes; the great gods' blessings attend you."

A right kingly sentiment this and worthy a scion of the Aeacidae.

39 XIII. Again, if under stress of circumstances individuals have made any promise to the enemy, they are bound to keep their word even then. For instance, in the First Punic War, when Regulus was taken prisoner by the Carthaginians, he was sent to Rome on parole to negotiate an exchange of prisoners; he came and, in the first place, it was he that made the motion in the Senate that the prisoners should not be restored; and in the second place, when his relatives and friends would have kept him back, he chose to return to a death by torture rather than prove false to his promise, though given to an enemy.

Fidelity to a promise; (1) Regulus

40 And again in the Second Punic War, after the Battle of Cannae, Hannibal sent to Rome ten Roman captives bound by an oath to return to him, if they did not succeed in ransoming his prisoners; and as long as any one of them lived, the censors kept them all degraded and disfranchised, because they were

(2) Hannibal's envoys.

censores, quoad quisque eorum vixit, qui peierassent, in aerariis reliquerunt nec minus illum, qui iuris iurandi fraude culpam invenerat. Cum enim Hannibalis permissu exisset de castris, rediit paulo post, quod se oblitum nescio quid diceret; deinde egressus e castris iure iurando se solutum putabat, et erat verbis, re non erat. Semper autem in fide quid senseris, non quid dixeris, cogitandum.

Maximum autem exemplum est iustitiae in hostem a maioribus nostris constitutum, cum a Pyrrho perfuga senatui est pollicitus se venenum regi daturum et eum necaturum, senatus et C. Fabricius perfugam Pyrrho dedidit. Ita ne hostis quidem et potentis et bellum ultro inferentis interitum cum scelere approbavit.] [1]

41 Ac de bellicis quidem officiis satis dictum est.

Meminerimus autem etiam adversus infimos iustitiam esse servandam. Est autem infima condicio et fortuna servorum, quibus non male praecipiunt qui ita iubent uti, ut mercennariis: operam exigendam, iusta praebenda.

Cum autem duobus modis, id est aut vi aut fraude, fiat iniuria, fraus quasi vulpeculae, vis leonis videtur; utrumque homine alienissimum, sed fraus odio digna

[1] *Secundo . . . re non erat* om. L c; *Secundo . . . approbavit* om. A B H a b p, Edd.

guilty of perjury in not returning. And they punished in like manner the one who had incurred guilt by an evasion of his oath: with Hannibal's permission this man left the camp and returned a little later on the pretext that he had forgotten something or other; and then, when he left the camp the second time, he claimed that he was released from the obligation of his oath; and so he was, according to the letter of it, but not according to the spirit. In the matter of a promise one must always consider the meaning and not the mere words.

Our forefathers have given us another striking example of justice toward an enemy: when a deserter from Pyrrhus promised the Senate to administer poison to the king and thus work his death, the Senate and Gaius Fabricius delivered the deserter up to Pyrrhus. Thus they stamped with their disapproval the treacherous murder even of an enemy who was at once powerful, unprovoked, aggressive, and successful.

41 With this I will close my discussion of the duties connected with war.

But let us remember that we must have regard for justice even towards the humblest. Now the humblest station and the poorest fortune are those of slaves; and they give us no bad rule who bid us treat our slaves as we should our employees: they must be required to work; they must be given their dues. **Justice toward slaves.**

While wrong may be done, then, in either of two ways, that is, by force or by fraud, both are bestial: fraud seems to belong to the cunning fox, force to the lion; both are wholly unworthy of man, but fraud is the more contemptible. But of all forms of **Injustice of hypocrisy.**

maiore. Totius autem iniustitiae nulla capitalior quam eorum, qui tum, cum maxime fallunt, id agunt, ut viri boni esse videantur.

De iustitia satis dictum.

Ch. VII 42 XIV. Deinceps, ut erat propositum, de beneficentia ac de liberalitate dicatur, qua quidem nihil est naturae hominis accommodatius, sed habet multas cautiones. Videndum est enim, primum ne obsit benignitas et iis ipsis, quibus benigne videbitur fieri et ceteris, deinde ne maior benignitas sit quam facultates, tum ut pro dignitate cuique tribuatur; id enim est iustitiae fundamentum, ad quam haec referenda sunt omnia. Nam et qui gratificantur cuipiam, quod obsit illi, cui prodesse velle videantur, non benefici neque liberales, sed perniciosi assentatores iudicandi sunt, et qui aliis nocent, ut in alios liberales sint, in eadem sunt iniustitia, ut si in suam rem aliena convertant.

43 Sunt autem multi, et quidem cupidi splendoris et gloriae, qui eripiunt aliis, quod aliis largiantur, iique arbitrantur se beneficos in suos amicos visum iri, si locupletent eos quacumque ratione. Id autem tantum abest ab [1] officio, ut nihil magis officio possit esse contrarium. Videndum est igitur, ut ea liberalitate utamur, quae prosit amicis, noceat nemini. Quare L. Sullae, C. Caesaris pecuniarum translatio a iustis

[1] *ab* c, Edd.; not in A B H L b.

injustice, none is more flagrant than that of the hypocrite who, at the very moment when he is most false, makes it his business to appear virtuous.

This must conclude our discussion of justice.

42 XIV. Next in order, as outlined above, let us speak of kindness and generosity. Nothing appeals more to the best in human nature than this, but it calls for the exercise of caution in many particulars: we must, in the first place, see to it that our act of kindness shall not prove an injury either to the object of our beneficence or to others; in the second place, that it shall not be beyond our means; and finally, that it shall be proportioned to the worthiness of the recipient; for this is the corner-stone of justice; and by the standard of justice all acts of kindness must be measured. For those who confer a harmful favour upon someone whom they seemingly wish to help are to be accounted not generous benefactors but dangerous sycophants; and likewise those who injure one man, in order to be generous to another, are guilty of the same injustice as if they diverted to their own accounts the property of their neighbours. **Justice and generosity.**

43 Now, there are many—and especially those who are ambitious for eminence and glory—who rob one to enrich another; and they expect to be thought generous towards their friends, if they put them in the way of getting rich, no matter by what means. Such conduct, however, is so remote from moral duty that nothing can be more completely opposed to duty. We must, therefore, take care to indulge only in such liberality as will help our friends and hurt no one. The conveyance of property by Lucius Sulla and Gaius Caesar from its rightful owners to **Generosity must be (1) hurtful to no one,**

dominis ad alienos non debet liberalis videri; nihil est enim liberale, quod non idem iustum.

44 Alter locus erat cautionis, ne benignitas maior esset quam facultates, quod, qui benigniores volunt esse, quam res patitur, primum in eo peccant, quod iniuriosi sunt in proximos; quas enim copias his [1] et suppeditari aequius est et relinqui, eas transferunt ad alienos. Inest autem in tali liberalitate cupiditas plerumque rapiendi et auferendi per iniuriam, ut ad largiendum suppetant copiae. Videre etiam licet plerosque non tam natura liberales quam quadam gloria ductos, ut benefici videantur, facere multa, quae proficisci ab ostentatione magis quam a voluntate videantur. Talis autem simulatio vanitati est coniunctior quam aut liberalitati aut honestati.

45 Tertium est propositum, ut in beneficentia dilectus esset dignitatis; in quo et mores eius erunt spectandi, in quem beneficium conferetur, et animus erga nos et communitas ac societas vitae et ad nostras utilitates officia ante collata; quae ut concurrant omnia, optabile est; si minus, plures causae maioresque ponderis plus habebunt.

46 XV. Quoniam autem vivitur non cum perfectis

[1] *his* H a, Edd.; *iis* A B b; *eis* L c.

the hands of strangers should, for that reason, not be regarded as generosity; for nothing is generous, if it is not at the same time just.

44 The second point for the exercise of caution was that our beneficence should not exceed our means; for those who wish to be more open-handed than their circumstances permit are guilty of two faults: first, they do wrong to their next of kin; for they transfer to strangers property which would more justly be placed at their service or bequeathed to them. And second, such generosity too often engenders a passion for plundering and misappropriating property, in order to supply the means for making large gifts. We may also observe that a great many people do many things that seem to be inspired more by a spirit of ostentation than by heart-felt kindness; for such people are not really generous but are rather influenced by a sort of ambition to make a show of being open-handed. Such a pose is nearer akin to hypocrisy than to generosity or moral goodness. (2) within our means,

45 The third rule laid down was that in acts of kindness we should weigh with discrimination the worthiness of the object of our benevolence; we should take into consideration his moral character, his attitude toward us, the intimacy of his relations to us, and our common social ties, as well as the services he has hitherto rendered in our interest. It is to be desired that all these considerations should be combined in the same person; if they are not, then the more numerous and the more important considerations must have the greater weight. (3) according to merit.

46 XV. Now, the men we live with are not perfect

hominibus planeque sapientibus, sed cum iis, in quibus praeclare agitur si sunt simulacra virtutis, etiam hoc intellegendum puto, neminem omnino esse neglegendum, in quo aliqua significatio virtutis appareat, colendum autem esse ita quemque maxime, ut quisque maxime virtutibus his lenioribus erit ornatus, modestia, temperantia, hac ipsa, de qua multa iam dicta sunt, iustitia. Nam fortis animus et magnus in homine non perfecto nec sapiente [1] ferventior plerumque est, illae virtutes bonum virum videntur potius attingere.

Atque haec in moribus.

47 De benivolentia autem, quam quisque habeat erga nos, primum illud est in officio, ut ei plurimum tribuamus, a quo plurimum diligamur,[2] sed benivolentiam non adulescentulorum more ardore quodam amoris, sed stabilitate potius et constantia iudicemus. Sin erunt merita, ut non ineunda, sed referenda sit gratia, maior quaedam cura adhibenda est; nullum enim officium referenda gratia magis necessarium est.

48 Quodsi ea, quae utenda acceperis, maiore mensura,
Op. 349-351 si modo possis, iubet reddere Hesiodus, quidnam beneficio provocati facere debemus? an imitari agros fertiles, qui multo plus efferunt quam acceperunt? Etenim si in eos, quos speramus nobis profuturos, non dubitamus officia conferre, quales in eos esse debemus, qui iam profuerunt? Nam cum duo genera

[1] *sapiente* MSS.; *sapienti* Wesenberg, Bt.
[2] *diligamur* A B² H L b c; *diligimur* B¹, Bt¹.

and ideally wise, but men who do very well, if there be found in them but the semblance of virtue. I therefore think that this is to be taken for granted, that no one should be entirely neglected who shows any trace of virtue; but the more a man is endowed with these finer virtues—temperance, self-control, and that very justice about which so much has already been said—the more he deserves to be favoured. I do not mention fortitude, for a courageous spirit in a man who has not attained perfection and ideal wisdom is generally too impetuous; it is those other virtues that seem more particularly to mark the good man.

So much in regard to the character of the object of our beneficence.

47 But as to the affection which anyone may have Motives to
for us, it is the first demand of duty that we do generosity: (1) love,
most for him who loves us most; but we should measure affection, not like youngsters, by the ardour of its passion, but rather by its strength and constancy. But if there shall be obligations already (2) requital,
incurred, so that kindness is not to begin with us, but to be requited, still greater diligence, it seems, is called for; for no duty is more imperative than that of proving one's gratitude.

48 But if, as Hesiod bids, one is to repay with interest, if possible, what one has borrowed in time of need, what, pray, ought we to do when challenged by an unsought kindness? Shall we not imitate the fruitful fields, which return more than they receive? For if we do not hesitate to confer favours upon those who we hope will be of help to us, how ought we to deal with those who have already helped us? For generosity is of two kinds: doing

liberalitatis sint, unum dandi beneficii, alterum reddendi, demus necne, in nostra potestate est, non reddere viro bono non licet, modo[1] id facere possit sine iniuria.

49 Acceptorum autem beneficiorum sunt dilectus habendi, nec dubium, quin maximo cuique plurimum debeatur. In quo tamen in primis, quo quisque animo, studio, benivolentia fecerit, ponderandum est. Multi enim faciunt multa temeritate quadam sine iudicio vel morbo in omnes vel repentino quodam quasi vento impetu animi incitati; quae beneficia aeque magna non sunt habenda atque ea, quae iudicio, considerate constanterque delata sunt.

Sed in collocando beneficio et in referenda gratia, si cetera paria sunt, hoc maxime officii est, ut quisque maxime opis indigeat, ita ei potissimum opitulari; quod contra fit a plerisque; a quo enim plurimum sperant,[2] etiamsi ille iis non eget, tamen ei potissimum inserviunt.

50 XVI. Optime autem societas hominum coniunctioque servabitur, si, ut quisque erit coniunctissimus, ita in eum benignitatis plurimum conferetur.

Sed, quae naturae principia sint communitatis et societatis humanae, repetendum videtur altius; est enim primum, quod cernitur in universi generis humani societate. Eius autem vinculum est ratio et

[1] *modo* A H L b c; *si modo* B.
[2] *sperant* Marg. A, Edd.; *spectant* A b (*spernant* Marg. b).

a kindness and requiting one. Whether we do the kindness or not is optional; but to fail to requite one is not allowable to a good man, provided he can make the requital without violating the rights of others.

49 Furthermore, we must make some discrimination between favours received; for, as a matter of course, the greater the favour, the greater is the obligation. But in deciding this we must above all give due weight to the spirit, the devotion, the affection, that prompted the favour. For many people often do favours impulsively for everybody without discrimination, prompted by a morbid sort of benevolence or by a sudden impulse of the heart, shifting as the wind. Such acts of generosity are not to be so highly esteemed as those which are performed with judgment, deliberation, and mature consideration.

But in bestowing a kindness, as well as in making a requital, the first rule of duty requires us—other things being equal—to lend assistance preferably to people in proportion to their individual need. Most people adopt the contrary course: they put themselves most eagerly at the service of the one from whom they hope to receive the greatest favours, even though he has no need of their help.

(3) self-interest,

50 XVI. The interests of society, however, and its common bonds will be best conserved, if kindness be shown to each individual in proportion to the closeness of his relationship.

(4) relationship.

The principles of human society.

But it seems we must trace back to their ultimate sources the principles of fellowship and society that Nature has established among men. The first principle is that which is found in the connection subsisting between all the members of the human race;

oratio, quae docendo, discendo, communicando, disceptando, iudicando conciliat inter se homines coniungitque naturali quadam societate; neque ulla re longius absumus a natura ferarum, in quibus inesse fortitudinem saepe dicimus, ut in equis, in leonibus, iustitiam, aequitatem, bonitatem non dicimus; sunt enim rationis et orationis expertes.

51 Ac latissime quidem patens hominibus inter ipsos, omnibus inter omnes societas haec est; in qua omnium rerum, quas ad communem hominum usum natura genuit, est servanda communitas, ut, quae discripta [1] sunt legibus et iure civili, haec ita teneantur, ut sit constitutum legibus ipsis,[2] cetera sic observentur, ut in Graecorum proverbio est, amicorum esse communia omnia.[a] Omnium [3] autem communia hominum videntur ea, quae sunt generis eius, quod ab Ennio positum in una re transferri in permultas potest:

(Telephus ?) Vahlen², Fab. Inc. 398

Homó, qui erranti cómiter monstrát viam,
Quasi lúmen de suo lúmine accendát, facit.
Nihiló minus ipsi lúcet,[4] cum illi accénderit.

Una ex re satis praecipit, ut, quicquid sine detri-
52 mento commodari possit, id tribuatur vel ignoto; ex quo sunt illa communia: non prohibere aqua profluente, pati ab igne ignem capere, si qui velit, consilium

[1] *discripta* H b, Edd.; *descripta* A B L a c.
[2] *legibus ipsis* Gulielmus, Edd.; *e* (*ex* c) *quibus ipsis* MSS.
[3] *Omnium* Zumpt, Edd.; *omnia* MSS.
[4] *ipsi lucet* Edd.; *ipsi luceat* A B H b c; *ipsi ut luceat* a.

---

[a] κοινὰ τὰ (τῶν) φίλων (Plato, Phaedr. 279 C; Aristotle, Eth. VIII, 11).

and that bond of connection is reason and speech, which by the processes of teaching and learning, of communicating, discussing, and reasoning associate men together and unite them in a sort of natural fraternity. In no other particular are we farther removed from the nature of beasts; for we admit that they may have courage (horses and lions, for example); but we do not admit that they have justice, equity, and goodness; for they are not endowed with reason or speech.

51 This, then, is the most comprehensive bond that unites together men as men and all to all; and under it the common right to all things that Nature has produced for the common use of man is to be maintained, with the understanding that, while everything assigned as private property by the statutes and by civil law shall be so held as prescribed by those same laws, everything else shall be regarded in the light indicated by the Greek proverb: "Amongst friends all things in common."[a] Furthermore, we find the common property of all men in things of the sort defined by Ennius; and, though restricted by him to one instance, the principle may be applied very generally:

> "Who kindly sets a wand'rer on his way
> Does e'en as if he lit another's lamp by his:
> No less shines his, when he his friend's hath lit."

In this example he effectively teaches us all to bestow even upon a stranger what it costs us nothing to give.

52 On this principle we have the following maxims:

"Deny no one the water that flows by;" "Let anyone who will take fire from our fire;" "Honest counsel give to one who is in doubt;"

fidele deliberanti dare, quae sunt iis utilia, qui accipiunt, danti non molesta. Quare et his utendum est et semper aliquid ad communem utilitatem afferendum. Sed quoniam copiae parvae singulorum sunt, eorum autem, qui his egeant, infinita est multitudo, vulgaris liberalitas referenda est ad illum Ennii finem: "Nihilo minus ipsi lucet," ut facultas sit, qua in nostros simus liberales.

53 XVII. Gradus autem plures sunt societatis hominum. Ut enim ab illa infinita discedatur, propior[1] est eiusdem gentis, nationis, linguae, qua maxime homines coniunguntur; interius etiam est eiusdem esse civitatis; multa enim sunt civibus inter se communia, forum, fana, porticus, viae, leges, iura, iudicia, suffragia, consuetudines praeterea et familiaritates multisque cum multis res rationesque contractae.

Artior vero colligatio est societatis propinquorum; ab illa enim immensa societate humani generis in
54 exiguum angustumque concluditur. Nam cum sit hoc natura commune animantium, ut habeant libidinem procreandi, prima societas in ipso coniugio est, proxima in liberis, deinde una domus, communia omnia; id autem est principium urbis et quasi seminarium rei publicae. Sequuntur fratrum coniunctiones, post consobrinorum sobrinorumque, qui cum una domo iam capi non possint, in alias domos tam-

[1] *propior* A a c (ex corr.), Edd.; *proprior* B H b.

for such acts are useful to the recipient and cause the giver no loss. We should, therefore, adopt these principles and always be contributing something to the common weal. But since the resources of individuals are limited and the number of the needy is infinite, this spirit of universal liberality must be regulated according to that test of Ennius—"No less shines his"—in order that we may continue to have the means for being generous to our friends.

53 XVII. Then, too, there are a great many degrees of closeness or remoteness in human society. To proceed beyond the universal bond of our common humanity, there is the closer one of belonging to the same people, tribe, and tongue, by which men are very closely bound together; it is a still closer relation to be citizens of the same city-state; for fellow-citizens have much in common—forum, temples, colonnades, streets, statutes, laws, courts, rights of suffrage, to say nothing of social and friendly circles and diverse business relations with many.

Degrees of social relationship: (1) citizenship,

But a still closer social union exists between kindred. Starting with that infinite bond of union of the human race in general, the conception is now confined
54 to a small and narrow circle. For since the reproductive instinct is by Nature's gift the common possession of all living creatures, the first bond of union is that between husband and wife; the next, that between parents and children; then we find one home, with everything in common. And this is the foundation of civil government, the nursery, as it were, of the state. Then follow the bonds between brothers and sisters, and next those of first and then of second cousins; and when they can no longer be sheltered under one roof, they go out into other

(2) kinship,

quam in colonias exeunt. Sequuntur conubia et affinitates, ex quibus etiam plures propinqui; quae propagatio et suboles origo est rerum publicarum. Sanguinis autem coniunctio et benivolentia devincit
55 homines *et* [1] caritate; magnum est enim eadem habere monumenta maiorum, eisdem uti sacris, sepulcra habere communia.

Sed omnium societatum nulla praestantior est, nulla firmior, quam cum viri boni moribus similes sunt familiaritate coniuncti; illud enim honestum, quod saepe dicimus, etiam si in alio cernimus, [tamen] [2] nos movet atque illi, in quo id inesse videtur, amicos
56 facit. Et quamquam omnis virtus nos ad se allicit facitque, ut eos diligamus, in quibus ipsa inesse videatur, tamen iustitia et liberalitas id maxime efficit. Nihil autem est amabilius nec copulatius quam morum similitudo bonorum; in quibus enim eadem studia sunt, eaedem voluntates, in iis fit ut aeque quisque altero delectetur ac se ipso, efficiturque id, quod Pythagoras vult in amicitia, ut [3] unus fiat ex pluribus.

Magna etiam illa communitas est, quae conficitur ex beneficiis ultro et citro datis acceptis, quae et mutua et grata dum sunt, inter quos ea sunt, firma devinciuntur societate.

57 Sed cum omnia ratione animoque lustraris, omnium societatum nulla est gravior, nulla carior quam ea, quae cum re publica est uni cuique nostrum. Cari

[1] *et* Perizonius, Edd.; not in MSS.
[2] *tamen* MSS., Müller; del. Unger, Bt., Heine.
[3] *efficiturque id quod P. ultimum in amicitia putavit ut* Nonius (s.v. ultimum) (i.e. Pythagoras's ideal of friendship is realized).

homes, as into colonies. Then follow between these,
in turn, marriages and connections by marriage, and
from these again a new stock of relations; and from
this propagation and after-growth states have their
beginnings. The bonds of common blood hold men
55 fast through good-will and affection; for it means
much to share in common the same family traditions,
the same forms of domestic worship, and the same
ancestral tombs.

But of all the bonds of fellowship, there is none (3) friendship
more noble, none more powerful than when good
men of congenial character are joined in intimate
friendship; for really, if we discover in another that
moral goodness on which I dwell so much, it attracts
us and makes us friends to the one in whose character
56 it seems to dwell. And while every virtue attracts
us and makes us love those who seem to possess it,
still justice and generosity do so most of all. Nothing,
moreover, is more conducive to love and intimacy
than compatibility of character in good men; for
when two people have the same ideals and the same
tastes, it is a natural consequence that each loves the
other as himself; and the result is, as Pythagoras
requires of ideal friendship, that several are united
in one.

Another strong bond of fellowship is effected by
mutual interchange of kind services; and as long as
these kindnesses are mutual and acceptable, those
between whom they are interchanged are united by
the ties of an enduring intimacy.

57 But when with a rational spirit you have surveyed (4) love of country.
the whole field, there is no social relation among
them all more close, none more dear than that
which links each one of us with our country. Parents

sunt parentes, cari liberi, propinqui, familiares, sed omnes omnium caritates patria una complexa est, pro qua quis bonus dubitet mortem oppetere, si ei sit profuturus? Quo est detestabilior istorum immanitas, qui lacerarunt omni scelere patriam et in ea funditus delenda occupati et sunt et fuerunt.

58 Sed si contentio quaedam et comparatio fiat, quibus plurimum tribuendum sit officii, principes sint patria et parentes, quorum beneficiis maximis obligati sumus, proximi liberi totaque domus, quae spectat in nos solos neque aliud ullum potest habere perfugium, deinceps bene convenientes propinqui, quibuscum communis etiam fortuna plerumque est.

Quam ob rem necessaria praesidia vitae debentur iis maxime, quos ante dixi, vita autem victusque communis, consilia, sermones, cohortationes, consolationes, interdum etiam obiurgationes in amicitiis vigent maxime, estque ea iucundissima amicitia, quam similitudo morum coniugavit.

59 XVIII. Sed in his omnibus officiis tribuendis videndum erit, quid cuique maxime necesse sit, et quid quisque vel sine nobis aut possit consequi aut non possit. Ita non iidem erunt necessitudinum gradus, qui temporum; suntque officia, quae aliis magis quam aliis debeantur; ut vicinum citius adiuveris in fructibus percipiendis quam aut fratrem aut

[a] Antony and his associates. [b] Caesar, Clodius, Catiline.

are dear; dear are children, relatives, friends; but one native land embraces all our loves; and who that is true would hesitate to give his life for her, if by his death he could render her a service? So much the more execrable are those monsters who have torn their fatherland to pieces with every form of outrage and who are [a] and have been [b] engaged in compassing her utter destruction.

58 Now, if a contrast and comparison were to be made to find out where most of our moral obligation is due, country would come first, and parents; for their services have laid us under the heaviest obligation; next come children and the whole family, who look to us alone for support and can have no other protection; finally, our kinsmen, with whom we live on good terms and with whom, for the most part, our lot is one.

All needful material assistance is, therefore, due first of all to those whom I have named; but intimate relationship of life and living, counsel, conversation, encouragement, comfort, and sometimes even reproof flourish best in friendships. And that friendship is sweetest which is cemented by congeniality of character.

**Duties may vary under varying circumstances.**

59 XVIII. But in the performance of all these duties we shall have to consider what is most needful in each individual case and what each individual person can or cannot procure without our help. In this way we shall find that the claims of social relationship, in its various degrees, are not identical with the dictates of circumstances; for there are obligations that are due to one individual rather than to another: for example, one would sooner assist a neighbour in gathering his harvest than either

familiarem, at, si lis in iudicio sit, propinquum potius et amicum quam vicinum defenderis. Haec igitur et talia circumspicienda sunt in omni officio [et consuetudo exercitatioque capienda],[1] ut boni ratiocinatores officiorum esse possimus et addendo deducendoque [2] videre, quae reliqui summa fiat, ex quo, quantum cuique debeatur, intellegas.

60 Sed ut nec medici nec imperatores nec oratores, quamvis artis praecepta perceperint, quicquam magna laude dignum sine usu et exercitatione consequi possunt, sic officii conservandi praecepta traduntur illa quidem, ut facimus ipsi, sed rei magnitudo usum quoque exercitationemque desiderat.

Atque ab iis [3] rebus, quae sunt in iure societatis humanae, quem ad modum ducatur honestum, ex quo aptum est officium, satis fere diximus.

61 Intelligendum autem est, cum proposita sint genera quattuor, e quibus honestas officiumque manaret, splendidissimum videri, quod animo magno elatoque humanasque res despiciente factum sit. Itaque in probris maxime in promptu est si quid tale dici potest:

Pac. inc. fab., Ribbeck², 210

> " Vós enim,[4] iuvenes, ánimum geritis múliebrem,
> ílla " virgo " viri " [5]

et si quid eius modi:

Enn. Aj., Vahlen², 18

> Salmácida, spolia síne sudore et sánguine.

[1] *et . . . capienda* om. Facciolati, Edd.
[2] *deducendoque* p; *ducendoque* A B H L a b (superscr. sec. m. *demendo*); *demendoque* c.
[3] *iis* Edd.; *his* MSS.
[4] *enim* A B H b c; *etenim* a.
[5] *illa* " *virgo* " *viri* " Ed.; *illa virgo viri* MSS.; *virago* Orelli.

[a] Cloelia (see Index).

a brother or a friend; but should it be a case in court, one would defend a kinsman and a friend rather than a neighbour. Such questions as these must, therefore, be taken into consideration in every act of moral duty [and we must acquire the habit and keep it up], in order to become good calculators of duty, able by adding and subtracting to strike a balance correctly and find out just how much is due to each individual.

60 But as neither physicians nor generals nor orators can achieve any signal success without experience and practice, no matter how well they may understand the theory of their profession, so the rules for the discharge of duty are formulated, it is true, as I am doing now, but a matter of such importance requires experience also and practice.

This must close our discussion of the ways in which moral goodness, on which duty depends, is developed from those principles which hold good in human society.

61 We must realize, however, that while we have set C. Fortitude. down four cardinal virtues from which as sources moral rectitude and moral duty emanate, that achievement is most glorious in the eyes of the world which is won with a spirit great, exalted, and superior to the vicissitudes of earthly life. And so, when we wish to hurl a taunt, the very first to rise to our lips is, if possible, something like this:

> "For ye, young men, show a womanish soul, yon maiden [a] a man's;"

and this:

> "Thou son of Salmacis, win spoils that cost nor sweat nor blood."

Contraque in laudibus, quae magno animo et fortiter excellenterque gesta sunt, ea nescio quo modo quasi pleniore ore laudamus. Hinc rhetorum campus de Marathone, Salamine, Plataeis, Thermopylis, Leuctris, hinc noster Cocles,[1] hinc Decii, hinc Cn. et P. Scipiones, hinc M. Marcellus, innumerabiles alii, maximeque ipse populus Romanus animi magnitudine excellit. Declaratur autem studium bellicae gloriae, quod statuas quoque videmus ornatu fere militari.

62 XIX. Sed ea animi elatio, quae cernitur in periculis et laboribus, si iustitia vacat pugnatque non pro salute communi, sed pro suis commodis, in vitio est; non modo enim id virtutis non est, sed est potius immanitatis omnem humanitatem repellentis. Itaque probe definitur a Stoicis fortitudo, cum eam virtutem esse dicunt propugnantem pro aequitate. Quocirca nemo, qui fortitudinis gloriam consecutus est insidiis et malitia, laudem est adeptus; nihil enim[2] honestum esse potest, quod iustitia vacat.

Menex. 246 E; Laches 197 B

63 Praeclarum igitur illud Platonis: "Non," inquit, "solum scientia, quae est remota ab iustitia, calliditas potius quam sapientia est appellanda, verum etiam animus paratus ad periculum, si sua cupiditate, non utilitate communi impellitur, audaciae potius nomen habeat quam fortitudinis." Itaque viros fortes et[3] magnanimos eosdem bonos et simplices, veritatis amicos minimeque fallaces esse volumus; quae sunt ex media laude iustitiae.

[1] *Leuctris, hinc noster Cocles* Baldwin, Edd.; *leutris stercocles* A B H a b; *leutrister chodes* c; *leutris stercodes* L.
[2] *enim* A C, Edd.; not in A B H L b, Bt[2].
[3] *et* a, Edd.; not in A B H L b c p.

When, on the other hand, we wish to pay a compliment, we somehow or other praise in more eloquent strain the brave and noble work of some great soul. Hence there is an open field for orators on the subjects of Marathon, Salamis, Plataea, Thermopylae, and Leuctra, and hence our own Cocles, the Decii, Gnaeus and Publius Scipio, Marcus Marcellus, and countless others, and, above all, the Roman People as a nation are celebrated for greatness of spirit. Their passion for military glory, moreover, is shown in the fact that we see their statues usually in soldier's garb.

**Fortitude in the light of justice.**

62 XIX. But if the exaltation of spirit seen in times of danger and toil is devoid of justice and fights for selfish ends instead of for the common good, it is a vice; for not only has it no element of virtue, but its nature is barbarous and revolting to all our finer feelings. The Stoics, therefore, correctly define courage as "that virtue which champions the cause of right." Accordingly, no one has attained to true glory who has gained a reputation for courage by treachery and cunning; for nothing that lacks justice can be morally right.

63 This, then, is a fine saying of Plato's: "Not only must all knowledge that is divorced from justice be called cunning rather than wisdom," he says, "but even the courage that is prompt to face danger, if it is inspired not by public spirit, but by its own selfish purposes, should have the name of effrontery rather than of courage." And so we demand that men who are courageous and high-souled shall at the same time be good and straightforward, lovers of truth, and foes to deception; for these qualities are the centre and soul of justice.

64 Sed illud odiosum est, quod in hac elatione et magnitudine animi facillime pertinacia et nimia cupiditas principatus innascitur. Ut enim apud Platonem est, omnem morem Lacedaemoniorum inflammatum esse cupiditate vincendi, sic, ut quisque animi magnitudine maxime excellet,[1] ita maxime vult princeps omnium vel potius solus esse. Difficile autem est, cum praestare omnibus concupieris, servare aequitatem, quae est iustitiae maxime propria. Ex quo fit, ut neque disceptatione vinci se nec ullo publico ac legitimo iure patiantur, exsistuntque in re publica plerumque largitores et factiosi, ut opes quam maximas consequantur et sint vi[2] potius superiores quam iustitia pares. Sed quo difficilius, hoc praeclarius; nullum enim est tempus, quod iustitia vacare debeat.

Laches 182 E

65 Fortes igitur et magnanimi sunt habendi, non qui faciunt, sed qui propulsant iniuriam. Vera autem et sapiens animi magnitudo honestum illud, quod maxime natura sequitur, in factis positum, non in gloria iudicat principemque se esse mavult quam videri; etenim qui ex errore imperitae multitudinis pendet, hic in magnis viris non est habendus. Facillime autem ad res iniustas impellitur, ut quisque altissimo animo est, gloriae cupiditate;[3] qui locus est sane lubricus, quod vix invenitur, qui laboribus susceptis periculisque aditis non quasi mercedem rerum gestarum desideret gloriam.

[1] *excellet* A B H L b c; *excellit* a, Bt.

[2] *vi* a, Edd.; *ut* A B H b; *utcumque* L c.

[3] *altissimo animo est, gloriae cupiditate* Pearce (confirmed by several MSS.), Edd.; *alt. an. et gloriae cupiditate* A B H b p; *est alt. an. et gloria et cupiditate* L c.

64 But the mischief is that from this exaltation and greatness of spirit spring all too readily self-will and excessive lust for power. For just as Plato tells us that the whole national character of the Spartans was on fire with passion for victory, so, in the same way, the more notable a man is for his greatness of spirit, the more ambitious he is to be the foremost citizen, or, I should say rather, to be sole ruler. But when one begins to aspire to pre-eminence, it is difficult to preserve that spirit of fairness which is absolutely essential to justice. The result is that such men do not allow themselves to be constrained either by argument or by any public and lawful authority; but they only too often prove to be bribers and agitators in public life, seeking to obtain supreme power and to be superiors through force rather than equals through justice. But the greater the difficulty, the greater the glory; for no occasion arises that can excuse a man for being guilty of injustice.

65 So then, not those who do injury but those who prevent it are to be considered brave and courageous. Moreover, true and philosophic greatness of spirit regards the moral goodness to which Nature most aspires as consisting in deeds, not in fame, and prefers to be first in reality rather than in name. And we must approve this view; for he who depends upon the caprice of the ignorant rabble cannot be numbered among the great. Then, too, the higher a man's ambition, the more easily he is tempted to acts of injustice by his desire for fame. We are now, to be sure, on very slippery ground; for scarcely can the man be found who has passed through trials and encountered dangers and does not then wish for glory as a reward for his achievements.

True greatness of spirit.

66 XX. Omnino fortis animus et magnus duabus rebus maxime cernitur, quarum una in rerum externarum despicientia ponitur, cum persuasum est[1] nihil hominem, nisi quod honestum decorumque sit, aut admirari aut optare aut expetere oportere nullique neque homini neque perturbationi animi nec fortunae succumbere. Altera est res, ut, cum ita sis affectus animo, ut supra dixi, res geras magnas illas quidem et maxime utiles, sed [ut] vehementer arduas plenasque laborum et periculorum cum vitae, tum multarum rerum, quae ad vitam pertinent.

67 Harum rerum duarum splendor omnis, amplitudo, addo etiam utilitatem, in posteriore est, causa autem et ratio efficiens magnos viros in priore; in eo est enim illud, quod excellentes animos et humana contemnentes facit. Id autem ipsum cernitur in duobus, si et solum id, quod honestum sit, bonum iudices et ab omni animi perturbatione liber sis. Nam et ea, quae eximia plerisque et praeclara videntur, parva ducere eaque ratione stabili firmaque contemnere fortis animi magnique ducendum est, et ea, quae videntur acerba, quae multa et varia in hominum vita fortunaque versantur, ita ferre, ut nihil a statu naturae discedas, nihil a dignitate sapientis, robusti
68 animi est magnaeque constantiae. Non est autem consentaneum, qui metu non frangatur, eum frangi cupiditate nec, qui invictum se a labore praestiterit, vinci a voluptate. Quam ob rem et haec vitanda[2]

[1] *persuasum est* Madvig (ad de Fin. p. 448 ff.), Edd.; *p. sit* MSS.

[2] *vitanda* Edd. (cum duobus codd. Guelpherbytanis); *videnda* MSS.

66 XX. The soul that is altogether courageous and great is marked above all by two characteristics: one of these is indifference to outward circumstances; for such a person cherishes the conviction that nothing but moral goodness and propriety deserves to be either admired or wished for or striven after, and that he ought not to be subject to any man or any passion or any accident of fortune. The second characteristic is that, when the soul is disciplined in the way above mentioned, one should do deeds not only great and in the highest degree useful, but extremely arduous and laborious and fraught with danger both to life and to many things that make life worth living.

Characteristic of Fortitude:

67 All the glory and greatness and, I may add, all the usefulness of these two characteristics of courage are centred in the latter; the rational cause that makes men great, in the former. For it is the former that contains the element that makes souls pre-eminent and indifferent to worldly fortune. And this quality is distinguished by two criteria: (1) if one account moral rectitude as the only good; and (2) if one be free from all passion. For we must agree that it takes a brave and heroic soul to hold as slight what most people think grand and glorious, and to disregard it from fixed and settled principles. And it requires strength of character and great singleness of purpose to bear what seems painful, as it comes to pass in many and various forms in human life, and to bear it so unflinchingly as not to be shaken in the least from one's natural state of the dignity of a
68 philosopher. Moreover, it would be inconsistent for the man who is not overcome by fear to be overcome by desire, or for the man who has shown himself invincible to toil to be conquered by pleasure. We

(1) Moral courage.

Indifference to outward fortunes.

et pecuniae fugienda cupiditas; nihil enim est tam angusti animi tamque parvi quam amare divitias, nihil honestius magnificentiusque quam pecuniam contemnere, si non habeas, si habeas, ad beneficentiam liberalitatemque conferre.

Cavenda etiam est gloriae cupiditas, ut supra dixi; eripit enim libertatem, pro qua magnanimis viris omnis debet esse contentio. Nec vero imperia expetenda ac potius aut non accipienda interdum aut deponenda non numquam.

69 Vacandum autem omni est animi perturbatione, cum cupiditate et metu, tum etiam aegritudine et voluptate nimia [1] et iracundia, ut tranquillitas animi et securitas adsit, quae affert cum constantiam, tum etiam dignitatem. Multi autem et sunt et fuerunt, qui eam, quam dico, tranquillitatem expetentes a negotiis publicis se removerint ad otiumque perfugerint; in his et nobilissimi philosophi longeque principes et quidam homines severi et graves nec populi nec principum mores ferre potuerunt, vixeruntque non nulli in agris delectati re sua familiari.
70 His idem propositum fuit, quod regibus, ut ne qua re egerent, ne cui parerent, libertate uterentur, cuius proprium est sic vivere, ut velis.

XXI. Quare cum hoc commune sit potentiae cupidorum cum iis, quos dixi, otiosis, alteri se

[1] *voluptate nimia* Orelli, Müller; *voluptate animi* A H L a b c; *vol. animi et securitas* (*et iracundia ut tr. animi* by a later hand on the margin) B; *voluptate* [*animi*], Bt., Heine.

---

[a] As Cicero did at the expiration of his consulship.

[b] As Sulla did in his dictatorship. The contrast to Caesar is the more striking for Cicero's not mentioning it.

[c] e.g. Plato, Aristotle, Zeno, Pythagoras, Anaxagoras.

[d] Such as Cicero's friend, Atticus, and Marcus Piso.

must, therefore, not only avoid the latter, but also beware of ambition for wealth; for there is nothing so characteristic of narrowness and littleness of soul as the love of riches; and there is nothing more honourable and noble than to be indifferent to money, if one does not possess it, and to devote it to beneficence and liberality, if one does possess it.

As I said before, we must also beware of ambition for glory; for it robs us of liberty, and in defence of liberty a high-souled man should stake everything. And one ought not to seek military authority; nay, rather it ought sometimes to be declined,[a] sometimes to be resigned.[b]

69 Again, we must keep ourselves free from every disturbing emotion, not only from desire and fear, but also from excessive pain and pleasure, and from anger, so that we may enjoy that calm of soul and freedom from care which bring both moral stability and dignity of character. But there have been many and still are many who, while pursuing that calm of soul of which I speak, have withdrawn from civic duty and taken refuge in retirement. Among such have been found the most famous and by far the foremost philosophers [c] and certain other [d] earnest, thoughtful men who could not endure the conduct of either the people or their leaders; some of them, too, lived in the country and found their pleasure in the manage-
70 ment of their private estates. Such men have had the same aims as kings—to suffer no want, to be subject to no authority, to enjoy their liberty, that is, in its essence, to live just as they please.

(3) Freedom from passion.

The retired life.

XXI. So, while this desire is common to men of political ambitions and men of retirement, of whom I have just spoken, the one class think they can

adipisci id posse arbitrantur, si opes magnas habeant, alteri, si contenti sint et suo et parvo. In quo neutrorum omnino contemnenda sententia est, sed et facilior et tutior et minus aliis gravis aut molesta vita est otiosorum, fructuosior autem hominum generi et ad claritatem amplitudinemque aptior eorum, qui se ad rem publicam et ad magnas res gerendas accommodaverunt.

71 Quapropter et iis forsitan concedendum sit rem publicam non capessentibus, qui excellenti ingenio doctrinae sese dediderunt, et iis, qui aut valetudinis imbecillitate aut aliqua graviore causa impediti a re publica recesserunt, cum eius administrandae potestatem aliis laudemque concederent. Quibus autem talis nulla sit causa, si despicere se dicant ea, quae plerique mirentur, imperia et magistratus, iis non modo non laudi, verum etiam vitio dandum puto; quorum iudicium in eo, quod gloriam contemnant et pro nihilo putent, difficile factu est non probare; sed videntur labores et molestias, tum offensionum et repulsarum quasi quandam ignominiam timere et infamiam. Sunt enim, qui in rebus contrariis parum sibi constent, voluptatem severissime contemnant, in dolore sint molliores, gloriam neglegant, frangantur infamia, atque ea quidem non satis constanter.

72 Sed iis, qui habent a natura adiumenta rerum gerendarum, abiecta omni cunctatione adipiscendi

attain their end if they secure large means; the other, if they are content with the little they have. And, in this matter, neither way of thinking is altogether to be condemned; but the life of retirement is easier and safer and at the same time less burdensome or troublesome to others, while the career of those who apply themselves to statecraft and to conducting great enterprises is more profitable to mankind and contributes more to their own greatness and renown.

**The life of public service *vs.* the life of retirement.**

71 So perhaps those men of extraordinary genius who have devoted themselves to learning must be excused for not taking part in public affairs; likewise, those who from ill-health or for some still more valid reason have retired from the service of the state and left to others the opportunity and the glory of its administration. But if those who have no such excuse profess a scorn for civil and military offices, which most people admire, I think that this should be set down not to their credit but to their discredit; for in so far as they care little, as they say, for glory and count it as naught, it is difficult not to sympathize with their attitude; in reality, however, they seem to dread the toil and trouble and also, perhaps, the discredit and humiliation of political failure and defeat. For there are people who in opposite circumstances do not act consistently: they have the utmost contempt for pleasure, but in pain they are too sensitive; they are indifferent to glory, but they are crushed by disgrace; and even in their inconsistency they show no great consistency.

**Public service a duty.**

72 But those whom Nature has endowed with the capacity for administering public affairs should put

magistratus et gerenda res publica est; nec enim aliter aut regi civitas aut declarari animi magnitudo potest. Capessentibus autem rem publicam nihilo[1] minus quam philosophis, haud scio an magis etiam et magnificentia et despicientia adhibenda est[2] rerum humanarum, quam saepe dico, et tranquillitas animi atque securitas, siquidem nec anxii futuri
73 sunt et cum gravitate constantiaque victuri. Quae faciliora sunt philosophis, quo minus multa patent in eorum vita, quae fortuna feriat, et quo minus multis rebus egent, et quia, si quid adversi eveniat, tam graviter cadere non possunt. Quocirca non sine causa maiores motus animorum concitantur maioraque studia efficiendi[3] rem publicam gerentibus quam quietis, quo magis iis et magnitudo est animi adhibenda et vacuitas ab angoribus.

Ad rem gerendam autem qui accedit, caveat, ne id modo consideret, quam illa res honesta sit, sed etiam ut habeat efficiendi facultatem; in quo ipso considerandum est, ne aut temere desperet propter ignaviam aut nimis confidat propter cupiditatem. In omnibus autem negotiis, prius quam aggrediare, adhibenda est praeparatio diligens.

74 XXII. Sed cum plerique arbitrentur res bellicas maiores esse quam urbanas, minuenda est haec opinio. Multi enim bella saepe quaesiverunt propter gloriae cupiditatem, atque id in magnis animis ingeniisque plerumque contingit, eoque magis, si sunt ad rem militarem apti et cupidi bellorum

[1] *nihilo* Wesenberg, Edd.; *nihil* MSS.

[2] *est* Manutius, Edd.; *sit* MSS.

[3] *maioraque studia efficiendi* Unger, Müller; *maioraque efficiendi* $A^1$ B H L b c; *maiorque cura efficiendi* a, Bt., Heine; *maioraque efficienda* $A^2$ p.

aside all hesitation, enter the race for public office, and take a hand in directing the government; for in no other way can a government be administered or greatness of spirit be made manifest. Statesmen, too, no less than philosophers—perhaps even more so—should carry with them that greatness of spirit and indifference to outward circumstances to which I so often refer, together with calm of soul and freedom from care, if they are to be free from worries
73 and lead a dignified and self-consistent life. This is easier for the philosophers; as their life is less exposed to the assaults of fortune, their wants are fewer; and, if any misfortune overtakes them, their fall is not so disastrous. Not without reason, therefore, are stronger emotions aroused in those who engage in public life than in those who live in retirement, and greater is their ambition for success; the more, therefore, do they need to enjoy greatness of spirit and freedom from annoying cares.

If anyone is entering public life, let him beware of thinking only of the honour that it brings; but let him be sure also that he has the ability to succeed. At the same time, let him take care not to lose heart too readily through discouragement nor yet to be over-confident through ambition. In a word, before undertaking any enterprise, careful preparation must be made.

**Victories of war *vs.* victories of peace.**

74 XXII. Most people think that the achievements of war are more important than those of peace; but this opinion needs to be corrected. For many men have sought occasions for war from the mere ambition for fame. This is notably the case with men of great spirit and natural ability, and it is the more likely to happen, if they are adapted to a soldier's

gerendorum; vere autem si volumus iudicare, multae res exstiterunt urbanae maiores clarioresque quam bellicae.

75 Quamvīs enim Themistocles iure laudetur et sit eius nomen quam Solonis illustrius citeturque Salamis clarissimae testis victoriae, quae anteponatur consilio Solonis ei, quo primum constituit Areopagitas, non minus praeclarum hoc quam illud iudicandum est; illud enim semel profuit, hoc semper proderit civitati; hoc consilio leges Atheniensium, hoc maiorum instituta servantur; et Themistocles quidem nihil dixerit, in quo ipse Areopagum adiuverit, at ille vere a[1] se adiutum Themistoclem; est enim bellum gestum consilio senatus eius, qui a Solone erat constitutus.

76 Licet eadem de Pausania Lysandroque dicere, quorum rebus gestis quamquam imperium Lacedaemoniis partum[2] putatur, tamen ne minima quidem ex parte Lycurgi legibus et disciplinae conferendi sunt; quin etiam ob has ipsas causas et parentiores habuerunt exercitus et fortiores. Mihi quidem neque pueris nobis M. Scaurus C. Mario neque, cum versaremur in re publica, Q. Catulus Cn. Pompeio cedere videbatur; parvi enim sunt foris arma, nisi est consilium domi; nec plus Africanus, singularis

[1] *a* Edd.; not in MSS.; *se adiutum* A B H b, Edd.; *adiuvit* L$^1$ c p; *se adiutum ab illo dixerit* (?) *Themistocles* L$^2$.

[2] *L. partum* Lambinus, Müller; *partum L.*, Bt.; om. *partum* A$^1$ B H L$^1$ a b; *L. dilatatum* A$^2$; *dilatatum L.* L$^2$ c.

life and fond of warfare. But if we will face the facts, we shall find that there have been many instances of achievement in peace more important and no less renowned than in war.

75 However highly Themistocles, for example, may be extolled—and deservedly—and however much more illustrious his name may be than Solon's, and however much Salamis may be cited as witness of his most glorious victory—a victory glorified above Solon's statesmanship in instituting the Areopagus—yet Solon's achievement is not to be accounted less illustrious than his. For Themistocles's victory served the state once and only once; while Solon's work will be of service for ever. For through his legislation the laws of the Athenians and the institutions of their fathers are maintained. And while Themistocles could not readily point to any instance in which he himself had rendered assistance to the Areopagus, the Areopagus might with justice assert that Themistocles had received assistance from it; for the war was directed by the counsels of that senate which Solon had created. **Themistocles *vs.* Solon.**

76 The same may be said of Pausanias and Lysander. Although it is thought that it was by their achievements that Sparta gained her supremacy, yet these are not even remotely to be compared with the legislation and discipline of Lycurgus. Nay, rather, it was due to these that Pausanias and Lysander had armies so brave and so well disciplined. For my own part, I do not consider that Marcus Scaurus was inferior to Gaius Marius, when I was a lad, or Quintus Catulus to Gnaeus Pompey, when I was engaged in public life. For arms are of little value in the field unless there is wise counsel at home. So, too, **Pausanias and Lysander *vs.* Lycurgus.**

et vir et imperator, in exscindenda Numantia rei publicae profuit quam eodem tempore P. Nasica privatus, cum Ti. Gracchum interemit; quamquam haec quidem res non solum ex domestica est ratione (attingit etiam bellicam, quoniam vi manuque confecta est), sed tamen id ipsum est gestum consilio urbano sine exercitu.

Cic., de temp. suis, iii

77 Illud autem optimum est, in quod invadi solere ab improbis et invidis audio:

"Cedant arma togae, concedat laurea laudi."

Ut enim alios omittam, nobis rem publicam gubernantibus nonne togae arma cesserunt? neque enim periculum in re publica fuit gravius umquam nec maius otium. Ita consiliis diligentiaque nostra celeriter de manibus audacissimorum civium delapsa arma ipsa ceciderunt. Quae res igitur gesta umquam
78 in bello tanta? qui triumphus conferendus? licet enim mihi, M. fili, apud te gloriari, ad quem et hereditas huius gloriae et factorum imitatio pertinet. Mihi quidem certe vir abundans bellicis laudibus, Cn. Pompeius, multis audientibus hoc tribuit, ut diceret frustra se triumphum tertium deportaturum fuisse, nisi meo in rem publicam beneficio, ubi triumpharet, esset habiturus.

Sunt igitur domesticae fortitudines non inferiores

---

[a] The praises of Cicero for his overthrow of the conspiracy of Catiline.

[b] The laurels of the triumphant general.

Africanus, though a great man and a soldier of extraordinary ability, did no greater service to the state by destroying Numantia than was done at the same time by Publius Nasica, though not then clothed with official authority, by removing Tiberius Gracchus. This deed does not, to be sure, belong wholly to the domain of civil affairs; it partakes of the nature of war also, since it was effected by violence; but it was, for all that, executed as a political measure without the help of an army.

77 The whole truth, however, is in this verse, against which, I am told, the malicious and envious are wont to rail: Cicero's great victory.

"Yield, ye arms, to the toga; to civic praises,[a] ye laurels."[b]

Not to mention other instances, did not arms yield to the toga, when I was at the helm of state? For never was the republic in more serious peril, never was peace more profound. Thus, as the result of my counsels and my vigilance, their weapons slipped suddenly from the hands of the most desperate traitors—dropped to the ground of their own accord! What achievement in war, then, was ever so great?
78 What triumph can be compared with that? For I may boast to you, my son Marcus; for to you belong the inheritance of that glory of mine and the duty of imitating my deeds. And it was to me, too, that Gnaeus Pompey, a hero crowned with the honours of war, paid this tribute in the hearing of many, when he said that his third triumph would have been gained in vain, if he were not to have through my services to the state a place in which to celebrate it.

There are, therefore, instances of civic courage

militaribus; in quibus plus etiam quam in his operae studiique ponendum est.

79 XXIII. Omnino illud honestum, quod ex animo excelso magnificoque quaerimus, animi efficitur, non corporis viribus. Exercendum tamen corpus et ita afficiendum est, ut oboedire consilio rationique possit in exsequendis negotiis et in labore tolerando. Honestum autem id, quod exquirimus, totum est positum in animi cura et cogitatione; in quo non minorem utilitatem afferunt, qui togati rei publicae praesunt, quam qui bellum gerunt. Itaque eorum consilio saepe aut non suscepta aut confecta bella sunt, non numquam etiam illata, ut M. Catonis bellum tertium Punicum, in quo etiam mortui valuit
80 auctoritas. Quare expetenda quidem magis est decernendi ratio quam decertandi fortitudo, sed cavendum, ne id bellandi magis fuga quam utilitatis ratione faciamus. Bellum autem ita suscipiatur, ut nihil aliud nisi pax quaesita videatur.

Fortis vero animi et constantis est non perturbari in rebus asperis nec tumultuantem de gradu deici, ut dicitur, sed praesenti animo uti et consilio nec a ratione discedere.

81 Quamquam hoc animi, illud etiam ingenii magni est, praecipere cogitatione futura et aliquanto [1] ante

[1] *aliquanto* Edd.; *aliquando* MSS.

that are not inferior to the courage of the soldier. Nay, the former calls for even greater energy and greater devotion than the latter.

79 XXIII. That moral goodness which we look for in a lofty, high-minded spirit is secured, of course, by moral, not by physical, strength. And yet the body must be trained and so disciplined that it can obey the dictates of judgment and reason in attending to business and in enduring toil. But that moral goodness which is our theme depends wholly upon the thought and attention given to it by the mind. And, in this way, the men who in a civil capacity direct the affairs of the nation render no less important service than they who conduct its wars: by their statesmanship oftentimes wars are either averted or terminated; sometimes also they are declared. Upon Marcus Cato's counsel, for example, the Third Punic War was undertaken, and in its conduct his influence

(2) Physical courage.

80 was dominant, even after he was dead. And so diplomacy in the friendly settlement of controversies is more desirable than courage in settling them on the battlefield; but we must be careful not to take that course merely for the sake of avoiding war rather than for the sake of public expediency. War, however, should be undertaken in such a way as to make it evident that it has no other object than to secure peace.

But it takes a brave and resolute spirit not to be disconcerted in times of difficulty or ruffled and thrown off one's feet, as the saying is, but to keep one's presence of mind and one's self-possession and not to swerve from the path of reason.

81 Now all this requires great personal courage; but it calls also for great intellectual ability by reflection

Courage and discretion.

constituere, quid accidere possit in utramque partem, et quid agendum sit, cum quid evenerit, nec committere, ut aliquando dicendum sit: "Non putaram."

Haec sunt opera magni animi et excelsi et prudentia consilioque fidentis; temere autem in acie versari et manu cum hoste confligere immane quiddam et beluarum simile est; sed cum tempus necessitasque postulat, decertandum manu est et mors servituti turpitudinique anteponenda.

Ch. xxii 82 XXIV. De evertendis autem diripiendisque urbibus valde considerandum est ne quid temere, ne quid crudeliter. Idque est magni viri, rebus agitatis punire sontes, multitudinem conservare, in omni fortuna recta atque honesta retinere. Ut enim sunt, quem ad modum supra dixi, qui urbanis rebus bellicas anteponant, sic reperias multos, quibus periculosa et calida [1] consilia quietis et cogitatis [2] splendidiora et maiora videantur.

83 Numquam omnino periculi fuga committendum est, ut imbelles timidique videamur, sed fugiendum illud etiam, ne offeramus nos periculis sine causa, quo esse nihil potest stultius. Quapropter in adeundis periculis consuetudo imitanda medicorum est, qui leviter aegrotantes leniter curant, gravioribus autem morbis periculosas curationes et ancipites adhibere coguntur. Quare in tranquillo tempestatem adversam

[1] *calida* Nonius, Edd.; *callida* MSS.

[2] *consilia quietis et cogitatis* Edd.; *consilia et quietis et cogitationis* A B H a b; *consilia et quietis cogitationibus* c p.

to anticipate the future, to discover some time in advance what may happen whether for good or for ill, and what must be done in any possible event, and never to be reduced to having to say "I had not thought of that."

These are the activities that mark a spirit strong, high, and self-reliant in its prudence and wisdom. But to mix rashly in the fray and to fight hand to hand with the enemy is but a barbarous and brutish kind of business. Yet when the stress of circumstances demands it, we must gird on the sword and prefer death to slavery and disgrace.

82 XXIV. As to destroying and plundering cities, let me say that great care should be taken that nothing be done in reckless cruelty or wantonness. And it is a great man's duty in troublous times to single out the guilty for punishment, to spare the many, and in every turn of fortune to hold to a true and honourable course. For whereas there are many, as I have said before, who place the achievements of war above those of peace, so one may find many to whom adventurous, hot-headed counsels seem more brilliant and more impressive than calm and well-considered measures.

83 We must, of course, never be guilty of seeming cowardly and craven in our avoidance of danger; but we must also beware of exposing ourselves to danger needlessly. Nothing can be more foolhardy than that. Accordingly, in encountering danger we should do as doctors do in their practice: in light cases of illness they give mild treatment; in cases of dangerous sickness they are compelled to apply hazardous and even desperate remedies. It is, therefore, only a madman who, in a calm, would pray

Courage in times of doubt and danger.

optare dementis est, subvenire autem tempestati quavis ratione sapientis, eoque magis, si plus adipiscare re explicata boni quam addubitata mali.

Periculosae autem rerum actiones partim iis [1] sunt, qui eas suscipiunt, partim rei publicae. Itemque alii de vita, alii de gloria et benivolentia civium in discrimen vocantur. Promptiores igitur debemus esse ad nostra pericula quam ad communia dimicareque paratius de honore et gloria quam de ceteris commodis.

84 Inventi autem multi sunt, qui non modo pecuniam, sed etiam vitam profundere pro patria parati essent, iidem gloriae iacturam ne minimam quidem facere vellent, ne re publica quidem postulante; ut Callicratidas, qui, cum Lacedaemoniorum dux fuisset Peloponnesiaco bello multaque fecisset egregie, vertit ad extremum omnia, cum consilio non paruit eorum, qui classem ab Arginusis removendam nec cum Atheniensibus dimicandum putabant; quibus ille respondit Lacedaemonios classe illa amissa aliam parare posse, se fugere sine suo dedecore non posse. Atque haec quidem Lacedaemoniis [2] plaga mediocris, illa pestifera, qua, cum Cleombrotus invidiam timens temere cum Epaminonda conflixisset, Lacedaemoniorum opes corruerunt.

[1] *iis* Edd.; *his* MSS.

[2] *quidem Lacedaemoniis* Edd., *quidem de Lacedaemoniis* MSS.

---

[a] Such as the esteem and good-will of fellow-citizens; life, liberty, and the pursuit of happiness; the existence of the state and all the advantages it brings.

for a storm; a wise man's way is, when the storm does come, to withstand it with all the means at his command, and especially, when the advantages to be expected in case of a successful issue are greater than the hazards of the struggle.

The dangers attending great affairs of state fall sometimes upon those who undertake them, sometimes upon the state. In carrying out such enterprises, some run the risk of losing their lives, others their reputation and the good-will of their fellow-citizens. It is our duty, then, to be more ready to endanger our own than the public welfare and to hazard honour and glory more readily than other advantages.[a] Patriotism and self-sacrifice.

84 Many, on the other hand, have been found who were ready to pour out not only their money but their lives for their country and yet would not consent to make even the slightest sacrifice of personal glory—even though the interests of their country demanded it. For example, when Callicratidas, as Spartan admiral in the Peloponnesian War, had won many signal successes, he spoiled everything at the end by refusing to listen to the proposal of those who thought he ought to withdraw his fleet from the Arginusae and not to risk an engagement with the Athenians. His answer to them was that "the Spartans could build another fleet, if they lost that one, but he could not retreat without dishonour to himself." And yet what he did dealt only a slight blow to Sparta; there was another which proved disastrous, when Cleombrotus in fear of criticism recklessly went into battle against Epaminondas. In consequence of that, the Spartan power fell.

Ann. xii, Vahlen², 370–372

Quanto Q. Maximus melius! de quo Ennius:

Unus homo nobis cunctando restituit rem.
Noenum rumores ponebat [1] ante salutem.
Ergo postque magisque viri nunc gloria claret.

Quod genus peccandi vitandum est etiam in rebus urbanis. Sunt enim, qui, quod sentiunt, etsi optimum sit, tamen invidiae metu non audeant [2] dicere.

85 XXV. Omnino qui rei publicae praefuturi sunt, duo Platonis praecepta teneant, unum, ut utilitatem civium sic tueantur, ut, quaecumque agunt, ad eam referant obliti commodorum suorum, alterum, ut totum corpus rei publicae curent, ne, dum partem aliquam tuentur, reliquas deserant. Ut enim tutela, sic procuratio rei publicae ad eorum utilitatem, qui commissi sunt, non ad eorum, quibus commissa est, gerenda est. Qui autem parti civium consulunt, partem neglegunt, rem perniciosissimam in civitatem inducunt, seditionem atque discordiam; ex quo evenit, ut alii populares, alii studiosi optimi cuiusque videantur, pauci universorum.

Rep. I, 342

Rep. IV, 420

86 Hinc apud Atheniensis magnae discordiae, in nostra re publica non solum seditiones, sed etiam pestifera bella civilia; quae gravis et fortis civis et

[1] *Noenum rumores ponebat* Lachmann (ad Lucr. III, 198); *Non enim rumores ponebat* MSS.; *Non ponebat enim* alii.

[2] *audeant* Ernesti; *audent* MSS., Bt.[1], Heine.

---

[a] Sacrificing public interests to personal glory.

[b] From the death of Pericles on.

[c] Such as the conspiracy of Catiline.

[d] The civil wars of Marius and Sulla, Caesar and Pompey.

How much better was the conduct of Quintus Maximus! Of him Ennius says:

"One man—and he alone—restored our state by delaying.
Not in the least did fame with him take precedence of safety;
Therefore now does his glory shine bright, and it grows ever brighter."

This sort of offence [a] must be avoided no less in political life. For there are men who for fear of giving offence do not dare to express their honest opinion, no matter how excellent.

**Public administration must be free from**

85 XXV. Those who propose to take charge of the affairs of government should not fail to remember two of Plato's rules: first, to keep the good of the people so clearly in view that regardless of their own interests they will make their every action conform to that; second, to care for the welfare of the whole body politic and not in serving the interests of some one party to betray the rest. For the administration of the government, like the office of a trustee, must be conducted for the benefit of those entrusted to one's care, not of those to whom it is entrusted. Now, those who care for the interests of a part of the citizens and neglect another part, introduce into the civil service a dangerous element—dissension and party strife. The result is that some are found to be loyal supporters of the democratic, others of the aristocratic party, and few of the nation as a whole.

**(1) partisanship**

86 As a result of this party spirit bitter strife arose at Athens,[b] and in our own country not only dissensions [c] but also disastrous civil wars [d] broke out.

in re publica dignus principatu fugiet atque oderit tradetque se totum rei publicae neque opes aut potentiam consectabitur totamque eam sic tuebitur, ut omnibus consulat; nec vero criminibus falsis in odium aut invidiam quemquam vocabit omninoque ita iustitiae honestatique adhaerescet, ut, dum ea conservet, quamvis graviter offendat mortemque oppetat potius quam deserat illa, quae dixi.

87 Miserrima omnino est ambitio honorumque contentio, de qua praeclare apud eundem est Platonem, (Rep. vi, 488 B; 489 C) "similiter facere eos, qui inter se contenderent, uter potius rem publicam administraret, ut si nautae certarent, quis eorum potissimum gubernaret." Idemque praecipit, ut (Rep. viii, 567 C; Leg. ix, 856 B) "eos adversarios existimemus, qui arma contra ferant, non eos, qui suo iudicio tueri rem publicam velint," qualis fuit inter P. Africanum et Q. Metellum sine acerbitate dissensio.

88 Nec vero audiendi, qui graviter inimicis irascendum putabunt idque magnanimi et fortis viri esse censebunt; nihil enim laudabilius, nihil magno et praeclaro viro dignius placabilitate atque clementia. In liberis vero populis et in iuris aequabilitate exer-

All this the citizen who is patriotic, brave, and worthy of a leading place in the state will shun with abhorrence; he will dedicate himself unreservedly to his country, without aiming at influence or power for himself; and he will devote himself to the state in its entirety in such a way as to further the interests of all. Besides, he will not expose anyone to hatred or disrepute by groundless charges, but he will surely cleave to justice and honour so closely that he will submit to any loss, however heavy, rather than be untrue to them, and will face death itself rather than renounce them.

87 A most wretched custom, assuredly, is our electioneering and scrambling for office. Concerning this also we find a fine thought in Plato: "Those who compete against one another," he says, "to see which of two candidates shall administer the government, are like sailors quarrelling as to which one of them shall do the steering." And he likewise lays down the rule that we should regard only those as adversaries who take up arms against the state, not those who strive to have the government administered according to their convictions. This was the spirit of the disagreement between Publius Africanus and Quintus Metellus: there was in it no trace of rancour. **(2) self-seeking,**

88 Neither must we listen to those who think that one should indulge in violent anger against one's political enemies and imagine that such is the attitude of a great-spirited, brave man. For nothing is more commendable, nothing more becoming in a pre-eminently great man than courtesy and forbearance. Indeed, in a free people, where all enjoy equal rights before the law, we **(3) vindictiveness,**

cenda etiam est facilitas et altitudo animi, quae dicitur, ne, si irascamur aut intempestive accedentibus aut impudenter rogantibus, in morositatem inutilem et odiosam incidamus. Et tamen ita probanda est mansuetudo atque clementia, ut adhibeatur rei publicae causa severitas, sine qua administrari civitas non potest. Omnis autem et animadversio et castigatio contumelia vacare debet neque ad eius, qui punitur [1] aliquem aut verbis castigat,[2] sed ad rei publicae utilitatem referri.

89 Cavendum est etiam, ne maior poena quam culpa sit, et ne isdem de causis alii plectantur, alii ne appellentur quidem. Prohibenda autem maxime est ira in puniendo; numquam enim, iratus qui accedet ad poenam, mediocritatem illam tenebit, quae est inter nimium et parum, quae placet Peripateticis, et recte placet, modo ne laudarent iracundiam et dicerent utiliter a natura datam. Illa vero omnibus in rebus repudianda est optandumque, ut ii, qui praesunt rei publicae, legum similes sint, quae ad puniendum non iracundia, sed aequitate dicuntur.

90 XXVI. Atque etiam in rebus prosperis et ad voluntatem nostram fluentibus superbiam magno-

[1] *punitur* Nonius, Edd.; *punit* a; *puniet* A B H b c.
[2] *castigat* MSS.; *fatigat* Nonius, Orelli.

---

[a] The quality elsewhere expressed by Cicero with βαθύτης—'depth,' 'reserve,' the art of concealing and controlling one's feelings under an outward serenity of manner.

must school ourselves to affability and what is called "mental poise"; [a] for if we are irritated when people intrude upon us at unseasonable hours or make unreasonable requests, we shall develop a sour, churlish temper, prejudicial to ourselves and offensive to others. And yet gentleness of spirit and forbearance are to be commended only with the understanding that strictness may be exercised for the good of the state; for without that, the government cannot be well administered. On the other hand, if punishment or correction must be administered, it need not be insulting; it ought to have regard to the welfare of the state, not to the personal satisfaction of the man who administers the punishment or reproof.

89 We should take care also that the punishment shall not be out of proportion to the offence, and that some shall not be chastised for the same fault for which others are not even called to account. In administering punishment it is above all necessary to allow no trace of anger. For if anyone proceeds in a passion to inflict punishment, he will never observe that happy mean which lies between excess and defect. This doctrine of the mean is approved by the Peripatetics—and wisely approved, if only they did not speak in praise of anger and tell us that it is a gift bestowed on us by Nature for a good purpose. But, in reality, anger is in every circumstance to be eradicated; and it is to be desired that they who administer the government should be like the laws, which are led to inflict punishment not by wrath but by justice. (4) anger.

90 XXVI. Again, when fortune smiles and the stream of life flows according to our wishes, let us diligently Fortitude in prosperity.

pere, fastidium arrogantiamque fugiamus. Nam ut adversas res, sic secundas immoderate ferre levitatis est, praeclaraque est aequabilitas in omni vita et idem semper vultus eademque frons, ut de Socrate itemque [1] de C. Laelio accepimus.[2] Philippum quidem, Macedonum regem, rebus gestis et gloria superatum a filio, facilitate et humanitate video superiorem fuisse; itaque alter semper magnus, alter saepe turpissimus; ut recte praecipere videantur, qui monent, ut, quanto superiores simus, tanto nos geramus summissius. Panaetius quidem Africanum, auditorem et familiarem suum, solitum ait dicere, "ut equos propter crebras contentiones proeliorum ferocitate exsultantes domitoribus tradere soleant, ut iis [3] facilioribus possint uti, sic homines secundis rebus effrenatos sibique praefidentes tamquam in gyrum rationis et doctrinae duci oportere, ut perspicerent rerum humanarum imbecillitatem varietatemque fortunae."

91 Atque etiam in secundissimis rebus maxime est utendum consilio amicorum iisque maior etiam quam ante tribuenda auctoritas. Isdemque temporibus cavendum est, ne assentatoribus patefaciamus auris neve [4] adulari nos sinamus, in quo falli facile est; tales enim nos esse putamus, ut iure laudemur; ex

[1] *itemque* H[2] a, Edd.; *idemque* A B H[1] L b c.
[2] *accepimus* B[2] a c, Edd.; *accipimus* A B[1] H b.
[3] *iis* Edd.; *his* MSS.
[4] *neve* Nonius, Edd.; *nec* MSS.

avoid all arrogance, haughtiness, and pride. For it is as much a sign of weakness to give way to one's feelings in success as it is in adversity. But it is a fine thing to keep an unruffled temper, an unchanging mien, and the same cast of countenance in every condition of life; this, history tells us, was characteristic of Socrates and no less of Gaius Laelius. Philip, king of Macedon, I observe, however surpassed by his son in achievements and fame, was superior to him in affability and refinement. Philip, accordingly, was always great; Alexander, often infamously bad. There seems to be sound advice, therefore, in this word of warning: "The higher we are placed, the more humbly should we walk." Panaetius tells us that Africanus, his pupil and friend, used to say: "As, when horses have become mettlesome and unmanageable on account of their frequent participation in battles, their owners put them in the hands of trainers to make them more tractable; so men, who through prosperity have become restive and over self-confident, ought to be put into the training-ring, so to speak, of reason and learning, that they may be brought to comprehend the frailty of human affairs and the fickleness of fortune."

**Humility.**

91 The greater our prosperity, moreover, the more should we seek the counsel of friends, and the greater the heed that should be given to their advice. Under such circumstances also we must beware of lending an ear to sycophants or allowing them to impose upon us with their flattery. For it is easy in this way to deceive ourselves, since we thus come to think ourselves duly entitled to praise; and to this frame of mind a thousand de-

quo nascuntur innumerabilia peccata, cum homines inflati opinionibus turpiter irridentur et in maximis versantur erroribus.

Sed haec quidem hactenus.

92 Illud autem sic est iudicandum, maximas geri res et maximi animi ab iis,[1] qui res publicas regant, quod earum administratio latissime pateat ad plurimosque pertineat; esse autem magni animi et fuisse multos etiam in vita otiosa, qui aut investigarent aut conarentur magna quaedam seseque suarum rerum finibus continerent aut interiecti inter philosophos et eos, qui rem publicam administrarent, delectarentur re sua familiari non eam quidem omni ratione exaggerantes neque excludentes ab eius usu suos potiusque et amicis impertientes et rei publicae, si quando usus esset. Quae primum bene parta[2] sit nullo neque turpi quaestu neque odioso, deinde augeatur ratione, diligentia, parsimonia,[3] tum quam plurimis, modo dignis, se utilem praebeat nec libidini potius luxuriaeque quam liberalitati et beneficentiae pareat.

Haec praescripta servantem licet magnifice, graviter animoseque vivere atque etiam simpliciter, fideliter, † vere hominum amice.

93 XXVII. Sequitur, ut de una reliqua parte honestatis dicendum sit, in qua verecundia et quasi

[1] *iis* Edd.; *his* MSS.
[2] *parta* B[1], Edd.; *parata* A B[2] H L a b c.
[3] *deinde . . . parsimonia* Edd., after Unger, transpose; in MSS. it follows *tum . . . pareat*.

[a] § 70.

lusions may be traced, when men are puffed up with conceit and expose themselves to ignominy and ridicule by committing the most egregious blunders.

So much for this subject.

92 To revert to the original question [a]—we must decide that the most important activities, those most indicative of a great spirit, are performed by the men who direct the affairs of nations; for such public activities have the widest scope and touch the lives of the most people. But even in the life of retirement there are and there have been many high-souled men who have been engaged in important inquiries or embarked on most important enterprises and yet kept themselves within the limits of their own affairs; or, taking a middle course between philosophers on the one hand and statesmen on the other, they were content with managing their own property—not increasing it by any and every means nor debarring their kindred from the enjoyment of it, but rather, if ever there were need, sharing it with their friends and with the state. Only let it, in the first place, be honestly acquired, by the use of no dishonest or fraudulent means; let it, in the second place, increase by wisdom, industry, and thrift; and, finally, let it be made available for the use of as many as possible (if only they are worthy) and be at the service of generosity and beneficence rather than of sensuality and excess.

**Greatness of mind in public and in private life.**

By observing these rules, one may live in magnificence, dignity, and independence, and yet in honour, truth and charity toward all.

93 XXVII. We have next to discuss the one remaining division of moral rectitude. That is the one

**D. Temperance.**

quidam ornatus vitae, temperantia et modestia omnisque sedatio perturbationum animi et rerum modus cernitur. Hoc loco continetur id, quod dici Latine decorum potest; Graece enim πρέπον dicitur. Huius[1] vis ea est, ut ab honesto non queat
94 separari; nam et, quod decet, honestum est et, quod honestum est, decet; qualis autem differentia sit honesti et decori, facilius intellegi quam explanari potest. Quicquid est enim, quod deceat, id tum apparet, cum antegressa est honestas. Itaque non solum in hac parte honestatis, de qua hoc loco disserendum est, sed etiam in tribus superioribus quid deceat apparet. Nam et ratione uti atque oratione prudenter et agere, quod agas, considerate omnique in re quid sit veri videre et tueri decet, contraque falli, errare, labi, decipi tam dedecet quam delirare et mente esse captum; et iusta omnia decora sunt, iniusta contra, ut turpia, sic indecora.

Similis est ratio fortitudinis. Quod enim viriliter animoque magno fit, id dignum viro et decorum videtur, quod contra, id ut turpe, sic indecorum.

95 Quare pertinet quidem ad omnem honestatem hoc, quod dico, decorum, et ita pertinet, ut non recondita quadam ratione cernatur, sed sit in promptu. Est enim quiddam, idque intellegitur

[1] *dicitur. Huius* Edd.; *dicitur decorum. huius* MSS.

---

[a] *Decorum,* Cicero's attempt to translate πρέπον, means an appreciation of the fitness of things, propriety in inward feeling or outward appearance, in speech, behaviour, dress, etc. *Decorum* is as difficult to translate into English as πρέπον is to reproduce in Latin; as an adjective, it is here rendered by 'proper,' as a noun, by 'propriety.'

in which we find considerateness and self-control, which give, as it were, a sort of polish to life; it embraces also temperance, complete subjection of all the passions, and moderation in all things. Under this head is further included what, in Latin, may be called *decorum* [a] (propriety); for in Greek it is called πρέπον.[a] Such is its essential nature, **Propriety.**

94 that it is inseparable from moral goodness; for what is proper is morally right, and what is morally right is proper. The nature of the difference between morality and propriety can be more easily felt than expressed. For whatever propriety may be, it is manifested only when there is pre-existing moral rectitude. And so, not only in this division of moral rectitude which we have now to discuss but also in the three preceding divisions, it is clearly brought out what propriety is. For to employ reason and speech rationally, to do with careful consideration whatever one does, and in everything to discern the truth and to uphold it—that is proper. To be mistaken, on the other hand, to miss the truth, to fall into error, to be led astray—that is as improper as to be deranged and lose one's mind. And all things just are proper; all things unjust, like all things immoral, are improper. **Propriety and the Cardinal Virtues.**

The relation of propriety to fortitude is similar. What is done in a manly and courageous spirit seems becoming to a man and proper; what is done in a contrary fashion is at once immoral and improper.

95 This propriety, therefore, of which I am speaking belongs to each division of moral rectitude; and its relation to the cardinal virtues is so close, that it is perfectly self-evident and does not require any abstruse process of reasoning to see it. For

in omni virtute, quod deceat; quod cogitatione magis a virtute potest quam re separari. Ut venustas et pulchritudo corporis secerni non potest a valetudine, sic hoc, de quo loquimur, decorum totum illud quidem est cum virtute confusum, sed mente et cogitatione distinguitur.

96 Est autem eius discriptio[1] duplex; nam et generale quoddam decorum intellegimus, quod in omni honestate versatur, et aliud huic subiectum, quod pertinet ad singulas partes honestatis. Atque illud superius sic fere definiri solet: decorum id esse, quod consentaneum sit hominis excellentiae in eo, in quo natura eius a reliquis animantibus differat. Quae autem pars subiecta generi est, eam sic definiunt, ut id decorum velint esse, quod ita naturae consentaneum sit, ut in eo moderatio et temperantia appareat cum specie quadam liberali.

Cic., Or. xxii, 71 97 XXVIII. Haec ita intellegi possumus existimare ex eo decoro, quod poetae sequuntur; de quo alio loco plura dici solent. Sed tum[2] servare illud poëtas, quod deceat, dicimus, cum id, quod quaque persona dignum est, et fit et dicitur; ut, si Aeacus aut Minos diceret:

Attius, Atreus, Ribbeck[3], 203

óderint, dum métuant,

aut:

natís sepulchro ipse ést parens,

[1] *discriptio* b, Edd.; *descriptio* A B H a; *distinctio* L c.
[2] *Sed tum* L c, Edd.; *sed ut tum* A B H b.

there is a certain element of propriety perceptible in every act of moral rectitude; and this can be separated from virtue theoretically better than it can be practically. As comeliness and beauty of person are inseparable from the notion of health, so this propriety of which we are speaking, while in fact completely blended with virtue, is mentally and theoretically distinguishable from it.

96 The classification of propriety, moreover, is two-fold: (1) we assume a general sort of propriety, which is found in moral goodness as a whole; then (2) there is another propriety, subordinate to this, which belongs to the several divisions of moral goodness. The former is usually defined somewhat as follows: "Propriety is that which harmonizes with man's superiority in those respects in which his nature differs from that of the rest of the animal creation." And they so define the special type of propriety which is subordinate to the general notion, that they represent it to be that propriety which harmonizes with Nature, in the sense that it manifestly embraces temperance and self-control, together with a certain deportment such as becomes a gentleman. Propriety defined.

97 XXVIII. That this is the common acceptation of propriety we may infer from that propriety which poets aim to secure. Concerning that, I have occasion to say more in another connection. Now, we say that the poets observe propriety, when every word or action is in accord with each individual character. For example, if Aeacus or Minos said: Poetic propriety.

> "Let them hate, if only they fear,"

or:

> "The father is himself his children's tomb,"

Ibid., 226 indecorum videretur, quod eos fuisse iustos accepimus; at Atreo dicente plausus excitantur; est enim digna persona oratio. Sed poëtae, quid quemque deceat, ex persona iudicabunt; nobis autem personam imposuit ipsa natura magna cum excellentia praestantiaque animantium reliquarum.[1]

98 Quocirca poëtae in magna varietate personarum, etiam vitiosis quid conveniat et quid deceat, videbunt, nobis autem cum a natura constantiae, moderationis, temperantiae, verecundiae partes datae sint, cumque eadem natura doceat non neglegere, quem ad modum nos adversus homines geramus, efficitur, ut et illud, quod ad omnem honestatem pertinet, decorum quam late fusum sit, appareat et hoc, quod spectatur in uno quoque genere virtutis. Ut enim pulchritudo corporis apta compositione membrorum movet oculos et delectat hoc ipso, quod inter se omnes partes cum quodam lepore consentiunt, sic hoc decorum, quod elucet in vita, movet approbationem eorum, quibuscum vivitur, ordine et constantia et moderatione dictorum omnium atque factorum.

99 Adhibenda est igitur quaedam reverentia adversus homines et optimi cuiusque et reliquorum. Nam neglegere, quid de se quisque sentiat, non solum arro-

[1] *reliquarum* $A^1$ $B^1$ H a b; *reliquorum* $A^2$ $B^2$ c.

that would seem improper, because we are told that they were just men. But when Atreus speaks those lines, they call forth applause; for the sentiment is in keeping with the character. But it will rest with the poets to decide, according to the individual characters, what is proper for each; but to us Nature herself has assigned a character of surpassing excellence, far superior to that of all other living creatures, and in accordance with that we shall have to decide what propriety requires.

98 The poets will observe, therefore, amid a great variety of characters, what is suitable and proper for all—even for the bad. But to us Nature has assigned the rôles of steadfastness, temperance, self-control, and considerateness of others; Nature also teaches us not to be careless in our behaviour towards our fellow-men. Hence we may clearly see how wide is the application not only of that propriety which is essential to moral rectitude in general, but also of the special propriety which is displayed in each particular subdivision of virtue. For, as physical beauty with harmonious symmetry of the limbs engages the attention and delights the eye, for the very reason that all the parts combine in harmony and grace, so this propriety, which shines out in our conduct, engages the approbation of our fellow-men by the order, consistency, and self-control it imposes upon every word and deed.

**Moral propriety.**

99 We should, therefore, in our dealings with people show what I may almost call reverence toward all men—not only toward the men who are the best, but toward others as well. For indifference to public opinion implies not merely self-sufficiency, but even total lack of principle. There is, too, a difference be-

**Considerateness.**

gantis est, sed etiam omnino dissoluti. Est autem, quod differat in hominum ratione habenda inter iustitiam et verecundiam. Iustitiae partes sunt non violare homines, verecundiae non offendere; in quo maxime vis perspicitur decori.

His igitur expositis, quale sit id, quod decere dicimus, intellectum puto.

100 Officium autem, quod ab eo ducitur, hanc primum habet viam, quae deducit ad convenientiam conservationemque naturae; quam si sequemur ducem, numquam aberrabimus sequemurque et id, quod acutum et perspicax natura est, et id, quod ad hominum consociationem accommodatum, et id, quod vehemens atque forte. Sed maxima vis decori in hac inest parte, de qua disputamus; neque enim solum corporis, qui ad naturam apti sunt, sed multo etiam magis animi motus probandi, qui item ad naturam accommodati sunt.

101 Duplex est enim vis animorum atque natura;[1] una pars in appetitu posita est, quae est ὁρμή Graece, quae hominem huc et illuc rapit, altera in ratione, quae docet et[2] explanat, quid faciendum fugiendumque[3] sit. Ita fit, ut ratio praesit, appetitus obtemperet.

XXIX. Omnis autem actio vacare debet temeritate et neglegentia nec vero agere quicquam, cuius non possit causam probabilem reddere; haec est enim fere discriptio[4] officii.

102 Efficiendum autem est, ut appetitus rationi

[1] *natura* Edd.; *naturae* MSS.
[2] *et* L c, Edd.; not in A B H b.
[3] *fugiendumque* A B H a b; *fugiendumve* L c p.
[4] *discriptio* B H, Bt.[1]; *descriptio* A L a b c, Bt.[2], Müller, Heine.

tween justice and considerateness in one's relations to one's fellow-men. It is the function of justice not to do wrong to one's fellow-men; of considerateness, not to wound their feelings; and in this the essence of propriety is best seen.

With the foregoing exposition, I think it is clear what the nature is of what we term propriety.

100 Further, as to the duty which has its source in propriety, the first road on which it conducts us leads to harmony with Nature and the faithful observance of her laws. If we follow Nature as our guide, we shall never go astray, but we shall be pursuing that which is in its nature clear-sighted and penetrating (Wisdom), that which is adapted to promote and strengthen society (Justice), and that which is strong and courageous (Fortitude). But the very essence of propriety is found in the division of virtue which is now under discussion (Temperance). For it is only when they agree with Nature's laws that we should give our approval to the movements not only of the body, but still more of the spirit.

Duties prescribed by propriety: (1) follow Nature,

101 Now we find that the essential activity of the spirit is twofold: one force is appetite (that is, ὁρμή, in Greek), which impels a man this way and that; the other is reason, which teaches and explains what should be done and what should be left undone. The result is that reason commands, appetite obeys.

(2) subject appetite to reason.

XXIX. Again, every action ought to be free from undue haste or carelessness; neither ought we to do anything for which we cannot assign a reasonable motive; for in these words we have practically a definition of duty.

102 The appetites, moreover, must be made to obey

oboediant eamque neque praecurrant nec propter pigritiam aut ignaviam deserant sintque tranquilli atque omni animi perturbatione careant; ex quo elucebit omnis constantia omnisque moderatio. Nam qui appetitus longius evagantur et tamquam exsultantes sive cupiendo sive fugiendo non satis a ratione retinentur, ii[1] sine dubio finem et modum transeunt; relinquunt enim et abiciunt oboedientiam nec rationi parent, cui sunt subiecti lege naturae; a quibus non modo animi perturbantur, sed etiam corpora. Licet ora ipsa cernere iratorum aut eorum, qui aut libidine aliqua aut metu commoti sunt aut voluptate nimia gestiunt; quorum omnium voltus, voces, motus statusque mutantur.

103 Ex quibus illud intellegitur, ut ad officii formam revertamur, appetitus omnes contrahendos sedandosque esse excitandamque animadversionem et diligentiam, ut ne quid temere ac fortuito, inconsiderate neglegenterque agamus. Neque enim ita generati a natura sumus, ut ad ludum et iocum facti esse videamur, ad severitatem potius et ad quaedam studia graviora atque maiora. Ludo autem et ioco uti illo quidem licet, sed sicut somno et quietibus ceteris tum, cum gravibus seriisque rebus satis fecerimus. Ipsumque genus iocandi non profusum nec immodestum, sed ingenuum et facetum esse debet. Ut enim pueris non omnem ludendi licentiam damus, sed eam, quae ab honestatis actionibus

[1] *ii* Edd.; *hi* a; *hii* H; *hij* c.

the reins of reason and neither allowed to run ahead of it nor from listlessness or indolence to lag behind; but people should enjoy calm of soul and be free from every sort of passion. As a result strength of character and self-control will shine forth in all their lustre. For when appetites overstep their bounds and, galloping away, so to speak, whether in desire or aversion, are not well held in hand by reason, they clearly overleap all bound and measure; for they throw obedience off and leave it behind and refuse to obey the reins of reason, to which they are subject by Nature's laws. And not only minds but bodies as well are disordered by such appetites. We need only to look at the faces of men in a rage or under the influence of some passion or fear or beside themselves with extravagant joy: in every instance their features, voices, motions, attitudes undergo a change.

**Self-control in (1) passions.**

103 From all this—to return to our sketch of duty—we see that all the appetites must be controlled and calmed and that we must take infinite pains not to do anything from mere impulse or at random, without due consideration and care. For Nature has not brought us into the world to act as if we were created for play or jest, but rather for earnestness and for some more serious and important pursuits. We may, of course, indulge in sport and jest, but in the same way as we enjoy sleep or other relaxations, and only when we have satisfied the claims of our earnest, serious tasks. Further than that, the manner of jesting itself ought not to be extravagant or immoderate, but refined and witty. For as we do not grant our children unlimited licence to play, but only such freedom as is not incompatible with

**(2) amusements.**

**(3) raillery.**

non sit aliena, sic in ipso ioco aliquod probi ingenii
104 lumen eluceat. Duplex omnino est iocandi genus, unum illiberale, petulans, flagitiosum, obscenum, alterum elegans, urbanum, ingeniosum, facetum. Quo genere non modo Plautus noster et Atticorum antiqua comoedia, sed etiam philosophorum Socraticorum libri referti sunt, multaque multorum facete dicta, ut ea, quae a sene Catone collecta sunt, quae vocant ἀποφθέγματα. Facilis igitur est distinctio ingenui et illiberalis ioci. Alter est, si tempore fit, ut si remisso animo, *gravissimo* homine dignus,[1] alter ne libero quidem, si rerum turpitudini adhibetur verborum [2] obscenitas.

Ludendi etiam est quidam modus retinendus, ut ne nimis omnia profundamus elatique voluptate in aliquam turpitudinem delabamur. Suppeditant autem et campus noster et studia venandi honesta exempla ludendi.

105 XXX. Sed pertinet ad omnem officii quaestionem semper in promptu habere, quantum natura hominis pecudibus reliquisque beluis antecedat; illae nihil sentiunt nisi voluptatem ad eamque feruntur omni impetu, hominis autem mens discendo alitur et cogitando, semper aliquid aut anquirit aut agit videndique et audiendi delectatione ducitur. Quin etiam, si quis est paulo ad voluptates propensior, modo ne sit ex pecudum genere (sunt enim quidam homines non re, sed nomine), sed si quis est paulo

[1] *fit, ut si remisso animo, gravissimo homine dignus* Ed.; *fit, ut* (*et* c) *remisso animo homine dignus* MSS.; *fit aut si rem. an. magno homine* Madvig; *fit, ut sit remissio animo, homine dignus* Unger.

[2] *turpitudini adhibetur verborum* A B H a b, Edd.; *turpitudo adhibetur et verborum* L c.

good conduct, so even in our jesting let the light
104 of a pure character shine forth. There are, generally speaking, two sorts of jest: the one, coarse, rude, vicious, indecent; the other, refined, polite, clever, witty. With this latter sort not only our own Plautus and the Old Comedy of Athens, but also the books of Socratic philosophy abound; and we have many witty sayings of many men—like those collected by old Cato under the title of *Bons Mots* (or Apophthegms). So the distinction between the elegant and the vulgar jest is an easy matter: the one kind, if well timed (for instance, in hours of mental relaxation), is becoming to the most dignified person; the other is unfit for any gentleman, if the subject is indecent and the words obscene.

Then, too, certain bounds must be observed in our amusements and we must be careful not to carry things too far and, swept away by our passions, lapse into some shameful excess. Our Campus, however, and the amusements of the chase are examples of wholesome recreation.

105 XXX. But it is essential to every inquiry about duty that we keep before our eyes how far superior man is by nature to cattle and other beasts: they have no thought except for sensual pleasure and this they are impelled by every instinct to seek; but man's mind is nurtured by study and meditation; he is always either investigating or doing, and he is captivated by the pleasure of seeing and hearing. Nay, even if a man is more than ordinarily
inclined to sensual pleasures, provided, of course, (4) pleasure.
that he be not quite on a level with the beasts of the field (for some people are men only in name, not in fact)—if, I say, he is a little too susceptible

erectior, quamvis voluptate capiatur, occultat et dissimulat appetitum voluptatis propter verecundiam.

106 Ex quo intellegitur corporis voluptatem non satis esse dignam hominis praestantia, eamque contemni et reici oportere; sin sit quispiam, qui aliquid tribuat voluptati, diligenter ei tenendum esse eius fruendae modum. Itaque victus cultusque corporis ad valetudinem referatur et ad vires, non ad voluptatem. Atque etiam si considerare volumus,[1] quae sit in natura excellentia et dignitas, intellegemus, quam sit turpe diffluere luxuria et delicate ac molliter vivere quamque honestum parce, continenter, severe, sobrie.

107 Intellegendum etiam est duabus quasi nos a natura indutos esse personis; quarum una communis est ex eo, quod omnes participes sumus rationis praestantiaeque eius, qua antecellimus bestiis, a qua omne honestum decorumque trahitur, et ex qua ratio inveniendi officii exquiritur, altera autem, quae proprie singulis est tributa. Ut enim in corporibus magnae dissimilitudines sunt (alios videmus velocitate ad cursum, alios viribus ad luctandum valere, itemque in formis aliis dignitatem inesse, aliis venustatem), sic in animis exsistunt maiores etiam varieta-
108 tes. Erat in L. Crasso, in L. Philippo multus lepos, maior etiam magisque de industria in C. Caesare

[1] *volumus* A $B^1$ $H^1$ b; *volemus* $B^2$ $H^2$, Bt., Heine; *velimus* L; *vellemus* c.

to the attractions of pleasure, he hides the fact, however much he may be caught in its toils, and for very shame conceals his appetite.

106 From this we see that sensual pleasure is quite unworthy of the dignity of man and that we ought to despise it and cast it from us; but if someone should be found who sets some value upon sensual gratification, he must keep strictly within the limits of moderate indulgence. One's physical comforts and wants, therefore, should be ordered according to the demands of health and strength, not according to the calls of pleasure. And if we will only bear in mind the superiority and dignity of our nature, we shall realize how wrong it is to abandon ourselves to excess and to live in luxury and voluptuousness, and how right it is to live in thrift, self-denial, simplicity, and sobriety.

**The universal and the individual nature of man.**

107 We must realize also that we are invested by Nature with two characters, as it were: one of these is universal, arising from the fact of our being all alike endowed with reason and with that superiority which lifts us above the brute. From this all morality and propriety are derived, and upon it depends the rational method of ascertaining our duty. The other character is the one that is assigned to individuals in particular. In the matter of physical endowment there are great differences: some, we see, excel in speed for the race, others in strength for wrestling; so in point of personal appearance, some have stateliness, others comeliness.

**Individual endowments.**

108 Diversities of character are greater still. Lucius Crassus and Lucius Philippus had a large fund of wit; Gaius Caesar, Lucius's son, had a still richer fund and employed it with more studied purpose.

L. filio; at isdem temporibus in M. Scauro et in M. Druso adulescente singularis severitas, in C. Laelio multa hilaritas, in eius familiari Scipione ambitio maior, vita tristior. De Graecis autem dulcem et facetum festivique sermonis atque in omni oratione simulatorem, quem *εἴρωνα* Graeci [1] nominarunt, Socratem accepimus, contra Pythagoram et Periclem summam auctoritatem consecutos sine ulla hilaritate. Callidum Hannibalem ex Poenorum, ex nostris ducibus Q. Maximum accepimus, facile celare, tacere, dissimulare, insidiari, praeripere hostium consilia. In quo genere Graeci Themistoclem et Pheraeum Iasonem ceteris anteponunt; in primisque versutum et callidum factum Solonis, qui, quo et tutior eius vita esset et plus aliquanto rei publicae prodesset, furere se simulavit.

109 Sunt his alii multum dispares, simplices et aperti, qui nihil ex occulto, nihil de insidiis agendum putant, veritatis cultores, fraudis inimici, itemque alii, qui [2] quidvis perpetiantur, cuivis deserviant, dum, quod velint, consequantur, ut Sullam et M. Crassum videbamus. Quo in genere versutissimum et patientissimum Lacedaemonium Lysandrum accepimus, contraque Callicratidam, qui praefectus classis proximus post Lysandrum fuit; itemque in sermonibus alium [quemque], quamvis [3] praepotens sit, efficere, ut unus

[1] *εἴρωνα Graeci* Edd.; *ironia graeci* A B H b; *ironian graeci* a; *greci mironian* c.

[2] *qui* A L c; *si* B H a b.

[3] *alium* [*quemque*] *quamvis* Ed.; *alium quemque quamvis* MSS.; *quemque alium quamvis* p; *aliquem, quamvis* Pearce, Bt.; *alium quamvis* Facciolati, Heine.

Contemporary with them, Marcus Scaurus and Marcus Drusus, the younger, were examples of unusual seriousness; Gaius Laelius, of unbounded jollity; while his intimate friend, Scipio, cherished more serious ideals and lived a more austere life. Among the Greeks, history tells us, Socrates was fascinating and witty, a genial conversationalist; he was what the Greeks call εἴρων—in every conversation, pretending to need information and professing admiration for the wisdom of his companion. Pythagoras and Pericles, on the other hand, reached the heights of influence and power without any seasoning of mirthfulness. We read that Hannibal, among the Carthaginian generals, and Quintus Maximus, among our own, were shrewd and ready at concealing their plans, covering up their tracks, disguising their movements, laying stratagems, forestalling the enemy's designs. In these qualities the Greeks rank Themistocles and Jason of Pherae above all others. Especially crafty and shrewd was the device of Solon, who, to make his own life safer and at the same time to do a considerably larger service for his country, feigned insanity.

109 Then there are others, quite different from these, straightforward and open, who think that nothing should be done by underhand means or treachery. They are lovers of truth, haters of fraud. There are others still who will stoop to anything, truckle to anybody, if only they may gain their ends. Such, we saw, were Sulla and Marcus Crassus. The most crafty and most persevering man of this type was Lysander of Sparta, we are told; of the opposite type was Callicratidas, who succeeded Lysander as admiral of the fleet. So we find that another, no matter how

de multis esse videatur; quod in Catulo, et in patre et in filio, itemque in Q. Mucio † Mancia[1] vidimus. Audivi ex maioribus natu hoc idem fuisse in P. Scipione Nasica, contraque patrem eius, illum qui Ti. Gracchi conatus perditos vindicavit, nullam comitatem habuisse sermonis [ne Xenocratem quidem, severissimum philosophorum,][2] ob eamque rem ipsam magnum et clarum fuisse.

Innumerabiles aliae dissimilitudines sunt naturae morumque, minime tamen vituperandorum.

110 XXXI. Admodum autem tenenda sunt sua cuique non vitiosa, sed tamen propria, quo facilius decorum illud, quod quaerimus, retineatur. Sic enim est faciendum, ut contra universam naturam nihil contendamus, ea tamen conservata propriam nostram sequamur, ut, etiamsi sint alia graviora atque meliora, tamen nos studia nostra nostrae naturae regula[3] metiamur; neque enim attinet naturae repugnare nec quicquam sequi, quod assequi non queas. Ex quo magis emergit, quale sit decorum illud, ideo quia nihil decet invita Minerva, ut aiunt, id est adversante et repugnante natura.

111 Omnino si quicquam est decorum, nihil est profecto magis quam aequabilitas *cum*[4] universae vitae,

[1] *et in patre et in filio* A B b, Edd.; *et in patre et filio* H a; *et patre et filio* L c. *itemque* B H², Bt.¹, Müller; *idemque* A H¹ L a b c, Bt.², Heine. *in Q Mucio † Mancia* Heine, Bt.²; *in q. mucio mantia* B; *in q. mutio mancia* H L c; *in q. mutio mantia* a; *inque mucio mantia* b; *inque mutio mantia* A; *in q. muntio mantia* p; *in Q. Mucio, Mancia* Müller.

[2] *ne* (*nec* c) *Xenocratem* (-*n* L c) . . . *philosophorum* MSS.; bracketed by Heumann, Edd.

[3] *studia nostra nostrae naturae regula* Ernesti, Bt., Heine; *studia nostra nostra* (corr. ex *nostri*) *regula* A; *studia nostrae regulae* B; *studia nostrae regulā* H; *studia nostra regula* a; *studia* (corr. in *studii*) *nostri regula* b; *studia nostra naturae regula* L c, Nonius; *studia nostrae naturae regula* Müller.

eminent he may be, will condescend in social intercourse to make himself appear but a very ordinary person. Such graciousness of manner we have seen in the case of Catulus—both father and son—and also of Quintus Mucius Mancia. I have heard from my elders that Publius Scipio Nasica was another master of this art; but his father, on the other hand—the man who punished Tiberius Gracchus for his nefarious undertakings—had no such gracious manner in social intercourse [ . . . ], and because of that very fact he rose to greatness and fame.

Countless other dissimilarities exist in natures and characters, and they are not in the least to be criticized.

110 XXXI. Everybody, however, must resolutely hold fast to his own peculiar gifts, in so far as they are peculiar only and not vicious, in order that propriety, which is the object of our inquiry, may the more easily be secured. For we must so act as not to oppose the universal laws of human nature, but, while safeguarding those, to follow the bent of our own particular nature; and even if other careers should be better and nobler, we may still regulate our own pursuits by the standard of our own nature. For it is of no avail to fight against one's nature or to aim at what is impossible of attainment. From this fact the nature of that propriety defined above comes into still clearer light, inasmuch as nothing is proper that "goes against the grain," as the saying is—that is, if it is in direct opposition to one's natural genius.

**Conduct must accord with individual endowments.**

111 If there is any such thing as propriety at all, it can be nothing more than uniform consistency

[a] *cum* Lambinus, Edd.; not in MSS.

tum singularum actionum, quam conservare non possis, si aliorum naturam imitans omittas tuam. Ut enim sermone eo debemus uti, qui innatus[1] est nobis, ne, ut quidam, Graeca verba inculcantes iure optimo rideamur, sic in actiones omnemque vitam
112 nullam discrepantiam conferre debemus. Atque haec differentia naturarum tantam habet vim, ut non numquam mortem sibi ipse consciscere alius debeat, alius [in eadem causa] non debeat.[2] Num enim alia in causa M. Cato fuit, alia ceteri, qui se in Africa Caesari tradiderunt? Atqui ceteris forsitan vitio datum esset, si se interemissent, propterea quod lenior eorum vita et mores fuerant faciliores, Catoni cum incredibilem tribuisset natura gravitatem eamque ipse perpetua constantia roboravisset semperque in proposito susceptoque consilio permansisset, moriendum potius quam tyranni vultus aspiciendus fuit.
113 Quam multa passus est Ulixes in illo errore diuturno, cum et mulieribus, si Circe et Calypso mulieres appellandae sunt, inserviret et in omni sermone omnibus affabilem [et iucundum][3] esse se vellet! domi vero etiam contumelias servorum ancillarumque pertulit, ut ad id aliquando, quod cupiebat, veniret. At Aiax, quo animo traditur, milies oppetere mortem quam illa perpeti maluisset.

Quae contemplantes expendere oportebit, quid

[1] *innatus* Bt., Edd.; *notus* MSS.

[2] *alius in eadem causa non debeat* L c p, Müller, Heine; not in A B H b; *alius non debeat* a; *alius* [*in eadem causa*] *non debeat* Bt., Ed.

[3] *et iocundum* L c p; not in A B H a b; [*et iucundum*] Bt., Ed.

in the course of our life as a whole and all its individual actions. And this uniform consistency one could not maintain by copying the personal traits of others and eliminating one's own. For as we ought to employ our mother-tongue, lest, like certain people who are continually dragging in Greek words, we draw well-deserved ridicule upon ourselves, so we ought not to introduce anything foreign into our
112 actions or our life in general. Indeed, such diversity of character carries with it so great significance that suicide may be for one man a duty, for another [under the same circumstances] a crime. Did Marcus Cato find himself in one predicament, and were the others, who surrendered to Caesar in Africa, in another? And yet, perhaps, they would have been condemned, if they had taken their lives; for their mode of life had been less austere and their characters more pliable. But Cato had been endowed by nature with an austerity beyond belief, and he himself had strengthened it by unswerving consistency and had remained ever true to his purpose and fixed resolve; and it was for him to die rather than to look upon the face of a tyrant. The same course may be right for one, wrong for another.

113 How much Ulysses endured on those long wanderings, when he submitted to the service even of women (if Circe and Calypso may be called women) and strove in every word to be courteous and complaisant to all! And, arrived at home, he brooked even the insults of his men-servants and maid-servants, in order to attain in the end the object of his desire. But Ajax, with the temper he is represented as having, would have chosen to meet death a thousand times rather than suffer such indignities!

If we take this into consideration, we shall see

quisque habeat sui, eaque moderari nec velle experiri, quam se aliena deceant; id enim maxime quemque decet, quod est cuiusque maxime suum.

114 *Suum* [1] quisque igitur noscat ingenium acremque se et bonorum et vitiorum suorum iudicem praebeat, ne scaenici plus quam nos videantur habere prudentiae. Illi enim non optimas, sed sibi accommodatissimas fabulas eligunt; qui voce freti sunt, Epigonos Medumque, qui gestu, Melanippam, Clytemnestram, semper Rupilius, quem ego memini, Antiopam, non saepe Aesopus Aiacem. Ergo histrio hoc videbit in scaena, non videbit sapiens vir in vita?

Ad quas igitur res aptissimi erimus, in iis potissimum elaborabimus; sin aliquando necessitas nos ad ea detruserit, quae nostri ingenii non erunt, omnis adhibenda erit cura, meditatio, diligentia, ut ea si non decore, at quam minime indecore facere possimus; nec tam [2] est enitendum, ut bona, quae nobis data non sint, sequamur, quam ut vitia fugiamus.

115 XXXII. Ac duabus iis personis, quas supra dixi, tertia adiungitur, quam casus aliqui aut tempus imponit; quarta etiam, quam nobismet ipsi iudicio nostro accommodamus. Nam regna, imperia, nobilitas, honores, divitiae,[3] opes eaque, quae sunt his contraria, in casu sita temporibus gubernantur; ipsi

[1] *Suum* Orelli; not in MSS.; but p has *ingenium suum.*
[2] *tam* L c, Edd.; *tam* (i.e. *tamen*) A B H b.
[3] *nobilitas, h., divitiae* Unger; *nobilitatem, h., divitias* MSS.

[a] The universal and the individual; § 107.

that it is each man's duty to weigh well what are his own peculiar traits of character, to regulate these properly, and not to wish to try how another man's would suit him. For the more peculiarly his own a man's character is, the better it fits him.

Let every one sustain his own character.

114 Everyone, therefore, should make a proper estimate of his own natural ability and show himself a critical judge of his own merits and defects; in this respect we should not let actors display more practical wisdom than we have. They select, not the best plays, but the ones best suited to their talents. Those who rely most upon the quality of their voice take the Epigoni and the Medus; those who place more stress upon the action choose the Melanippa and the Clytaemnestra; Rupilius, whom I remember, always played in the Antiope, Aesopus rarely in the Ajax. Shall a player have regard to this in choosing his rôle upon the stage, and a wise man fail to do so in selecting his part in life?

We shall, therefore, work to the best advantage in that rôle to which we are best adapted. But if at some time stress of circumstances shall thrust us aside into some uncongenial part, we must devote to it all possible thought, practice, and pains, that we may be able to perform it, if not with propriety, at least with as little impropriety as possible; and we need not strive so hard to attain to points of excellence that have not been vouchsafed to us as to correct the faults we have.

115 XXXII. To the two above-mentioned characters [a] is added a third, which some chance or some circumstance imposes, and a fourth also, which we assume by our own deliberate choice. Regal powers and military commands, nobility of birth and political office, wealth and influence, and their opposites

autem gerere quam personam velimus, a nostra voluntate proficiscitur. Itaque se alii ad philosophiam, alii ad ius civile, alii ad eloquentiam applicant, ipsarumque virtutum in alia alius mavult excellere.

116 Quorum vero patres aut maiores aliqua gloria praestiterunt, ii student plerumque eodem in genere laudis excellere, ut Q. Mucius P. f. in iure civili, Pauli filius Africanus in re militari. Quidam autem ad eas laudes, quas a patribus acceperunt, addunt aliquam suam, ut hic idem Africanus eloquentia cumulavit bellicam gloriam; quod idem fecit Timotheus Cononis filius, qui cum belli laude non inferior fuisset quam pater, ad eam laudem doctrinae et ingenii gloriam adiecit. Fit autem interdum, ut non nulli omissa imitatione maiorum suum quoddam institutum consequantur, maximeque in eo plerumque elaborant ii,[1] qui magna sibi proponunt obscuris orti maioribus.

117 Haec igitur omnia, cum quaerimus, quid deceat, complecti animo et cogitatione debemus; in primis autem constituendum est, quos nos et quales esse velimus et in quo genere vitae, quae deliberatio est omnium difficillima. Ineunte enim adulescentia, cum est maxima imbecillitas consilii, tum id sibi quisque genus aetatis degendae constituit, quod maxime adamavit; itaque ante implicatur aliquo

[1] *ii* Edd.; *hii* A H b; *hij* c; *hi* B a.

depend upon chance and are, therefore, controlled by circumstances. But what rôle we ourselves may choose to sustain is decided by our own free choice. And so some turn to philosophy, others to the civil law, and still others to oratory, while in case of the virtues themselves one man prefers to excel in one, another in another.

Selection of a career:

116 They, whose fathers or forefathers have achieved distinction in some particular field, often strive to attain eminence in the same department of service: for example, Quintus, the son of Publius Mucius, in the law; Africanus, the son of Paulus, in the army. And to that distinction which they have severally inherited from their fathers some have added lustre of their own; for example, that same Africanus, who crowned his inherited military glory with his own eloquence. Timotheus, Conon's son, did the same: he proved himself not inferior to his father in military renown and added to that distinction the glory of culture and intellectual power. It happens sometimes, too, that a man declines to follow in the footsteps of his fathers and pursues a vocation of his own. And in such callings those very frequently achieve signal success who, though sprung from humble parentage, have set their aims high.

(1) inheritance,

(2) choice,

117 All these questions, therefore, we ought to bear thoughtfully in mind, when we inquire into the nature of propriety; but above all we must decide who and what manner of men we wish to be and what calling in life we would follow; and this is the most difficult problem in the world. For it is in the years of early youth, when our judgment is most immature, that each of us decides that his calling in life shall be that to which he has taken a special liking. And thus he becomes engaged in some

certo genere cursuque vivendi, quam potuit, quod optimum esset, iudicare.

118 Nam quod[1] Herculem Prodicus[2] dicit, ut est apud Xenophontem, cum primum pubesceret, quod tempus a natura ad deligendum, quam quisque viam vivendi sit ingressurus, datum est, exisse in solitudinem atque ibi sedentem diu secum multumque dubitasse, cum duas cerneret vias, unam Voluptatis, alteram Virtutis, utram ingredi melius esset, hoc Herculi " Iovis satu edito " potuit fortasse contingere, nobis non item,[3] qui imitamur, quos cuique visum est, atque ad eorum studia institutaque impellimur; plerumque autem parentium praeceptis imbuti ad eorum consuetudinem moremque deducimur; alii multitudinis iudicio feruntur, quaeque maiori parti pulcherrima videntur, ea maxime exoptant; non nulli tamen sive felicitate quadam sive bonitate naturae sine[4] parentium disciplina rectam vitae secuti sunt viam.

Mem. II, i, 21-34

119 XXXIII. Illud autem maxime rarum genus est eorum, qui aut excellenti[5] ingenii magnitudine aut praeclara eruditione atque doctrina aut utraque re ornati spatium etiam deliberandi habuerunt, quem potissimum vitae cursum sequi vellent; in qua deliberatione ad suam cuiusque naturam consilium est omne revocandum. Nam cum in omnibus, quae aguntur, ex eo, quo modo quisque natus est, ut supra dictum est, quid deceat, exquirimus, tum in tota

[1] *Nam quod* L c, Edd.; *namque* A B H a b.
[2] *Prodicus* Manutius, Edd.; *prodigus* L c; *prodigum* B H b.
[3] *item* Edd.; *idem* MSS.
[4] *sine* Stuerenburg, Edd. plerique; *sive* MSS., Bt.[1]
[5] *excellenti* L c; *excellente* A B H a b; *excellentis* p.

particular calling and career in life, before he is fit to decide intelligently what is best for him.

118 For we cannot all have the experience of Hercules, as we find it in the words of Prodicus in Xenophon: "When Hercules was just coming into youth's estate (the time which Nature has appointed unto every man for choosing the path of life on which he would enter), he went out into a desert place. And as he saw two paths, the path of Pleasure and the path of Virtue, he sat down and debated long and earnestly which one it were better for him to take." This might, perhaps, happen to a Hercules, "scion of the seed of Jove"; but it cannot well happen to us; for we copy each the model he fancies, and we are constrained to adopt their pursuits and vocations. But usually, we are so imbued with the teachings of our parents, that we fall irresistibly into their manners and customs. Others drift with the current of popular opinion and make especial choice of those callings which the majority find most attractive. Some, however, as the result either of some happy fortune or of natural ability, enter upon the right path of life, without parental guidance.

Hercules at the parting of the ways.

(3) accident,

119 XXXIII. There is one class of people that is very rarely met with: it is composed of those who are endowed with marked natural ability, or exceptional advantages of education and culture, or both, and who also have time to consider carefully what career in life they prefer to follow; and in this deliberation the decision must turn wholly upon each individual's natural bent. For we try to find out from each one's native disposition, as was said above, just what is proper for him; and this we require not only in case of each individual act but also in ordering the whole course of one's life; and this last is a matter to

(4) natural bias

vita constituenda multo est ei rei[1] cura maior adhibenda, ut constare in perpetuitate vitae possimus nobismet ipsis nec in ullo officio claudicare.

120 Ad hanc autem rationem quoniam maximam vim natura habet, fortuna proximam, utriusque omnino habenda ratio est in deligendo genere vitae, sed naturae magis; multo enim et firmior est et constantior, ut fortuna non numquam tamquam ipsa mortalis cum immortali natura pugnare videatur. Qui igitur ad naturae suae non vitiosae genus consilium vivendi omne contulerit, is constantiam teneat (id enim maxime decet), nisi forte se intellexerit errasse in deligendo genere vitae. Quod si acciderit (potest autem accidere), facienda morum institutorumque mutatio est. Eam mutationem si tempora adiuvabunt, facilius commodiusque faciemus; sin minus, sensim erit pedetemptimque facienda, ut amicitias, quae minus delectent et minus probentur, magis decere censent sapientes sensim diluere quam
121 repente praecidere. Commutato autem genere vitae omni ratione curandum est, ut id bono consilio fecisse videamur.

Sed quoniam paulo ante dictum est imitandos esse maiores, primum illud exceptum sit, ne vitia sint imitanda, deinde si natura non feret, ut quaedam imitari possit[2] (ut superioris filius Africani, qui hunc Paulo natum adoptavit, propter infirmitatem

[1] *est ei rei* Gruter, Edd.; *est eius rei* L c p; *est rei* A B H b; *est ei* a.
[2] *possit* J. M. Heusinger, Edd.; *possint* MSS.

which still greater care must be given, in order that we may be true to ourselves throughout all our lives and not falter in the discharge of any duty.

120 But since the most powerful influence in the choice of a career is exerted by Nature, and the next most powerful by Fortune, we must, of course, take account of them both in deciding upon our calling in life; but, of the two, Nature claims the more attention. For Nature is so much more stable and steadfast, that for Fortune to come into conflict with Nature seems like a combat between a mortal and a goddess. If, therefore, anyone has conformed his whole plan of life to the kind of nature that is his (that is, his better nature), let him go on with it consistently—for that is the essence of Propriety—unless, perchance, he should discover that he has made a mistake in choosing his life work. If this should happen (and it can easily happen), he must change his vocation and mode of life. If circumstances favour such change, it will be effected with greater ease and convenience. If not, it must be made gradually, step by step, just as, when friendships become no longer pleasing or desirable, it is more proper (so wise men think) to undo the bond

**Change of vocation.**

121 little by little than to sever it at a stroke. And when we have once changed our calling in life, we must take all possible care to make it clear that we have done so with good reason.

But whereas I said a moment ago that we have to follow in the steps of our fathers, let me make the following exceptions: first, we need not imitate their faults; second, we need not imitate certain other things, if our nature does not permit such imitation; for example, the son of the elder Africanus (that Scipio who adopted the younger Africanus,

valetudinis non tam potuit patris similis esse, quam ille fuerat sui); si igitur non poterit sive causas defensitare sive populum contionibus tenere sive bella gerere, illa tamen praestare debebit, quae erunt in ipsius potestate, iustitiam, fidem, liberalitatem, modestiam, temperantiam, quo minus ab eo id, quod desit, requiratur. Optima autem hereditas a patribus traditur liberis omnique patrimonio praestantior gloria virtutis rerumque gestarum, cui dedecori esse nefas [et vitium] [1] iudicandum est.

122 XXXIV. Et quoniam officia non eadem disparibus aetatibus tribuuntur aliaque sunt iuvenum, alia seniorum, aliquid etiam de hac distinctione dicendum est.

Est igitur adulescentis maiores natu vereri exque iis deligere optimos et probatissimos, quorum consilio atque auctoritate nitatur; ineuntis enim aetatis inscitia senum constituenda et regenda prudentia est. Maxime autem haec aetas a libidinibus arcenda est exercendaque in labore patientiaque et animi et corporis, ut eorum et in bellicis et in civilibus officiis vigeat industria. Atque etiam cum relaxare animos et dare se iucunditati volent, caveant intemperantiam, meminerint verecundiae, quod erit facilius, si *ne* in eius modi quidem rebus maiores natu nolent [2] interesse.

123 Senibus autem labores corporis minuendi, exerci-

[1] *et* (*sed* b) *vitium* A B H a b; [*et vitium*] Bt.[2], Ed.; *et vicium* c; *et impium* L p, Bt.[1], Heine.

[2] *si ne in . . . nolent* Stuerenburg, Edd.; *si in . . . nolint* A B H a b; *si in . . . volent* L c; *si in . . . non nolint* Lambinus.

the son of Paulus) could not on account of ill-health be so much like his father as Africanus had been like his. If, then, a man is unable to conduct cases at the bar or to hold the people spell-bound with his eloquence or to conduct wars, still it will be his duty to practise these other virtues, which are within his reach—justice, good faith, generosity, temperance, self-control—that his deficiencies in other respects may be less conspicuous. The noblest heritage, however, that is handed down from fathers to children, and one more precious than any inherited wealth, is a reputation for virtue and worthy deeds; and to dishonour this must be branded as a sin and a shame.

122 XXXIV. Since, too, the duties that properly belong to different times of life are not the same, but some belong to the young, others to those more advanced in years, a word must be said on this distinction also.

It is, then, the duty of a young man to show deference to his elders and to attach himself to the best and most approved of them, so as to receive the benefit of their counsel and influence. For the inexperience of youth requires the practical wisdom of age to strengthen and direct it. And this time of life is above all to be protected against sensuality and trained to toil and endurance of both mind and body, so as to be strong for active duty in military and civil service. And even when they wish to relax their minds and give themselves up to enjoyment they should beware of excesses and bear in mind the rules of modesty. And this will be easier, if the young are not unwilling to have their elders join them even in their pleasures.

**Duties of (1) youth,**

123 The old, on the other hand, should, it seems, have their physical labours reduced; their mental activi-

**(2) age,**

tationes animi etiam augendae videntur; danda vero opera, ut et amicos et iuventutem et maxime rem publicam consilio et prudentia quam plurimum adiuvent. Nihil autem magis cavendum est senectuti, quam ne languori se desidiaeque dedat; luxuria vero cum omni aetati turpis, tum senectuti foedissima est; sin autem etiam libidinum intemperantia accessit, duplex malum est, quod et ipsa senectus dedecus concipit et facit adulescentium impudentiorem intemperantiam.

124 Ac ne illud quidem alienum est, de magistratuum, de privatorum, [de civium,][1] de peregrinorum officiis dicere.

Est igitur proprium munus magistratus intellegere se gerere personam civitatis debereque eius dignitatem et decus sustinere, servare leges, iura discribere,[2] ea fidei suae commissa meminisse.

Privatum autem oportet aequo et pari cum civibus iure vivere neque summissum et abiectum neque se efferentem,[3] tum in re publica ea velle, quae tranquilla et honesta sint; talem enim solemus et sentire bonum civem et dicere.

125 Peregrini autem atque incolae officium est nihil praeter suum negotium agere, nihil de alio anquirere minimeque esse in aliena re publica curiosum.

Ita fere officia reperientur, cum quaeretur, quid deceat, et quid aptum sit personis, temporibus,

[1] *de civium* MSS.; [*de civium*] Hieron., Wolff, Edd.
[2] *discribere* Bt., Ed., Heine; *describere* MSS.
[3] *efferentem* A H[1] L a b c; *ecferentem* B H[2], Ed.

ties should be actually increased. They should endeavour, too, by means of their counsel and practical wisdom to be of as much service as possible to their friends and to the young, and above all to the state. But there is nothing against which old age has to be more on its guard than against surrendering to feebleness and idleness, while luxury, a vice in any time of life, is in old age especially scandalous. But if excess in sensual indulgence is added to luxurious living, it is a twofold evil; for old age not only disgraces itself; it also serves to make the excesses of the young more shameless.

124 At this point it is not at all irrelevant to discuss the duties of magistrates, of private individuals, [of native citizens,] and of foreigners.

It is, then, peculiarly the place of a magistrate to bear in mind that he represents the state and that it is his duty to uphold its honour and its dignity, to enforce the law, to dispense to all their constitutional rights, and to remember that all this has been committed to him as a sacred trust. **(3) magistrates**

The private individual ought first, in private relations, to live on fair and equal terms with his fellow-citizens, with a spirit neither servile and grovelling nor yet domineering; and second, in matters pertaining to the state, to labour for her peace and honour; for such a man we are accustomed to esteem and call a good citizen. **(4) private citizens,**

125 As for the foreigner or the resident alien, it is his duty to attend strictly to his own concerns, not to pry into other people's business, and under no condition to meddle in the politics of a country not his own. **(5) aliens.**

In this way I think we shall have a fairly clear view of our duties when the question arises what is proper and what is appropriate to each character, **Duty and Propriety.**

aetatibus. Nihil est autem, quod tam deceat, quam in omni re gerenda consilioque capiendo servare constantiam.

126 XXXV. Sed quoniam decorum illud in omnibus factis, dictis, in corporis denique motu et statu cernitur idque positum est in tribus rebus, formositate, ordine, ornatu ad actionem apto, difficilibus ad eloquendum, sed satis erit intellegi, in his autem tribus continetur cura etiam illa, ut probemur iis, quibuscum apud quosque vivamus, his quoque de rebus pauca dicantur.

Principio corporis nostri magnam natura ipsa videtur habuisse rationem, quae formam nostram reliquamque figuram, in qua esset species honesta, eam posuit in promptu, quae partes autem corporis ad naturae necessitatem datae aspectum essent deformem habiturae atque foedum,[1] eas contexit atque
127 abdidit. Hanc naturae tam diligentem fabricam imitata est hominum verecundia. Quae enim natura occultavit, eadem omnes, qui sana mente sunt, removent ab oculis ipsique necessitati dant operam ut quam occultissime pareant; quarumque partium corporis usus sunt necessarii, eas neque partes neque earum usus suis nominibus appellant; quodque facere turpe non est,[2] modo occulte, id dicere obscenum est. Itaque nec actio rerum illarum aperta petulantia vacat nec orationis obscenitas.

[1] *foedum* Klotz, Müller, Heine; *formam* A B H a b; *turpem* L c, Bt.

[2] *turpe non est* a, Edd.; *non turpe est* L; *non turpe* (om. *est*) c; *turpe non turpe est* A B H b (the first *turpe* crossed out in A B).

circumstance, and age. But there is nothing so essentially proper as to maintain consistency in the performance of every act and in the conception of every plan.

126 XXXV. But the propriety to which I refer shows itself also in every deed, in every word, even in every movement and attitude of the body. And in outward, visible propriety there are three elements—beauty, tact, and taste; these conceptions are difficult to express in words, but it will be enough for my purpose if they are understood. In these three elements is included also our concern for the good opinion of those with whom and amongst whom we live. For these reasons I should like to say a few words about this kind of propriety also. Propriety in bodily actions.

First of all, Nature seems to have had a wonderful plan in the construction of our bodies. Our face and our figure generally, in so far as it has a comely appearance, she has placed in sight; but the parts of the body that are given us only to serve the needs of Nature and that would present an unsightly and unpleasant appearance she has covered up and
127 concealed from view. Man's modesty has followed this careful contrivance of Nature's; all right-minded people keep out of sight what Nature has hidden and take pains to respond to Nature's demands as privately as possible; and in the case of those parts of the body which only serve Nature's needs, neither the parts nor the functions are called by their real names. To perform these functions—if only it be done in private—is nothing immoral; but to speak of them is indecent. And so neither public performance of those acts nor vulgar mention of them is free from indecency. Modesty.

128 Nec vero audiendi sunt Cynici, aut si qui fuerunt Stoici paene Cynici, qui reprehendunt et irrident, quod ea, quae turpia [1] non sint, verbis flagitiosa ducamus, illa autem, quae turpia [2] sint, nominibus appellemus suis. Latrocinari, fraudare, adulterare re [3] turpe est, sed dicitur non obscene; liberis dare operam re honestum est, nomine obscenum; pluraque in eam sententiam ab eisdem contra verecundiam disputantur. Nos autem naturam sequamur et ab omni, quod abhorret ab oculorum auriumque approbatione, fugiamus; status incessus, sessio accubitio, vultus oculi manuum motus teneat illud decorum.

129 Quibus in rebus duo maxime sunt fugienda, ne quid effeminatum aut molle et ne quid durum aut rusticum sit. Nec vero histrionibus oratoribusque concedendum est, ut iis haec apta sint, nobis dissoluta. Scaenicorum quidem mos tantam habet vetere disciplina verecundiam, ut in scaenam sine subligaculo prodeat nemo; verentur enim, ne, si quo casu evenerit, ut corporis partes quaedam aperiantur, aspiciantur non decore. Nostro quidem more cum parentibus puberes filii, cum soceris generi non lavantur. Retinenda igitur est huius generis verecundia, praesertim natura ipsa magistra et duce.

130 XXXVI. Cum autem pulchritudinis duo genera sint, quorum in altero venustas sit, in altero dignitas,

[1] *quae turpia* B b, Edd.; *quae re turpia* L c; *quae . . . autem* om. H.
[2] *quae turpia* B H b, Edd.; *quae re turpia* L c.
[3] *re* B H, Edd.; not in A L b c p.

128 But we should give no heed to the Cynics (or to some Stoics who are practically Cynics) who censure and ridicule us for holding that the mere mention of some actions that are not immoral is shameful, while other things that are immoral we call by their real names. Robbery, fraud, and adultery, for example, are immoral in deed, but it is not indecent to name them. To beget children in wedlock is in deed morally right; to speak of it is indecent. And they assail modesty with a great many other arguments to the same purport. But as for us, let us follow Nature and shun everything that is offensive to our eyes or our ears. So, in standing or walking, in sitting or reclining, in our expression, our eyes, or the movements of our hands, let us preserve what we have called "propriety."

129 In these matters we must avoid especially the two extremes: our conduct and speech should not be effeminate and over-nice, on the one hand, nor coarse and boorish, on the other. And we surely must not admit that, while this rule applies to actors and orators, it is not binding upon us. As for stage-people, their custom, because of its traditional discipline, carries modesty to such a point that an actor would never step out upon the stage without a breech-cloth on, for fear he might make an improper exhibition, if by some accident certain parts of his person should happen to become exposed. And in our own custom, grown sons do not bathe with their fathers, nor sons-in-law with their fathers-in-law. We must, therefore, keep to the path of this sort of modesty, especially when Nature is our teacher and guide.

**Propriety: (1) in outward appearance;**

130 XXXVI. Again, there are two orders of beauty: in the one, loveliness predominates; in the other,

venustatem muliebrem ducere debemus, dignitatem virilem. Ergo et a forma removeatur omnis viro non dignus ornatus, et huic simile vitium in gestu motuque caveatur. Nam et palaestrici motus sunt saepe odiosiores, et histrionum non nulli gestus ineptiis non vacant,[1] et in utroque genere quae sunt recta et simplicia, laudantur. Formae autem dignitas coloris bonitate tuenda est, color exercitationibus corporis. Adhibenda praeterea munditia est non odiosa neque exquisita nimis, tantum quae fugiat agrestem et inhumanam neglegentiam. Eadem ratio est habenda vestitus, in quo, sicut in plerisque rebus, mediocritas optima est.

131 Cavendum autem est, ne aut tarditatibus utamur *in* [2] ingressu mollioribus, ut pomparum ferculis similes esse videamur, aut in festinationibus suscipiamus nimias celeritates, quae cum fiunt, anhelitus moventur, vultus mutantur, ora torquentur; ex quibus magna significatio fit non adesse constantiam. Sed multo etiam magis elaborandum est, ne animi motus a natura recedant; quod assequemur, si cavebimus, ne in perturbationes atque exanimationes incidamus, et si attentos animos ad decoris conservationem tenebimus.

132 Motus autem animorum duplices sunt, alteri cogi-

[1] *ineptiis non vacant* A B H a b; *inepti non vacant offensione* L c p.
[2] *in* Edd.; not in MSS.

dignity; of these, we ought to regard loveliness as the attribute of woman, and dignity as the attribute of man. Therefore, let all finery not suitable to a man's dignity be kept off his person, and let him guard against the like fault in gesture and action. The manners taught in the palaestra,[a] for example, are often rather objectionable, and the gestures of actors on the stage are not always free from affectation; but simple, unaffected manners are commendable in both instances. Now dignity of mien is also to be enhanced by a good complexion; the complexion is the result of physical exercise. We must besides present an appearance of neatness—not too punctilious or exquisite, but just enough to avoid boorish and ill-bred slovenliness. We must follow the same principle in regard to dress. In this, as in most things, the best rule is the golden mean.

131 We must be careful, too, not to fall into a habit of listless sauntering in our gait, so as to look like carriers in festal processions, or of hurrying too fast, when time presses. If we do this, it puts us out of breath, our looks are changed, our features distorted; and all this is clear evidence of a lack of poise. But it is much more important that we succeed in keeping our mental operations in harmony with Nature's laws. And we shall not fail in this if we guard against violent excitement or depression, and if we keep our minds intent on the observance of propriety. (2) in inward self-control.

132 Our mental operations, moreover, are of two

[a] The Greek palaestra, a public school of wrestling and athletics, adopted by the Romans became a place of exercise where the youth were trained in gestures and attitudes, a nursery of foppish manners.

tationis, alteri appetitus; cogitatio in vero exquirendo maxime versatur, appetitus impellit ad agendum. Curandum est igitur, ut cogitatione ad res quam optimas utamur, appetitum rationi oboedientem praebeamus.

XXXVII. Et quoniam magna vis orationis est, eaque duplex, altera contentionis, altera sermonis, contentio disceptationibus tribuatur iudiciorum, contionum, senatus, sermo in circulis, disputationibus, congressionibus familiarium versetur, sequatur etiam convivia. Contentionis praecepta rhetorum sunt, nulla sermonis, quamquam haud scio an possint haec quoque esse. Sed discentium studiis inveniuntur magistri, huic autem qui studeant, sunt nulli, rhetorum turba referta omnia; quamquam, quae[1] verborum sententiarumque praecepta sunt, eadem ad sermonem pertinebunt.

133 Sed cum orationis indicem vocem habeamus, in voce autem duo sequamur, ut clara sit, ut suavis, utrumque omnino a natura petundum est, verum alterum exercitatio augebit, alterum imitatio presse loquentium et leniter.

Nihil fuit in Catulis, ut eos exquisito iudicio putares uti litterarum, quamquam erant litterati; sed et alii; hi autem optime uti lingua Latina putaban-

[1] *quae* $A^2$ c, Edd.; *quoniam* (per compend.) $A^1$ B H a b.

kinds: some have to do with thought, others with impulse. Thought is occupied chiefly with the discovery of truth; impulse prompts to action. We must be careful, therefore, to employ our thoughts on themes as elevating as possible and to keep our impulses under the control of reason.

XXXVII. The power of speech in the attainment of propriety is great, and its function is twofold: the first is oratory; the second, conversation. Oratory is the kind of discourse to be employed in pleadings in court and speeches in popular assemblies and in the senate; conversation should find its natural place in social gatherings, in informal discussions, and in intercourse with friends; it should also seek admission at dinners. There are rules for oratory laid down by rhetoricians; there are none for conversation; and yet I do not know why there should not be. But where there are students to learn, teachers are found; there are, however, none who make conversation a subject of study, whereas pupils throng about the rhetoricians everywhere. And yet the same rules that we have for words and sentences in rhetoric will apply also to conversation.

**Propriety in speech: oratory and conversation.**

133 Now since we have the voice as the organ of speech, we should aim to secure two properties for it: that it be clear, and that it be musical. We must, of course, look to Nature for both gifts. But distinctness may be improved by practice; the musical qualities, by imitating those who speak with smooth and articulate enunciation.

There was nothing in the two Catuli to lead one to suppose that they had a refined literary taste; they were men of culture, it is true; and so were others; but the Catuli were looked upon as the perfect

tur; sonus erat dulcis, litterae neque expressae neque oppressae, ne aut obscurum esset aut putidum, sine contentione vox nec languens nec canora. Uberior oratio L. Crassi nec minus faceta, sed bene loquendi de Catulis opinio non minor. Sale vero et facetiis Caesar, Catuli patris frater, vicit omnes, ut in illo ipso forensi genere dicendi contentiones aliorum sermone vinceret.

In omnibus igitur his elaborandum est, si in omni re quid deceat exquirimus.

134 Sit ergo hic sermo, in quo Socratici maxime excellunt, lenis minimeque pertinax, insit in eo lepos; nec vero, tamquam in possessionem suam venerit, excludat alios, sed cum reliquis in rebus, tum in sermone communi vicissitudinem non iniquam putet; ac videat in primis, quibus de rebus loquatur; si seriis, severitatem adhibeat, si iocosis, leporem; in primisque provideat, ne sermo vitium aliquod indicet inesse in moribus; quod maxime tum solet evenire, cum studiose de absentibus detrahendi causa aut per ridiculum aut severe maledice contumelioseque dicitur.

135 Habentur autem plerumque sermones aut de domesticis negotiis aut de re publica aut de artium

masters of the Latin tongue. Their pronunciation was charming; their words were neither mouthed nor mumbled: they avoided both indistinctness and affectation; their voices were free from strain, yet neither faint nor shrill. More copious was the speech of Lucius Crassus and not less brilliant, but the reputation of the two Catuli for eloquence was fully equal to his. But in wit and humour Caesar, the elder Catulus's half-brother, surpassed them all: even at the bar he would with his conversational style defeat other advocates with their elaborate orations.

If, therefore, we are aiming to secure propriety in every circumstance of life, we must master all these points.

134 Conversation, then, in which the Socratics are the best models, should have these qualities. It should be easy and not in the least dogmatic; it should have the spice of wit. And the one who engages in conversation should not debar others from participating in it, as if he were entering upon a private monopoly; but, as in other things, so in a general conversation he should think it not unfair for each to have his turn. He should observe, first and foremost, what the subject of conversation is. If it is grave, he should treat it with seriousness; if humorous, with wit. And above all, he should be on the watch that his conversation shall not betray some defect in his character. This is most likely to occur, when people in jest or in earnest take delight in making malicious and slanderous statements about the absent, on purpose to injure their reputations.

Conversation as an art.

135 The subjects of conversation are usually affairs of the home or politics or the practice of the professions

studiis atque doctrina. Danda igitur opera est, ut, etiamsi aberrare ad alia coeperit, ad haec revocetur oratio, sed utcumque aderunt; neque enim isdem [1] de rebus nec omni tempore nec similiter delectamur. Animadvertendum est etiam, quatenus sermo delectationem habeat, et, ut incipiendi ratio fuerit, ita sit desinendi modus.

136 XXXVIII. Sed quo modo in omni vita rectissime praecipitur, ut perturbationes fugiamus, id est motus animi nimios rationi non optemperantes, sic eius modi motibus sermo debet vacare, ne aut ira exsistat aut cupiditas aliqua aut pigritia aut ignavia aut tale aliquid appareat, maximeque curandum est, ut eos, quibuscum sermonem conferemus, et vereri et diligere videamur.

Obiurgationes etiam non numquam incidunt necessariae, in quibus utendum est fortasse et vocis contentione maiore et verborum gravitate acriore, id agendum etiam, ut ea facere videamur irati. Sed, ut ad urendum et secandum, sic ad hoc genus castigandi raro invitique veniemus nec umquam nisi necessario, si nulla reperietur alia medicina; sed tamen ira procul absit, cum qua nihil recte fieri, nihil considerate potest.
137 Magnam autem partem [2] clementi castigatione licet uti, gravitate tamen adiuncta, ut severitas adhibeatur et contumelia repellatur, atque etiam illud ipsum, quod acerbitatis habet obiurgatio, significandum est, ipsius id causa, qui obiurgetur, esse susceptum.

[1] *enim isdem* (*hisdem* B H) A B H b, Müller; *enim omnes isdem* L c, most Edd.

[2] *magnam autem partem* Lambinus, Edd.; *magna autem parte* MSS.

and learning. Accordingly, if the talk begins to drift off to other channels, pains should be taken to bring it back again to the matter in hand—but with due consideration to the company present; for we are not all interested in the same things at all times or in the same degree. We must observe, too, how far the conversation is agreeable and, as it had a reason for its beginning, so there should be a point at which to close it tactfully.

136 XXXVIII. But as we have a most excellent rule for every phase of life, to avoid exhibitions of passion, that is, mental excitement that is excessive and uncontrolled by reason; so our conversation ought to be free from such emotions: let there be no exhibition of anger or inordinate desire, of indolence or indifference, or anything of the kind. We must also take the greatest care to show courtesy and consideration toward those with whom we converse. Propriety of speech,

It may sometimes happen that there is need of administering reproof. On such occasions we should, perhaps, use a more emphatic tone of voice and more forcible and severe terms and even assume an appearance of being angry. But we shall have recourse to this sort of reproof, as we do to cautery and amputation, rarely and reluctantly—never at all, unless it is unavoidable and no other remedy can be discovered. We may seem angry, but anger should be far from us; for in anger nothing right or judi-
137 cious can be done. In most cases, we may apply a mild reproof, so combined, however, with earnestness, that, while severity is shown, offensive language is avoided. Nay more, we must show clearly that even that very harshness which goes with our reproof is designed for the good of the person reproved. (1) in reproofs,

Rectum est autem etiam in illis contentionibus, quae cum inimicissimis fiunt, etiamsi nobis indigna audiamus, tamen gravitatem retinere, iracundiam pellere. Quae enim cum aliqua perturbatione fiunt, ea nec constanter fieri possunt neque iis, qui adsunt, probari.

Deforme etiam est de se ipsum praedicare falsa praesertim et cum irrisione audientium imitari militem gloriosum.

138 XXXIX. Et quoniam omnia persequimur, volumus quidem certe, dicendum est etiam, qualem hominis honorati et principis domum placeat esse, cuius finis est usus,[1] ad quem accommodanda est aedificandi descriptio et tamen adhibenda commoditatis dignitatisque diligentia.

Cn. Octavio, qui primus ex illa familia consul factus est, honori fuisse accepimus, quod praeclaram aedificasset in Palatio et plenam dignitatis domum; quae cum vulgo viseretur, suffragata domino, novo homini, ad consulatum putabatur; hanc Scaurus demolitus accessionem adiunxit aedibus. Itaque ille in suam domum consulatum primus attulit, hic, summi et clarissimi viri filius, in domum multiplicatam non repulsam solum rettulit, sed ignominiam
139 etiam et[2] calamitatem. Ornanda enim est dignitas domo, non ex domo tota quaerenda, nec domo dominus, sed domino domus honestanda est, et, ut

[1] *est usus* L c, Edd.; *et usus* B H a b.
[2] *et* L c, Edd.; not in B H b.

The right course, moreover, even in our differences with our bitterest enemies, is to maintain our dignity and to repress our anger, even though we are treated outrageously. For what is done under some degree of excitement cannot be done with perfect self-respect or the approval of those who witness it. (2) in disputes,

It is bad taste also to talk about oneself—especially if what one says is not true—and, amid the derision of one's hearers, to play "The Braggart Captain."[a] (3) in self-praise.

138 XXXIX. But since I am investigating this subject in all its phases (at least, that is my purpose), I must discuss also what sort of house a man of rank and station should, in my opinion, have. Its prime object is serviceableness. To this the plan of the building should be adapted; and yet careful attention should be paid to its convenience and distinction. The proper home.

We have heard that Gnaeus Octavius—the first of that family to be elected consul—distinguished himself by building upon the Palatine an attractive and imposing house. Everybody went to see it, and it was thought to have gained votes for the owner, a new man, in his canvass for the consulship. That house Scaurus demolished, and on its site he built an addition to his own house. Octavius, then, was the first of his family to bring the honour of a consulship to his house; Scaurus, though the son of a very great and illustrious man, brought to the same house, when enlarged, not only defeat, but dis-
139 grace and ruin. The truth is, a man's dignity may be enhanced by the house he lives in, but not wholly secured by it; the owner should bring honour to his

[a] Like Pyrgopolinices in the *Miles Gloriosus* of Plautus, or Thraso in the *Eunuchus* of Terence.

in ceteris habenda ratio non sua solum, sed etiam aliorum, sic in domo clari hominis, in quam et hospites multi recipiendi et admittenda hominum cuiusque modi multitudo, adhibenda cura est laxitatis; aliter ampla domus dedecori saepe domino fit,[1] si est in ea solitudo, et maxime, si aliquando alio domino solita est frequentari. Odiosum est enim, cum a praetereuntibus dicitur:

Inc. inc. fab., Ribbeck², 184–185

o domus ántiqua, heu[2] quam díspari
dominháre domino!

quod quidem his temporibus in multis licet dicere.

140 Cavendum autem est, praesertim si ipse aedifices, ne extra modum sumptu et magnificentia prodeas; quo in genere multum mali etiam in exemplo est. Studiose enim plerique praesertim in hanc partem facta principum imitantur, ut L. Luculli, summi viri, virtutem quis? at quam multi villarum magnificentiam imitati! quarum quidem certe est adhibendus modus ad mediocritatemque[3] revocandus. Eademque mediocritas ad omnem usum cultumque vitae transferenda est.

Sed haec hactenus.

[1] *fit* Bt., Ed.; *sit* B H a b; *est* L (corr. ex *sit* b). Müller, Heine; not in c.

[2] *heu* Edd.; *et* MSS.; *ei* Schenkl.

[3] *mediocritatemque*: *que* italicized by Ed., but attested by B H L b c.

house, not the house to its owner. And, as in everything else a man must have regard not for himself alone but for others also, so in the home of a distinguished man, in which numerous guests must be entertained and crowds of every sort of people received, care must be taken to have it spacious. But if it is not frequented by visitors, if it has an air of lonesomeness, a spacious palace often becomes a discredit to its owner. This is sure to be the case if at some other time, when it had a different owner, it used to be thronged. For it is unpleasant, when passers-by remark:

> " O good old house, alas! how different
> The owner who now owneth thee! "

And in these times that may be said of many a house! [a]

140 One must be careful, too, not to go beyond proper bounds in expense and display, especially if one is building for oneself. For much mischief is done in this way, if only in the example set. For many people imitate zealously the foibles of the great, particularly in this direction: for example, who copies the virtues of Lucius Lucullus, excellent man that he was? But how many there are who have copied the magnificence of his villas! Some limit should surely be set to this tendency and it should be reduced at least to a standard of moderation; and by that same standard of moderation the comforts and wants of life generally should be regulated.

But enough on this part of my theme.

[a] Members of Caesar's party were now occupying the houses that had been the homes of Pompey's friends. Antony, for example, lived in Pompey's house.

141 In omni autem actione suscipienda tria sunt tenenda, primum ut appetitus rationi pareat, quo nihil est ad officia conservanda accommodatius, deinde ut animadvertatur, quanta illa res sit, quam efficere velimus, ut neve maior neve minor cura et opera suscipiatur, quam causa postulet. Tertium est, ut caveamus, ut ea, quae pertinent ad liberalem speciem et dignitatem,[1] moderata[2] sint. Modus autem est optimus decus ipsum tenere, de quo ante diximus, nec progredi longius. Horum tamen trium praestantissimum est appetitum optemperare rationi.

142 XL. Deinceps de ordine rerum et de opportunitate temporum dicendum est. Haec autem scientia continentur ea, quam Graeci *εὐταξίαν* nominant, non hanc, quam interpretamur modestiam, quo in verbo modus inest, sed illa est *εὐταξία*, in qua intellegitur ordinis conservatio. Itaque, ut eandem nos modestiam appellemus, sic definitur a Stoicis, ut modestia sit scientia rerum earum, quae agentur aut dicentur, loco suo collocandarum. Ita videtur eadem vis ordinis et collocationis fore; nam et ordinem sic definiunt: compositionem rerum aptis et accommodatis locis; locum autem actionis opportunitatem[3] temporis esse dicunt; tempus autem actionis opportunum[4] Graece *εὐκαιρία*, Latine appellatur occasio. Sic fit, ut modestia haec, quam ita interpretamur, ut

[1] *ad liberalem speciem et dignitatem* B H b, Edd.; *ad liberalitatem specie et dignitate* L c p.
[2] *moderata* L c p, Edd.; *moderanda* B H a b.
[3] *oportunitate(m)* Ed. [4] *oportunum* Ed.

141 In entering upon any course of action, then, we must hold fast to three principles: first, that impulse shall obey reason; for there is no better way than this to secure the observance of duties; second, that we estimate carefully the importance of the object that we wish to accomplish, so that neither more nor less care and attention may be expended upon it than the case requires; the third principle is that we be careful to observe moderation in all that is essential to the outward appearance and dignity of a gentleman. Moreover, the best rule for securing this is strictly to observe that propriety which we have discussed above, and not to overstep it. Yet of these three principles, the one of prime importance is to keep impulse subservient to reason.

**Three rules for the duty of propriety.**

142 XL. Next, then, we must discuss orderliness of conduct and seasonableness of occasions. These two qualities are embraced in that science which the Greeks call εὐταξία—not that εὐταξία which we translate with *moderation* [*modestia*], derived from *moderate*; but this is the εὐταξία by which we understand *orderly conduct*. And so, if we may call it also *moderation*, it is defined by the Stoics as follows: "Moderation is the science of disposing aright everything that is done or said." So the essence of orderliness and of right-placing, it seems, will be the same; for *orderliness* they define also as "the arrangement of things in their suitable and appropriate places." By "place of action," moreover, they mean *seasonableness of circumstance*; and the *seasonable circumstance* for an action is called in Greek εὐκαιρία, in Latin *occasio* (occasion). So it comes about that in this sense *moderation*, which we

**Orderliness—the right thing at the right time.**

dixi, scientia sit opportunitatis [1] idoneorum ad agendum temporum.

143 Sed potest eadem esse prudentiae definitio, de
Ch. vi qua principio diximus; hoc autem loco de moderatione et temperantia et harum similibus virtutibus quaerimus. Itaque, quae erant prudentiae propria, suo loco dicta sunt; quae autem harum virtutum, de quibus iam diu loquimur, quae pertinent ad verecundiam et ad eorum approbationem, quibuscum vivimus, nunc dicenda sunt.

144 Talis est igitur ordo actionum adhibendus, ut, quem ad modum in oratione constanti, sic in vita omnia sint apta inter se et convenientia; turpe enim valdeque vitiosum in re severa convivio digna [2] aut delicatum aliquem inferre sermonem. Bene Pericles, cum haberet collegam in praetura Sophoclem poëtam iique de communi officio convenissent et casu formosus puer praeteriret dixissetque Sophocles: "O puerum pulchrum, Pericle!" "At enim praetorem, Sophocle, decet non solum manus, sed etiam oculos abstinentes habere." Atqui [3] hoc idem Sophocles si in athletarum probatione dixisset, iusta reprehensione caruisset. Tanta vis est et loci et temporis. Ut, si qui, cum causam sit acturus, in itinere aut in ambulatione secum ipse meditetur, aut si quid aliud attentius cogitet, non reprehendatur, at

[1] *oportunitatis* Ed.
[2] *convivio digna* B H a b, Edd.; *convivio dignum* c; *convivii dicta* L p.
[3] *Atqui* Müller, Heine; *atque* MSS., Bt.

explain as I have indicated, is the science of doing the right thing at the right time.

143 A similar definition can be given for prudence, of which I have spoken in an early chapter. But in this part we are considering temperance and self-control and related virtues. Accordingly, the properties which, as we found, are peculiar to prudence were discussed in their proper place, while those are to be discussed now which are peculiar to these virtues of which we have for some time been speaking and which relate to considerateness and to the approbation of our fellow-men.

144 Such orderliness of conduct is, therefore, to be observed, that everything in the conduct of our life shall balance and harmonize, as in a finished speech. For it is unbecoming and highly censurable, when upon a serious theme, to introduce such jests as are proper at a dinner, or any sort of loose talk. When Pericles was associated with the poet Sophocles as his colleague in command and they had met to confer about official business that concerned them both, a handsome boy chanced to pass and Sophocles said: "Look, Pericles; what a pretty boy!" How pertinent was Pericles's reply: "Hush, Sophocles, a general should keep not only his hands but his eyes under control." And yet, if Sophocles had made this same remark at a trial of athletes, he would have incurred no just reprimand. So great is the significance of both place and circumstance. For example, if anyone, while on a journey or on a walk, should rehearse to himself a case which he is preparing to conduct in court, or if he should under similar circumstances apply his closest thought to some other subject, he would not be open to censure:

Seasonableness of speech.

hoc idem si in convivio faciat, inhumanus videatur inscitia temporis.

145 Sed ea, quae multum ab humanitate discrepant, ut si qui in foro cantet, aut si qua est alia magna perversitas, facile apparet nec magnopere admonitionem et praecepta desiderat; quae autem parva videntur esse delicta neque a multis intellegi possunt, ab iis [1] est diligentius declinandum. Ut in fidibus aut tibiis, quamvis paulum discrepent, tamen id a sciente animadverti solet, sic videndum [2] est in vita ne forte quid discrepet, vel multo etiam magis, quo maior et melior actionum quam sonorum concentus est.

146 XLI. Itaque, ut in fidibus musicorum aures vel minima sentiunt, sic nos, si acres ac diligentes esse volumus animadversores[que] [3] vitiorum, magna saepe intellegemus ex parvis. Ex oculorum optutu, superciliorum aut remissione aut contractione, ex maestitia, ex hilaritate, ex risu, ex locutione, ex reticentia, ex contentione vocis, ex summissione, ex ceteris similibus facile iudicabimus, quid eorum apte fiat, quid ab officio naturaque discrepet. Quo in genere non est incommodum, quale quidque eorum sit, ex aliis iudicare, ut, si quid dedeceat in illis,[4] vitemus ipsi; fit enim nescio quo modo, ut magis in aliis cernamus quam in nobismet ipsis, si quid delinquitur. Itaque facillime corriguntur in discendo, quorum vitia imitantur emendandi causa magistri.

[1] *iis* Edd.; *his* MSS.

[2] *videndum* L c, Edd.; *vivendum* B H a b.

[3] *animadversores*[*que*] Ed.; *animadversoresque* MSS.; * *animadversoresque* Bt.; *animadversores* Orelli. Müller, Heine.

[4] *dedeceat* a c, Edd.; *deceat* H L b; *non deceat* B. *in illis* a Bt.[1], Ed.; *in illos* B H b c; *illos* L, Bt.[2]

but if he should do that same thing at a dinner, he would be thought ill-bred, because he ignored the proprieties of the occasion.

145 But flagrant breaches of good breeding, like singing in the streets or any other gross misconduct, are easily apparent and do not call especially for admonition and instruction. But we must even more carefully avoid those seemingly trivial faults which pass unnoticed by the many. However slightly out of tune a harp or flute may be, the fault is still detected by a connoisseur; so we must be on the watch lest haply something in our life be out of tune—nay, rather, far greater is the need for painstaking, inasmuch as harmony of actions is far better and far more important than harmony of sounds. The little things that count.

146 XLI. As, therefore, a musical ear detects even the slightest falsity of tone in a harp, so we, if we wish to be keen and careful observers of moral faults, shall often draw important conclusions from trifles. We observe others and from a glance of the eyes, from a contracting or relaxing of the brows, from an air of sadness, from an outburst of joy, from a laugh, from speech, from silence, from a raising or lowering of the voice, and the like, we shall easily judge which of our actions is proper, and which is out of accord with duty and Nature. And, in the same manner, it is not a bad plan to judge of the nature of our every action by studying others, that so we may ourselves avoid anything that is unbecoming in them. For it happens somehow or other that we detect another's failings more readily than we do our own; and so in the school-room those pupils learn most easily to do better whose faults the masters mimic for the sake of correcting them. We correct our faults (1) by observing others,

147 Nec vero alienum est ad ea eligenda, quae dubitationem afferunt, adhibere doctos homines vel etiam usu peritos et, quid iis de quoque officii genere placeat, exquirere. Maior enim pars eo fere deferri solet, quo a natura ipsa deducitur. In quibus videndum est, non modo quid quisque loquatur, sed etiam quid quisque sentiat atque etiam de qua causa quisque sentiat. Ut enim pictores et ii, qui signa fabricantur, et vero etiam poëtae suum quisque opus a vulgo considerari vult, ut, si quid reprehensum sit a pluribus, id corrigatur, iique et secum et ab aliis,[1] quid in eo peccatum sit, exquirunt, sic aliorum iudicio permulta nobis et facienda et non facienda et mutanda et corrigenda sunt.

148 Quae vero more agentur institutisque civilibus, de iis nihil est praecipiendum; illa enim ipsa praecepta sunt, nec quemquam hoc errore duci oportet, ut, si quid Socrates aut Aristippus contra morem consuetudinemque civilem fecerint locutive sint, idem sibi arbitretur licere; magnis illi et divinis bonis hanc licentiam assequebantur. Cynicorum vero ratio tota est eicienda; est enim inimica verecundiae, sine qua nihil rectum esse potest, nihil honestum.

149 Eos autem, quorum vita perspecta in rebus honestis atque magnis est, bene de re publica sentientes ac bene meritos aut merentes sic ut [2] aliquo honore aut

[1] *et ab aliis* a, Bt., Ed.; *aliis* B H b; *et cum aliis* c; *et ex aliis* Unger, Müller.

[2] *sic ut* L p, Nonius; not in B H b c.

147 Nor is it out of place in making a choice between duties involving a doubt, to consult men of learning or practical wisdom and to ascertain what their views are on any particular question of duty. For the majority usually drift as the current of their own natural inclinations carries them; and in deriving counsel from one of these, we have to see not only what our adviser says, but also what he thinks, and what his reasons are for thinking as he does. For, as painters and sculptors and even poets, too, wish to have their works reviewed by the public, in order that, if any point is generally criticized, it may be improved; and as they try to discover both by themselves and with the help of others what is wrong in their work; so through consulting the judgment of others we find that there are many things to be done and left undone, to be altered and improved. (2) by the criticisms of the wise.

148 But no rules need to be given about what is done in accordance with the established customs and conventions of a community; for these are in themselves rules; and no one ought to make the mistake of supposing that, because Socrates or Aristippus did or said something contrary to the manners and established customs of their city, he has a right to do the same; it was only by reason of their great and superhuman virtues that those famous men acquired this special privilege. But the Cynics' whole system of philosophy must be rejected, for it is inimical to moral sensibility, and without moral sensibility nothing can be upright, nothing morally good. The laws of the state are rules of duty.

149 It is, furthermore, our duty to honour and reverence those whose lives are conspicuous for conduct in keeping with their high moral standards, and who, as true patriots, have rendered or are now rendering Special rules.

imperio affectos observare et colere debemus, tribuere etiam multum senectuti, cedere iis, qui magistratum habebunt, habere dilectum civis et peregrini in ipsoque peregrino, privatimne an publice venerit. Ad summam, ne agam de singulis, communem totius generis hominum conciliationem et consociationem colere, tueri, servare debemus.

150 XLII. Iam de artificiis et quaestibus, qui liberales habendi, qui sordidi sint, haec fere accepimus. Primum improbantur ii quaestus, qui in odia hominum incurrunt, ut portitorum, ut faeneratorum. Illiberales autem et sordidi quaestus mercennariorum omnium, quorum operae, non quorum artes emuntur; est enim in illis ipsa merces auctoramentum servitutis. Sordidi etiam putandi, qui mercantur a mercatoribus, quod statim vendant; nihil enim proficiant, nisi admodum mentiantur; nec vero est quicquam turpius vanitate. Opificesque omnes in sordida arte versantur; nec enim quicquam ingenuum habere potest officina. Minimeque artes eae probandae, quae ministrae sunt voluptatum:

Eunuchus II, 26 Cetárii, laniı́, coqui, fartóres, piscatóres,

efficient service to their country, just as much as if they were invested with some civil or military authority; it is our duty also to show proper respect to old age, to yield precedence to magistrates, to make a distinction between a fellow-citizen and a foreigner, and, in the case of the foreigner himself, to discriminate according to whether he has come in an official or a private capacity. In a word, not to go into details, it is our duty to respect, defend, and maintain the common bonds of union and fellowship subsisting between all the members of the human race.

150 XLII. Now in regard to trades and other means of livelihood, which ones are to be considered becoming to a gentleman and which ones are vulgar, we have been taught, in general, as follows. First, those means of livelihood are rejected as undesirable which incur people's ill-will, as those of tax-gatherers and usurers. Unbecoming to a gentleman, too, and vulgar are the means of livelihood of all hired workmen whom we pay for mere manual labour, not for artistic skill; for in their case the very wage they receive is a pledge of their slavery. Vulgar we must consider those also who buy from wholesale merchants to retail immediately; for they would get no profits without a great deal of downright lying; and verily, there is no action that is meaner than misrepresentation. And all mechanics are engaged in vulgar trades; for no workshop can have anything liberal about it. Least respectable of all are those trades which cater for sensual pleasures:

Occupations: (1) vulgar,

> "Fishmongers, butchers, cooks, and poulterers,
> And fishermen,"

ut ait Terentius; adde huc, si placet, unguentarios, saltatores, totumque ludum talarium.

151 Quibus autem artibus aut prudentia maior inest aut non mediocris utilitas quaeritur, ut medicina, ut architectura, ut doctrina rerum honestarum, eae sunt iis, quorum ordini conveniunt, honestae. Mercatura autem, si tenuis est, sordida putanda est; sin magna et copiosa, multa undique apportans multisque sine vanitate impertiens, non est admodum vituperanda, atque etiam, si satiata quaestu vel contenta potius, ut saepe ex alto in portum, ex ipso portu se in agros possessionesque contulit, videtur iure optimo posse laudari. Omnium autem rerum, ex quibus aliquid acquiritur, nihil est agri cultura melius, nihil uberius, nihil dulcius, nihil homine
C.M. XV-XVII libero [1] dignius; de qua quoniam in Catone Maiore satis multa diximus, illim [2] assumes, quae ad hunc locum pertinebunt.

152 XLIII. Sed ab iis partibus, quae sunt honestatis, quem ad modum officia ducerentur, satis expositum videtur. Eorum autem ipsorum, quae honesta sunt, potest incidere saepe contentio et comparatio, de duobus honestis utrum honestius, qui locus a Panaetio est praetermissus. Nam cum omnis honestas manet a partibus quattuor, quarum una sit cognitionis, altera communitatis, tertia magnani-

[1] *homine libero* Edd.; *homine nihil libero* B H L a b c.
[2] *illim* B[1], Edd.; *illum* H; *illa* B[2] p; *illinc* a b c; *illic* L.

as Terence says. Add to these, if you please, the perfumers, dancers, and the whole *corps de ballet.*[a]

151 But the professions in which either a higher degree of intelligence is required or from which no small benefit to society is derived—medicine and architecture, for example, and teaching—these are proper for those whose social position they become. Trade, if it is on a small scale, is to be considered vulgar; but if wholesale and on a large scale, importing large quantities from all parts of the world and distributing to many without misrepresentation, it is not to be greatly disparaged. Nay, it even seems to deserve the highest respect, if those who are engaged in it, satiated, or rather, I should say, satisfied with the fortunes they have made, make their way from the port to a country estate, as they have often made it from the sea into port. But of all the occupations by which gain is secured, none is better than agriculture, none more profitable, none more delightful, none more becoming to a freeman. But since I have discussed this quite fully in my Cato Major, you will find there the material that applies to this point. (2) liberal.

152 XLIII. Now, I think I have explained fully enough how moral duties are derived from the four divisions of moral rectitude. But between those very actions which are morally right, a conflict and comparison may frequently arise, as to which of two moral actions is morally better—a point overlooked by Panaetius. For, since all moral rectitude springs from four sources (one of which is prudence; the second, social instinct; the third, courage; the fourth, tem- Comparative estimate of duties.

[a] The *ludus talarius* was a kind of low variety show, with loose songs and dances and bad music.

mitatis, quarta moderationis, haec in deligendo officio saepe inter se comparentur necesse est.

153 Placet igitur aptiora esse naturae ea officia, quae ex communitate, quam ea, quae ex cognitione ducantur, idque hoc argumento confirmari potest, quod, si contigerit ea vita sapienti, ut omnium rerum affluentibus copiis [quamvis] omnia,[1] quae cognitione digna sint, summo otio secum ipse consideret et contempletur, tamen, si solitudo tanta sit, ut hominem videre non possit, excedat e vita. Princepsque omnium virtutum illa sapientia, quam σοφίαν Graeci vocant—prudentiam enim, quam Graeci φρόνησιν dicunt, aliam quandam intellegimus, quae est rerum expetendarum fugiendarumque scientia; illa autem sapientia, quam principem dixi, rerum est divinarum et humanarum scientia, in qua continetur deorum et hominum communitas et societas inter ipsos; ea si maxima est, ut est certe, necesse est, quod a communitate ducatur officium, id esse maximum. Etenim cognitio contemplatioque naturae manca quodam modo atque inchoata sit, si nulla actio rerum consequatur. Ea autem actio in hominum commodis tuendis maxime cernitur; pertinet igitur ad socie-

[1] *copiis [quamvis] omnia* Ed.; *copiis quamvis omnia* MSS.; *copiis omnia* Lambinus, Bt., Müller, Heine.

---

[a] Cicero is guilty of a curious fallacy. If it follows from his premises, (1) some one virtue is the highest virtue, and (2) the duties derived from the highest virtue are the highest duties, and if (3) wisdom is the highest virtue, then it can only follow that the duties derived from wisdom are the highest duties. But Cicero throws in a fourth premise that the "bonds of union between gods and men and the relations of man to man" are derived from wisdom, and therewith side-

perance), it is often necessary in deciding a question of duty that these virtues be weighed against one another.

153 My view, therefore, is that those duties are closer to Nature which depend upon the social instinct than those which depend upon knowledge; and this view can be confirmed by the following argument: (1) suppose that a wise man should be vouchsafed such a life that, with an abundance of everything pouring in upon him, he might in perfect peace study and ponder over everything that is worth knowing, still, if the solitude were so complete that he could never see a human being, he would die. And then, the foremost of all virtues is wisdom—what the Greeks call σοφία; for by prudence, which they call φρόνησις, we understand something else, namely, the practical knowledge of things to be sought for and of things to be avoided. (2) Again, that wisdom which I have given the foremost place is the knowledge of things human and divine, which is concerned also with the bonds of union between gods and men and the relations of man to man. If wisdom is the most important of the virtues, as it certainly is, it necessarily follows that that duty which is connected with the social obligation is the most important duty.[a] And (3) service is better than mere theoretical knowledge, for the study and knowledge of the universe would somehow be lame and defective, were no practical results to follow. Such results, moreover, are best seen in the safeguarding of human interests. It is

Justice vs. Wisdom.

tracks wisdom and gives the duties derived from the social instinct the place from which wisdom has been shunted.

Cicero could not refrain from introducing a bit of theoretical speculation that has no value for his practical position—it actually prejudices it and confuses the reader.

tatem generis humani; ergo haec cognitioni anteponenda est.

154 Atque id optimus quisque re ipsa[1] ostendit et iudicat. Quis enim est tam cupidus in perspicienda cognoscendaque rerum natura, ut, si ei tractanti contemplantique res cognitione dignissimas subito sit allatum periculum discrimenque patriae, cui subvenire opitularique possit, non illa omnia relinquat atque abiciat, etiamsi dinumerare se stellas aut metiri mundi magnitudinem posse arbitretur? atque hoc idem in parentis, in amici re aut periculo fecerit.

155 Quibus rebus intellegitur studiis officiisque scientiae praeponenda esse officia iustitiae, quae pertinent ad hominum utilitatem,[2] qua nihil homini esse debet antiquius.

XLIV. Atque illi, quorum studia vitaque omnis in rerum cognitione versata est, tamen ab augendis hominum utilitatibus et commodis non recesserunt; nam et erudiverunt multos, quo meliores cives utilioresque rebus suis publicis essent, ut Thebanum Epaminondam Lysis Pythagoreus, Syracosium Dionem Plato multique multos, nosque ipsi, quicquid ad rem publicam attulimus, si modo aliquid attulimus, a doctoribus atque doctrina instructi ad eam et ornati

156 accessimus. Neque solum vivi atque praesentes studiosos discendi erudiunt atque docent, sed hoc

[1] *re ipsa* B H a b, Bt., Ed.; *re ab se* L c (i.e. *reapse* Orelli, Müller, Heine); *ab ipsa re* p.

[2] *utilitatem* B H a b; *caritatem* L c p (affection).

essential, then, to human society; and it should, therefore, be ranked above speculative knowledge.

154 Upon this all the best men agree, as they prove by their conduct. For who is so absorbed in the investigation and study of creation, but that, even though he were working and pondering over tasks never so much worth mastering and even though he thought he could number the stars and measure the length and breadth of the universe, he would drop all those problems and cast them aside, if word were suddenly brought to him of some critical peril to his country, which he could relieve or repel? And he would do the same to further the interests of parent or friend or to save him from danger.

155 From all this we conclude that the duties prescribed by justice must be given precedence over the pursuit of knowledge and the duties imposed by it; for the former concern the welfare of our fellow-men; and nothing ought to be more sacred in men's eyes than that.

**Wisdom in the service of Justice.**

XLIV. And yet scholars, whose whole life and interests have been devoted to the pursuit of knowledge, have not, after all, failed to contribute to the advantages and blessings of mankind. For they have trained many to be better citizens and to render larger service to their country. So, for example, the Pythagorean Lysis taught Epaminondas of Thebes; Plato, Dion of Syracuse; and many, many others. As for me myself, whatever service I have rendered to my country—if, indeed, I have rendered any—I came to my task trained and equipped for it by my
156 teachers and what they taught me. And not only while present in the flesh do they teach and train those who are desirous of learning, but by the written

idem etiam post mortem monumentis litterarum assequuntur. Nec enim locus ullus est praetermissus ab iis, qui ad leges, qui ad mores, qui ad disciplinam rei publicae pertineret, ut otium suum ad nostrum negotium contulisse videantur. Ita illi ipsi doctrinae studiis et sapientiae dediti ad hominum utilitatem suam prudentiam intellegentiamque potissimum conferunt; ob eamque etiam causam eloqui copiose, modo prudenter, melius est quam vel acutissime sine eloquentia cogitare, quod cogitatio in se ipsa vertitur, eloquentia complectitur eos, quibuscum communitate iuncti sumus.

157 Atque ut apium examina non fingendorum favorum causa congregantur, sed, cum congregabilia natura sint, fingunt favos, sic homines, ac multo etiam magis, natura congregati adhibent agendi cogitandique[1] sollertiam. Itaque, nisi ea virtus, quae constat ex hominibus tuendis, id est ex societate generis humani, attingat cognitionem rerum, solivaga cognitio et ieiuna videatur, itemque magnitudo animi remota communitate[2] coniunctioneque humana feritas sit quaedam et immanitas. Ita fit, ut vincat cognitionis studium consociatio hominum atque communitas.

Plato, Rep. II, 369 B; Arist., Pol. I, 1253 A

158 Nec verum est, quod dicitur a quibusdam, propter necessitatem vitae, quod ea, quae natura desideraret, consequi sine aliis atque efficere non possemus,

[1] *cogitandique* L c p, Edd.; *congregandique* B H a b.

[2] *communitate* p (per compendium), Bt.[2], Müller, Heine; *comitate* A B H L a b c.

memorials of their learning they continue the same service after they are dead. For they have overlooked no point that has a bearing upon laws, customs, or political science; in fact, they seem to have devoted their retirement to the benefit of us who are engaged in public business. The principal thing done, therefore, by those very devotees of the pursuits of learning and science is to apply their own practical wisdom and insight to the service of humanity. And for that reason also much speaking (if only it contain wisdom) is better than speculation never so profound without speech; for mere speculation is self-centred, while speech extends its benefits to those with whom we are united by the bonds of society.

157 And again, as swarms of bees do not gather for the sake of making honeycomb but make the honeycomb because they are gregarious by nature, so human beings—and to a much higher degree—exercise their skill together in action and thought because they are naturally gregarious. And so, if that virtue [Justice] which centres in the safeguarding of human interests, that is, in the maintenance of human society, were not to accompany the pursuit of knowledge, that knowledge would seem isolated and barren of results. In the same way, courage [Fortitude], if unrestrained by the uniting bonds of society, would be but a sort of brutality and savagery. Hence it follows that the claims of human society and the bonds that unite men together take precedence of the pursuit of speculative knowledge.

**Justice more valuable than Wisdom and Fortitude.**

158 And it is not true, as certain people maintain, that the bonds of union in human society were instituted in order to provide for the needs of daily life; for, they say, without the aid of others we could not

idcirco initam esse cum hominibus communitatem et societatem; quodsi omnia nobis, quae ad victum cultumque pertinent, quasi virgula divina, ut aiunt, suppeditarentur, tum optimo quisque ingenio negotiis omnibus omissis totum se in cognitione et scientia collocaret. Non est ita; nam et solitudinem fugeret et socium studii quaereret, tum docere tum discere vellet, tum audire tum dicere. Ergo omne officium, quod ad coniunctionem hominum et ad societatem tuendam valet, anteponendum est illi officio, quod cognitione et scientia continetur.

159 XLV. Illud forsitan quaerendum sit, num haec communitas, quae maxime est apta naturae, sit etiam moderationi modestiaeque semper anteponenda. Non placet; sunt enim quaedam partim ita foeda, partim ita flagitiosa, ut ea ne conservandae quidem patriae causa sapiens facturus sit. Ea Posidonius collegit permulta, sed ita taetra quaedam, ita obscena, ut dictu quoque videantur turpia. Haec igitur non suscipiet rei publicae causa, ne res publica quidem pro se suscipi volet. Sed hoc[1] commodius se res habet, quod non potest accidere tempus, ut intersit rei publicae quicquam illorum facere sapientem.

160 Quare hoc quidem effectum sit, in officiis deligendis id[2] genus officiorum excellere, quod teneatur hominum societate. [Etenim cognitionem prudentiam-

[1] *hoc* L c p, Edd.; *haec* B H a b.
[2] *id* a, Edd.; *ut* b; *hoc* B H L c p.

secure for ourselves or supply to others the things that Nature requires; but if all that is essential to our wants and comfort were supplied by some magic wand, as in the stories, then every man of first-rate ability could drop all other responsibility and devote himself exclusively to learning and study. Not at all. For he would seek to escape from his loneliness and to find someone to share his studies; he would wish to teach, as well as to learn; to hear, as well as to speak. Every duty, therefore, that tends effectively to maintain and safeguard human society should be given the preference over that duty which arises from speculation and science alone.

159 XLV. The following question should, perhaps, be asked: whether this social instinct, which is the deepest feeling in our nature, is always to have precedence over temperance and moderation also. I think not. For there are some acts either so repulsive or so wicked, that a wise man would not commit them, even to save his country. Posidonius has made a large collection of them; but some of them are so shocking, so indecent, that it seems immoral even to mention them. The wise man, therefore, will not think of doing any such thing for the sake of his country; no more will his country consent to have it done for her. But the problem is the more easily disposed of because the occasion cannot arise when it could be to the state's interest to have the wise man do any of those things. **Justice *vs.* Temperance.**

160 This, then, may be regarded as settled: in choosing between conflicting duties, that class takes precedence which is demanded by the interests of human society. [And this is the natural sequence; for discreet action will presuppose learning and prac- Order of precedence of duties.

que sequetur considerata actio; ita fit, ut agere considerate pluris sit quam cogitare prudenter.][1]

Atque haec quidem hactenus. Patefactus enim locus est ipse, ut non difficile sit in exquirendo officio, quid cuique sit praeponendum, videre. In ipsa autem communitate sunt gradus officiorum, ex quibus, quid cuique praestet, intellegi possit, ut prima dis immortalibus, secunda patriae, tertia parentibus, deinceps gradatim reliquis debeantur.

161 Quibus ex rebus breviter disputatis intellegi potest non solum id homines solere dubitare, honestumne an turpe sit, sed etiam duobus propositis honestis utrum honestius sit. Hic locus a Panaetio est, ut supra dixi, praetermissus. Sed iam ad reliqua pergamus.

[1] *Etenim . . . prudenter* bracketed by Unger.

tical wisdom; it follows, therefore, that discreet action is of more value than wise (but inactive) speculation.]

So much must suffice for this topic. For, in its essence, it has been made so clear, that in determining a question of duty it is not difficult to see which duty is to be preferred to any other. Moreover, even in the social relations themselves there are gradations of duty so well defined that it can easily be seen which duty takes precedence of any other: our first duty is to the immortal gods; our second, to country; our third, to parents; and so on, in a descending scale, to the rest.

161 From this brief discussion, then, it can be understood that people are often in doubt not only whether an action is morally right or wrong, but also, when a choice is offered between two moral actions, which one is morally better. This point, as I remarked above, has been overlooked by Panaetius. But let us now pass on to what remains.

# BOOK II

## EXPEDIENCY

# LIBER SECUNDUS

1 I. Quem ad modum officia ducerentur ab honestate, Marce fili, atque ab omni genere virtutis, satis explicatum arbitror libro superiore. Sequitur, ut haec officiorum genera persequar, quae pertinent ad vitae cultum et ad earum rerum, quibus utuntur homines, facultatem, ad opes, ad copias [; in quo tum quaeri dixi, quid utile, quid inutile, tum ex utilibus quid utilius aut quid maxime utile].[1] De quibus dicere aggrediar, si pauca prius de instituto ac de iudicio meo dixero.

2 Quamquam enim libri nostri complures non modo ad legendi, sed etiam ad scribendi studium excitaverunt, tamen interdum vereor, ne quibusdam bonis viris philosophiae nomen sit invisum mirenturque in ea tantum me operae et temporis ponere.

Ego autem, quam diu res publica per eos gerebatur, quibus se ipsa commiserat, omnis meas curas cogitationesque in eam conferebam; cum autem dominatu unius omnia tenerentur neque esset usquam consilio aut auctoritati locus, socios denique tuendae rei publicae, summos viros, amisissem, nec me angoribus dedidi, quibus essem confectus, nisi

[1] *in quo . . . maxime utile* bracketed by Heumann, Facciolati, Edd.; *tum ex . . . maxime utile* not in B H a b.

# BOOK II

1 I. I believe, Marcus, my son, that I have fully explained in the preceding book how duties are derived from moral rectitude, or rather from each of virtue's four divisions. My next step is to trace out those kinds of duty which have to do with the comforts of life, with the means of acquiring the things that people enjoy, with influence, and with wealth. [In this connection, the question is, as I said: (1) what is expedient, and what is inexpedient; and (2) of several expedients, which is of more and which of most importance.] These questions I shall proceed to discuss, after I have said a few words in vindication of my present purpose and my principles of philosophy. Statement of subject.

2 Although my books have aroused in not a few men the desire not only to read but to write, yet I sometimes fear that what we term philosophy is distasteful to certain worthy gentlemen, and that they wonder that I devote so much time and attention to it. Why Cicero wrote on philosophy.

Now, as long as the state was administered by the men to whose care she had voluntarily entrusted herself, I devoted all my effort and thought to her. But when everything passed under the absolute control of a despot and there was no longer any room for statesmanship or authority of mine; and finally when I had lost the friends [a] who had been associated with me in the task of serving the interests of the state, and who were men of the highest standing, I did not resign myself to grief, by which I should have been overwhelmed, had I not struggled

[a] Such as Pompey, Cato, Hortensius, and Piso.

iis restitissem, nec rursum indignis homine docto voluptatibus.

3 Atque utinam res publica stetisset, quo coeperat, statu nec in homines non tam commutandarum quam evertendarum rerum cupidos incidisset! Primum enim, ut stante re publica facere solebamus, in agendo plus quam in scribendo operae poneremus, deinde ipsis scriptis non ea, quae nunc, sed actiones nostras mandaremus, ut saepe fecimus. Cum autem res publica, in qua omnis mea cura, cogitatio, opera poni solebat, nulla esset omnino, illae scilicet litterae
4 conticuerunt forenses et senatoriae. Nihil agere autem cum animus non posset, in his studiis ab initio versatus aetatis existimavi honestissime molestias [1] posse deponi, si me ad philosophiam rettulissem. Cui cum multum adulescens discendi causa temporis tribuissem, posteaquam honoribus inservire coepi meque totum rei publicae tradidi, tantum erat philosophiae loci, quantum superfuerat amicorum et rei publicae temporibus; [2] id autem omne consumebatur in legendo, scribendi otium non erat.

5 II. Maximis igitur in malis hoc tamen boni assecuti videmur, ut ea litteris mandaremus, quae nec erant satis nota nostris et erant cognitione dignissima. Quid enim est, per deos, optabilius sapientia,

[1] *molestias* L c p, Nonius, Edd.; not in B H a b.
[2] *temporibus* Victorius, Edd.; *temporis* B H a b; *tempori* L c p.

against it; neither, on the other hand, did I surrender myself to a life of sensual pleasure unbecoming to a philosopher.

3 I would that the government had stood fast in the position it had begun to assume and had not fallen into the hands of men who desired not so much to reform as to abolish the constitution. For then, in the first place, I should now be devoting my energies more to public speaking than to writing, as I used to do when the republic stood; and in the second place, I should be committing to written form not these present essays but my public speeches, as I often formerly did. But when the republic, to which all my care and thought and effort used to be devoted, was no more, then, of course, my voice was
4 silenced in the forum and in the senate. And since my mind could not be wholly idle, I thought, as I had been well-read along these lines of thought from my early youth, that the most honourable way for me to forget my sorrows would be by turning to philosophy. As a young man, I had devoted a great deal of time to philosophy as a discipline; but after I began to fill the high offices of state and devoted myself heart and soul to the public service, there was only so much time for philosophical studies as was left over from the claims of my friends and of the state; all of this was spent in reading; I had no leisure for writing.

5 II. Therefore, amid all the present most awful calamities I yet flatter myself that I have won this good out of evil—that I may commit to written form matters not at all familiar to our countrymen but still very much worth their knowing. For what, in the name of heaven, is more to be desired

Why philosophy is worth while.

quid praestantius, quid homini melius, quid homine dignius? Hanc igitur qui expetunt,[1] philosophi nominantur, nec quicquam aliud est philosophia, si interpretari velis, praeter studium sapientiae. Sapientia autem est, ut a veteribus philosophis definitum est, rerum divinarum et humanarum causarumque, quibus eae res continentur, scientia; cuius studium qui vituperat, haud sane intellego, quidnam sit,
6 quod laudandum putet. Nam sive oblectatio quaeritur animi requiesque curarum, quae conferri cum eorum studiis potest, qui semper aliquid anquirunt, quod spectet et valeat ad bene beateque vivendum? sive ratio constantiae virtutisque ducitur, aut haec ars est aut nulla omnino, per quam eas assequamur. Nullam dicere maximarum rerum artem esse, cum minimarum sine arte nulla sit, hominum est parum considerate loquentium atque in maximis rebus errantium. Si autem est aliqua disciplina virtutis, ubi ea quaeretur, cum ab hoc discendi genere discesseris?

Sed haec, cum ad philosophiam cohortamur, accuratius disputari solent, quod alio quodam libro fecimus; hoc autem tempore tantum nobis declarandum fuit, cur orbati rei publicae muneribus ad hoc nos studium potissimum contulissemus.

Hortensius, de Div., II, 1.

7 Occurritur autem nobis, et quidem a doctis et

[1] *expetunt* L c p, Edd.; *expetant* H; *expectant* B a b.

than wisdom? What is more to be prized? What is better for a man, what more worthy of his nature? Those who seek after it are called philosophers; and philosophy is nothing else, if one will translate the word into our idiom, than "the love of wisdom." Wisdom, moreover, as the word has been defined by the philosophers of old, is "the knowledge of things human and divine and of the causes by which those things are controlled." And if the man lives who would belittle the study of philosophy, I quite fail to see what in the world he would see fit to
6 praise. For if we are looking for mental enjoyment and relaxation, what pleasure can be compared with the pursuits of those who are always studying out something that will tend toward and effectively promote a good and happy life? Or, if regard is had for strength of character and virtue, then this is the method by which we can attain to those qualities, or there is none at all. And to say that there is no "method" for securing the highest blessings, when none even of the least important concerns is without its method, is the language of people who talk without due reflection and who blunder in matters of the utmost importance. Furthermore, if there is really a way to learn virtue, where shall one look for it, when one has turned aside from this field of learning?

Now, when I am advocating the study of philosophy, I usually discuss this subject at greater length, as I have done in another of my books. For the present I meant only to explain why, deprived of the tasks of public service, I have devoted myself to this particular pursuit.

7 But people raise other objections against me—

eruditis quaerentibus, satisne constanter facere videamur, qui, cum percipi nihil posse dicamus, tamen et aliis de rebus disserere soleamus et hoc ipso tempore praecepta officii persequamur. Quibus vellem satis cognita esset nostra sententia. Non enim sumus ii, quorum vagetur animus errore nec habeat umquam, quid sequatur. Quae enim esset ista mens vel quae vita potius non modo disputandi, sed etiam vivendi ratione sublata? Nos autem, ut ceteri alia certa, alia incerta esse dicunt, sic ab his dissentientes alia probabilia, contra alia dicimus.

8 Quid est igitur, quod me impediat ea, quae probabilia mihi videantur, sequi, quae contra, improbare atque affirmandi arrogantiam vitantem fugere temeritatem, quae a sapientia dissidet plurimum? Contra autem omnia disputatur [1] a nostris, quod hoc ipsum probabile elucere non posset,[2] nisi ex utraque parte causarum esset facta contentio.

II, 20 ff. Sed haec explanata sunt in Academicis nostris satis, ut arbitror, diligenter. Tibi autem, mi Cicero, quamquam in antiquissima nobilissimaque philosophia Cratippo auctore versaris iis simillimo, qui ista

[1] *disputatur* Edd.; *disputantur* MSS.
[2] *posset* a c; *possit* B H b.

and that, too, philosophers and scholars—asking whether I think I am quite consistent in my conduct: for although our school maintains that nothing can be known for certain, yet, they urge, I make a habit of presenting my opinions on all sorts of subjects and at this very moment am trying to formulate rules of duty. But I wish that they had a proper understanding of our position. For we Academicians are not men whose minds wander in uncertainty and never know what principles to adopt. For what sort of mental habit, or rather what sort of life would that be which should dispense with all rules for reasoning or even for living? Not so with us; but, as other schools maintain that some things are certain, others uncertain, we, differing with them, say that some things are probable, others improbable. **Position of the New Academy.**

8 What, then, is to hinder me from accepting what seems to me to be probable, while rejecting what seems to be improbable, and from shunning the presumption of dogmatism, while keeping clear of that recklessness of assertion which is as far as possible removed from true wisdom? And as to the fact that our school argues against everything, that is only because we could not get a clear view of what is "probable," unless a comparative estimate were made of all the arguments on both sides.

But this subject has been, I think, quite fully set forth in my "Academics." And although, my dear Cicero, you are a student of that most ancient and celebrated school of philosophy, with Cratippus as your master—and he deserves to be classed with the founders of that illustrious sect[a]—still I wish our

[a] Aristotle and Theophrastus.

praeclara pepererunt, tamen haec nostra finitima vestris ignota esse nolui.

Sed iam ad instituta pergamus.

9 III. Quinque igitur rationibus propositis officii persequendi, quarum duae ad decus honestatemque pertinerent, duae ad commoda vitae, copias, opes, facultates, quinta ad eligendi iudicium, si quando ea, quae dixi, pugnare inter se viderentur, honestatis pars confecta est, quam quidem tibi cupio esse notissimam.

Hoc autem, de quo nunc agimus, id ipsum est, quod "utile" appellatur. In quo verbo lapsa consuetudo deflexit de via sensimque eo deducta est, ut honestatem ab utilitate secernens constitueret esse honestum aliquid, quod utile non esset, et utile, quod non honestum, qua nulla pernicies maior hominum vitae potuit afferri.

10 Summa quidem auctoritate philosophi severe sane atque honeste haec tria genera confusa [1] cogitatione distinguunt. [Quicquid enim iustum sit, id etiam utile esse censent, itemque quod honestum, idem iustum; ex quo efficitur, ut, quicquid honestum sit, idem sit utile.] [2] Quod qui parum perspiciunt, ii saepe versu-

[1] *haec tria genera confusa* B H a b, Bt.[2], Heine; *haec tria genere confusa* c, Bt.[1], Müller; *haec tria genera, re confusa* J. F. Heusinger.

[2] *Quicquid . . . sit utile* bracketed by Unger, Bt.[2], Müller, Heine.

school, which is closely related to yours, not to be unknown to you.

Let us now proceed to the task in hand.

9 III. Five principles, accordingly, have been laid down for the pursuance of duty: two of them have to do with propriety and moral rectitude; two, with the external conveniences of life—means, wealth, influence; the fifth, with the proper choice, if ever the four first mentioned seem to be in conflict. The division treating of moral rectitude, then, has been completed, and this is the part with which I desire you to be most familiar.

Expediency and Moral Rectitude identical.

The principle with which we are now dealing is that one which is called Expediency. The usage of this word has been corrupted and perverted and has gradually come to the point where, separating moral rectitude from expediency, it is accepted that a thing may be morally right without being expedient, and expedient without being morally right. No more pernicious doctrine than this could be introduced into human life.

10 There are, to be sure, philosophers of the very highest reputation who distinguish theoretically between these three conceptions,[a] although they are indissolubly blended together; and they do this, I assume, on moral, conscientious principles. [For whatever is just, they hold, is also expedient; and, in like manner, whatever is morally right is also just. It follows, then, that whatever is morally right is also expedient.] Those who fail to comprehend that

[a] That is, they make a false distinction between (1) moral rectitude that is at the same time expedient; (2) moral rectitude that is (apparently) not expedient; and (3) the expedient that is (apparently) not morally right.

tos homines et callidos admirantes malitiam sapientiam iudicant. Quorum error eripiendus est opinioque omnis ad eam spem traducenda, ut honestis consiliis iustisque factis, non fraude et malitia se intellegant ea, quae velint, consequi posse.

11 Quae ergo ad vitam hominum tuendam pertinent, partim sunt inanima, ut aurum, argentum, ut ea, quae gignuntur e terra, ut alia generis eiusdem, partim animalia, quae habent suos impetus et rerum appetitus. Eorum autem alia [1] rationis expertia sunt, alia ratione utentia; expertes rationis equi, boves, reliquae pecudes, [apes,] [2] quarum opere efficitur aliquid ad usum hominum atque vitam; ratione autem utentium duo genera ponunt, deorum unum, alterum hominum. Deos placatos pietas efficiet et sanctitas, proxime autem et secundum deos homines hominibus maxime utiles esse possunt.

12 Earumque item rerum, quae noceant et obsint, eadem divisio est. Sed quia deos nocere non putant, iis exceptis homines hominibus obesse plurimum arbitrantur.

Ea enim ipsa, quae inanima diximus, pleraque sunt hominum operis effecta; quae nec haberemus, nisi manus et ars accessisset, nec iis sine hominum administratione uteremur. Neque enim valetudinis curatio neque navigatio neque agri cultura neque frugum fructuumque reliquorum perceptio et

[1] *alia* H² (inserted above the line) a, Edd.; not in B H¹ b; *partim* c.
[2] *apes* MSS.; bracketed by Facciolati, Edd.

theory do often, in their admiration for shrewd and clever men, take craftiness for wisdom. But they must be disabused of this error and their way of thinking must be wholly converted to the hope and conviction that it is only by moral character and righteousness, not by dishonesty and craftiness, that they may attain to the objects of their desires.

11 Of the things, then, that are essential to the sustenance of human life, some are inanimate (gold and silver, for example, the fruits of the earth, and so forth), and some are animate and have their own peculiar instincts and appetites. Of these again some are rational, others irrational. Horses, oxen, and the other cattle, [bees,] whose labour contributes more or less to the service and subsistence of man, are not endowed with reason; of rational beings two divisions are made—gods and men. Worship and purity of character will win the favour of the gods; and next to the gods, and a close second to them, men can be most helpful to men. Classification of expedients.

12 The same classification may likewise be made of the things that are injurious and hurtful. But, as people think that the gods bring us no harm, they decide (leaving the gods out of the question) that men are most hurtful to men.

As for mutual helpfulness, those very things which we have called inanimate are for the most part themselves produced by man's labours; we should not have them without the application of manual labour and skill nor could we enjoy them without the intervention of man. And so with many other things: for without man's industry there could have been no provisions for health, no navigation, no agriculture, no ingathering or storing of the Necessity of man's helpfulness to man.

conservatio sine hominum opera ulla esse potuisset.
13 Iam vero et earum rerum, quibus abundaremus, exportatio et earum, quibus egeremus, invectio certe nulla esset, nisi his [1] muneribus homines fungerentur. Eademque ratione nec lapides ex terra exciderentur ad usum nostrum necessarii, nec " ferrum, aes, aurum, argentum " effoderetur " penitus abditum " sine hominum labore et manu.

(Attius, Prometheus?), Inc, inc. fab. Ribbeck², 154.

IV. Tecta vero, quibus et frigorum vis pelleretur et calorum molestiae sedarentur, unde aut initio generi humano dari potuissent aut postea subveniri,[2] si aut vi tempestatis aut terrae motu aut vetustate cecidissent, nisi communis vita ab hominibus harum rerum auxilia
14 petere didicisset? Adde ductus aquarum, derivationes fluminum, agrorum irrigationes, moles oppositas fluctibus, portus manu factos, quae unde sine hominum opere habere possemus? Ex quibus multisque aliis perspicuum est, qui fructus quaeque utilitates ex rebus iis, quae sint inanimae, percipiantur, eas nos nullo modo sine hominum manu atque opera capere potuisse.

Qui denique ex bestiis fructus aut quae commoditas, nisi homines adiuvarent, percipi posset? Nam et qui principes inveniendi fuerunt, quem ex quaque belua usum habere possemus, homines certe fuerunt, nec hoc tempore sine hominum opera aut pascere eas aut domare aut tueri aut tempestivos fructus ex iis capere possemus; ab eisdemque et, quae nocent,[3] interficiuntur et, quae usui possunt esse, capiuntur.
15 Quid enumerem artium multitudinem, sine quibus vita omnino nulla esse potuisset? Qui enim aegris

[1] *his* H, Edd.; *iis* B L b; *hijs* c.
[2] *subveniri* L c, Müller, Heine; *subvenire* B H a b, Bt., Ed.
[3] *et, quae nocent* Bt.[2]; *et eae, quae nocent* B H b, Bt.[1]; *et ea quae nocent* L; *ea quae nocent* c.

13 fruits of the field or other kinds of produce. Then, too, there would surely be no exportation of our superfluous commodities or importation of those we lack, did not men perform these services. By the same process of reasoning, without the labour of man's hands, the stone needful for our use would not be quarried from the earth, nor would "iron, copper, gold, and silver, hidden far within," be mined.

**Mutual helpfulness the key to civilization.**

IV. And how could houses ever have been provided in the first place for the human race, to keep out the rigours of the cold and alleviate the discomforts of the heat; or how could the ravages of furious tempest or of earthquake or of time upon them afterward have been repaired, had not the bonds of social life taught men in such events to
14 look to their fellow-men for help? Think of the aqueducts, canals, irrigation works, breakwaters, artificial harbours; how should we have these without the work of man? From these and many other illustrations it is obvious that we could not in any way, without the work of man's hands, have received the profits and the benefits accruing from inanimate things.

Finally, of what profit or service could animals be, without the co-operation of man? For it was men who were the foremost in discovering what use could be made of each beast; and to-day, if it were not for man's labour, we could neither feed them nor break them in nor take care of them nor yet secure the profits from them in due season. By man, too, noxious beasts are destroyed, and those that can be of use are captured.

15 Why should I recount the multitude of arts without which life would not be worth living at all? For

subveniretur,[1] quae esset oblectatio valentium, qui victus aut cultus, nisi tam multae nobis artes ministrarent? quibus rebus exculta hominum vita tantum distat [2] a victu et cultu bestiarum. Urbes vero sine hominum coetu non potuissent nec aedificari nec frequentari; ex quo leges moresque constituti, tum iuris aequa discriptio [3] certaque vivendi disciplina; quas res et mansuetudo animorum consecuta et verecundia est effectumque, ut esset vita munitior, atque ut dando et accipiendo mutuandisque facultatibus et commodandis [4] nulla re egeremus.

16 V. Longiores hoc loco sumus, quam necesse est. Quis est enim, cui non perspicua sint illa, quae pluribus verbis a Panaetio commemorantur, neminem neque ducem bello [5] nec principem domi magnas res et salutares sine hominum studiis gerere potuisse? Commemoratur ab eo Themistocles, Pericles, Cyrus, Agesilaus, Alexander, quos negat sine adiumentis hominum tantas res efficere potuisse. Utitur in re non dubia testibus non necessariis.

Atque ut magnas utilitates adipiscimur conspiratione hominum atque consensu, sic nulla tam detestabilis pestis est, quae non homini ab homine nascatur. Est Dicaearchi liber de interitu hominum,

[1] *qui . . . subveniretur* Gernhard, Edd.; *qui . . . subveniret* B H; *quis . . . subveniret* L c; *quid . . . subveniret* a b.

[2] *distat* L c p, Müller, Heine; *destitit* B H a b, Bt.

[3] *discriptio* H b; *descriptio* B a c.

[4] *mutuandisque facultatibus et commodandis* Nonius, Bt.[2], Müller; *mutandisque facultatibus et commodis* MSS., Bt.[1], Heine.

[5] *bello* B H a b, Müller, Heine; *belli* L c p, Bt.

how would the sick be healed? What pleasure would the hale enjoy? What comforts should we have, if there were not so many arts to minister to our wants? In all these respects the civilized life of man is far removed from the standard of the comforts and wants of the lower animals. And, without the association of men, cities could not have been built or peopled. In consequence of city life, laws and customs were established, and then came the equitable distribution of private rights and a definite social system. Upon these institutions followed a more humane spirit and consideration for others, with the result that life was better supplied with all it requires, and by giving and receiving, by mutual exchange of commodities and conveniences, we succeeded in meeting all our wants.

16 V. I have dwelt longer on this point than was necessary. For who is there to whom those facts which Panaetius narrates at great length are not self-evident—namely, that no one, either as a general in war or as a statesman at home, could have accomplished great things for the benefit of the state, without the hearty co-operation of other men? He cites the deeds of Themistocles, Pericles, Cyrus, Agesilaus, Alexander, who, he says, could not have achieved so great success without the support of other men. He calls in witnesses, whom he does not need, to prove a fact that no one questions.

**Man's hurtfulness to man.**

And yet, as, on the one hand, we secure great advantages through the sympathetic co-operation of our fellow-men; so, on the other, there is no curse so terrible but it is brought down by man upon man. There is a book by Dicaearchus on "The Destruction of Human Life." He was a famous

Peripatetici magni et copiosi, qui collectis ceteris causis eluvionis, pestilentiae, vastitatis, beluarum etiam repentinae multitudinis, quarum impetu docet quaedam hominum genera esse consumpta, deinde comparat, quanto plures deleti sint homines hominum impetu, id est bellis aut seditionibus, quam omni reliqua calamitate.

17 Cum igitur hic locus nihil habeat dubitationis, quin homines plurimum hominibus et prosint et obsint, proprium hoc statuo esse virtutis, conciliare animos hominum et ad usus suos adiungere. Itaque, quae in rebus inanimis quaeque in usu et [1] tractatione beluarum fiunt utiliter ad hominum vitam, artibus ea tribuuntur operosis, hominum autem studia ad amplificationem nostrarum rerum prompta ac parata [virorum praestantium] [2] sapientia et virtute excitan-
18 tur. Etenim virtus omnis tribus in rebus fere vertitur, quarum una est in perspiciendo, quid in quaque re verum sincerumque sit, quid consentaneum cuique, quid consequens, ex quo quaeque gignantur, quae cuiusque rei causa sit, alterum cohibere motus animi turbatos, quos Graeci *πάθη* nominant, appetitionesque, quas illi *ὁρμάς*, oboedientes efficere rationi, tertium iis, quibuscum congregemur, uti moderate et scienter, quorum studiis ea, quae natura desiderat, expleta cumulataque habeamus, per eosdemque, si quid importetur nobis incommodi, propulsemus ulciscamurque eos, qui nocere nobis conati sint,

[1] *usu et* L c p; not in B H a b; bracketed by Bt.[1]
[2] *virorum praestantium* bracketed by Ed.

and eloquent Peripatetic, and he gathered together all the other causes of destruction—floods, epidemics, famines, and sudden incursions of wild animals in myriads, by whose assaults, he informs us, whole tribes of men have been wiped out. And then he proceeds to show by way of comparison how many more men have been destroyed by the assaults of men—that is, by wars or revolutions—than by any and all other sorts of calamity.

17 Since, therefore, there can be no doubt on this point, that man is the source of both the greatest help and the greatest harm to man, I set it down as the peculiar function of virtue to win the hearts of men and to attach them to one's own service. And so those benefits that human life derives from inanimate objects and from the employment and use of animals are ascribed to the industrial arts; the co-operation of men, on the other hand, prompt and ready for the advancement of our interests, is secured through wisdom and virtue [in men of superior

**Co-operation and the virtues.**

18 ability]. And, indeed, virtue in general may be said to consist almost wholly in three properties: the first is [Wisdom,] the ability to perceive what in any given instance is true and real, what its relations are, its consequences, and its causes; the second is [Temperance,] the ability to restrain the passions (which the Greeks call πάθη) and make the impulses (ὁρμαί) obedient to reason; and the third is [Justice,] the skill to treat with consideration and wisdom those with whom we are associated, in order that we may through their co-operation have our natural wants supplied in full and overflowing measure, that we may ward off any impending trouble, avenge ourselves upon those who have attempted to

tantaque poena afficiamus, quantam aequitas humanitasque patitur.

19 VI. Quibus autem rationibus hanc facultatem assequi possimus, ut hominum studia complectamur eaque teneamus, dicemus, neque ita multo post, sed pauca ante dicenda sunt.

Magnam vim esse in fortuna in utramque partem, vel secundas ad res vel adversas, quis ignorat? Nam et, cum prospero flatu eius utimur, ad exitus pervehimur optatos et, cum reflavit, affligimur. Haec igitur ipsa fortuna ceteros casus rariores habet, primum ab inanimis procellas, tempestates, naufragia, ruinas, incendia, deinde a bestiis ictus, morsus, im-
20 petus; haec ergo, ut dixi, rariora. At vero interitus exercituum, ut proxime trium, saepe multorum, clades imperatorum, ut nuper summi et singularis viri, invidiae praeterea multitudinis atque ob eas bene meritorum saepe civium expulsiones, calamitates, fugae, rursusque secundae res, honores, imperia, victoriae, quamquam fortuita sunt, tamen sine hominum opibus et studiis neutram in partem effici possunt.

Hoc igitur cognito dicendum est, quonam modo hominum studia ad utilitates nostras allicere atque excitare possimus. Quae si longior fuerit oratio,

injure us, and visit them with such retribution as justice and humanity will permit.

19 VI. I shall presently discuss the means by which we can gain the ability to win and hold the affections of our fellow-men; but I must say a few words by way of preface.

**Co-operation *vs.* Fortune.**

Who fails to comprehend the enormous, two-fold power of Fortune for weal and for woe? When we enjoy her favouring breeze, we are wafted over to the wished-for haven; when she blows against us, we are dashed to destruction. Fortune herself, then, does send those other less usual calamities, arising, first, from inanimate Nature—hurricanes, storms, shipwrecks, catastrophes, conflagrations; second, from wild beasts—kicks, bites, and attacks. But these, as I have said, are comparatively rare.
20 But think, on the one side, of the destruction of armies (three lately, and many others at many different times), the loss of generals (of a very able and eminent commander recently), the hatred of the masses, too, and the banishment that as a consequence frequently comes to men of eminent services, their degradation and voluntary exile; think, on the other hand, of the successes, the civil and military honours, and the victories;—though all these contain an element of chance, still they cannot be brought about, whether for good or for ill, without the influence and the co-operation of our fellow-men.

With this understanding of the influence of Fortune, I may proceed to explain how we can win the affectionate co-operation of our fellows and enlist it in our service. And if the discussion of this point is unduly prolonged, let the length be compared

cum magnitudine utilitatis comparetur; ita fortasse etiam brevior videbitur.

21 Quaecumque igitur homines homini tribuunt ad eum augendum atque honestandum, aut benivolentiae gratia faciunt, cum aliqua de causa quempiam diligunt, aut honoris, si cuius virtutem suspiciunt, quemque dignum fortuna quam amplissima putant, aut cui fidem habent et bene rebus suis consulere arbitrantur, aut cuius opes metuunt, aut contra, a quibus aliquid exspectant, ut cum reges popularesve homines largitiones aliquas proponunt, aut postremo pretio ac mercede ducuntur, quae sordidissima est illa quidem ratio et inquinatissima et iis, qui ea tenentur, et illis, qui ad eam [1] confugere conantur;
22 male enim se res habet, cum, quod virtute effici debet, id temptatur pecunia. Sed quoniam non numquam hoc subsidium necessarium est, quem ad modum sit utendum eo, dicemus, si prius iis [2] de rebus, quae virtuti propiores sunt, dixerimus.

Atque etiam subiciunt se homines imperio alterius et potestati de causis pluribus. Ducuntur enim aut benivolentia aut beneficiorum magnitudine aut dignitatis praestantia aut spe sibi id utile futurum aut metu ne vi parere cogantur, aut spe largitionis

[1] *eam* c, Edd.; *ea* B H a b.
[2] *iis* Edd.; *his* B H a b; *hijs* c.

with the importance of the object in view. It will then, perhaps, seem even too short.

How men are led to promote another's interests.

21 Whenever, then, people bestow anything upon a fellow-man to raise his estate or his dignity, it may be from any one of several motives: (1) it may be out of good-will, when for some reason they are fond of him; (2) it may be from esteem, if they look up to his worth and think him deserving of the most splendid fortune a man can have; (3) they may have confidence in him and think that they are thus acting for their own interests; or (4) they may fear his power; (5) they may, on the contrary, hope for some favour—as, for example, when princes or demagogues bestow gifts of money; or, finally, (6) they may be moved by the promise of payment or reward. This last is, I admit, the meanest and most sordid motive of all, both for those who are swayed by it and for those who venture to
22 resort to it. For things are in a bad way, when that which should be obtained by merit is attempted by money. But since recourse to this kind of support is sometimes indispensable, I shall explain how it should be employed; but first I shall discuss those qualities which are more closely allied to merit.

Now, it is by various motives that people are led to submit to another's authority and power: they may be influenced (1) by good-will; (2) by gratitude for generous favours conferred upon them; (3) by the eminence of that other's social position or by the hope that their submission will turn to their own account; (4) by fear that they may be compelled perforce to submit; (5) they may be captivated by the hope of gifts of money and by liberal promises; or, finally,

promissisque [1] capti aut postremo, ut saepe in nostra re publica videmus, mercede conducti.

23 VII. Omnium autem rerum nec aptius est quicquam ad opes tuendas ac tenendas quam diligi nec alienius quam timeri. Praeclare enim Ennius:

(Thyestes?) Fab. inc. Valhen², 402.

Quém metuunt, odérunt; quem quisque ódit, periisse éxpetit.

Multorum autem odiis nullas opes posse obsistere, si antea fuit ignotum, nuper est cognitum. Nec vero huius tyranni solum, quem armis oppressa pertulit civitas ac paret cum maxime mortuo,[2] interitus declarat, quantum odium hominum valeat [3] ad pestem, sed reliquorum similes exitus tyrannorum, quorum haud fere quisquam talem interitum effugit; malus enim est custos diuturnitatis metus contraque benivolentia fidelis vel ad perpetuitatem.

24 Sed iis, qui vi oppressos imperio coercent, sit sane adhibenda saevitia, ut eris[4] in famulos, si aliter teneri non possunt; qui vero in libera civitate ita se instruunt, ut metuantur, iis [5] nihil potest esse dementius. Quamvis enim sint demersae leges alicuius opibus, quamvis timefacta libertas, emergunt tamen haec aliquando aut iudiciis tacitis aut occultis de honore suffragiis. Acriores autem morsus sunt inter-

[1] *promissisque* L c, Edd.; *promissionisque* B H a b; *promissionibusque* alii.

[2] *ac paret cum maxime mortuo* Halm, Müller, Heine; *paretque cum maxime mortuo* c¹, Bt.; *paretque, c. m. m.* L; *apparet, cuius maxime mortui* b; *apparet cuius maxime portui* B H a.

[3] *valeat* c; *valet* B H a b.

[4] *ut eris* Baiter; *ut eriis* B; *uteris* L; *utere hiis* H; *utere iis* b; *utere his* a; *utantur eis* c.

[5] *iis* Edd.; *his* B H L a; *hijs* c; *hiis* b.

(6) they may be bribed with money, as we have frequently seen in our own country.

23 VII. But, of all motives, none is better adapted to secure influence and hold it fast than love; nothing is more foreign to that end than fear. For Ennius says admirably: The motive of love *vs.* that of fear.

" Whom they fear they hate. And whom one hates, one hopes to see him dead."

And we recently discovered, if it was not known before, that no amount of power can withstand the hatred of the many. The death of this tyrant,[a] whose yoke the state endured under the constraint of armed force and whom it still obeys more humbly than ever, though he is dead, illustrates the deadly effects of popular hatred; and the same lesson is taught by the similar fate of all other despots, of whom practically no one has ever escaped such a death. For fear is but a poor safeguard of lasting power; while affection, on the other hand, may be trusted to keep it safe for ever. Hatred of tyranny.

24 But those who keep subjects in check by force would of course have to employ severity—masters, for example, toward their servants, when these cannot be held in control in any other way. But those who in a free state deliberately put themselves in a position to be feared are the maddest of the mad. For let the laws be never so much overborne by some one individual's power, let the spirit of freedom be never so intimidated, still sooner or later they assert themselves either through unvoiced public sentiment, or through secret ballots disposing of some high office of state. Freedom suppressed and again regained bites with keener fangs than freedom never

[a] Julius Caesar.

missae libertatis quam retentae. Quod igitur latissime patet neque ad incolumitatem solum, sed etiam ad opes et potentiam valet plurimum, id amplectamur, ut metus absit, caritas retineatur. Ita facillime, quae volemus, et privatis in rebus et in re publica consequemur.

Etenim qui se metui volent, a quibus metuentur,
25 eosdem metuant ipsi necesse est. Quid enim censemus superiorem illum Dionysium quo cruciatu timoris angi solitum, qui cultros metuens tonsorios candente carbone sibi adurebat capillum? quid Alexandrum Pheraeum quo animo vixisse arbitramur? qui, ut scriptum legimus, cum uxorem Theben admodum diligeret, tamen ad eam ex epulis in cubiculum veniens barbarum, et eum quidem, ut scriptum est, compunctum notis Thraeciis, destricto gladio iubebat anteire praemittebatque de stipatoribus suis, qui scrutarentur arculas muliebres et, ne quod in vestimentis telum occultaretur, exquirerent. O miserum, qui fideliorem et barbarum et stigmatiam putaret quam coniugem! Nec eum fefellit; ab ea est enim ipsa propter pelicatus suspicionem interfectus.

Nec vero ulla vis imperii tanta est, quae premente
26 metu possit esse diuturna. Testis est Phalaris, cuius est praeter ceteros nobilitata crudelitas, qui non ex insidiis interiit, ut is, quem modo dixi, Alexander, non a paucis, ut hic noster, sed in quem universa Agrigentinorum multitudo impetum fecit.

Quid? Macedones nonne Demetrium reliquerunt

endangered. Let us, then, embrace this policy, which appeals to every heart and is the strongest support not only of security but also of influence and power —namely, to banish fear and cleave to love. And thus we shall most easily secure success both in private and in public life.

Furthermore, those who wish to be feared must inevitably be afraid of those whom they intimidate.
25 What, for instance, shall we think of the elder Dionysius? With what tormenting fears he used to be racked! For through fear of the barber's razor he used to have his hair singed off with a glowing coal. In what state of mind do we fancy Alexander of Pherae lived? We read in history that he dearly loved his wife Thebe; and yet, whenever he went from the banquet-hall to her in her chamber, he used to order a barbarian—one, too, tattooed like a Thracian, as the records state—to go before him with a drawn sword; and he used to send ahead some of his bodyguard to pry into the lady's caskets and to search and see whether some weapon were not concealed in her wardrobe. Unhappy man! To think a barbarian, a branded slave, more faithful than his own wife! Nor was he mistaken. For he was murdered by her own hand, because she suspected him of infidelity.

**The wretchedness of fear.**

And indeed no power is strong enough to be last-
26 ing, if it labours under the weight of fear. Witness Phalaris, whose cruelty is notorious beyond that of all others. He was slain, not treacherously (like that Alexander whom I named but now), not by a few conspirators (like that tyrant of ours), but the whole population of Agrigentum rose against him with one accord.

Again, did not the Macedonians abandon Deme-

universique se ad Pyrrhum contulerunt? Quid? Lacedaemonios iniuste imperantes nonne repente omnes fere socii deseruerunt spectatoresque se otiosos praebuerunt Leuctricae calamitatis?

VIII. Externa libentius in tali re quam domestica recordor. Verum tamen, quam diu imperium populi Romani beneficiis tenebatur, non iniuriis, bella aut pro sociis aut de imperio gerebantur, exitus erant bellorum aut mites aut necessarii, regum, populorum, nationum portus erat et refugium senatus,
27 nostri autem magistratus imperatoresque ex hac una re maximam laudem capere studebant, si provincias,
(27) si socios aequitate et fide defendissent; itaque illud patrocinium orbis terrae verius quam imperium poterat nominari.

Sensim hanc consuetudinem et disciplinam iam antea minuebamus, post vero Sullae victoriam penitus amisimus; desitum est enim videri quicquam in socios iniquum, cum exstitisset in cives tanta crudelitas. Ergo in illo secuta est honestam causam non honesta victoria; est enim ausus dicere, hasta posita cum bona in foro venderet et bonorum virorum et locupletium et certe civium, "praedam se suam

trius and march over as one man to Pyrrhus? And again, when the Spartans exercised their supremacy tyrannically, did not practically all the allies desert them and view their disaster at Leuctra, as idle spectators?

The old Republic and the new despotism.

VIII. I prefer in this connection to draw my illustrations from foreign history rather than from our own. Let me add, however, that as long as the empire of the Roman People maintained itself by acts of service, not of oppression, wars were waged in the interest of our allies or to safeguard our supremacy; the end of our wars was marked by acts of clemency or by only a necessary degree of severity; the senate was a haven of refuge for kings, tribes,
27 and nations; and the highest ambition of our magistrates and generals was to defend our provinces and
(27) allies with justice and honour. And so our government could be called more accurately a protectorate of the world than a dominion.

This policy and practice we had begun gradually to modify even before Sulla's time; but since his victory we have departed from it altogether. For the time had gone by when any oppression of the allies could appear wrong, seeing that atrocities so outrageous were committed against Roman citizens. In Sulla's case, therefore, an unrighteous victory disgraced a righteous cause. For when he had planted his spear [a] and was selling under the hammer in the forum the property of men who were patriots and men of wealth and, at least, Roman citizens, he had the effrontery to announce that "he was selling

[a] The Romans were accustomed to set up a spear as a sign of an auction-sale—a symbol derived from the sale of booty taken in war.

vendere." Secutus est, qui in causa impia, victoria etiam foediore non singulorum civium bona publicaret, sed universas provincias regionesque uno calamitatis iure comprehenderet.

28 Itaque vexatis ac perditis exteris nationibus ad exemplum amissi imperii portari in triumpho Massiliam vidimus et ex ea urbe triumphari, sine qua numquam nostri imperatores ex Transalpinis bellis triumpharunt. Multa praeterea commemorarem nefaria in socios, si hoc uno quicquam sol vidisset indignius. Iure igitur plectimur. Nisi enim multorum impunita scelera tulissemus, numquam ad unum tanta pervenisset licentia; a quo quidem rei familiaris ad paucos, cupiditatum ad multos improbos
29 venit hereditas. Nec vero umquam bellorum civilium semen et causa deerit, dum homines perditi hastam illam cruentam et meminerint et sperabunt; quam P.[1] Sulla cum vibrasset dictatore propinquo suo, idem sexto tricesimo anno post a sceleratiore hasta non recessit; alter autem, qui in illa dictatura scriba fuerat, in hac fuit quaestor urbanus. Ex quo debet intellegi talibus praemiis propositis numquam defutura bella civilia.

Itaque parietes modo urbis stant et manent, iique ipsi iam extrema scelera metuentes, rem vero publicam penitus amisimus. Atque in has clades incidimus (redeundum est enim ad propositum), dum metui

[1] *P. c*, Edd.; *L.* B H a b.

his spoils." After him came one who, in an unholy cause, made an even more shameful use of victory; for he did not stop at confiscating the property of individual citizens, but actually embraced whole provinces and countries in one common ban of ruin.

28 And so, when foreign nations had been oppressed and ruined, we have seen a model of Marseilles carried in a triumphal procession, to serve as proof to the world that the supremacy of the people had been forfeited; and that triumph we saw celebrated over a city without whose help our generals have never gained a triumph for their wars beyond the Alps. I might mention many other outrages against our allies, if the sun had ever beheld anything more infamous than this particular one. Justly, therefore, are we being punished. For if we had not allowed the crimes of many to go unpunished, so great licence would never have centred in one individual. His estate descended by inheritance to but a few indi-

The wages of the sin of Rome.

29 viduals, his ambitions to many scoundrels. And never will the seed and occasion of civil war be wanting, so long as villains remember that blood-stained spear and hope to see another. As Publius Sulla wielded that spear, when his kinsman was dictator, so again thirty-six years later he did not shrink from a still more criminal spear. And still another Sulla, who was a mere clerk under the former dictatorship, was under the later one a city quaestor. From this, one would realize that, if such rewards are offered, civil wars will never cease to be.

And so in Rome only the walls of her houses remain standing—and even they wait now in fear of the most unspeakable crimes—but our republic we have lost for ever. But to return to my subject: it is

quam cari esse et diligi malumus. Quae si populo Romano iniuste imperanti accidere potuerunt, quid debent putare singuli? Quod cum perspicuum sit, benivolentiae vim esse magnam, metus imbecillam, sequitur, ut disseramus, quibus rebus facillime possimus eam, quam volumus, adipisci cum honore et fide caritatem.

30 Sed ea non pariter omnes egemus; nam ad cuiusque vitam institutam accommodandum est, a multisne opus sit an satis sit a paucis diligi. Certum igitur hoc sit, idque et primum et maxime necessarium, familiaritates habere fidas amantium nos amicorum et nostra mirantium; haec enim una [1] res prorsus, ut non multum differat inter summos et mediocris viros, aeque [2] utrisque est propemodum comparanda.

31 Honore et gloria et benivolentia civium fortasse non aeque omnes egent, sed tamen, si cui haec suppetunt, adiuvant aliquantum cum ad cetera, tum ad amicitias comparandas.

IX. Sed de amicitia alio libro dictum est, qui inscribitur Laelius; nunc dicamus de gloria, quamquam ea quoque de re duo sunt nostri libri, sed attingamus, quandoquidem ea in rebus maioribus administrandis adiuvat plurimum.

Summa igitur et perfecta gloria constat ex tribus

[1] *enim una* Baiter; *enim est una* MSS.
[2] *aeque* Lund; *eaque* MSS.

while we have preferred to be the object of fear rather than of love and affection, that all these misfortunes have fallen upon us. And if such retribution could overtake the Roman People for their injustice and tyranny, what ought private individuals to expect? And since it is manifest that the power of good-will is so great and that of fear is so weak, it remains for us to discuss by what means we can most readily win the affection, linked with honour and confidence, which we desire.

30 But we do not all feel this need to the same extent; for it must be determined in conformity with each individual's vocation in life whether it is essential for him to have the affection of many or whether the love of a few will suffice. Let this then be settled as the first and absolute essential—that we have the devotion of friends, affectionate and loving, who value our worth. For in just this one point there is but little difference between the greatest and the ordinary man; and friendship is to be cultivated almost equally by both. The acquisition of friends.

31 All men do not, perhaps, stand equally in need of political honour, fame, and the good-will of their fellow-citizens; nevertheless, if these honours come to a man, they help in many ways, and especially in the acquisition of friends.

IX. But friendship has been discussed in another book of mine, entitled "Laelius." Let us now take up the discussion of Glory, although I have published two books [a] on that subject also. Still, let us touch briefly on it here, since it is of very great help in the conduct of more important business. The attainment of glory.

The highest, truest glory depends upon the fol-

[a] Now lost, though they were still known to Petrarch.

his: si diligit multitudo, si fidem habet, si cum admiratione quadam honore dignos putat. Haec autem, si est simpliciter breviterque dicendum, quibus rebus pariuntur a singulis, eisdem fere a multitudine. Sed est alius quoque quidam aditus ad multitudinem, ut in universorum animos tamquam influere possimus.

32 Ac primum de illis tribus, quae ante dixi, benivolentiae praecepta videamus; quae quidem capitur beneficiis maxime, secundo autem loco voluntate benefica benivolentia movetur, etiamsi res forte non suppetit; vehementer autem amor multitudinis commovetur ipsa fama et opinione liberalitatis, beneficentiae, iustitiae, fidei omniumque earum virtutum, quae pertinent ad mansuetudinem morum ac facilitatem. Etenim illud ipsum, quod honestum decorumque dicimus, quia per se nobis placet animosque omnium natura et specie sua commovet maximeque quasi perlucet ex iis, quas commemoravi, virtutibus, idcirco illos, in quibus eas virtutes esse remur, a natura ipsa diligere cogimur. Atque hae quidem causae diligendi gravissimae; possunt enim praeterea non nullae esse leviores.

33 Fides autem ut habeatur, duabus rebus effici potest, si existimabimur adepti coniunctam cum iustitia prudentiam. Nam et iis fidem habemus,

lowing three things: the affection, the confidence, and the mingled admiration and esteem of the people. Such sentiments, if I may speak plainly and concisely, are awakened in the masses in the same way as in individuals. But there is also another avenue of approach to the masses, by which we can, as it were, steal into the hearts of all at once. How to gain popularity:

32 But of the three above-named requisites, let us look first at good-will and the rules for securing it. Good-will is won principally through kind services [a]; next to that, it is elicited by the will to do a kind service, even though nothing happen to come of it. Then, too, the love of people generally is powerfully attracted by a man's mere name and reputation for generosity, kindness, justice, honour, and all those virtues that belong to gentleness of character and affability of manner. And because that very quality which we term moral goodness and propriety is pleasing to us by and of itself and touches all our hearts both by its inward essence and its outward aspect and shines forth with most lustre through those virtues named above, we are, therefore, compelled by Nature herself to love those in whom we believe those virtues to reside. Now these are only the most powerful motives to love—not all of them; there may be some minor ones besides. (1) through good-will,

33 Secondly, the command of confidence can be secured on two conditions: (1) if people think us possessed of practical wisdom combined with a sense of justice. For we have confidence in those who we think have more understanding than ourselves, who, (2) through confidence.

[a] Cicero means by "kind services" the services of the lawyer; he was forbidden by law to accept a fee; his services, if he contributed them, were "acts of kindness."

quos plus intellegere quam nos arbitramur quosque et futura prospicere credimus et, cum res agatur in discrimenque ventum sit, expedire rem et consilium ex tempore capere posse; hanc enim utilem homines existimant veramque prudentiam. Iustis autem et fidis [1] hominibus, id est bonis viris, ita fides habetur, ut nulla sit in iis [2] fraudis iniuriaeque suspicio. Itaque his salutem nostram, his fortunas, his liberos rectissime committi arbitramur.

34 Harum igitur duarum ad fidem faciendam iustitia plus pollet, quippe cum ea sine prudentia satis habeat auctoritatis, prudentia sine iustitia nihil valet ad faciendam fidem. Quo enim quis versutior et callidior, hoc invisior et suspectior est detracta opinione probitatis. Quam ob rem intellegentiae iustitia coniuncta, quantum volet, habebit ad faciendam fidem virium; iustitia sine prudentia multum poterit, sine iustitia nihil valebit prudentia.

35 X. Sed ne quis sit admiratus, cur, cum inter omnes philosophos constet a meque ipso saepe disputatum sit, qui unam haberet, omnes habere virtutes, nunc ita seiungam, quasi possit quisquam, qui non idem prudens sit, iustus esse, alia est illa, cum veritas ipsa limatur in disputatione, subtilitas, alia, cum ad opinionem communem omnis accommodatur oratio. Quam ob rem, ut volgus, ita nos hoc loco

[1] *et fidis* MSS.; del. Facciolati, Pearce; [*et fidis*] Bt., Ed.
[2] *iis* B; *his* H a b; *hijs* c.

we believe, have better insight into the future, and who, when an emergency arises and a crisis comes, can clear away the difficulties and reach a safe decision according to the exigencies of the occasion; for that kind of wisdom the world accounts genuine and practical. But (2) confidence is reposed in men who are just and true—that is, good men—on the definite assumption that their characters admit of no suspicion of dishonesty or wrong-doing. And so we believe that it is perfectly safe to entrust our lives, our fortunes, and our children to their care.

34 Of these two qualities, then, justice has the greater power to inspire confidence; for even without the aid of wisdom, it has considerable weight; but wisdom without justice is of no avail to inspire confidence; for take from a man his reputation for probity, and the more shrewd and clever he is, the more hated and mistrusted he becomes. Therefore, justice combined with practical wisdom will command all the confidence we can desire; justice without wisdom will be able to do much; wisdom without justice will be of no avail at all. Justice *vs.* Wisdom;

35 X. But I am afraid someone may wonder why I am now separating the virtues—as if it were possible for anyone to be just who is not at the same time wise; for it is agreed upon among all philosophers, and I myself have often argued, that he who has one virtue has them all. The explanation of my apparent inconsistency is that the precision of speech we employ, when abstract truth is critically investigated in philosophic discussion, is one thing; and that employed, when we are adapting our language entirely to popular thinking, is another. And therefore I am speaking here in the popular sense, when

loquimur, ut alios fortes, alios viros bonos, alios prudentes esse dicamus; popularibus enim verbis est agendum et usitatis, cum loquimur[1] de opinione populari, idque eodem modo fecit Panaetius. Sed ad propositum revertamur.

36 Erat igitur ex iis[2] tribus, quae ad gloriam pertinerent, hoc tertium, ut cum admiratione hominum honore ab iis[3] digni iudicaremur. Admirantur igitur communiter illi quidem omnia, quae magna et praeter opinionem suam animadverterunt, separatim autem, in singulis si perspiciunt necopinata quaedam bona. Itaque eos viros suspiciunt maximisque efferunt laudibus, in quibus existimant se excellentes quasdam et singulares perspicere virtutes, despiciunt autem eos et contemnunt, in quibus nihil virtutis, nihil animi, nihil nervorum putant. Non enim omnes eos contemnunt, de quibus male existimant. Nam quos improbos, maledicos, fraudulentos putant et ad faciendam iniuriam instructos, eos haud contemnunt quidem,[4] sed de iis[5] male existimant. Quam ob rem, ut ante dixi, contemnuntur ii,[6] qui "nec sibi nec alteri," ut dicitur, in quibus nullus labor, nulla industria, nulla cura est.

37 Admiratione autem afficiuntur ii, qui anteire ceteris virtute putantur et cum omni carere dedecore, tum vero iis vitiis, quibus alii non facile possunt obsistere. Nam et voluptates, blandissimae dominae, maioris partis animos[7] a virtute detorquent et, dolorum cum admoventur faces, praeter modum plerique

[1] *loquimur* B; *loquamur* H a b; *loquemur* c.

[2] *iis* Bt.; *his* B H; *hijs* c; not in a b.

[3] *iis* Bt.; *his* B H a b; *hijs* c.

[4] *haud contemnunt quidem* b, Bt.[2]; *contemnunt quidem nautiquam* B H a p, Bt.[1], Heine; *contemnunt quidem nequaquam* c; *non contemnunt quidem* Madvig, Müller.

[5] *iis* B, Edd.; *his* H a b; *hijs* c.

I call some men brave, others good, and still others wise; for in dealing with popular conceptions we must employ familiar words in their common acceptation; and this was the practice of Panaetius likewise. But let us return to the subject.

36 The third, then, of the three conditions I named as essential to glory is that we be accounted worthy of the esteem and admiration of our fellow-men. While people admire in general everything that is great or better than they expect, they admire in particular the good qualities that they find unexpectedly in individuals. And so they reverence and extol with the highest praises those men in whom they see certain pre-eminent and extraordinary talents; and they look down with contempt upon those who they think have no ability, no spirit, no energy. For they do not despise all those of whom they think ill. For some men they consider unscrupulous, slanderous, fraudulent, and dangerous; they do not despise them, it may be; but they do think ill of them. And therefore, as I said before, those are despised who are "of no use to themselves or their neighbours," as the saying is, who are idle, lazy, and indifferent. (3) through esteem and admiration.

37 On the other hand, those are regarded with admiration who are thought to excel others in ability and to be free from all dishonour and also from those vices which others do not easily resist. For sensual pleasure, a most seductive mistress, turns the hearts of the greater part of humanity away from virtue; and when the fiery trial of affliction draws near, most people are terrified beyond measure.

[6] *ii* B b; *hii* H; *hi* a; *hij* c. So § 37.

[7] *maioris partis animos* c, Edd.; *maiores partis animi* B; *maiores partes animi* H a b.

exterrentur; vita mors, divitiae paupertas omnes homines vehementissime permovent. Quae qui in utramque partem excelso animo magnoque despiciunt, cumque aliqua iis ampla et honesta res obiecta est, totos ad se convertit et rapit, tum quis non admiretur splendorem pulchritudinemque virtutis?

38 XI. Ergo et haec animi despicientia admirabilitatem magnam facit et maxime iustitia, ex qua una virtute viri boni appellantur, mirifica quaedam multitudini videtur, nec iniuria; nemo enim iustus esse potest, qui mortem, qui dolorem, qui exsilium, qui egestatem timet, aut qui ea, quae sunt his contraria, aequitati anteponit. Maximeque admirantur eum, qui pecunia non movetur; quod in quo viro perspectum sit, hunc igni spectatum arbitrantur.

Itaque illa tria, quae proposita sunt ad gloriam, omnia iustitia conficit, et benivolentiam, quod prodesse vult plurimis, et ob eandem causam fidem et admirationem, quod eas res spernit et neglegit, ad quas plerique inflammati aviditate rapiuntur.

39 Ac mea quidem sententia omnis ratio atque institutio vitae adiumenta hominum desiderat, in primisque ut habeat, quibuscum possit familiares conferre sermones; quod est difficile, nisi speciem prae te boni viri feras. Ergo etiam solitario homini atque in agro vitam agenti opinio iustitiae necessaria est, eoque etiam magis, quod, eam si non habebunt, [iniusti habebuntur,][1] nullis praesidiis saepti multis

[1] *iniusti habebuntur* B H b; bracketed by Facciolati, Edd.

Life and death, wealth and want affect all men most powerfully. But when men, with a spirit great and exalted, can look down upon such outward circumstances, whether prosperous or adverse, and when some noble and virtuous purpose, presented to their minds, converts them wholly to itself and carries them away in its pursuit, who then could fail to admire in them the splendour and beauty of virtue?

38 XI. As, then, this superiority of mind to such externals inspires great admiration, so justice, above all, on the basis of which alone men are called "good men," seems to people generally a quite marvellous virtue—and not without good reason; for no one can be just who fears death or pain or exile or poverty, or who values their opposites above equity. And people admire especially the man who is uninfluenced by money; and if a man has proved himself in this direction, they think him tried as by fire.

**Justice is the best way to popularity.**

Those three requisites, therefore, which were presupposed as the means of obtaining glory, are all secured by justice: (1) good-will, for it seeks to be of help to the greatest number; (2) confidence, for the same reason; and (3) admiration, because it scorns and cares nothing for those things, with a consuming passion for which most people are carried away.

39 Now, in my opinion at least, every walk and vocation in life calls for human co-operation—first and above all, in order that one may have friends with whom to enjoy social intercourse. And this is not easy, unless one is looked upon as a good man. So, even to a man who shuns society and to one who spends his life in the country a reputation for justice is essential—even more so than to others; for they who do not have it [but are considered unjust] will

I, 96. 40 afficientur iniuriis. Atque iis[1] etiam, qui vendunt emunt, conducunt locant contrahendisque negotiis implicantur, iustitia ad rem gerendam necessaria est, cuius tanta vis est, ut ne illi quidem, qui maleficio et scelere pascuntur, possint sine ulla particula iustitiae vivere. Nam qui eorum cuipiam, qui una latrocinantur, furatur aliquid aut eripit, is sibi ne in latrocinio quidem relinquit locum, ille autem, qui archipirata dicitur, nisi aequabiliter praedam dispertiat, aut interficiatur a sociis aut relinquatur; quin etiam leges latronum esse dicuntur, quibus pareant, quas observent. Itaque propter aequabilem praedae partitionem et Bardulis Illyrius latro, de quo est apud Theopompum, magnas opes habuit et multo maiores Viriathus Lusitanus; cui quidem etiam exercitus nostri imperatoresque cesserunt; quem C. Laelius, is qui Sapiens usurpatur, praetor fregit et comminuit ferocitatemque eius ita repressit, ut facile bellum reliquis traderet.

Cum igitur tanta vis iustitiae sit, ut ea etiam latronum opes firmet atque augeat, quantam eius vim inter leges et iudicia et in constituta re publica fore putamus?

41 XII. Mihi quidem non apud Medos solum, ut ait Herodotus, sed etiam apud maiores nostros iustitiae fruendae causa videntur olim bene morati reges constituti. Nam cum premeretur inops[2] multitudo ab iis, qui maiores opes habebant, ad unum aliquem

[1] *iis* Edd.; *his* B H a b, not in c.

[2] *inops* inferior MSS., Edd.; *in otio* (i.e. "at will") B H a b p; *inicio* (= *initio*) c.

have no defence to protect them and so will be
40 the victims of many kinds of wrong. So also to buyers and sellers, to employers and employed, and to those who are engaged in commercial dealings generally, justice is indispensable for the conduct of business. Its importance is so great, that not even those who live by wickedness and crime can get on without some small element of justice. For if a robber takes anything by force or by fraud from another member of the gang, he loses his standing even in a band of robbers; and if the one called the "Pirate Captain" should not divide the plunder impartially, he would be either deserted or murdered by his comrades. Why, they say that robbers even have a code of laws to observe and obey. And so, because of his impartial division of booty, Bardulis, the Illyrian bandit, of whom we read in Theopompus, acquired great power, Viriathus, of Lusitania, much greater. He actually defied even our armies and generals. But Gaius Laelius—the one surnamed "the Wise"—in his praetorship crushed his power, reduced him to terms, and so checked his intrepid daring, that he left to his successors an easy conquest.

Honour among thieves.

Since, therefore, the efficacy of justice is so great that it strengthens and augments the power even of robbers, how great do we think its power will be in a constitutional government with its laws and courts?

Kings chosen for the sake of justice.

41 XII. Now it seems to me, at least, that not only among the Medes, as Herodotus tells us, but also among our own ancestors, men of high moral character were made kings in order that the people might enjoy justice. For, as the masses in their helplessness were oppressed by the strong, they appealed for protection to some one man who was

confugiebant virtute praestantem; qui cum prohiberet iniuria tenuiores, aequitate constituenda summos cum infimis[1] pari iure retinebat.[2] Eademque
42 constituendarum legum fuit causa, quae regum. Ius enim semper est quaesitum aequabile; neque enim aliter esset ius. Id si ab uno iusto et bono viro consequebantur, erant eo contenti; cum id minus contingeret, leges sunt inventae, quae cum omnibus semper una atque eadem voce loquerentur.

Ergo hoc quidem perspicuum est, eos ad imperandum deligi solitos, quorum de iustitia magna esset opinio multitudinis. Adiuncto vero, ut idem etiam prudentes haberentur, nihil erat, quod homines iis auctoribus non posse consequi se arbitrarentur. Omni igitur ratione colenda et retinenda iustitia est cum ipsa per sese (nam aliter iustitia non esset), tum propter amplificationem honoris et gloriae.

Sed ut pecuniae non quaerendae solum ratio est, verum etiam collocandae, quae perpetuos sumptus suppeditet, nec solum necessarios, sed etiam liberales, sic gloria et quaerenda et collocanda ratione est.
Xen. Mem. II, 6, 39. 43 Quamquam praeclare Socrates hanc viam ad gloriam proximam et quasi compendiariam dicebat esse, si quis id ageret, ut, qualis haberi vellet, talis esset. Quodsi qui simulatione et inani ostentatione et ficto non modo sermone, sed etiam voltu stabilem se gloriam consequi posse rentur, vehementer errant.

[1] *infimis* c, Edd.; *infirmis* B a b; *infirmos* H.
[2] *retinebat* c, Edd.; *pertinebat* B H a p; *pertinebant* b.

conspicuous for his virtue; and, as he shielded the weaker classes from wrong, he managed by establishing equitable conditions to hold the higher and the lower classes in an equality of right. The reason for making constitutional laws was the same as that for
42 making kings. For what people have always sought is equality of rights before the law. For rights that were not open to all alike would be no rights. If the people secured their end at the hands of one just and good man, they were satisfied with that; but when such was not their good fortune, laws were invented, to speak to all men at all times in one and the same voice.

This, then, is obvious: nations used to select for their rulers those men whose reputation for justice was high in the eyes of the people. If in addition they were also thought wise, there was nothing that men did not think they could secure under such leadership. Justice is, therefore, in every way to be cultivated and maintained, both for its own sake (for otherwise it would not be justice) and for the enhancement of personal honour and glory.

But as there is a method not only of acquiring money but also of investing it so as to yield an income to meet our continuously recurring expenses—both for the necessities and for the more refined comforts of life—so there must be a method of gaining glory and turning it to account. And yet, as
43 Socrates used to express it so admirably, "the nearest way to glory—a short cut, as it were—is to strive to be what you wish to be thought to be." For if anyone thinks that he can win lasting glory by pretence, by empty show, by hypocritical talk and looks, he is very much mistaken. True glory strikes

**The way to glory is Justice.**

Vera gloria radices agit atque etiam propagatur, ficta omnia celeriter tamquam flosculi decidunt, nec simulatum potest quicquam esse diuturnum. Testes sunt permulti in utramque partem, sed brevitatis causa familia contenti erimus una. Ti. enim Gracchus P. f. tam diu laudabitur, dum memoria rerum Romanarum manebit; at eius filii nec vivi probabantur bonis et mortui numerum optinent iure caesorum.

XIII. Qui igitur adipisci veram gloriam[1] volet, iustitiae fungatur officiis. Ea quae essent, dictum
I, 20-41. est in libro superiore.

44 (XIII.) Sed ut facillime, quales simus, tales esse videamur, etsi in eo ipso vis maxima est, ut simus ii, qui haberi velimus, tamen quaedam praecepta danda sunt. Nam si quis ab ineunte aetate habet causam celebritatis et nominis aut a patre acceptam, quod tibi, mi Cicero, arbitror contigisse, aut aliquo casu atque fortuna, in hunc oculi omnium coniciuntur atque in eum, quid agat, quem ad modum vivat, inquiritur et, tamquam in clarissima luce versetur, ita nullum obscurum potest nec dictum eius esse nec
45 factum. Quorum autem prima aetas propter humilitatem et obscuritatem in hominum ignoratione versatur, ii,[2] simul ac iuvenes esse coeperunt, magna spectare et ad ea rectis studiis debent contendere;

[1] *veram gloriam* Edd.; *veram iustitiae gloriam* MSS.
[2] *ii* B, Edd.; *hi* H; *iis* b; *hij* c; *his* a.

deep root and spreads its branches wide; but all pretences soon fall to the ground like fragile flowers, and nothing counterfeit can be lasting. There are very many witnesses to both facts; but, for brevity's sake, I shall confine myself to one family: Tiberius Gracchus, Publius's son, will be held in honour as long as the memory of Rome shall endure; but his sons were not approved by patriots while they lived, and since they are dead they are numbered among those whose murder was justifiable.

XIII. If, therefore, anyone wishes to win true glory, let him discharge the duties required by justice. And what they are has been set forth in the course of the preceding book. **Ways of winning a good name:**

44 (XIII.) But, although the very essence of the problem is that we actually be what we wish to be thought to be, still some rules may be laid down to enable us most easily to secure the reputation of being what we are. For, if anyone in his early youth has the responsibility of living up to a distinguished name acquired either by inheritance from his father (as, I think, my dear Cicero, is your good fortune) or by some chance or happy combination of circumstances, the eyes of the world are turned upon him; his life and character are scrutinized; and, as if he moved in a blaze of light, not a word and not a deed of his

45 can be kept a secret. Those, on the other hand, whose humble and obscure origin has kept them unknown to the world in their early years ought, as soon as they approach young manhood, to set a high ideal before their eyes and to strive with unswerving zeal towards its realization. This they will do with the better heart, because that time of life is

quod eo firmiore animo facient, quia non modo non invidetur illi aetati, verum etiam favetur.

Prima igitur est adulescenti commendatio ad gloriam, si qua ex bellicis rebus comparari potest, in qua multi apud maiores nostros exstiterunt; semper enim fere bella gerebantur. Tua autem aetas incidit in id bellum, cuius altera pars sceleris nimium habuit, altera felicitatis parum. Quo tamen in bello cum te Pompeius alae [alteri] [1] praefecisset, magnam laudem et a summo viro et ab exercitu consequebare equitando, iaculando, omni militari labore tolerando. Atque ea quidem tua laus pariter cum re publica cecidit.

Mihi autem haec oratio suscepta non de te est, sed de genere toto; quam ob rem pergamus ad ea, quae restant.

46 Ut igitur in reliquis rebus multo maiora opera sunt animi quam corporis, sic eae res, quas ingenio ac ratione persequimur, gratiores sunt quam illae, quas viribus. Prima igitur commendatio proficiscitur a modestia cum [2] pietate in parentes, in suos benivolentia. Facillime autem et in optimam partem cognoscuntur adulescentes, qui se ad claros et sapientes viros bene consulentes rei publicae contulerunt; quibuscum si frequentes sunt, opinionem afferunt populo eorum fore se similes, quos sibi ipsi

[1] *alteri* MSS.: om. Graevius, Edd.
[2] *cum* Victorius, Edd.; *tum* MSS.

accustomed to find favour rather than to meet with opposition.

Well, then, the first thing to recommend to a young man in his quest for glory is that he try to win it, if he can, in a military career. Among our forefathers many distinguished themselves as soldiers; for warfare was almost continuous then. The period of your own youth, however, has coincided with that war in which the one side was too prolific in crime, the other in failure. And yet, when Pompey placed you in command of a cavalry squadron in this war, you won the applause of that great man and of the army for your skill in riding and spear-throwing and for endurance of all the hardships of the soldier's life. But that credit accorded to you came to nothing along with the fall of the republic. (1) by a military career,

The subject of this discussion, however, is not your personal history, but the general theme. Let us, therefore, proceed to the sequel.

46 As, then, in everything else brain-work is far more important than mere hand-work, so those objects which we strive to attain through intellect and reason gain for us a higher degree of gratitude than those which we strive to gain by physical strength. The best recommendation, then, that a young man can have to popular esteem proceeds from self-restraint, filial affection, and devotion to kinsfolk. (2) by personal character,
Next to that, young men win recognition most easily and most favourably, if they attach themselves to men who are at once wise and renowned as well as patriotic counsellors in public affairs. And if they associate constantly with such men, they inspire in the public the expectation that they will be like them, seeing that they have themselves selected them (3) by association with the great,

47 delegerint ad imitandum. P. Rutili adulescentiam ad opinionem et innocentiae et iuris scientiae P. Muci commendavit domus. Nam L. quidem Crassus, cum esset admodum adulescens, non aliunde mutuatus est, sed sibi ipse peperit maximam laudem ex illa accusatione nobili et gloriosa, et, qua [1] aetate qui exercentur, laude affici solent, ut de Demosthene accepimus, ea aetate L. Crassus ostendit id se in foro optime iam facere, quod etiam tum poterat domi cum laude meditari.

48 XIV. Sed cum duplex ratio sit orationis, quarum in altera sermo sit, in altera contentio, non est id quidem dubium, quin contentio [orationis] [2] maiorem vim habeat ad gloriam (ea est enim, quam eloquentiam dicimus); sed tamen difficile dictu est, quantopere conciliet animos comitas affabilitasque sermonis. Exstant epistulae et Philippi ad Alexandrum et Antipatri ad Cassandrum et Antigoni ad Philippum filium, trium prudentissimorum (sic enim accepimus); quibus praecipiunt, ut oratione benigna multitudinis animos ad benivolentiam alliciant militesque blande appellando [sermone] [3] deliniant. Quae autem in multitudine cum contentione habetur oratio, ea saepe universam excitat [gloriam]; [4] magna est enim admiratio copiose sapienterque dicentis; quem qui audiunt, intellegere etiam et sapere plus quam cete-

[1] *et, qua* Manutius, Edd.; *ex qua* MSS.

[2] *orationis* MSS., Ed.; bracketed by Fleckeisen, Bt.², Müller, Heine.

[3] *blande appellando sermone* a c, Edd.; *blando appellando sermone* B H b; *blande appellando* Gulielmus (with three inferior MSS.), Bt., Heine; [*sermone*] Ed.

[4] *excitat gloriam* MSS.; *excitat* [*gloriam*] Ed.; *excitat* Lange.

[a] At the age of 21 Crassus conducted the case against Gaius Papirius Carbo, a former supporter of the Gracchi.

47 for imitation. His frequent visits to the home of Publius Mucius assisted young Publius Rutilius to gain a reputation for integrity of character and for ability as a jurisconsult. Not so, however, Lucius Crassus; for, though he was a mere boy, he looked to no one else for assistance, but by his own unaided ability he won for himself in that brilliant and famous prosecution[a] a splendid reputation as an orator. And at an age when young men are accustomed with their school exercises to win applause as students of oratory, this Roman Demosthenes, Lucius Crassus, was already proving himself in the law-courts a master of the art which he might even then have been studying at home with credit to himself.

48 XIV. But as the classification of discourse is a twofold one—conversation, on the one side; oratory, on the other—there can be no doubt that of the two this debating power (for that is what we mean by eloquence) counts for more toward the attainment of glory; and yet, it is not easy to say how far an affable and courteous manner in conversation may go toward winning the affections. We have, for instance, the letters of Philip to Alexander, of Antipater to Cassander, and of Antigonus to Philip the Younger. The authors of these letters were, as we are informed, three of the wisest men in history; and in them they instruct their sons to woo the hearts of the populace to affection by words of kindness and to keep their soldiers loyal by a winning address. But the speech that is delivered in a debate before an assembly often stirs the hearts of thousands at once; for the eloquent and judicious speaker is received with high admiration, and his hearers think

(4) by eloquence.

[a] The prosecution was so ably conducted that Carbo committed suicide to escape certain condemnation.

ros arbitrantur. Si vero inest in oratione mixta modestia gravitas, nihil admirabilius fieri potest, eoque magis, si ea sunt in adulescente.

49 Sed cum sint plura causarum genera, quae eloquentiam desiderent, multique in nostra re publica adulescentes et apud iudices et apud populum [1] et apud senatum dicendo laudem assecuti sint, maxima est admiratio in iudiciis.

Quorum ratio duplex est. Nam ex accusatione et ex defensione constat; quarum etsi laudabilior est defensio, tamen etiam accusatio probata persaepe est. Dixi paulo ante de Crasso; idem fecit adulescens M. Antonius. Etiam P. Sulpici eloquentiam accusatio illustravit, cum seditiosum et inutilem
50 civem, C. Norbanum, in iudicium vocavit. Sed hoc quidem non est saepe faciendum nec umquam nisi aut rei publicae causa, ut ii, quos ante dixi, aut ulciscendi, ut duo Luculli, aut patrocinii, ut nos pro Siculis, pro Sardis in Albucio Iulius. In accusando etiam M'. Aquilio L. Fufi cognita industria est. Semel igitur aut non saepe certe. Sin erit, cui faciendum sit saepius, rei publicae tribuat hoc muneris, cuius inimicos ulcisci saepius non est repre-

[1] *et apud populum* c, Edd.; not in B H a b.

him understanding and wise beyond all others. And, if his speech have also dignity combined with moderation, he will be admired beyond all measure, especially if these qualities are found in a young man.

49 But while there are occasions of many kinds that call for eloquence, and while many young men in our republic have obtained distinction by their speeches in the courts, in the popular assemblies, and in the senate, yet it is the speeches before our courts that excite the highest admiration.

Prosecution *vs.* defence.

The classification of forensic speeches also is a twofold one: they are divided into arguments for the prosecution and arguments for the defence. And while the side of the defence is more honourable, still that of the prosecution also has very often established a reputation. I spoke of Crassus a moment ago; Marcus Antonius, when a youth, had the same success. A prosecution brought the eloquence of Publius Sulpicius into favourable notice, when he brought an action against Gaius Norbanus, a sedi-
50 tious and dangerous citizen. But this should not be done often—never, in fact, except in the interest of the state (as in the cases of those above mentioned) or to avenge wrongs (as the two Luculli, for example, did) or for the protection of our provincials (as I did in the defence of the Sicilians, or Julius in the prosecution of Albucius in behalf of the Sardinians). The activity of Lucius Fufius in the impeachment of Manius Aquilius is likewise famous. This sort of work, then, may be done once in a lifetime, or at all events not often. But if it shall be required of anyone to conduct more frequent prosecutions, let him do it as a service to his country; for it is no disgrace to be often employed in the prosecution of her

hendendum; modus tamen adsit. Duri enim hominis vel potius vix hominis videtur periculum capitis inferre multis. Id cum periculosum ipsi est, tum etiam sordidum ad famam, committere, ut accusator nominere; quod contigit M. Bruto summo genere nato, illius filio, qui iuris civilis in primis peritus fuit.

51 Atque etiam hoc praeceptum officii diligenter tenendum est, ne quem umquam innocentem iudicio capitis arcessas; id enim sine scelere fieri nullo pacto potest. Nam quid est tam inhumanum quam eloquentiam a natura ad salutem hominum et ad conservationem datam ad bonorum pestem perniciemque convertere? Nec tamen, ut hoc fugiendum est, item est habendum religioni nocentem aliquando, modo ne nefarium [1] impiumque, defendere; vult hoc multitudo, patitur consuetudo, fert etiam humanitas. Iudicis est semper in causis verum sequi, patroni non numquam veri simile, etiamsi minus sit verum, defendere; quod scribere, praesertim cum de philosophia scriberem, non auderem, nisi idem placeret gravissimo Stoicorum, Panaetio. Maxime autem et gloria paritur et gratia defensionibus, eoque maior, si quando accidit, ut ei subveniatur, qui potentis alicuius opibus circumveniri urguerique videatur, ut nos et saepe alias et adulescentes contra L. Sullae

[1] *modo ne nefarium* L c, Edd.; *modo nefarium* Nonius; *et nefarium* B H a b.

---

[a] A "capital charge" meant to the Roman a charge endangering a person's *caput*, or civil status. A conviction on such a charge resulted in his civil degradation and the loss of his privileges as a Roman citizen.

enemies. And yet a limit should be set even to that. For it requires a heartless man, it seems, or rather one who is well-nigh inhuman, to be arraigning one person after another on capital charges.[a] It is not only fraught with danger to the prosecutor himself, but is damaging to his reputation, to allow himself to be called a prosecutor. Such was the effect of this epithet upon Marcus Brutus, the scion of a very noble family and the son of that Brutus who was an eminent authority in the civil law.

51 Again, the following rule of duty is to be carefully observed: never prefer a capital charge against any person who may be innocent. For that cannot possibly be done without making oneself a criminal. For what is so unnatural as to turn to the ruin and destruction of good men the eloquence bestowed by Nature for the safety and protection of our fellow-men? And yet, while we should never prosecute the innocent, we need not have scruples against undertaking on occasion the defence of a guilty person, provided he be not infamously depraved and wicked. For people expect it; custom sanctions it; humanity also accepts it. It is always the business of the judge in a trial to find out the truth; it is sometimes the business of the advocate to maintain what is plausible, even if it be not strictly true, though I should not venture to say this, especially in an ethical treatise, if it were not also the position of Panaetius, that strictest of Stoics. Then, too, briefs for the defence are most likely to bring glory and popularity to the pleader, and all the more so, if ever it falls to him to lend his aid to one who seems to be oppressed and persecuted by the influence of someone in power. This I have done on many other occasions; and once

**Spare the innocent; defend the guilty.**

dominantis opes pro Sex. Roscio Amerino fecimus, quae, ut scis, exstat oratio.

52 XV. Sed expositis adulescentium officiis, quae valeant ad gloriam adipiscendam, deinceps de beneficentia[1] ac de liberalitate dicendum est; cuius est ratio duplex; nam aut opera benigne fit indigentibus aut pecunia. Facilior est haec posterior, locupleti praesertim, sed illa lautior ac splendidior et viro forti claroque dignior. Quamquam enim in utroque inest gratificandi liberalis voluntas, tamen altera ex arca, altera ex virtute depromitur, largitioque, quae fit ex re familiari, fontem ipsum benignitatis exhaurit. Ita benignitate benignitas tollitur; qua quo in plures
53 usus sis, eo minus in multos uti possis. At qui opera, id est virtute et industria, benefici et liberales erunt, primum, quo pluribus profuerint, eo plures ad benigne faciendum adiutores habebunt, dein consuetudine beneficentiae paratiores erunt et tamquam exercitatiores ad bene de multis promerendum.

Praeclare in[2] epistula[3] quadam Alexandrum filium Philippus accusat, quod largitione benivolentiam Macedonum consectetur: "Quae te, malum!" inquit, "ratio in istam spem induxit, ut eos tibi fideles pu-

[1] *beneficentia* Edd.; *beneficientia* MSS. (ubique).
[2] *in* B H a b; not in L c p.
[3] *epistula* H, Heine; *epistola* B L a b c.

in particular, in my younger days, I defended Sextus Roscius of Ameria against the power of Lucius Sulla when he was acting the tyrant. The speech is published, as you know.

52 XV. Now that I have set forth the moral duties of a young man, in so far as they may be exerted for the attainment of glory, I must next in order discuss kindness and generosity. The manner of showing it is twofold: kindness is shown to the needy either by personal service, or by gifts of money. The latter way is the easier, especially for a rich man; but the former is nobler and more dignified and more becoming to a strong and eminent man. For, although both ways alike betray a generous wish to oblige, still in the one case the favour makes a draft upon one's bank account, in the other upon one's personal energy; and the bounty which is drawn from one's material substance tends to exhaust the very fountain of liberality. Liberality is thus forestalled by liberality: for the more people one has helped with
53 gifts of money, the fewer one can help. But if people are generous and kind in the way of personal service—that is, with their ability and personal effort—various advantages arise: first, the more people they assist, the more helpers they will have in works of kindness; and second, by acquiring the habit of kindness they are better prepared and in better training, as it were, for bestowing favours upon many.

Generosity of two kinds:

In one of his letters Philip takes his son Alexander sharply to task for trying by gifts of money to secure the good-will of the Macedonians: "What in the mischief induced you to entertain such a hope," he says, "as that those men would be loyal subjects to

tares fore, quos pecunia corrupisses? An tu id agis, ut Macedones non te regem suum, sed ministrum et praebitorem [1] sperent fore?"

Bene "ministrum et praebitorem," [2] quia sordidum regi, melius etiam, quod largitionem "corruptelam" dixit esse; fit enim deterior, qui accipit, atque ad idem semper exspectandum paratior.

54 Hoc ille filio, sed praeceptum putemus omnibus.

Quam ob rem id quidem non dubium est, quin illa benignitas, quae constet ex opera et industria, et honestior sit et latius pateat et possit prodesse pluribus; non numquam tamen est largiendum, nec hoc benignitatis genus omnino repudiandum est et saepe idoneis hominibus indigentibus de re familiari impertiendum, sed diligenter atque moderate; multi enim patrimonia effuderunt inconsulte largiendo. Quid autem est stultius quam, quod libenter facias, curare, ut id diutius facere non possis? Atque etiam sequuntur largitionem rapinae; cum enim dando egere coeperunt, alienis bonis manus afferre coguntur. Ita, cum benivolentiae comparandae causa benefici esse velint, non tanta studia assequuntur eorum, quibus dederunt, quanta odia eorum, quibus ademerunt.

55 Quam ob rem nec ita claudenda res est familiaris, ut eam benignitas aperire non possit, nec ita reseranda, ut pateat omnibus; modus adhibeatur, isque

[1] *praebitorem* B H L b c p; *praebitorem putant* a.
[2] *sperent . . . praebitorem* L c p, Edd.; not in B H a b.

---

[a] Julius Caesar was a striking example of this.
[b] Cicero evidently had in mind such instances as Sulla, Caesar, Antony, and Catiline—*alieni appetens, sui profusus* (Sall., Cat. V).

you whom you had corrupted with money? Or are you trying to do what you can to lead the Macedonians to expect that you will be not their king but their steward and purveyor?"

"Steward and purveyor" was well said, because it was degrading for a prince; better still, when he called the gift of money "corruption." For the recipient goes from bad to worse and is made all the more ready to be constantly looking for one bribe after another.

54 It was to his son that Philip gave this lesson; but let us all take it diligently to heart.

That liberality, therefore, which consists in personal service and effort is more honourable, has wider application, and can benefit more people. There can be no doubt about that. Nevertheless, we should sometimes make gifts of money; and this kind of liberality is not to be discouraged altogether. We must often distribute from our purse to the worthy poor, but we must do so with discretion and moderation. For many [a] have squandered their patrimony by indiscriminate giving. But what is worse folly than to do the thing you like in such a way that you can no longer do it at all? Then, too, lavish giving leads to robbery; [b] for when through over-giving men begin to be impoverished, they are constrained to lay their hands on the property of others. And so, when men aim to be kind for the sake of winning good-will, the affection they gain from the objects of their gifts is not so great as the hatred they incur from those whom they despoil.

(1) gifts of money,

55 One's purse, then, should not be closed so tightly that a generous impulse cannot open it, nor yet so loosely held as to be open to everybody. A limit

referatur ad facultates. Omnino meminisse debemus, id quod a nostris hominibus saepissime usurpatum iam in proverbii consuetudinem venit, " largitionem fundum non habere "; etenim quis potest modus esse, cum et idem, qui consuerunt, et idem illud alii desiderent?

XVI. Omnino duo sunt genera largorum, quorum alteri prodigi, alteri liberales: prodigi, qui epulis et viscerationibus et gladiatorum muneribus, ludorum venationumque apparatu pecunias profundunt in eas res, quarum memoriam aut brevem aut nullam
56 omnino sint relicturi, liberales autem, qui suis facultatibus aut captos a praedonibus redimunt aut aes alienum suscipiunt amicorum aut in filiarum collocatione adiuvant aut opitulantur in re vel quaerenda
(56) vel augenda. Itaque miror, quid in mentem venerit Theophrasto in eo libro, quem de divitiis scripsit; in quo multa praeclare, illud absurde: est enim multus in laudanda magnificentia et apparatione popularium munerum taliumque sumptuum facultatem fructum divitiarum putat. Mihi autem ille fructus liberalitatis, cuius pauca exempla posui, multo et maior videtur et certior.

Not found in our Aristotle.

Quanto Aristoteles gravius et verius nos reprehendit! qui has pecuniarum effusiones non admiremur, quae fiunt ad multitudinem deliniendam. *Ait*

should be observed and that limit should be determined by our means. We ought, in a word, to remember the phrase, which, through being repeated so very often by our countrymen, has come to be a common proverb: "Bounty has no bottom." For indeed what limit can there be, when those who have been accustomed to receive gifts claim what they have been in the habit of getting, and those who have not wish for the same bounty?

**Extravagant waste of the public games**

XVI. There are, in general, two classes of those who give largely: the one class is the lavish, the other the generous. The lavish are those who squander their money on public banquets, doles of meat among the people, gladiatorial shows, magnificent games, and wild-beast fights—vanities of which but a brief recollection will remain, or none at all.
56 The generous, on the other hand, are those who employ their own means to ransom captives from brigands, or who assume their friends' debts or help in providing dowries for their daughters, or assist them in acquiring property or increasing what they
(56) have. And so I wonder what Theophrastus could have been thinking about when he wrote his book on "Wealth." It contains much that is fine; but his position is absurd, when he praises at great length the magnificent appointments of the popular games, and it is in the means for indulging in such expenditures that he finds the highest privilege of wealth. But to me the privilege it gives for the exercise of generosity, of which I have given a few illustrations, seems far higher and far more certain.

How much more true and pertinent are Aristotle's words, as he rebukes us for not being amazed at this extravagant waste of money, all to win the favour of

*enim*,[1] "qui ab hoste obsidentur, si emere aquae sextarium cogerentur[2] mina, hoc primo incredibile nobis videri, omnesque mirari, sed cum attenderint, veniam necessitati dare, in his immanibus iacturis infinitisque sumptibus nihil nos magnopere mirari, cum praesertim neque necessitati subveniatur nec dignitas augeatur ipsaque illa delectatio multitudinis ad breve exiguumque tempus *capiatur*,[3] eaque a levissimo quoque, in quo tamen ipso una cum satietate memoria
57 quoque moriatur voluptatis." Bene etiam colligit, "haec pueris et mulierculis et servis et servorum simillimis liberis esse grata, gravi vero homini et ea, quae fiunt, iudicio certo ponderanti probari posse nullo modo."

Quamquam intellego in nostra civitate inveterasse iam bonis temporibus, ut splendor aedilitatum ab optimis viris postuletur.[4] Itaque et P. Crassus cum cognomine dives, tum copiis functus est aedilicio maximo munere, et paulo post L. Crassus cum omnium hominum moderatissimo Q. Mucio magnificentissima aedilitate functus est, deinde C. Claudius App. f., multi post, Luculli, Hortensius, Silanus; omnes autem P. Lentulus me consule vicit superiores; hunc est Scaurus imitatus; magnificentissima

[1] *Ait enim* Ed.; *at hi* a; *at hii* H; *at ii* B b; *at hij* c.
[2] *cogerentur* B H a b; *cogantur* L c p.
[3] *capiatur* Beier; not in MSS.
[4] *postuletur* B H a b, Heine; *postularetur* L c p, Bt.

the populace. "If people in time of siege," he says, "are required to pay a mina for a pint of water, this seems to us at first beyond belief, and all are amazed; but, when they think about it, they make allowances for it on the plea of necessity. But in the matter of this enormous waste and unlimited expenditure we are not very greatly astonished, and that, too, though by it no extreme need is relieved, no dignity is enhanced, and the very gratification of the populace is but for a brief, passing moment; such pleasure as it is, too, is confined to the most frivolous, and even in these the very memory of their enjoyment dies as
57 soon as the moment of gratification is past." His conclusion, too, is excellent: "This sort of amusement pleases children, silly women, slaves, and the servile free; but a serious-minded man who weighs such matters with sound judgment cannot possibly approve of them."

**Magnificent entertainments expected of an aedile.**

And yet I realize that in our country, even in the good old times, it had become a settled custom to expect magnificent entertainments from the very best men in their year of aedileship. So both Publius Crassus, who was not merely surnamed "The Rich" but was rich in fact, gave splendid games in his aedileship; and a little later Lucius Crassus (with Quintus Mucius, the most unpretentious man in the world, as his colleague) gave most magnificent entertainments in his aedileship. Then came Gaius Claudius, the son of Appius, and, after him, many others—the Luculli, Hortensius, and Silanus. Publius Lentulus, however, in the year of my consulship, eclipsed all that had gone before him, and Scaurus emulated him. And my friend Pompey's exhibitions in his second consulship were the most magnificent

vero nostri Pompei munera secundo consulatu; in quibus omnibus quid mihi placeat, vides.

58 XVII. Vitanda tamen suspicio est avaritiae. Mamerco, homini divitissimo, praetermissio aedilitatis consulatus repulsam attulit. Quare et, si postulatur a populo, bonis viris si non desiderantibus, at tamen approbantibus faciundum est, modo pro facultatibus, nos ipsi ut fecimus, et, si quando aliqua res maior atque utilior populari largitione acquiritur, ut Oresti nuper prandia in semitis decumae nomine magno honori fuerunt. Ne M.[1] quidem Seio vitio datum est, quod in caritate asse modium populo dedit; magna enim se et inveterata invidia nec turpi iactura, quando erat aedilis, nec maxima liberavit. Sed honori summo nuper nostro Miloni fuit, qui gladiatoribus emptis rei publicae causa, quae salute nostra continebatur, omnes P. Clodi conatus furoresque compressit.

Causa igitur largitionis est, si aut necesse est aut
59 utile. In his[2] autem ipsis mediocritatis regula optima est. L. quidem Philippus Q. f., magno vir ingenio in primisque clarus, gloriari solebat se sine

[1] *M.* Orelli, Ed.; *Marco* MSS.
[2] *his* H, Edd.; *hijs* c; *iis* B b; *is* L.

[a] The *as* was a copper coin worth somewhat less than a penny. Selling grain to the people at such a price was practically giving it away to purchase their good-will.

of all. And so you see what I think about all this sort of thing.

58 XVII. Still we should avoid any suspicion of penuriousness. Mamercus was a very wealthy man, and his refusal of the aedileship was the cause of his defeat for the consulship. If, therefore, such entertainment is demanded by the people, men of right judgment must at least consent to furnish it, even if they do not like the idea. But in so doing they should keep within their means, as I myself did. They should likewise afford such entertainment, if gifts of money to the people are to be the means of securing on some occasion some more important or more useful object. Thus Orestes recently won great honour by his public dinners given in the streets, on the pretext of their being a tithe-offering. Neither did anybody find fault with Marcus Seius for supplying grain to the people at an *as* [a] the peck at a time when the market-price was prohibitive; for he thus succeeded in disarming the bitter and deep-seated prejudice of the people against him at an outlay neither very great nor discreditable to him in view of the fact that he was aedile at the time. But the highest honour recently fell to my friend Milo, who bought a band of gladiators for the sake of the country, whose preservation then depended upon my recall from exile, and with them put down the desperate schemes, the reign of terror, of Publius Clodius.

**Justification of such extravagance.**

The justification for gifts of money, therefore, is
59 either necessity or expediency. And, in making them even in such cases, the rule of the golden mean is best. To be sure, Lucius Philippus, the son of Quintus, a man of great ability and unusual renown, used to

**The golden mean is best.**

ullo munere adeptum esse omnia, quae haberentur amplissima. Dicebat idem Cotta, Curio. Nobis quoque licet in hoc quodam modo gloriari; nam pro amplitudine honorum, quos cunctis suffragiis adepti sumus nostro quidem anno, quod contigit eorum nemini, quos modo nominavi, sane exiguus sumptus aedilitatis fuit.

60 Atque etiam illae impensae meliores, muri, navalia, portus, aquarum ductus omniaque, quae ad usum rei publicae pertinent. Quamquam, quod praesens tamquam in manum datur, iucundius est; tamen haec in posterum gratiora. Theatra, porticus, nova templa verecundius reprehendo propter Pompeium, sed doctissimi non probant, ut et hic ipse Panaetius, quem multum in his libris secutus sum, non interpretatus, et Phalereus Demetrius, qui Periclem, principem Graeciae, vituperat, quod tantam pecuniam in praeclara illa propylaea coniecerit. Sed de hoc genere toto in iis libris, quos de re publica scripsi, diligenter est disputatum.

The portion here referred to is lost.

Tota igitur ratio talium largitionum genere vitiosa est, temporibus necessaria, et tum ipsum et ad facultates accommodanda et mediocritate moderanda est.

61 XVIII. In illo autem altero genere largiendi, quod

[a] The saving clause is added, because Cicero never filled the office of Censor.

make it his boast that without giving any entertainments he had risen to all the positions looked upon as the highest within the gift of the state. Cotta could say the same, and Curio. I, too, may make this boast my own—to a certain extent;[a] for in comparison with the eminence of the offices to which I was unanimously elected at the earliest legal age—and this was not the good fortune of any one of those just mentioned—the outlay in my aedileship was very inconsiderable.

**Lavish expenditure on public works.**

60 Again, the expenditure of money is better justified when it is made for walls, docks, harbours, aqueducts, and all those works which are of service to the community. There is, to be sure, more of present satisfaction in what is handed out, like cash down; nevertheless public improvements win us greater gratitude with posterity. Out of respect for Pompey's memory I am rather diffident about expressing any criticism of theatres, colonnades, and new temples; and yet the greatest philosophers do not approve of them—our Panaetius himself, for example, whom I am following, not slavishly translating, in these books; so, too, Demetrius of Phalerum, who denounces Pericles, the foremost man of Greece, for throwing away so much money on the magnificent, far-famed Propylaea. But this whole theme is discussed at length in my books on "The Republic."

To conclude, the whole system of public bounties in such extravagant amount is intrinsically wrong; but it may under certain circumstances be necessary to make them; even then they must be proportioned to our ability and regulated by the golden mean.

**General rules of beneficence.**

61 XVIII. Now, as touching that second division of

a liberalitate proficiscitur, non uno modo in disparibus causis affecti esse debemus. Alia causa est eius, qui calamitate premitur, et eius, qui res me-
62 liores quaerit nullis suis rebus adversis. Propensior benignitas esse debebit in calamitosos, nisi forte erunt digni calamitate. In iis tamen, qui se adiuvari volent, non ne affligantur, sed ut altiorem gradum ascendant, restricti omnino esse nullo modo debemus, sed in deligendis idoneis iudicium et diligentiam adhibere. Nam praeclare Ennius:

Fab. inc. Vahlen², 409.

Bene fácta male locáta male facta árbitror.

63 Quod autem tributum est bono viro et grato, in eo cum ex ipso fructus est, tum etiam ex ceteris. Temeritate enim remota gratissima est liberalitas, eoque eam studiosius plerique laudant, quod summi cuiusque bonitas commune perfugium est omnium. Danda igitur opera est, ut iis beneficiis quam plurimos afficiamus, quorum memoria liberis posterisque prodatur, ut iis ingratis esse non liceat. Omnes enim immemorem beneficii oderunt eamque iniuriam in deterrenda liberalitate sibi etiam fieri eumque, qui faciat, communem hostem tenuiorum putant.

Atque haec benignitas etiam rei publicae est utilis, redimi e servitute captos, locupletari tenuiores; quod

gifts of money, those which are prompted by a spirit of generosity, we ought to look at different cases differently. The case of the man who is overwhelmed by misfortune is different from that of the one who is seeking to better his condition, though
62 he suffers from no actual distress. It will be the duty of charity to incline more to the unfortunate, unless, perchance, they deserve their misfortune. But of course we ought by no means to withhold our assistance altogether from those who wish for aid, not to save them from utter ruin but to enable them to reach a higher degree of fortune. But, in selecting worthy cases, we ought to use judgment and discretion. For, as Ennius says so admirably,

"Good deeds misplaced, methinks, are evil deeds."

63 Furthermore, the favour conferred upon a man who is good and grateful finds its reward, in such a case, not only in his own good-will but in that of others. For, when generosity is not indiscriminate giving, it wins most gratitude and people praise it with more enthusiasm, because goodness of heart in a man of high station becomes the common refuge of everybody. Pains must, therefore, be taken to benefit as many as possible with such kindnesses that the memory of them shall be handed down to children and to children's children, so that they too may not be ungrateful. For all men detest ingratitude and look upon the sin of it as a wrong committed against themselves also, because it discourages generosity; and they regard the ingrate as the common foe of all the poor.

Ransoming prisoners from servitude and relieving the poor is a form of charity that is a service to the

quidem volgo solitum fieri ab ordine nostro in oratione Crassi scriptum copiose videmus. Hanc ergo[1] consuetudinem benignitatis largitioni munerum longe[2] antepono; haec est gravium hominum atque magnorum, illa quasi assentatorum populi multitudinis levitatem voluptate quasi titillantium.

64 Conveniet autem cum in dando munificum esse, tum in exigendo non acerbum in omnique re contrahenda, vendundo emendo, conducendo locando, vicinitatibus et confiniis, aequum, facilem, multa multis de suo iure cedentem, a litibus vero, quantum liceat et nescio an paulo plus etiam, quam liceat, abhorrentem. Est enim non modo liberale paulum non numquam de suo iure decedere, sed interdum etiam fructuosum. Habenda autem ratio est rei familiaris, quam quidem dilabi[3] sinere flagitiosum est, sed ita, ut illiberalitatis avaritiaeque absit suspicio; posse enim liberalitate uti non spoliantem se patrimonio nimirum est pecuniae fructus maximus.

Recte etiam a Theophrasto est laudata hospitalitas; est enim, ut mihi quidem videtur, valde decorum patere domus hominum illustrium hospitibus illustribus, idque etiam rei publicae est ornamento, homines externos hoc liberalitatis genere in urbe nostra non egere. Est autem etiam vehementer

[1] *ergo* B H a b, Müller; *ego* L c p, Lactantius, Bt., Heine.
[2] *longe* L c p, Lactantius, Edd.; not in B H a b.
[3] *dilabi* L c, Ed., Heine; *delabi* B H a b, Bt.

state as well as to the individual. And we find in one of Crassus's orations the full proof given that such beneficence used to be the common practice of our order. This form of charity, then, I much prefer to the lavish expenditure of money for public exhibitions. The former is suited to men of worth and dignity, the latter to those shallow flatterers, if I may call them so, who tickle with idle pleasure, so to speak, the fickle fancy of the rabble.

64 It will, moreover, befit a gentleman to be at the same time liberal in giving and not inconsiderate in exacting his dues, but in every business relation—in buying or selling, in hiring or letting, in relations arising out of adjoining houses and lands—to be fair, reasonable, often freely yielding much of his own right, and keeping out of litigation as far as his interests will permit and perhaps even a little farther. For it is not only generous occasionally to abate a little of one's rightful claims, but it is sometimes even advantageous. We should, however, have a care for our personal property, for it is discreditable to let it run through our fingers; but we must guard it in such a way that there shall be no suspicion of meanness or avarice. For the greatest privilege of wealth is, beyond all peradventure, the opportunity it affords for doing good, without sacrificing one's fortune.

Another expression of beneficence is hospitality.

Hospitality also is a theme of Theophrastus's praise, and rightly so. For, as it seems to me at least, it is most proper that the homes of distinguished men should be open to distinguished guests. And it is to the credit of our country also that men from abroad do not fail to find hospitable entertainment of this kind in our city. It is, moreover, a very

utile iis, qui honeste posse multum volunt, per hospites apud externos populos valere opibus et gratia. Theophrastus quidem scribit Cimonem Athenis etiam in suos curiales Laciadas hospitalem fuisse; ita enim instituisse et vilicis imperavisse, ut omnia praeberentur, quicumque Laciades in villam suam devertisset.

65 XIX. Quae autem opera, non largitione beneficia dantur, haec tum in universam rem publicam, tum in singulos cives conferuntur. Nam in iure cavere [, consilio iuvare,] [1] atque hoc scientiae genere prodesse quam plurimis vehementer et ad opes augendas pertinet et ad gratiam.

Itaque cum multa praeclara maiorum, tum quod optime constituti iuris civilis summo semper in honore fuit cognitio atque interpretatio; quam quidem ante hanc confusionem temporum in possessione sua principes retinuerunt, nunc, ut honores, ut omnes dignitatis gradus, sic huius scientiae splendor deletus est, idque eo indignius, quod eo tempore hoc contigit, cum is esset, qui omnes superiores, quibus honore par esset, scientia facile vicisset. Haec igitur opera grata multis et ad beneficiis obstringendos homines accommodata.

[1] *consilio iuvare* MSS., Ed.; bracketed by Muther, Müller, Heine.

---

[a] Acts of kindness and personal service mean to Cicero throughout this discussion the services of the lawyer, which were voluntary and gratis.

[b] This eminent jurist was Servius Sulpicius Lemonia Rufus, a close friend of Cicero, author of the well-known letter of condolence to Cicero on the death of his daughter Tullia.

great advantage, too, for those who wish to obtain a powerful political influence by honourable means to be able through their social relations with their guests to enjoy popularity and to exert influence abroad. For an instance of extraordinary hospitality, Theophrastus writes that at Athens Cimon was hospitable even to the Laciads, the people of his own deme; for he instructed his bailiffs to that end and gave them orders that every attention should be shown to any Laciad who should ever call at his country home.

(2) personal service.

65 XIX. Again, the kindnesses shown not by gifts of money but by personal service [a] are bestowed sometimes upon the community at large, sometimes upon individual citizens. To protect a man in his legal rights [, to assist him with counsel,] and to serve as many as possible with that sort of knowledge tends greatly to increase one's influence and popularity.

The profession of the law.

Thus, among the many admirable ideas of our ancestors was the high respect they always accorded to the study and interpretation of the excellent body of our civil law. And down to the present unsettled times the foremost men of the state have kept this profession exclusively in their own hands; but now the prestige of legal learning has departed along with offices of honour and positions of dignity; and this is the more deplorable, because it has come to pass in the lifetime of a man [b] who in knowledge of the law would easily have surpassed all his predecessors, while in honour he is their peer. Service such as this, then, finds many to appreciate it and is calculated to bind people closely to us by our good services.

66 Atque huic arti finitima est dicendi [gravior] facultas [1] et gratior et ornatior. Quid enim eloquentia praestabilius vel admiratione audientium vel spe indigentium vel eorum, qui defensi sunt, gratia? Huic [quoque] ergo [2] a maioribus nostris est in toga dignitatis [3] principatus datus. Diserti igitur hominis et facile laborantis, quodque in patriis est moribus, multorum causas et non gravate et gratuito defendentis beneficia et patrocinia late patent.

67 Admonebat me res, ut hoc quoque loco intermissionem eloquentiae, ne dicam interitum, deplorarem, ni vererer, ne de me ipso aliquid viderer queri. Sed tamen videmus, quibus exstinctis oratoribus quam in paucis spes, quanto in paucioribus facultas, quam in multis sit audacia. Cum autem omnes non possint, ne multi quidem, aut iuris periti esse aut diserti, licet tamen opera prodesse multis beneficia petentem, commendantem iudicibus, magistratibus, vigilantem pro re alterius, eos ipsos, qui aut consuluntur aut defendunt, rogantem; quod qui faciunt, plurimum gratiae consequuntur, latissimeque eorum manat industria.

68 Iam illud non sunt admonendi (est enim in promptu), ut animadvertant, cum iuvare alios velint, ne quos offendant. Saepe enim aut eos laedunt,

[1] *dicendi gravior facultas* B H b; *gravior facultas* L c p; *dicendi [gravior] facultas* Ed.; *dicendi facultas* Lambinus.

[2] *huic quoque ergo* B H L b c, Bt.; *huic ergo* Facciolati; *huic [quoque] ergo* Ed.

[3] *in toga dignitatis* L c p, Edd.; *in tota dignitatis* B H b; *in tota dignitate* a.

66 Closely connected with this profession, furthermore, is the gift of eloquence; it is at once more popular and more distinguished. For what is better than eloquence to awaken the admiration of one's hearers or the hopes of the distressed or the gratitude of those whom it has protected? It was to eloquence, therefore, that our fathers assigned the foremost rank among the civil professions. The door of opportunity for generous patronage to others, then, is wide open to the orator whose heart is in his work and who follows the custom of our forefathers in undertaking the defence of many clients without reluctance and without compensation. **Eloquence at the bar.**

67 My subject suggests that at this point I express once more my regret at the decadence, not to say the utter extinction, of eloquence; and I should do so, did I not fear that people would think that I were complaining on my own account. We see, nevertheless, what orators have lost their lives and how few of any promise are left, how far fewer there are who have ability, and how many there are who have nothing but presumption. But though not all—no, not even many—can be learned in the law or eloquent as pleaders, still anybody may be of service to many by canvassing in their support for appointments, by witnessing to their character before juries and magistrates, by looking out for the interests of one and another, and by soliciting for them the aid of jurisconsults or of advocates. Those who perform such services win the most gratitude and find a most extensive sphere for their activities. **The decline of eloquence.**

68 Of course, those who pursue such a course do not need to be warned (for the point is self-evident) to be careful when they seek to oblige some, not to **A warning to eloquence.**

quos non debent, aut eos, quos non expedit; si imprudentes, neglegentiae est, si scientes, temeritatis. Utendum etiam est excusatione adversus eos, quos invitus offendas, quacumque possis, quare id, quod feceris, necesse fuerit nec aliter facere potueris, ceterisque operis et officiis erit id, quod violatum videbitur,[1] compensandum.

69 XX. Sed cum in hominibus iuvandis aut mores spectari aut fortuna soleat, dictu quidem est proclive, itaque volgo loquuntur, se in beneficiis collocandis mores hominum, non fortunam sequi. Honesta oratio est; sed quis est tandem, qui inopis et optimi viri causae non anteponat in opera danda gratiam fortunati et potentis? a quo enim expeditior et celerior remuneratio fore videtur, in eum fere est voluntas nostra propensior. Sed animadvertendum est diligentius, quae natura rerum sit. Nimirum enim inops ille, si bonus est vir, etiamsi referre gratiam non potest, habere certe potest. Commode autem, quicumque dixit, "pecuniam qui habeat, non reddidisse, qui reddiderit, non habere, gratiam autem et, qui rettulerit, habere [2] et, qui habeat, rettulisse."

At qui se locupletes, honoratos, beatos putant, ii ne obligari quidem beneficio volunt; quin etiam beneficium se dedisse arbitrantur, cum ipsi quamvis

[1] *videbitur* L c p, Edd.; not in B H b; *est*, a.
[2] *gratiam . . . habere* L c p, Edd.; not in B H a b.

offend others. For oftentimes they hurt those whom they ought not or those whom it is inexpedient to offend. If they do it inadvertently, it is carelessness; if designedly, inconsiderateness. A man must apologize also, to the best of his ability, if he has involuntarily hurt anyone's feelings, and explain why what he has done was unavoidable and why he could not have done otherwise; and he must by future services and kind offices atone for the apparent offence.

69 XX. Now in rendering helpful service to people, we usually consider either their character or their circumstances. And so it is an easy remark, and one commonly made, to say that in investing kindnesses we look not to people's outward circumstances, but to their character. The phrase is admirable! But who is there, pray, that does not in performing a service set the favour of a rich and influential man above the cause of a poor, though most worthy, person? For, as a rule, our will is more inclined to the one from whom we expect a prompter and speedier return. But we should observe more carefully how the matter really stands: the poor man of whom we spoke cannot return a favour in kind, of course, but if he is a good man he can do it at least in thankfulness of heart. As someone has happily said, "A man has not repaid money, if he still has it; if he has repaid it, he has ceased to have it. But a man still has the sense of favour, if he has returned the favour; and if he has the sense of the favour, he has repaid it."

The basis for personal service is character not fortune.

On the other hand, they who consider themselves wealthy, honoured, the favourites of fortune, do not wish even to be put under obligations by our kind services. Why, they actually think that they have

magnum aliquod acceperint, atque etiam a se aut postulari aut exspectari aliquid suspicantur, patrocinio vero se [1] usos aut clientes appellari mortis instar
70 putant. At vero ille tenuis, cum, quicquid factum sit, se spectatum, non fortunam putet,[2] non modo illi, qui est meritus, sed etiam illis, a quibus exspectat (eget enim multis), gratum se videri studet neque vero verbis auget suum munus, si quo forte fungitur, sed etiam extenuat. Videndumque illud est, quod, si opulentum fortunatumque defenderis, in uno illo aut, si [3] forte, in liberis eius manet gratia; sin autem inopem, probum tamen et modestum, omnes non improbi humiles, quae magna in populo multitudo
71 est, praesidium sibi paratum vident. Quam ob rem melius apud bonos quam apud fortunatos beneficium collocari puto.

Danda omnino opera est, ut omni generi satis facere possimus; sed si res in contentionem veniet, nimirum Themistocles est auctor adhibendus; qui cum consuleretur, utrum bono viro pauperi an minus probato diviti filiam collocaret: "Ego vero," inquit, "malo virum, qui pecunia egeat, quam pecuniam, quae viro." Sed corrupti mores depravatique sunt

[1] *vero se* B H a b; *vero tuo se* L c p.
[2] *putet* Ed.; *putat* MSS.
[3] *si* L c p, Edd.; not in B H a b.

conferred a favour by accepting one, however great; and they even suspect that a claim is thereby set up against them or that something is expected in return. Nay more, it is bitter as death to them to have
70 accepted a patron or to be called clients. Your man of slender means, on the other hand, feels that whatever is done for him is done out of regard for himself and not for his outward circumstances. Hence **The poor man's gratitude.**
he strives to show himself grateful not only to the one who has obliged him in the past but also to those from whom he expects similar favours in the future —and he needs the help of many; and his own service, if he happens to render any in return, he does not exaggerate, but he actually depreciates it. This fact, furthermore, should not be overlooked—that, if one defends a wealthy favourite of fortune, the favour does not extend further than to the man himself or, possibly, to his children. But, if one defends a man who is poor but honest and upright, all the lowly who are not dishonest—and there is a large proportion of that sort among the people—look upon such an advocate as a tower of defence raised up for
71 them. I think, therefore, that kindness to the good is a better investment than kindness to the favourites of fortune.

We must, of course, put forth every effort to oblige all sorts and conditions of men, if we can. But if it comes to a conflict of duty on this point, we must, I should say, follow the advice of Themistocles: when someone asked his advice whether he should give his daughter in marriage to a man who was poor but honest or to one who was rich but less esteemed, he said: "For my part, I prefer a man without money to money without a man." But the moral sense of **Wealth no inducement nor a bar to personal service.**

admiratione divitiarum; quarum magnitudo quid ad unum quemque nostrum pertinet? Illum fortasse adiuvat, qui habet. Ne id quidem semper; sed fac iuvare; utentior[1] sane sit, honestior vero quo modo? Quodsi etiam bonus erit vir, ne impediant divitiae, quo minus iuvetur, modo ne adiuvent, sitque omne iudicium, non quam locuples, sed qualis quisque sit!

Extremum autem praeceptum in beneficiis operaque danda, ne quid contra aequitatem contendas, ne quid pro iniuria; fundamentum enim est perpetuae commendationis et famae iustitia, sine qua nihil potest esse laudabile.

72 XXI. Sed, quoniam de eo genere beneficiorum dictum est, quae ad singulos spectant, deinceps de iis, quae ad universos quaeque ad rem publicam pertinent, disputandum est. Eorum autem ipsorum partim[2] eius modi sunt, ut ad universos cives pertineant, partim, singulos ut attingant; quae sunt etiam gratiora. Danda opera est omnino, si possit, utrisque, nec minus, ut etiam singulis consulatur, sed ita, ut ea res aut prosit aut certe ne obsit rei publicae. C. Gracchi frumentaria magna largitio; exhauriebat igitur aerarium; modica M. Octavi et rei publicae

[1] *utentior* MSS., Bt.[1], Heine; *potentior* later MSS.; *opulentior* one MS. (C. Lange), Lambinus, Bt.[2], Müller.

[2] *partim* L c p, Edd.; *quae* (*que* = *quae* H) *partim* B H a b.

to-day is demoralized and depraved by our worship of wealth. Of what concern to any one of us is the size of another man's fortune? It is, perhaps, an advantage to its possessor; but not always even that. But suppose it is; he may, to be sure, have more money to spend; but how is he any the better man for that? Still, if he is a good man, as well as a rich one, let not his riches be a hindrance to his being aided, if only they are not the motive to it; but in conferring favours our decision should depend entirely upon a man's character, not on his wealth.

The supreme rule, then, in the matter of kindnesses to be rendered by personal service is never to take up a case in opposition to the right nor in defence of the wrong. For the foundation of enduring reputation and fame is justice, and without justice there can be nothing worthy of praise.

**Service to the state through personal service to individuals.**

72 XXI. Now, since we have finished the discussion of that kind of helpful services which concern individuals, we must next take up those which touch the whole body politic and the state. Of these public services, some are of such a nature that they concern the whole body of citizens; others, that they affect individuals only. And these latter are the more productive of gratitude. If possible, we should by all means attend to both kinds of service; but we must take care in protecting the interests of individuals that what we do for them shall be beneficial, or at least not prejudicial, to the state. Gaius Gracchus inaugurated largesses of grain on an extensive scale; this had a tendency to exhaust the exchequer. Marcus Octavius inaugurated a moderate dole; this was both practicable for the state and necessary for

tolerabilis et plebi necessaria; ergo et civibus et rei publicae salutaris.

73 In primis autem videndum erit ei, qui rem publicam administrabit, ut suum quisque teneat neque de bonis privatorum publice deminutio fiat. Perniciose enim Philippus, in tribunatu cum legem agrariam ferret, quam tamen antiquari facile passus est et in eo vehementer se moderatum praebuit—sed cum in agendo multa populariter, tum illud male, " non esse in civitate duo milia hominum, qui rem haberent." Capitalis oratio est, ad aequationem bonorum pertinens; qua peste quae potest esse maior? Hanc enim ob causam maxime, ut sua tenerentur, res publicae civitatesque constitutae sunt. Nam, etsi duce natura congregabantur homines, tamen spe custodiae rerum suarum urbium praesidia quaerebant.

74 Danda etiam opera est, ne, quod apud maiores nostros saepe fiebat propter aerarii tenuitatem assiduitatemque bellorum, tributum sit conferendum, idque ne eveniat, multo ante erit providendum. Sin quae necessitas huius muneris alicui rei publicae obvenerit (malo enim [1] quam nostrae ominari; neque tamen de

[1] *malo enim* B H L b p; *malo enim alii* a; *malo enim aliene* (= *alienae*) c.

the commons; it was, therefore, a blessing both to the citizens and to the state.

73 The man in an administrative office, however, must make it his first care that everyone shall have what belongs to him and that private citizens suffer no invasion of their property rights by act of the state. It was a ruinous policy that Philippus proposed when in his tribuneship he introduced his agrarian bill. However, when his law was rejected, he took his defeat with good grace and displayed extraordinary moderation. But in his public speeches on the measure he often played the demagogue, and that time viciously, when he said that "there were not in the state two thousand people who owned any property." That speech deserves unqualified condemnation, for it favoured an equal distribution of property; and what more ruinous policy than that could be conceived? For the chief purpose in the establishment of constitutional state and municipal governments was that individual property rights might be secured. For, although it was by Nature's guidance that men were drawn together into communities, it was in the hope of safeguarding their possessions that they sought the protection of cities. **The statesman's duty toward (1) property rights,**

74 The administration should also put forth every effort to prevent the levying of a property tax, and to this end precautions should be taken long in advance. Such a tax was often levied in the times of our forefathers on account of the depleted state of their treasury and their incessant wars. But, if any state (I say "any," for I would rather speak in general terms than forebode evils to our own; however, I am not discussing our own state but states in general)—if any state ever has to face a crisis requiring the **(2) taxation,**

nostra, sed de omni re publica disputo), danda erit opera, ut omnes intellegant, si salvi esse velint, necessitati esse parendum. Atque etiam omnes, qui rem publicam gubernabunt, consulere debebunt, ut earum rerum copia sit, quae sunt[1] necessariae. Quarum qualis comparatio fieri soleat et debeat, non est necesse disputare; est enim in promptu; tantum locus attingendus fuit.

75 Caput autem est in omni procuratione negotii et muneris publici, ut avaritiae pellatur etiam minima suspicio. "Utinam," inquit C. Pontius Samnis, "ad illa tempora me fortuna reservavisset et tum essem natus, quando Romani dona accipere[2] coepissent! non essem passus diutius eos imperare." Ne illi multa saecula exspectanda fuerunt; modo enim hoc malum in hanc rem publicam invasit. Itaque facile patior tum potius Pontium fuisse, siquidem in illo tantum fuit roboris. Nondum centum et decem anni sunt, cum de pecuniis repetundis a L. Pisone lata lex est, nulla antea cum fuisset. At vero postea tot leges et proximae quaeque duriores, tot rei, tot damnati, tantum [Italicum][3] bellum propter iudiciorum metum excitatum, tanta sublatis legibus et iudiciis expilatio direptioque sociorum, ut imbecillitate aliorum, non nostra virtute valeamus.

76 XXII. Laudat Africanum Panaetius, quod fuerit abstinens. Quidni laudet? Sed in illo alia maiora;

[1] *sunt* B H b, Bt.[2]; *sunt ad victum* L c p, Bt.[1], Heine.
[2] *dona accipere* B H L a c p; *accipere dona* b, Ed.
[3] *tantum* [*Italicum*] Bake, Edd.; *tantum Italicum* L c p; *tantum Iliacum* B H; *tanti militari cum* b.

---

[a] The Italian or Social War, B.C. 100–88.
[b] During the dictatorships of Sulla and Caesar.

imposition of such a burden, every effort must be made to let all the people realize that they must bow to the inevitable, if they wish to be saved. And it will also be the duty of those who direct the affairs of the state to take measures that there shall be an abundance of the necessities of life. It is needless to discuss the ordinary ways and means; for the duty is self-evident; it is necessary only to mention the matter. (3) necessities of life,

75 But the chief thing in all public administration and public service is to avoid even the slightest suspicion of self-seeking. "I would," says Gaius Pontius, the Samnite, "that fortune had withheld my appearance until a time when the Romans began to accept bribes, and that I had been born in those days! I should then have suffered them to hold their supremacy no longer." Aye, but he would have had many generations to wait; for this plague has only recently infected our nation. And so I rejoice that Pontius lived then instead of now, seeing that he was so mighty a man! It is not yet a hundred and ten years since the enactment of Lucius Piso's bill to punish extortion; there had been no such law before. But afterward came so many laws, each more stringent than the other, so many men were accused and so many convicted, so horrible a war[a] was stirred up on account of the fear of what our courts would do to still others, so frightful was the pillaging and plundering of the allies when the laws and courts were suppressed,[b] that now we find ourselves strong not in our own strength but in the weakness of others. (4) official integrity.

76 XXII. Panaetius praises Africanus for his integrity in public life. Why should he not? But Africanus

laus abstinentiae [1] non hominis est solum, sed etiam temporum illorum. Omni Macedonum gaza, quae fuit maxima, potitus [est] [2] Paulus tantum in aerarium pecuniae invexit, ut unius imperatoris praeda finem attulerit tributorum. At hic nihil domum suam intulit [3] praeter memoriam nominis sempiternam. Imitatus patrem Africanus nihilo locupletior Carthagine eversa. Quid? qui eius collega fuit in censura, L. Mummius, numquid copiosior, cum copiosissimam urbem funditus sustulisset? Italiam ornare quam domum suam maluit; quamquam Italia ornata domus ipsa mihi videtur ornatior.

77 Nullum igitur vitium taetrius est, ut eo, unde egressa est, referat se oratio, quam avaritia, praesertim in principibus et rem publicam gubernantibus. Habere enim quaestui rem publicam non modo turpe est, sed sceleratum etiam et nefarium. Itaque, quod Apollo Pythius oraclum edidit, Spartam nulla re alia nisi avaritia esse perituram, id videtur non solum Lacedaemoniis, sed etiam omnibus opulentis populis praedixisse. Nulla autem re conciliare facilius benivolentiam multitudinis possunt ii, qui rei publicae praesunt, quam abstinentia et continentia.

Plut., Inst. Lacon. 239 F.

78 Qui vero se populares volunt ob eamque causam aut agrariam rem temptant, ut possessores pellantur suis sedibus, aut pecunias creditas debitoribus con-

[1] *abstinentiae* L c p, Edd.; *sapientiae* B H a b.
[2] *potitus* J. F. Heusinger; *potitus* [*est*] Edd.; *potitus est* MSS.
[3] *intulit* B H b, Edd.; *detulit* L c p.

[a] Nearly two million pounds sterling.

had other and greater virtues. The boast of official integrity belongs not to that man alone but also to his times. When Paulus got possession of all the wealth of Macedon—and it was enormous—he brought into our treasury so much money [a] that the spoils of a single general did away with the need for a tax on property in Rome for all time to come. But to his own house he brought nothing save the glory of an immortal name. Africanus emulated his father's example and was none the richer for his overthrow of Carthage. And what shall we say of Lucius Mummius, his colleague in the censorship? Was he one penny the richer when he had destroyed to its foundations the richest of cities? He preferred to adorn Italy rather than his own house. And yet by the adornment of Italy his own house was, as it seems to me, still more splendidly adorned.

77 There is, then, to bring the discussion back to the point from which it digressed, no vice more offensive than avarice, especially in men who stand foremost and hold the helm of state. For to exploit the state for selfish profit is not only immoral; it is criminal, infamous. And so the oracle, which the Pythian Apollo uttered, that "Sparta should not fall from any other cause than avarice," seems to be a prophecy not to the Lacedaemonians alone, but to all wealthy nations as well. They who direct the affairs of state, then, can win the good-will of the masses by no other means more easily than by self-restraint and self-denial. **Integrity *vs.* avarice.**

78 But they who pose as friends of the people, and who for that reason either attempt to have agrarian laws passed, in order that the occupants may be driven out of their homes, or propose that money **The menace of agrarian laws.**

donandas putant, labefactant fundamenta rei publicae, concordiam primum, quae esse non potest, cum aliis adimuntur, aliis condonantur pecuniae, deinde aequitatem, quae tollitur omnis, si habere suum cuique non licet. Id enim est proprium, ut supra
§73. dixi, civitatis atque urbis, ut sit libera et non solli-
79 cita suae rei cuiusque custodia. Atque in hac pernicie rei publicae ne illam quidem consequuntur, quam putant, gratiam; nam cui res erepta est, est inimicus, cui data est, etiam dissimulat se accipere voluisse et maxime in pecuniis creditis occultat suum gaudium, ne videatur non fuisse solvendo; at vero ille, qui accepit [1] iniuriam, et meminit et prae se fert dolorem suum, nec, si plures sunt ii, quibus inprobe datum est, quam illi, quibus iniuste ademptum est, idcirco plus etiam valent; non enim numero haec iudicantur, sed pondere. Quam autem habet aequitatem, ut agrum multis annis aut etiam saeculis ante possessum, qui nullum habuit, habeat, qui autem habuit, amittat?

80 XXIII. Ac [2] propter hoc iniuriae genus Lacedaemonii Lysandrum ephorum expulerunt, Agim regem, quod numquam antea apud eos acciderat, necaverunt, exque eo tempore tantae discordiae secutae sunt, ut

[1] *accepit* L c, Edd.; *accipit* B H a b p.
[2] *Ac* Edd.; *at* MSS.

loaned should be remitted to the borrowers, are undermining the foundations of the commonwealth: first of all, they are destroying harmony, which cannot exist when money is taken away from one party and bestowed upon another; and second, they do away with equity, which is utterly subverted, if the rights of property are not respected. For, as I said above, it is the peculiar function of the state and the city to guarantee to every man the free and undisturbed control of his own particular property.

79 And yet, when it comes to measures so ruinous to public welfare, they do not gain even that popularity which they anticipate. For he who has been robbed of his property is their enemy; he to whom it has been turned over actually pretends that he had no wish to take it; and most of all, when his debts are cancelled, the debtor conceals his joy, for fear that he may be thought to have been insolvent; whereas the victim of the wrong both remembers it and shows his resentment openly. Thus even though they to whom property has been wrongfully awarded be more in number than they from whom it has been unjustly taken, they do not for that reason have more influence; for in such matters influence is measured not by numbers but by weight. And how is it fair that a man who never had any property should take possession of lands that had been occupied for many years or even generations, and that he who had them before should lose possession of them?

80 XXIII. Now, it was on account of just this sort of wrong-doing that the Spartans banished their ephor Lysander, and put their king Agis to death—an act without precedent in the history of Sparta. From that time on—and for the same reason—dissensions

**Instances of agrarian legislation.**

et tyranni exsisterent et optimates exterminarentur et praeclarissime constituta res publica dilaberetur; nec vero solum ipsa cecidit, sed etiam reliquam Graeciam evertit contagionibus malorum,[1] quae a Lacedaemoniis profectae manarunt latius. Quid? nostros Gracchos, Ti. Gracchi summi viri filios, Africani nepotes, nonne agrariae contentiones perdiderunt?

81 At vero Aratus Sicyonius iure laudatur, qui, cum eius civitas quinquaginta annos a tyrannis teneretur, profectus Argis Sicyonem clandestino introitu urbe est potitus, cumque tyrannum Nicoclem improviso oppressisset,[2] sescentos exsules, qui locupletissimi fuerant eius civitatis, restituit remque publicam adventu suo liberavit. Sed cum magnam animadverteret in bonis et possessionibus difficultatem, quod et eos, quos ipse restituerat, quorum bona alii possederant, egere iniquissimum esse arbitrabatur et quinquaginta annorum possessiones moveri[3] non nimis aequum putabat, propterea quod tam longo spatio multa hereditatibus, multa emptionibus, multa dotibus tenebantur sine iniuria, iudicavit neque illis adimi nec iis non satis fieri, quorum illa
82 fuerant, oportere. Cum igitur statuisset opus esse ad eam rem constituendam pecunia, Alexandream se proficisci velle dixit remque integram ad

[1] *malorum* L c p, Edd.; *maiorum* B H a b.
[2] *oppressisset* L c p, Edd.; *pressisset* B H a b.
[3] *moveri* L c p, Edd.; *movere* B H a b.

so serious ensued that tyrants arose, the nobles were sent into exile, and the state, though most admirably constituted, crumbled to pieces. Nor did it fall alone, but by the contagion of the ills that, starting in Lacedaemon, spread widely and more widely, it dragged the rest of Greece down to ruin. What shall we say of our own Gracchi, the sons of that famous Tiberius Gracchus and grandsons of Africanus? Was it not strife over the agrarian issue that caused their downfall and death?

81 Aratus of Sicyon, on the other hand, is justly praised. When his city had been kept for fifty years in the power of its tyrants, he came over from Argos to Sicyon, secretly entered the city and took it by surprise; he fell suddenly upon the tyrant Nicocles, recalled from banishment six hundred exiles who had been the wealthiest men of the city, and by his coming made his country free. But he found great difficulty in the matter of property and its occupancy; for he considered it most unjust, on the one hand, that those men should be left in want whom he had restored and of whose property others had taken possession; and he thought it hardly fair, on the other hand, that tenure of fifty years' standing should be disturbed. For in the course of that long period many of those estates had passed into innocent hands by right of inheritance, many by purchase, many by dower. He therefore decided that it would be wrong either to take the property away from the present incumbents or to let them keep it
82 without compensation to its former possessors. So, when he had come to the conclusion that he must have money to meet the situation, he announced that he meant to make a trip to Alexandria and gave

Aratus of Sicyon.

reditum suum iussit esse, isque celeriter ad Ptolomaeum, suum hospitem, venit, qui tum regnabat alter post Alexandream conditam. Cui [1] cum exposuisset patriam se liberare velle causamque docuisset, a rege opulento vir summus facile impetravit, ut grandi pecunia adiuvaretur. Quam cum Sicyonem attulisset, adhibuit sibi in consilium quindecim principes, cum quibus causas cognovit et eorum, qui aliena tenebant, et eorum, qui sua amiserant, perfecitque aestimandis possessionibus, ut persuaderet aliis, ut pecuniam accipere mallent, possessionibus cederent, aliis, ut commodius putarent numerari sibi, quod tanti esset, quam suum recuperare. Ita perfectum est, ut omnes concordia constituta sine querella discederent.

83 O virum magnum dignumque, qui in re publica nostra natus esset! Sic par est agere cum civibus, non, ut bis iam vidimus, hastam in foro ponere et bona civium voci subicere [2] praeconis. At ille Graecus, id quod fuit sapientis et praestantis viri, omnibus consulendum putavit, eaque est summa ratio et sapientia boni civis, commoda civium non divellere atque omnis aequitate eadem continere. Habitent

[1] *Cui* Edd.; *qui* MSS.
[2] *subicere* L c p, Edd.; *subiacere* B H a b.

orders that matters should remain as they were until his return. And so he went in haste to his friend Ptolemy, then upon the throne, the second king after the founding of Alexandria. To him he explained that he wished to restore constitutional liberty to his country and presented his case to him. And, being a man of the highest standing, he easily secured from that wealthy king assistance in the form of a large sum of money. And, when he had returned with this to Sicyon, he called into counsel with him fifteen of the foremost men of the city. With them he investigated the cases both of those who were holding possession of other people's property and of those who had lost theirs. And he managed by a valuation of the properties to persuade some that it was more desirable to accept money and surrender their present holdings; others he convinced that it was more to their interest to take a fair price in cash for their lost estates than to try to recover possession of what had been their own. As a result, harmony was preserved, and all parties went their way without a word of complaint.

Justice the corner-stone of statecraft

83 A great statesman, and worthy to have been born in our commonwealth! That is the right way to deal with one's fellow-citizens, and not, as we have already witnessed on two occasions, to plant the spear in the forum and knock down the property of citizens under the auctioneer's hammer. But yon Greek, like a wise and excellent man, thought that he must look out for the welfare of all. And this is the highest statesmanship and the soundest wisdom on the part of a good citizen, not to divide the interests of the citizens but to unite all on the basis of impartial justice. "Let them live in their neighbour's

gratis in alieno. Quid ita? ut, cum ego emerim, aedificarim, tuear, impendam, tu me invito fruare meo? Quid est aliud aliis sua eripere, aliis dare
84 aliena? Tabulae vero novae quid habent argumenti, nisi ut emas mea pecunia fundum, eum tu habeas, ego non habeam pecuniam?

XXIV. Quam ob rem ne sit aes alienum, quod rei publicae noceat, providendum est, quod multis rationibus caveri potest, non, si fuerit, ut locupletes suum perdant, debitores lucrentur alienum; nec enim ulla res vehementius rem publicam continet quam fides, quae esse nulla potest, nisi erit necessaria solutio rerum creditarum. Numquam vehementius actum est quam me consule, ne solveretur; armis et castris temptata res est ab omni genere hominum et ordine; quibus ita restiti, ut hoc totum malum de re publica tolleretur. Numquam nec maius aes alienum fuit nec melius nec facilius dissolutum est; fraudandi enim spe sublata solvendi necessitas consecuta est. At vero hic nunc victor, tum quidem victus, quae cogitarat, ea [1] perfecit, cum eius iam nihil interesset. Tanta in eo peccandi libido fuit, ut hoc ipsum eum delectaret, peccare, etiamsi causa non esset.

[1] *cogitarat, ea* B H a b, Bt.[2], Müller; *cogitarat, cum ipsius intererat, tum ea* c p, Bt.[1], Heine.

---

[a] An assumed appeal to one of Caesar's edicts.

[b] Caesar, it seems, had had some part in the schemes of Catiline in B.C. 63 and possibly in the plot of B.C. 66–65. When his conquests in Gaul had freed him from his debts and made him rich, his party, with his consent, passed (B.C. 49) the obnoxious legislation here referred to—that all interest in arrears should be remitted, and that that which had been paid should be deducted from the principal.

house rent-free."[a] Why so? In order that, when I have bought, built, kept up, and spent my money upon a place, you may without my consent enjoy what belongs to me? What else is that but to rob one man of what belongs to him and to give to
84 another what does not belong to him? And what is the meaning of an abolition of debts, except that you buy a farm with my money; that you have the farm, and I have not my money?

Economics of debts.

XXIV. We must, therefore, take measures that there shall be no indebtedness of a nature to endanger the public safety. It is a menace that can be averted in many ways; but should a serious debt be incurred, we are not to allow the rich to lose their property, while the debtors profit by what is their neighbour's. For there is nothing that upholds a government more powerfully than its credit; and it can have no credit, unless the payment of debts is enforced by law. Never were measures for the repudiation of debts more strenuously agitated than in my consulship. Men of every sort and rank attempted with arms and armies to force the project through. But I opposed them with such energy that this plague was wholly eradicated from the body politic. Indebtedness was never greater; debts were never liquidated more easily or more fully; for the hope of defrauding the creditor was cut off and payment was enforced by law. But the present victor, though vanquished then, still carried out his old design, when it was no longer of any personal advantage to him.[b] So great was his passion for wrong-doing that the very doing of wrong was a joy to him for its own sake, even when there was no motive for it.

85 Ab hoc igitur genere largitionis, ut aliis detur, aliis auferatur, aberunt ii, qui rem publicam tuebuntur, in primisque operam dabunt, ut iuris et iudiciorum aequitate suum quisque teneat et neque tenuiores propter humilitatem circumveniantur neque locupletibus ad sua vel tenenda vel recuperanda obsit invidia, praeterea, quibuscumque rebus vel belli vel domi poterunt, rem publicam augeant imperio, agris, vectigalibus.

Haec magnorum hominum sunt, haec apud maiores nostros factitata, haec genera officiorum qui persequentur,[1] cum summa utilitate rei publicae magnam ipsi adipiscentur et gratiam et gloriam.

86 In his autem utilitatum praeceptis Antipater Tyrius Stoicus, qui Athenis nuper est mortuus, duo praeterita censet esse a Panaetio, valetudinis curationem et pecuniae; quas res a summo philosopho praeteritas arbitror, quod essent faciles; sunt certe utiles. Sed valetudo sustentatur notitia sui corporis et observatione, quae res aut prodesse soleant aut obesse, et continentia in victu omni atque cultu corporis tuendi causa [praetermittendis voluptatibus],[2] postremo arte eorum, quorum ad scientiam haec pertinent.

[1] *persequentur* c; *persequuntur* b, Bt.[2]; *persecuntur* B H p, Bt.[1], Heine.

[2] *praetermittendis voluptatibus* MSS.; del. Heine, Edd.

85 Those, then, whose office it is to look after the interests of the state will refrain from that form of liberality which robs one man to enrich another. Above all, they will use their best endeavours that everyone shall be protected in the possession of his own property by the fair administration of the law and the courts, that the poorer classes shall not be oppressed because of their helplessness, and that envy shall not stand in the way of the rich, to prevent them from keeping or recovering possession of what justly belongs to them; they must strive, too, by whatever means they can, in peace or in war, to advance the state in power, in territory, and in revenues.

**Administration of the courts in equity**

Such service calls for great men; it was commonly rendered in the days of our ancestors; if men will perform duties such as these, they will win popularity and glory for themselves and at the same time render eminent service to the state.

**Sanitation.**

86 Now, in this list of rules touching expediency, Antipater of Tyre, a Stoic philosopher who recently died at Athens, claims that two points were overlooked by Panaetius—the care of health and of property. I presume that the eminent philosopher overlooked these two items because they present no difficulty. At all events they are expedient. Although they are a matter of course, I will still say a few words on the subject. Individual health is preserved by studying one's own constitution, by observing what is good or bad for one, by constant self-control in supplying physical wants and comforts (but only to the extent necessary to self-preservation), by forgoing sensual pleasures, and finally, by the professional skill of those to whose science these matters belong.

87 Res autem familiaris quaeri debet iis rebus, a quibus abest turpitudo, conservari autem diligentia et parsimonia, eisdem etiam rebus augeri. Has res commodissime Xenophon Socraticus persecutus est in eo libro, qui Oeconomicus inscribitur, quem nos, ista fere aetate cum essemus, qua es tu nunc, e Graeco in Latinum convertimus. [1] Sed toto hoc de genere, de quaerenda, de collocanda pecunia (vellem [2] etiam de utenda), commodius a quibusdam optimis viris ad Ianum [3] medium sedentibus quam ab ullis philosophis ulla in schola disputatur. Sunt tamen ea cognoscenda; pertinent enim ad utilitatem, de qua hoc libro disputatum est.[1]

88 XXV. Sed utilitatum comparatio, quoniam hic locus erat quartus, a Panaetio praetermissus, saepe est necessaria. Nam et corporis commoda cum externis [et externa cum corporis] [4] et ipsa inter se corporis et externa cum externis comparari solent. Cum externis corporis hoc modo comparantur, valere ut malis quam dives esse, [cum corporis externa hoc modo, dives esse potius quam maximis corporis viribus,] [5] ipsa inter se corporis sic, ut bona valetudo voluptati anteponatur, vires celeritati, externorum autem, ut gloria divitiis, vectigalia urbana rusticis.
89 Ex quo genere comparationis illud est Catonis senis:

[1] *Sed . . . disputatum est* transposed from § 90 by Unger, Edd.
[2] *vellem* c p, Bt.[1], Ed.; not in B H a b, Bt.[2]
[3] *Ianum* c, Edd.; *ianuae* B H a b p.
[4] [*et . . . corporis*] bracketed by Unger, Edd.
[5] [*cum corporis . . . corporis viribus*] bracketed by Unger, Edd.

87 As for property, it is a duty to make money, but only by honourable means; it is a duty also to save it and increase it by care and thrift. These principles Xenophon, a pupil of Socrates, has set forth most happily in his book entitled "Oeconomicus." When I was about your present age, I translated it from the Greek into Latin. Finance.

But this whole subject of acquiring money, investing money (I wish I could include also spending money), is more profitably discussed by certain worthy gentlemen on "Change" than could be done by any philosophers of any school. For all that, we must take cognizance of them; for they come fitly under the head of expediency, and that is the subject of the present book.

88 XXV. But it is often necessary to weigh one expediency against another;—for this, as I stated, is a fourth point overlooked by Panaetius. For not only are physical advantages regularly compared with outward advantages [and outward, with physical], but physical advantages are compared with one another, and outward with outward. Physical advantages are compared with outward advantages in some such way as this: one may ask whether it is more desirable to have health than wealth; [external advantages with physical, thus: whether it is better to have wealth than extraordinary bodily strength;] while the physical advantages may be weighed against one another, so that good health is preferred to sensual pleasure, strength to agility. Outward advantages also may be weighed against one another: glory, for example, may be preferred to riches, an income derived from city property to one derived from the Comparison of expediencies.
89 farm. To this class of comparisons belongs that

a quo cum quaereretur, quid maxime in re familiari expediret, respondit: " Bene pascere "; quid secundum: " Satis bene pascere "; quid tertium: [1] " Male pascere "; quid quartum: " Arare "; et cum ille, qui quaesierat, dixisset: " Quid faenerari? ", tum Cato: " Quid hominem," inquit, " occidere? "

Ex quo et multis aliis intellegi debet utilitatum comparationes fieri solere, recteque hoc adiunctum esse quartum exquirendorum officiorum genus.[2]

Reliqua deinceps persequemur.

[1] *quid tertium :* " *Male pascere* " c p, Edd.; not in B H a b.
[2] *officiorum genus.* Here follows in MSS. *Sed toto . . . disputatum est* transposed to § 87.

famous saying of old Cato's: when he was asked what was the most profitable feature of an estate, he replied: "Raising cattle successfully." What next to that? "Raising cattle with fair success." And next? "Raising cattle with but slight success." And fourth? "Raising crops." And when his questioner said, "How about money-lending?" Cato replied: "How about murder?"

From this as well as from many other incidents we ought to realize that expediencies have often to be weighed against one another and that it is proper for us to add this fourth division in the discussion of moral duty.

Let us now pass on to the remaining problems.

# BOOK III

## THE CONFLICT BETWEEN THE RIGHT AND THE EXPEDIENT

# LIBER TERTIUS

1 I. P. Scipionem, M.[1] fili, eum, qui primus Africanus appellatus est, dicere solitum scripsit Cato, qui fuit eius fere aequalis, numquam se minus otiosum esse, quam cum otiosus, nec minus solum, quam cum solus esset. Magnifica vero vox et magno viro ac sapiente digna; quae declarat illum et in otio de negotiis cogitare et in solitudine secum loqui solitum, ut neque cessaret umquam et interdum colloquio alterius non egeret. Ita duae res, quae languorem afferunt ceteris, illum acuebant, otium et solitudo. Vellem nobis hoc idem vere dicere liceret; sed si minus imitatione tantam ingenii praestantiam consequi possumus, voluntate certe proxime accedimus; nam et a re publica forensibusque negotiis armis impiis vique prohibiti otium persequimur et ob eam causam urbe relicta rura peragrantes saepe soli sumus.

2 Sed nec hoc otium cum Africani otio nec haec solitudo cum illa comparanda est. Ille enim requiescens a rei publicae pulcherrimis muneribus otium sibi sumebat aliquando et e[2] coetu hominum frequentiaque interdum tamquam in portum se in soli-

[1] *M.* Nonius; *Marce* MSS.
[2] *e* c, Edd.; *a* a; not in B H b.

# BOOK III

1 I. Cato, who was of about the same years, Marcus, my son, as that Publius Scipio who first bore the surname of Africanus, has given us the statement that Scipio used to say that he was never less idle than when he had nothing to do and never less lonely than when he was alone. An admirable sentiment, in truth, and becoming to a great and wise man. It shows that even in his leisure hours his thoughts were occupied with public business and that he used to commune with himself when alone; and so not only was he never unoccupied, but he sometimes had no need for company. The two conditions, then, that prompt others to idleness—leisure and solitude—only spurred him on. I wish I could say the same of myself and say it truly. But if by imitation I cannot attain to such excellence of character, in aspiration, at all events, I approach it as nearly as I can; for as I am kept by force of armed treason away from practical politics and from my practice at the bar, I am now leading a life of leisure. For that reason I have left the city and, wandering in the country from place to place, I am often alone. Preface: Scipio and Cicero.

2 But I should not compare this leisure of mine with that of Africanus, nor this solitude with his. For he, to find leisure from his splendid services to his country, used to take a vacation now and then and to retreat from the assemblies and the throngs of men into solitude, as into a haven of rest. But

tudinem recipiebat, nostrum autem otium negotii inopia, non requiescendi studio constitutum est. Exstincto enim senatu deletisque iudiciis quid est quod dignum nobis aut in curia aut in foro agere
3 possimus? Ita, qui in maxima celebritate atque in oculis civium quondam vixerimus, nunc fugientes conspectum sceleratorum, quibus omnia redundant, abdimus nos, quantum licet, et saepe soli sumus. Sed quia sic ab hominibus doctis accepimus, non solum ex malis eligere minima oportere, sed etiam excerpere ex his ipsis,[1] si quid inesset boni, propterea et otio fruor, non illo quidem, quo debebat is,[2] qui quondam peperisset otium civitati, nec eam solitudinem languere patior, quam mihi affert necessitas, non voluntas.

4 Quamquam Africanus maiorem laudem meo iudicio assequebatur. Nulla enim eius ingenii monumenta mandata litteris, nullum opus otii, nullum solitudinis munus exstat; ex quo intellegi debet illum mentis agitatione investigationeque earum rerum, quas cogitando consequebatur, nec otiosum nec solum umquam fuisse; nos autem, qui non tantum roboris habemus, ut cogitatione tacita a[3] solitudine abstrahamur, ad hanc scribendi operam omne studium curamque convertimus. Itaque plura brevi tempore eversa quam multis annis stante re publica scripsimus.

[1] *ex his ipsis* c, Edd.; *ex his* a; *ex ipsis* B H b.
[2] *debebat is* c, Edd.; *debeat* B H b; *debeat is* corr. in *debeat* a.
[3] *a* c, Edd.; not in B H a b.

my leisure is forced upon me by want of public business, not prompted by any desire for repose. For now that the senate has been abolished and the courts have been closed, what is there, in keeping with my self-respect, that I can do either in the senate- The orator's retirement.
3 chamber or in the forum? So, although I once lived amid throngs of people and in the greatest publicity, I am now shunning the sight of the miscreants with whom the world abounds and withdrawing from the public eye as far as I may, and I am often alone. But I have learned from philosophers that among evils one ought not only to choose the least, but also to extract even from these any element of good that they may contain. For that reason, I am turning my leisure to account—though it is not such repose as the man should be entitled to who once brought the state repose from civil strife—and I am not letting this solitude, which necessity and not my will imposes on me, find me idle.

4 And yet, in my judgment, Africanus earned the higher praise. For no literary monuments of his genius have been published, we have no work produced in his leisure hours, no product of his solitude. From this fact we may safely infer that, because of the activity of his mind and the study of those problems to which he used to direct his thought, he was never unoccupied, never lonely. But I have not strength of mind enough by means of silent meditation to forget my solitude; and so I have turned all my attention and endeavour to this kind of literary work. I have, accordingly, written more in this short time since the downfall of the republic than I did in the course of many years, while the republic stood.

5 II. Sed cum tota philosophia, mi Cicero, frugifera et fructuosa nec ulla pars eius inculta ac deserta sit, tum nullus feracior in ea locus est nec uberior [1] quam de officiis, a quibus constanter honesteque vivendi praecepta ducuntur. Quare, quamquam a Cratippo nostro, principe huius memoriae philosophorum, haec te assidue audire atque accipere confido, tamen conducere arbitror talibus aures tuas vocibus undique circumsonare, nec eas, si fieri possit, quicquam aliud
6 audire. Quod cum omnibus est faciendum, qui vitam honestam ingredi cogitant, tum haud scio an nemini potius quam tibi; sustines enim non parvam exspectationem imitandae industriae nostrae, magnam honorum, non nullam fortasse nominis. Suscepisti onus praeterea grave et Athenarum et Cratippi; ad quos cum tamquam ad mercaturam bonarum artium sis profectus, inanem redire turpissimum est dedecorantem et urbis auctoritatem et magistri. Quare, quantum coniti animo potes, quantum labore contendere, si discendi labor est potius quam voluptas, tantum fac ut efficias neve committas, ut, cum [2] omnia suppeditata sint a nobis, tute tibi defuisse videare.

Sed haec hactenus; multa enim saepe ad te

[1] *uberior* c, Edd.; *uerior* B H a b.
[2] *ut, cum* c, Edd.; *ut ne, cum* B H a b.

5 II. But, my dear Cicero, while the whole field of philosophy is fertile and productive and no portion of it barren and waste, still no part is richer or more fruitful than that which deals with moral duties; for from these are derived the rules for leading a consistent and moral life. And therefore, although you are, as I trust, diligently studying and profiting by these precepts under the direction of our friend Cratippus, the foremost philosopher of the present age, I still think it well that your ears should be dinned with such precepts from every side and that, if it could be, they should hear nothing else.

**Young Cicero admonished to diligence in his studies.**

6 These precepts must be laid to heart by all who look forward to a career of honour, and I am inclined to think that no one needs them more than you. For you will have to fulfil the eager anticipation that you will imitate my industry, the confident expectation that you will emulate my course of political honours, and the hope that you will, perhaps, rival my name and fame. You have, besides, incurred a heavy responsibility on account of Athens and Cratippus: for, since you have gone to them for the purchase, as it were, of a store of liberal culture, it would be a great discredit to you to return empty-handed, thereby disgracing the high reputation of the city and of your master. Therefore, put forth the best mental effort of which you are capable; work as hard as you can (if learning is work rather than pleasure); do your very best to succeed; and do not, when I have put all the necessary means at your disposal, allow it to be said that you have failed to do your part.

But enough of this. For I have written again and again for your encouragement. Let us now

cohortandi gratia scripsimus; nunc ad reliquam partem propositae divisionis revertamur.

7 Panaetius igitur, qui sine controversia de officiis accuratissime disputavit, quemque nos correctione quadam adhibita potissimum secuti sumus, tribus generibus propositis, in quibus deliberare homines et consultare de officio solerent, uno, cum dubitarent, honestumne id esset, de quo ageretur, an turpe, altero, utilene esset an inutile, tertio, si id, quod speciem haberet honesti, pugnaret cum eo, quod utile videretur, quo modo ea discerni oporteret, de duobus generibus primis tribus libris explicavit, de tertio autem genere deinceps se scripsit dicturum nec
8 exsolvit id, quod promiserat. Quod eo magis miror, quia scriptum a discipulo eius Posidonio est triginta annis vixisse Panaetium, posteaquam illos libros edidisset. Quem locum miror a Posidonio breviter esse tactum in quibusdam commentariis, praesertim cum scribat nullum esse locum in tota philosophia tam necessarium.

9 Minime vero assentior iis, qui negant eum locum a Panaetio praetermissum, sed consulto relictum, nec omnino scribendum fuisse, quia numquam posset utilitas cum honestate pugnare. De quo alterum potest habere dubitationem, adhibendumne fuerit hoc genus, quod in divisione Panaeti tertium est, an plane omittendum, alterum dubitari non potest, quin

return to the remaining section of our subject as outlined.

7 Panaetius, then, has given us what is unquestionably the most thorough discussion of moral duties that we have, and I have followed him in the main—but with slight modifications. He classifies under three general heads the ethical problems which people are accustomed to consider and weigh: first, the question whether the matter in hand is morally right or morally wrong; second, whether it is expedient or inexpedient; third, how a decision ought to be reached, in case that which has the appearance of being morally right clashes with that which seems to be expedient. He has treated the first two heads at length in three books; but, while he has stated that he meant to discuss the third head in its proper

**Panaetius on Moral Duties.**

8 turn, he has never fulfilled his promise. And I wonder the more at this, because Posidonius, a pupil of his, records that Panaetius was still alive thirty years after he published those three books. And I am surprised that Posidonius has but briefly touched upon this subject in certain memoirs of his, and especially, as he states that there is no other topic in the whole range of philosophy so essentially important as this.

9 Now, I cannot possibly accept the view of those who say that that point was not overlooked but purposely omitted by Panaetius, and that it was not one that ever needed discussion, because there never can be such a thing as a conflict between expediency and moral rectitude. But with regard to this assertion, the one point may admit of doubt—whether that question which is third in Panaetius's classification ought to have been included or omitted altogether;

**Why Panaetius omitted the "Conflict" of the moral and the expedient.**

a Panaetio susceptum sit, sed relictum. Nam qui e divisione tripertita duas partes absolverit, huic necesse est restare tertiam; praeterea in extremo libro tertio de hac parte pollicetur se deinceps esse
10 dicturum. Accedit eodem testis locuples Posidonius, qui etiam scribit in quadam epistula P. Rutilium Rufum dicere solere, qui Panaetium audierat, ut nemo pictor esset inventus, qui in Coa Venere eam partem, quam Apelles inchoatam reliquisset, absolveret (oris enim pulchritudo reliqui corporis imitandi spem auferebat), sic ea, quae Panaetius praetermisisset [et non perfecisset] [1] propter eorum, quae perfecisset, praestantiam neminem persecutum.

11 III. Quam ob rem de iudicio Panaeti dubitari non potest; rectene autem hanc tertiam partem ad exquirendum officium adiunxerit an secus, de eo fortasse disputari potest. Nam, sive honestum solum bonum est, ut Stoicis placet, sive, quod honestum est, id ita summum bonum est, quem ad modum Peripateticis vestris videtur, ut omnia ex altera parte collocata vix minimi momenti instar habeant, dubitandum non est, quin numquam possit utilitas cum honestate contendere. Itaque accepimus Socratem exsecrari solitum eos, qui primum haec natura cohaerentia opinione distraxissent. Cui quidem ita sunt Stoici assensi, ut et, quicquid honestum esset, id

[1] *et non perfecisset* MSS.; del. Muretus; bracketed by Edd.

but the other point is not open to debate—that it was included in Panaetius's plan but left unwritten. For, if a writer has finished two divisions of a threefold subject, the third must necessarily remain for him to do. Besides, he promises at the close of the third book that he will discuss this division also in its
10 proper turn. We have also in Posidonius a competent witness to the fact. He writes in one of his letters that Publius Rutilius Rufus, who also was a pupil of Panaetius's, used to say that "as no painter had been found to complete that part of the Venus of Cos which Apelles had left unfinished (for the beauty of her face made hopeless any attempt adequately to represent the rest of the figure), so no one, because of the surpassing excellence of what Panaetius did complete, would venture to supply what he had left undone."

The conflict between Expediency and Moral Rectitude only apparent.

11 III. In regard to Panaetius's real intentions, therefore, no doubt can be entertained. But whether he was or was not justified in adding this third division to the inquiry about duty may, perhaps, be a matter for debate. For whether moral goodness is the only good, as the Stoics believe, or whether, as your Peripatetics think, moral goodness is in so far the highest good that everything else gathered together into the opposing scale would have scarcely the slightest weight, it is beyond question that expediency can never conflict with moral rectitude. And so, we have heard, Socrates used to pronounce a curse upon those who first drew a conceptual distinction between things naturally inseparable. With this doctrine the Stoics are in agreement in so far as they maintain that if anything is morally right, it is

utile esse censerent nec utile quicquam, quod non honestum.

12 Quodsi is esset Panaetius, qui virtutem propterea colendam diceret, quod ea efficiens utilitatis esset, ut ii, qui res expetendas vel voluptate vel indolentia metiuntur, liceret ei dicere utilitatem aliquando cum honestate pugnare; sed cum sit is, qui id solum bonum iudicet, quod honestum sit, quae autem huic repugnent specie quadam utilitatis, eorum neque accessione meliorem vitam fieri nec decessione peiorem, non videtur debuisse eius modi deliberationem introducere, in qua, quod utile videretur,
13 cum eo, quod honestum est, compararetur. Etenim quod summum bonum a Stoicis dicitur, convenienter naturae vivere, id habet hanc, ut opinor, sententiam: cum virtute congruere semper, cetera autem, quae secundum naturam essent, ita legere, si ea virtuti non repugnarent. Quod cum ita sit, putant quidam hanc comparationem non recte introductam, nec omnino de eo genere quicquam praecipiendum fuisse.

Atque[1] illud quidem honestum, quod proprie vereque dicitur, id in sapientibus est solis neque a virtute divelli umquam potest; in iis autem, in quibus sapientia perfecta non est, ipsum illud quidem perfectum honestum nullo modo, similitu-
14 dines honesti esse possunt. Haec enim officia, de quibus his libris disputamus, media Stoici appellant; ea communia sunt et late patent; quae et ingenii

[1] *Atque* MSS., Bt.[1], Müller, Heine; *atqui* Fleckeisen, Bt.[2], Ed.

---

[a] See Note on I, 8.

expedient, and if anything is not morally right, it is not expedient.

12 But if Panaetius were the sort of man to say that virtue is worth cultivating only because it is productive of advantage, as do certain philosophers who measure the desirableness of things by the standard of pleasure or of absence of pain, he might argue that expediency sometimes clashes with moral rectitude. But since he is a man who judges that the morally right is the only good, and that those things which come in conflict with it have only the appearance of expediency and cannot make life any better by their presence nor any worse by their absence, it follows that he ought not to have raised a question involving the weighing of what seems expedient against
13 what is morally right. Furthermore, when the Stoics speak of the supreme good as "living conformably to Nature," they mean, as I take it, something like this: that we are always to be in accord with virtue, and from all other things that may be in harmony with Nature to choose only such as are not incompatible with virtue. This being so, some people are of the opinion that it was not right to introduce this counterbalancing of right and expediency and that no practical instruction should have been given on this question at all.

And yet moral goodness, in the true and proper sense of the term, is the exclusive possession of the wise and can never be separated from virtue; but those who have not perfect wisdom cannot possibly have perfect moral goodness, but only a semblance
14 of it. And indeed these duties under discussion in these books the Stoics call "mean duties";[a] they are a common possession and have wide application; and

The "absolute" and the "mean."

bonitate multi assequuntur et progressione discendi. Illud autem officium, quod rectum idem appellant, perfectum atque absolutum est et, ut idem dicunt, omnes numeros habet nec praeter sapientem cadere
15 in quemquam potest. Cum autem aliquid actum est, in quo media officia compareant,[1] id cumulate videtur esse perfectum, propterea quod volgus quid absit a perfecto, non fere intellegit; quatenus autem intellegit, nihil putat praetermissum; quod idem [2] in poematis, in picturis usu venit in aliisque compluribus, ut delectentur imperiti laudentque ea, quae laudanda non sint, ob eam, credo, causam, quod insit in iis [3] aliquid probi, quod capiat ignaros, qui quidem,[4] quid in una quaque re vitii sit, nequeant iudicare; itaque, cum sunt docti a peritis, desistunt facile sententia.

IV. Haec igitur officia, de quibus his libris disserimus, quasi secunda quaedam honesta esse dicunt, non sapientium modo propria, sed cum omni homi-
16 num genere communia. Itaque iis omnes, in quibus est virtutis indoles, commoventur. Nec vero, cum duo Decii aut duo Scipiones fortes viri commemorantur, aut cum Fabricius [aut Aristides] [5] iustus nominatur, aut ab illis fortitudinis aut ab hoc [6] iustitiae tamquam a sapiente petitur exemplum; nemo enim

[1] *compareant* Anemoecius, Edd.; *comparant* B H a b; *appareant* c; *comparent* p.

[2] *idem* Nonius, Müller, Heine; *autem* B H a b; *item* c, Bt.

[3] *iis* Baiter, Müller, Heine; *his* B H a b; *hijs* c.

[4] *qui quidem* many MSS., Bt.[1], Müller; *qui idem* B H a b c; *qui* [*idem*] Bt.[2], Heine.

[5] *aut Aristides* (*Aristidesve* p) MSS., Lactantius; bracketed by J. M. Heusinger, Edd.

[6] *hoc* Lactantius; Edd.; *his* MSS.

[a] I.e., fills all the requirements of absolute perfection—an allusion to the Pythagorean doctrine that specific numbers stand for perfection of specific kinds; "absolute duty" combines them all.

many people attain to the knowledge of them through natural goodness of heart and through advancement in learning. But that duty which those same Stoics call "right" is perfect and absolute and "satisfies all the numbers,"[a] as that same school says, and is
15 attainable by none except the wise man. On the other hand, when some act is performed in which we see "mean" duties manifested, that is generally regarded as fully perfect, for the reason that the common crowd does not, as a rule, comprehend how far it falls short of real perfection; but, as far as their comprehension does go, they think there is no deficiency. This same thing ordinarily occurs in the estimation of poems, paintings, and a great many other works of art: ordinary people enjoy and praise things that do not deserve praise. The reason for this, I suppose, is that those productions have some point of excellence which catches the fancy of the uneducated, because these have not the ability to discover the points of weakness in any particular piece of work before them. And so, when they are instructed by experts, they readily abandon their former opinion.

**Absolute goodness and imperfect humanity,**

IV. The performance of the duties, then, which I am discussing in these books, is called by the Stoics a sort of second-grade moral goodness, not the peculiar property of their wise men, but shared by them with
16 all mankind. Accordingly, such duties appeal to all men who have a natural disposition to virtue. And when the two Decii or the two Scipios are mentioned as "brave men" or Fabricius [or Aristides] is called "the just," it is not at all that the former are quoted as perfect models of courage or the latter as a perfect model of justice, as if we had in one of them the ideal "wise man." For no one of them was wise in

horum sic sapiens, ut sapientem volumus intellegi, nec ii, qui sapientes habiti et nominati, M. Cato et C. Laelius, sapientes fuerunt, ne illi quidem septem, sed ex mediorum officiorum frequentia similitudinem quandam gerebant speciemque sapientium.

17 Quocirca nec id, quod vere honestum est, fas est cum utilitatis repugnantia comparari, nec id, quod communiter appellamus honestum, quod colitur ab iis, qui bonos se viros haberi volunt, cum emolumentis umquam est comparandum, tamque id honestum, quod in nostram intellegentiam cadit, tuendum conservandumque nobis est quam illud, quod proprie dicitur vereque est honestum, sapientibus; aliter enim teneri non potest, si qua ad virtutem est facta progressio.

Sed haec quidem de iis, qui conservatione officiorum existimantur boni.

18 Qui autem omnia metiuntur emolumentis et commodis neque ea volunt praeponderari honestate, ii solent in deliberando honestum cum eo, quod utile putant, comparare, boni viri non solent. Itaque existimo Panaetium, cum dixerit homines solere in hac comparatione dubitare, hoc ipsum sensisse, quod dixerit, "solere" modo, non etiam "oportere." Etenim non modo pluris putare, quod utile videatur,

the sense in which we wish to have "wise" understood; neither were Marcus Cato and Gaius Laelius wise, though they were so considered and were surnamed "the wise." Not even the famous Seven were "wise." But because of their constant observance of "mean" duties they bore a certain semblance and likeness to wise men.

17 For these reasons it is unlawful either to weigh true morality against conflicting expediency, or common morality, which is cultivated by those who wish to be considered good men, against what is profitable; but we every-day people must observe and live up to that moral right which comes within the range of our comprehension as jealously as the truly wise men have to observe and live up to that which is morally right in the technical and true sense of the word. For otherwise we cannot maintain such progress as we have made in the direction of virtue.

So much for those who have won a reputation for being good men by their careful observance of duty.

**Moral rectitude and apparent expediency.**

18 Those, on the other hand, who measure everything by a standard of profits and personal advantage and refuse to have these outweighed by considerations of moral rectitude are accustomed, in considering any question, to weigh the morally right against what they think the expedient; good men are not. And so I believe that when Panaetius stated that people were accustomed to hesitate to do such weighing, he meant precisely what he said—merely that "such was their custom," not that such was their duty. And he gave it no approval; for it is most immoral to think more highly of the apparently expedient than of the morally right, or even to set

quam quod honestum sit,[1] sed etiam haec inter se comparare et in his addubitare turpissimum est.

Quid ergo est, quod non numquam dubitationem afferre soleat considerandumque videatur? Credo, si quando dubitatio accidit, quale sit id, de quo con-
19 sideretur. Saepe enim tempore fit, ut, quod turpe plerumque haberi soleat, inveniatur non esse turpe; exempli causa ponatur aliquid, quod pateat latius: Quod potest maius esse[2] scelus quam non modo hominem, sed etiam familiarem hominem occidere? Num igitur se astrinxit scelere, si qui tyrannum occidit quamvis familiarem? Populo quidem Romano non videtur, qui ex omnibus praeclaris factis illud pulcherrimum existimat. Vicit ergo utilitas honestatem? Immo vero honestas utilitatem secuta est.[3]

Itaque, ut sine ullo errore diiudicare possimus, si quando cum illo, quod honestum intellegimus, pugnare id videbitur, quod appellamus utile, formula quaedam constituenda est; quam si sequemur in comparatione rerum, ab officio numquam recedemus.
20 Erit autem haec formula Stoicorum rationi disciplinaeque maxime consentanea; quam quidem his libris propterea sequimur, quod, quamquam et a veteribus Academicis et a Peripateticis vestris, qui quondam idem erant, qui Academici, quae honesta sunt, anteponuntur iis, quae videntur utilia, tamen splendidius

[1] *sit* c, Bt.[2], Müller; not in B H a b, Bt.[1]; *est* Heine.
[2] *esse* c, Edd.; not in B H a b.
[3] *utilitatem secuta est* MSS., Müller, Heine; *utilitatem; honestatem utilitas secuta est* Baiter, Ed.

these over against each other and to hesitate to choose between them.

Occasion for doubt.

What, then, is it that may sometimes give room for a doubt and seem to call for consideration? It is, I believe, when a question arises as to the char-
19 acter of an action under consideration. For it often happens, owing to exceptional circumstances, that what is accustomed under ordinary circumstances to be considered morally wrong is found not to be morally wrong. For the sake of illustration, let us assume some particular case that admits of wider application: what more atrocious crime can there be than to kill a fellow-man, and especially an intimate friend? But if anyone kills a tyrant—be he never so intimate a friend—he has not laden his soul with guilt, has he? The Roman People, at all events, are not of that opinion; for of all glorious deeds they hold such an one to be the most noble. Has expediency, then, prevailed over moral rectitude? Not at all; moral rectitude has gone hand in hand with expediency.

Need of a rule for guidance.

Some general rule, therefore, should be laid down to enable us to decide without error, whenever what we call the expedient seems to clash with what we feel to be morally right; and, if we follow that rule in comparing courses of conduct, we shall never
20 swerve from the path of duty. That rule, moreover, shall be in perfect harmony with the Stoics' system and doctrines. It is their teachings that I am following in these books, and for this reason: the older Academicians and your Peripatetics (who were once the same as the Academicians) give what is morally right the preference over what seems expedient; and yet the discussion of

haec ab eis disseruntur,[1] quibus, quicquid honestum est, idem utile videtur nec utile quicquam, quod non honestum, quam ab iis,[2] quibus et honestum aliquid non utile et utile[3] non honestum. Nobis autem nostra Academia magnam licentiam dat, ut, quodcumque maxime probabile occurrat, id nostro iure liceat defendere. Sed redeo ad formulam.

21 V. Detrahere igitur alteri aliquid et hominem hominis incommodo suum commodum augere magis est contra naturam quam mors, quam paupertas, quam dolor, quam cetera, quae possunt aut corpori accidere aut rebus externis. Nam principio tollit convictum humanum et societatem. Si enim sic erimus affecti, ut propter suum quisque emolumentum spoliet aut violet alterum, disrumpi necesse est, eam quae maxime est secundum naturam, humani
22 generis societatem. Ut, si unum quodque membrum sensum hunc haberet, ut posse putaret se valere, si proximi membri valetudinem ad se traduxisset, debilitari et interire totum corpus necesse esset, sic, si unus quisque nostrum ad se rapiat commoda aliorum detrahatque, quod cuique possit, emolumenti sui gratia, societas hominum et communitas evertatur necesse est. Nam sibi ut quisque malit, quod ad usum vitae pertineat, quam alteri acquirere, concessum est non repugnante natura,

[1] *disseruntur* certain MSS., C. Lange and Fr. Fabricius, Müller, Heine; *disserentur* MSS., Bt.

[2] *iis* Edd.; *his* (*hijs* c) MSS.

[3] *et honestum . . . et utile* Lambinus, Bt.[2], Müller, Heine; *et honestum . . . aut utile* B H a b; *aut honestum . . . aut utile* c, Bt.[1]

these problems, if conducted by those who consider whatever is morally right also expedient and nothing expedient that is not at the same time morally right, will be more illuminating than if conducted by those who think that something not expedient may be morally right and that something not morally right may be expedient. But our New Academy allows us wide liberty, so that it is within my right to defend any theory that presents itself to me as most probable. But to return to my rule.

21 V. Well then, for a man to take something from his neighbour and to profit by his neighbour's loss is more contrary to Nature than is death or poverty or pain or anything else that can affect either our person or our property. For, in the first place, injustice is fatal to social life and fellowship between man and man. For, if we are so disposed that each, to gain some personal profit, will defraud or injure his neighbour, then those bonds of human society, which are most in accord with Nature's laws, must of

**Wrongful gains are against the laws: (1) of nature**

22 necessity be broken. Suppose, by way of comparison, that each one of our bodily members should conceive this idea and imagine that it could be strong and well if it should draw off to itself the health and strength of its neighbouring member, the whole body would necessarily be enfeebled and die; so, if each one of us should seize upon the property of his neighbours and take from each whatever he could appropriate to his own use, the bonds of human society must inevitably be annihilated. For, without any conflict with Nature's laws, it is granted that everybody may prefer to secure for himself rather than for his neighbour what is essential for the conduct of life; but Nature's laws do forbid us to increase

illud natura non patitur, ut aliorum spoliis nostras facultates, copias, opes augeamus.

23 Neque vero hoc solum natura, id est iure gentium, sed etiam legibus populorum, quibus in singulis civitatibus res publica continetur, eodem modo constitutum est, ut non liceat sui commodi causa nocere alteri; hoc enim spectant leges, hoc volunt, incolumem esse civium coniunctionem; quam qui dirimunt, eos morte, exsilio, vinclis, damno coërcent.

Atque hoc multo magis efficit ipsa naturae ratio, quae est lex divina et humana; cui parere qui velit (omnes autem parebunt, qui secundum naturam volent vivere), numquam committet, ut alienum appetat et id, quod alteri detraxerit, sibi adsumat.
24 Etenim multo magis est secundum naturam excelsitas animi et magnitudo itemque comitas, iustitia, liberalitas quam voluptas, quam vita, quam divitiae; quae quidem contemnere et pro nihilo ducere comparantem cum utilitate communi magni animi et excelsi est. [Detrahere autem de altero sui commodi causa magis est contra naturam quam mors, quam dolor, quam cetera generis eiusdem.] [1]

25 Itemque magis est secundum naturam pro omnibus gentibus, si fieri possit, conservandis aut iuvandis maximos labores molestiasque suscipere imitantem Herculem illum, quem hominum fama beneficiorum memor in concilio caelestium collocavit, quam vivere

[1] *Detrahere . . . generis eiusdem* MSS.; bracketed by Baiter, Edd.

our means, wealth, and resources by despoiling others.

23 But this principle is established not by Nature's laws alone (that is, by the common rules of equity), but also by the statutes of particular communities, in accordance with which in individual states the public interests are maintained. In all these it is with one accord ordained that no man shall be allowed for the sake of his own advantage to injure his neighbour. For it is to this that the laws have regard; this is their intent, that the bonds of union between citizens should not be impaired; and any attempt to destroy these bonds is repressed by the penalty of death, exile, imprisonment, or fine. (2) of nations

Again, this principle follows much more effectually directly from the Reason which is in Nature, which is the law of gods and men. If anyone will hearken to that voice (and all will hearken to it who wish to live in accord with Nature's laws), he will never be guilty of coveting anything that is his neighbour's or of appropriating to himself what he has taken (3) of gods and men.

24 from his neighbour. Then, too, loftiness and greatness of spirit, and courtesy, justice, and generosity are much more in harmony with Nature than are selfish pleasure, riches, and life itself; but it requires a great and lofty spirit to despise these latter and count them as naught, when one weighs them over against the common weal. [But for anyone to rob his neighbour for his own profit is more contrary to Nature than death, pain, and the like.] Self-seeking *vs.* self-sacrifice.

25 In like manner it is more in accord with Nature to emulate the great Hercules and undergo the greatest toil and trouble for the sake of aiding or saving the world, if possible, than to live in seclusion,

in solitudine non modo sine ullis molestiis, sed etiam in maximis voluptatibus abundantem omnibus copiis, ut excellas etiam pulchritudine et viribus.

Quocirca optimo quisque et splendidissimo ingenio longe illam vitam huic anteponit. Ex quo efficitur hominem naturae oboedientem homini nocere non posse.

26 Deinde, qui alterum violat, ut ipse aliquid commodi consequatur, aut nihil existimat se facere contra naturam aut magis fugiendam [1] censet mortem, paupertatem, dolorem, amissionem etiam liberorum, propinquorum, amicorum quam facere cuiquam iniuriam. Si nihil existimat contra naturam fieri hominibus violandis, quid cum eo disseras, qui omnino hominem ex homine tollat? sin fugiendum id quidem censet, sed [2] multo illa peiora, mortem, paupertatem, dolorem, errat in eo, quod ullum aut corporis aut fortunae vitium vitiis animi gravius existimat.

VI. Ergo unum debet esse omnibus propositum, ut eadem sit utilitas unius cuiusque et universorum; quam si ad se quisque rapiet, dissolvetur omnis humana consortio.

27 Atque etiam, si hoc natura praescribit, ut homo

[1] *fugiendam* b, Ed.; *fugienda* B H a c.
[2] *sed* c, Edd.; *et* B H a b.

not only free from all care, but revelling in pleasures and abounding in wealth, while excelling others also in beauty and strength. Thus Hercules denied himself and underwent toil and tribulation for the world, and, out of gratitude for his services, popular belief has given him a place in the council of the gods.

The better and more noble, therefore, the character with which a man is endowed, the more does he prefer the life of service to the life of pleasure. Whence it follows that man, if he is obedient to Nature, cannot do harm to his fellow-man.

26 Finally, if a man wrongs his neighbour to gain some advantage for himself, he must either imagine that he is not acting in defiance of Nature or he must believe that death, poverty, pain, or even the loss of children, kinsmen, or friends, is more to be shunned than an act of injustice against another. If he thinks he is not violating the laws of Nature, when he wrongs his fellow-men, how is one to argue with the individual who takes away from man all that makes him man? But if he believes that, while such a course should be avoided, the other alternatives are much worse—namely, death, poverty, pain—he is mistaken in thinking that any ills affecting either his person or his property are more serious than those affecting his soul.

**The interest of society is the interest of the individual.**

VI. This, then, ought to be the chief end of all men, to make the interest of each individual and of the whole body politic identical. For, if the individual appropriates to selfish ends what should be devoted to the common good, all human fellowship will be destroyed.

27 And further, if Nature ordains that one man shall

homini, quicumque sit, ob eam ipsam causam, quod is homo sit, consultum velit, necesse est secundum eandem naturam omnium utilitatem esse communem. Quod si ita est, una continemur omnes et eadem lege naturae, idque ipsum si ita est, certe violare alterum naturae lege prohibemur. Verum
28 autem primum; verum igitur extremum. Nam illud quidem absurdum est, quod quidam dicunt, parenti se aut fratri nihil detracturos sui commodi causa, aliam rationem esse civium reliquorum. Hi sibi nihil iuris, nullam societatem communis utilitatis causa statuunt esse cum civibus, quae sententia omnem societatem distrahit civitatis.

Qui autem civium rationem dicunt habendam, externorum negant, ii [1] dirimunt communem humani generis societatem; qua sublata beneficentia, liberalitas, bonitas, iustitia funditus tollitur; quae qui tollunt, etiam adversus deos immortales impii iudicandi sunt. Ab iis enim constitutam inter homines societatem evertunt, cuius societatis artissimum vinculum est magis arbitrari esse contra naturam hominem homini detrahere sui commodi causa quam omnia incommoda subire vel externa vel corporis . . . vel etiam ipsius animi, quae vacent iustitia; [2] haec enim una virtus omnium est domina et regina virtutum.

[1] *ii* Bt., Ed.; *hi* B a b; *hii* H p *hij* c.
[2] *quae vacent iustitia* MSS., Ed., Heine; *quae vacent iniustitia* cod. Ubaldini, Bt.[1]; *quae non v. iustitia* O.

---

[a] I.e., there are no circumstances of loss or gain that can warrant a violation of justice.

desire to promote the interests of a fellow-man, whoever he may be, just because he is a fellow-man, then it follows, in accordance with that same Nature, that there are interests that all men have in common. And, if this is true, we are all subject to one and the same law of Nature; and, if this also is true, we are certainly forbidden by Nature's law to wrong our neighbour. Now the first assumption is true;
28 therefore the conclusion is likewise true. For that is an absurd position which is taken by some people, who say that they will not rob a parent or a brother for their own gain, but that their relation to the rest of their fellow-citizens is quite another thing. Such people contend in essence that they are bound to their fellow-citizens by no mutual obligations, social ties, or common interests. This attitude demolishes the whole structure of civil society.

Better endure any loss than wrong a fellow man for gain.

Others again who say that regard should be had for the rights of fellow-citizens, but not of foreigners, would destroy the universal brotherhood of mankind; and, when this is annihilated, kindness, generosity, goodness, and justice must utterly perish; and those who work all this destruction must be considered as wickedly rebelling against the immortal gods. For they uproot the fellowship which the gods have established between human beings, and the closest bond of this fellowship is the conviction that it is more repugnant to Nature for man to rob a fellow-man for his own gain than to endure all possible loss, whether to his property or to his person . . . or even to his very soul—so far as these losses are not concerned with justice;[a] for this virtue is the sovereign mistress and queen of all the virtues.

29 Forsitan quispiam dixerit: Nonne igitur sapiens, si fame ipse conficiatur, abstulerit cibum alteri homini ad nullam rem utili? [Minime vero; non enim mihi est vita mea utilior quam animi talis affectio, neminem ut violem commodi mei gratia.][1] Quid? si Phalarim, crudelem tyrannum et immanem, vir bonus, ne ipse frigore conficiatur, vestitu spoliare possit, nonne faciat?

30 Haec ad iudicandum sunt facillima. Nam, si quid ab homine ad nullam partem utili utilitatis tuae causa detraxeris, inhumane feceris contraque naturae legem; sin autem is tu sis, qui multam utilitatem rei publicae atque hominum societati, si in vita remaneas, afferre possis, si quid ob eam causam alteri detraxeris, non sit reprehendendum. Sin autem id non sit eius modi, suum cuique incommodum ferendum est potius quam de alterius commodis detrahendum. Non igitur magis est contra naturam morbus aut egestas aut quid eius modi quam detractio atque appetitio alieni, sed communis utilitatis dere-
31 lictio contra naturam est; est enim iniusta. Itaque lex ipsa naturae, quae utilitatem hominum conservat et continet, decernet profecto, ut ab homine inerti atque inutili ad sapientem, bonum, fortem virum transferantur res ad vivendum necessariae, qui si occiderit, multum de communi utilitate detraxerit, modo hoc ita faciat, ut ne ipse de se bene existimans seseque diligens hanc causam habeat ad iniuriam.

[1] Bracketed by Unger, Edd.

29 But, perhaps, someone may say: "Well, then, suppose a wise man were starving to death, might he not take the bread of some perfectly useless member of society?" [Not at all; for my life is not more precious to me than that temper of soul which would keep me from doing wrong to anybody for my own advantage.] "Or again; supposing a righteous man were in a position to rob the cruel and inhuman tyrant Phalaris of clothing, might he not do it to keep himself from freezing to death?"

30 These cases are very easy to decide. For, if merely for one's own benefit one were to take something away from a man, though he were a perfectly worthless fellow, it would be an act of meanness and contrary to Nature's law. But suppose one would be able, by remaining alive, to render signal service to the state and to human society—if from that motive one should take something from another, it would not be a matter for censure. But, if such is not the case, each one must bear his own burden of distress rather than rob a neighbour of his rights. We are not to say, therefore, that sickness or want or any evil of that sort is more repugnant to Nature than to covet and to appropriate what is one's neighbour's; but we do maintain that disregard of the common interests
31 is repugnant to Nature; for it is unjust. And therefore Nature's law itself, which protects and conserves human interests, will surely determine that a man who is wise, good, and brave, should in emergency have the necessaries of life transferred to him from a person who is idle and worthless; for the good man's death would be a heavy loss to the common weal; only let him beware that self-esteem and self-love do not find in such a transfer of possessions

**The interests of society must decide about exceptions.**

Ita semper officio fungetur utilitati consulens hominum et ei, quam saepe commemoro, humanae societati.

32 Nam quod ad Phalarim attinet, perfacile iudicium est. Nulla est enim societas nobis cum tyrannis, et potius summa distractio est, neque est contra naturam spoliare eum, si possis, quem est honestum necare, atque hoc omne genus pestiferum atque impium ex hominum communitate exterminandum est. Etenim, ut membra quaedam amputantur, si et ipsa sanguine et tamquam spiritu carere coeperunt et nocent reliquis partibus corporis, sic ista in figura hominis feritas et immanitas beluae a communi tamquam humanitatis corpore [1] segreganda est.

Huius generis quaestiones sunt omnes eae, in quibus ex tempore officium exquiritur.

33 VII. Eius modi igitur credo res Panaetium persecuturum fuisse, nisi aliqui casus aut occupatio eius consilium peremisset. Ad quas ipsas consultationes superioribus libris satis multa praecepta sunt, ex quibus [2] perspici possit, quid sit propter turpitudinem fugiendum, quid sit, quod idcirco fugiendum non sit, quod omnino turpe non sit.

Sed quoniam operi inchoato, prope tamen absoluto tamquam fastigium imponimus, ut geometrae solent non omnia docere, sed postulare, ut quaedam sibi concedantur, quo facilius, quae volunt, explicent, sic

[1] *humanitatis corpore* Muret, cod. Guelf., Ed., Bt., Heine; *humanitate corporis* MSS., Müller; Unger strikes out *corporis*.

[2] *superioribus . . . ex quibus* Walker, Bt.², Ed.; *ex superioribus . . . quibus* MSS., Bt.¹; *superioribus . . . quibus* Heine.

a pretext for wrong-doing. But, thus guided in his decision, the good man will always perform his duty, promoting the general interests of human society on which I am so fond of dwelling.

32 As for the case of Phalaris, a decision is quite simple: we have no ties of fellowship with a tyrant, but rather the bitterest feud; and it is not opposed to Nature to rob, if one can, a man whom it is morally right to kill;—nay, all that pestilent and abominable race should be exterminated from human society. And this may be done by proper measures; for, as certain members are amputated, if they show signs themselves of being bloodless and virtually lifeless and thus jeopardize the health of the other parts of the body, so those fierce and savage monsters in human form should be cut off from what may be called the common body of humanity.

**No duty due to a tyrant.**

Of this sort are all those problems in which we have to determine what moral duty is, as it varies with varying circumstances.

33 VII. It is subjects of this sort that I believe Panaetius would have followed up, had not some accident or business interfered with his design. For the elucidation of these very questions there are in his former books rules in plenty, from which one can learn what should be avoided because of its immorality and what does not have to be avoided for the reason that it is not immoral at all.

We are now putting the capstone, as it were, upon our structure, which is unfinished, to be sure, but still almost completed; and, as mathematicians make a practice of not demonstrating every proposition, but require that certain axioms be assumed as true, in order more easily to explain their meaning, so, my

ego a te postulo, mi Cicero, ut mihi concedas, si potes, nihil praeter id, quod honestum sit, propter se esse expetendum. Sin hoc non licet per Cratippum, at illud certe dabis, quod honestum sit, id esse maxime propter se expetendum. Mihi utrumvis satis est et tum hoc, tum illud probabilius videtur nec praeterea quicquam probabile.

34 Ac primum in hoc Panaetius defendendus est, quod non utilia cum honestis pugnare aliquando posse dixerit (neque enim ei fas erat), sed ea, quae viderentur utilia. Nihil vero utile, quod non idem honestum, nihil honestum, quod non idem utile sit, saepe testatur negatque ullam pestem maiorem in vitam hominum invasisse quam eorum opinionem, qui ista distraxerint. Itaque, non ut aliquando anteponeremus utilia honestis, sed ut ea sine errore diiudicaremus, si quando incidissent,[1] induxit eam, quae videretur esse, non quae esset, repugnantiam. Hanc igitur partem relictam explebimus nullis adminiculis, sed, ut dicitur, Marte nostro. Neque enim quicquam est de hac parte post Panaetium explicatum, quod quidem mihi probaretur, de iis, quae in manus meas venerunt.[2]

[1] *ea . . . incidissent* MSS., Bt.[1], Heine, Ed.; *eam* [repugnantiam] . . . *incidisset* Unger, Bt.[2]

[2] *venerunt* Manutius, Edd.; *venerint* MSS.

---

[a] As a Peripatetic, Cratippus insisted that there was *natural* good as well as *moral* good; thus health, honour, etc., were good and worth seeking for their own sake, though in less degree than virtue. But the Stoics (and Cicero is now speaking as a Stoic) called all those other blessings not "good" nor "worth seeking for their own sake," but "indifferent."

[b] With this he waves aside, without even the honour of mentioning them, the Epicureans, Cyrenaics, etc.

[c] Because he was a Stoic.

dear Cicero, I ask you to assume with me, if you can, that nothing is worth the seeking for its own sake except what is morally right. But if Cratippus [a] does not permit this assumption, you will still grant this at least—that what is morally right is the object most worth the seeking for its own sake. Either alternative is sufficient for my purposes; first the one and then the other seems to me the more probable; and, besides these, there is no other alternative that seems probable at all.[b]

**Moral Right the only good or the chief good.**

34 In the first place, I must undertake the defence of Panaetius on this point; for he has said, not that the truly expedient could under certain circumstances clash with the morally right (for he could not have said that conscientiously [c]), but only that what *seemed* expedient could do so. For he often bears witness to the fact that nothing is really expedient that is not at the same time morally right, and nothing morally right that is not at the same time expedient; and he says that no greater curse has ever assailed human life than the doctrine of those who have separated these two conceptions. And so he introduced an apparent, not a real, conflict between them, not to the end that we should under certain circumstances give the expedient preference over the moral, but that, in case they ever should get in each other's way, we might decide between them without uncertainty. This part, therefore, which was passed over by Panaetius, I will carry to completion without any auxiliaries, but fighting my own battle, as the saying is. For, of all that has been worked out on this line since the time of Panaetius, nothing that has come into my hands is at all satisfactory to me.

**Vindication of Panaetius: nothing can be expedient that is not morally right.**

35 VIII. Cum igitur aliqua species utilitatis obiecta est, commoveri necesse est; sed si, cum animum attenderis, turpitudinem videas adiunctam ei rei, quae speciem utilitatis attulerit, tum non utilitas relinquenda est, sed intellegendum, ubi turpitudo sit, ibi utilitatem esse non posse. Quodsi nihil est tam contra naturam quam turpitudo (recta enim et convenientia et constantia natura desiderat aspernaturque contraria) nihilque tam secundum naturam quam utilitas, certe in eadem re utilitas et turpitudo [1] esse non potest.

Itemque, si ad honestatem nati sumus eaque aut sola expetenda est, ut Zenoni visum est, aut certe omni pondere gravior habenda quam reliqua omnia, quod Aristoteli placet, necesse est, quod honestum sit, id esse aut solum aut summum bonum; quod autem bonum, id certe utile; ita, quicquid honestum, id utile.

36 Quare error hominum non proborum, cum aliquid, quod utile visum est, arripuit, id continuo secernit ab honesto. Hinc sicae, hinc venena, hinc falsa testamenta nascuntur, hinc furta, peculatus, expilationes direptionesque sociorum et civium, hinc opum nimiarum, potentiae non ferendae, postremo etiam in liberis civitatibus regnandi exsistunt cupiditates, quibus nihil nec taetrius nec foedius excogitari potest.

[1] *re utilitas et turp.* c, Edd.; *re utili turpitudo* B H a b.

35 VIII. Now when we meet with expediency in some specious form or other, we cannot help being influenced by it. But if upon closer inspection one sees that there is some immorality connected with what presents the appearance of expediency, then one is not necessarily to sacrifice expediency but to recognize that there can be no expediency where there is immorality. But if there is nothing so repugnant to Nature as immorality (for Nature demands right and harmony and consistency and abhors their opposites), and if nothing is so thoroughly in accord with Nature as expediency, then surely expediency and immorality cannot co-exist in one and the same object. **Expediency and immorality incompatible.**

Again: if we are born for moral rectitude and if that is either the only thing worth seeking, as Zeno thought, or at least to be esteemed as infinitely outweighing everything else, as Aristotle holds, then it necessarily follows that the morally right is either the sole good or the supreme good. Now, that which is good is certainly expedient; consequently, that which is morally right is also expedient. **The morally right is also expedient.**

36 Thus it is the error of men who are not strictly upright to seize upon something that seems to be expedient and straightway to dissociate that from the question of moral right. To this error the assassin's dagger, the poisoned cup, the forged wills owe their origin; this gives rise to theft, embezzlement of public funds, exploitation and plundering of provincials and citizens; this engenders also the lust for excessive wealth, for despotic power, and finally for making oneself king even in the midst of a free people; and anything more atrocious or repulsive than such a passion cannot be conceived. For **The evils resulting from contrary view.**

Emolumenta enim rerum fallacibus iudiciis vident, poenam non dico legum, quam saepe perrumpunt, sed ipsius turpitudinis, quae acerbissima est, non vident.

37 Quam ob rem hoc quidem deliberantium genus pellatur e medio (est enim totum sceleratum et impium), qui deliberant, utrum id sequantur, quod honestum esse videant, an se scientes scelere contaminent; in ipsa enim dubitatione facinus inest, etiamsi ad id non pervenerint. Ergo ea deliberanda omnino non sunt, in quibus est turpis ipsa deliberatio.

Atque etiam ex omni deliberatione celandi et occultandi spes opinioque removenda est. Satis enim nobis, si modo in philosophia aliquid profecimus, persuasum esse debet, si omnes deos hominesque celare possimus, nihil tamen avare, nihil iniuste, nihil libidinose, nihil incontinenter esse faciendum.

Rep. II, 359 C 38 IX. Hinc ille Gyges inducitur a Platone, qui, cum terra discessisset magnis quibusdam imbribus, descendit in illum hiatum aëneumque equum, ut ferunt fabulae, animadvertit, cuius in lateribus fores essent; quibus apertis corpus hominis mortui vidit magnitudine invisitata [1] anulumque aureum in digito; quem ut detraxit, ipse induit (erat autem regius pastor), tum in concilium se pastorum recepit. Ibi cum palam eius anuli ad palmam converterat, a nullo videbatur, ipse autem omnia videbat; idem rursus

[1] *invisitata* B H[1], Edd.; *inusitata* H[2] a b c.

with a false perspective they see the material rewards but not the punishment—I do not mean the penalty of the law, which they often escape, but the heaviest penalty of all, their own demoralization.

37 Away, then, with questioners of this sort (for their whole tribe is wicked and ungodly), who stop to consider whether to pursue the course which they see is morally right or to stain their hands with what they know is crime. For there is guilt in their very deliberation, even though they never reach the performance of the deed itself. Those actions, therefore, should not be considered at all, the mere consideration of which is itself morally wrong.

**Moral rectitude and secret sin.**

Furthermore, in any such consideration we must banish any vain hope and thought that our action may be covered up and kept secret. For if we have only made some real progress in the study of philosophy, we ought to be quite convinced that, even though we may escape the eyes of gods and men, we must still do nothing that savours of greed or of injustice, of lust or of intemperance.

**The story of Gyges and his ring.**

38 IX. By way of illustrating this truth Plato introduces the familiar story of Gyges: Once upon a time the earth opened in consequence of heavy rains; Gyges went down into the chasm and saw, so the story goes, a horse of bronze; in its side was a door. On opening this door he saw the body of a dead man of enormous size with a gold ring upon his finger. He removed this and put it on his own hand and then repaired to an assembly of the shepherds, for he was a shepherd of the king. As often as he turned the bezel of the ring inwards toward the palm of his hand, he became invisible to everyone, while he himself saw everything; but as often as he turned

videbatur, cum in locum anulum inverterat. Itaque hac opportunitate anuli usus reginae stuprum intulit eaque adiutrice regem dominum interemit, sustulit, quos obstare arbitrabatur, nec in his eum facinoribus quisquam potuit videre. Sic repente anuli beneficio rex exortus est Lydiae.

Hunc igitur ipsum anulum si habeat sapiens, nihilo[1] plus sibi licere putet peccare, quam si non haberet;[2] honesta enim bonis viris, non occulta quaeruntur.

39 Atque hoc loco philosophi quidam, minime mali illi quidem, sed non satis acuti, fictam et commenticiam fabulam prolatam dicunt a Platone; quasi vero ille aut factum id esse aut fieri potuisse defendat! Haec est vis huius anuli et huius exempli: si nemo sciturus, nemo ne suspicaturus quidem sit, cum aliquid divitiarum, potentiae, dominationis, libidinis causa feceris, si id dis hominibusque futurum sit semper ignotum, sisne facturus. Negant id fieri posse. Nequaquam[3] potest id quidem; sed quaero, quod negant posse, id si posset, quidnam facerent. Urguent rustice sane; negant enim posse et in eo perstant; hoc verbum quid valeat, non vident. Cum enim quaerimus, si celare possint, quid facturi sint, non quaerimus, possintne celare, sed tamquam tormenta quaedam adhibemus, ut, si responderint se

[1] *ni(c)hilo* c, Edd.; *nihil* B H a b.
[2] *peccare . . . haberet* MSS.; bracketed by Madv., Bt.
[3] *nequaquam* Manutius, Bt., Ed., Heine; *quamquam* (and yet it is possible) MSS., Müller.

it back to its proper position, he became visible again. And so, with the advantage which the ring gave him, he debauched the queen, and with her assistance he murdered his royal master and removed all those who he thought stood in his way, without anyone's being able to detect him in his crimes. Thus, by virtue of the ring, he shortly rose to be king of Lydia.

Now, suppose a wise man had just such a ring, he would not imagine that he was free to do wrong any more than if he did not have it; for good men aim to secure not secrecy but the right.

39 And yet on this point certain philosophers, who are not at all vicious but who are not very discerning, declare that the story related by Plato is fictitious and imaginary. As if he affirmed that it was actually true or even possible! But the force of the illustration of the ring is this: if nobody were to know or even to suspect the truth, when you do anything to gain riches or power or sovereignty or sensual gratification—if your act should be hidden for ever from the knowledge of gods and men, would you do it? The condition, they say, is impossible. Of course it is. But my question is, if that were possible which they declare to be impossible, what, pray, would one do? They press their point with right boorish obstinacy: they assert that it is impossible and insist upon it; they refuse to see the meaning of my words, "if possible." For when we ask what they would do, if they could escape detection, we are not asking whether they can escape detection; but we put them as it were upon the rack: should they answer that, if impunity were assured, they would do what was most to their selfish interest,

The moral of the story.

impunitate proposita facturos, quod expediat, facinorosos se esse fateantur, si negent, omnia turpia per se ipsa fugienda esse concedant.

Sed iam ad propositum revertamur.

40 X. Incidunt multae saepe causae, quae conturbent animos utilitatis specie, non cum hoc deliberetur, relinquendane sit honestas propter utilitatis magnitudinem (nam id quidem improbum est), sed illud, possitne id, quod utile videatur, fieri non turpiter. Cum Collatino collegae Brutus imperium abrogabat, poterat videri facere id iniuste; fuerat enim in regibus expellendis socius Bruti consiliorum et adiutor. Cum autem consilium hoc principes cepissent, cognationem Superbi nomenque Tarquiniorum et memoriam regni esse tollendam, quod erat utile, patriae consulere, id erat ita honestum, ut etiam ipsi Collatino placere deberet. Itaque utilitas valuit propter honestatem, sine qua ne utilitas quidem esse potuisset.

At in eo rege, qui urbem condidit, non item;
41 species enim utilitatis animum pepulit eius; cui cum visum esset utilius solum quam cum altero regnare, fratrem interemit. Omisit hic et pietatem et humanitatem, ut id, quod utile videbatur neque erat,

[a] Romulus.
[b] Remus.

that would be a confession that they are criminally minded; should they say that they would not do so, they would be granting that all things in and of themselves immoral should be avoided.

But let us now return to our theme.

40 X. Many cases oftentimes arise to perplex our minds with a specious appearance of expediency: the question raised in these cases is not whether moral rectitude is to be sacrificed to some considerable advantage (for that would of course be wrong), but whether the apparent advantage can be secured without moral wrong. When Brutus deposed his colleague Collatinus from the consular office, his treatment of him might have been thought unjust; for Collatinus had been his associate, and had helped him with word and deed in driving out the royal family. But when the leading men of the state had determined that all the kindred of Superbus and the very name of the Tarquins and every reminder of the monarchy should be obliterated, then the course that was expedient—namely, to serve the country's interests—was so pre-eminently right, that it was even Collatinus's own duty to acquiesce in its justice. And so expediency gained the day because of its moral rightness; for without moral rectitude there could have been no possible expediency.

**Conflicts between: (1) apparent Expediency and Justice,**

Not so in the case of the king [a] who founded the
41 city: it was the specious appearance of expediency that actuated him; and when he decided that it was more expedient for him to reign alone than to share the throne with another, he slew his brother.[b] He threw to the winds his brotherly affection and his human feelings, to secure what seemed to him—but was not—expedient; and yet in defence of his deed

assequi posset, et tamen muri causam[1] opposuit, speciem honestatis nec probabilem nec sane idoneam. Peccavit igitur, pace vel Quirini vel Romuli dixerim.

42 Nec tamen nostrae nobis utilitates omittendae sunt aliisque tradendae, cum iis[2] ipsi egeamus, sed suae cuique utilitati, quod sine alterius iniuria fiat, serviendum est. Scite Chrysippus, ut multa: " Qui stadium," inquit, " currit, eniti et contendere debet, quam maxime possit, ut vincat, supplantare eum, quicum[3] certet, aut manu depellere nullo modo debet; sic in vita sibi quemque petere, quod pertineat ad usum, non iniquum est, alteri deripere ius non est."

43 Maxime autem perturbantur officia in amicitiis, quibus et non tribuere, quod recte possis, et tribuere, quod non sit aequum, contra officium est. Sed huius generis totius breve et non difficile praeceptum est. Quae enim videntur utilia, honores, divitiae, voluptates, cetera generis eiusdem, haec amicitiae numquam anteponenda sunt. At neque contra rem publicam neque contra ius iurandum ac fidem amici causa vir bonus faciet, ne si iudex quidem erit de ipso amico; ponit enim personam amici, cum induit iudicis. Tantum dabit amicitiae, ut veram amici

[1] *causam* c, Edd.; *causa* B H a b.
[2] *iis* Bt., Ed., Heine; *his* B H a b; *hijs* c.
[3] *quicum* MSS., Bt., Heine; *quocum* Ed.

---

[a] I.e., whether he be god or man.

he offered the excuse about his wall—a specious show of moral rectitude, neither reasonable nor adequate at all. He committed a crime, therefore, with due respect to him let me say so, be he Quirinus or Romulus.[a]

42 And yet we are not required to sacrifice our own interests and surrender to others what we need for ourselves, but each one should consider his own interests, as far as he may without injury to his neighbour's. "When a man enters the foot-race," says Chrysippus with his usual aptness, "it is his duty to put forth all his strength and strive with all his might to win; but he ought never with his foot to trip, or with his hand to foul a competitor. Thus in the stadium of life, it is not unfair for anyone to seek to obtain what is needful for his own advantage, but he has no right to wrest it from his neighbour."

**(2) Individual and general interests.**

43 It is in the case of friendships, however, that men's conceptions of duty are most confused; for it is a breach of duty either to fail to do for a friend what one rightly can do, or to do for him what is not right. But for our guidance in all such cases we have a rule that is short and easy to master: apparent advantages—political preferment, riches, sensual pleasures, and the like—should never be preferred to the obligations of friendship. But an upright man will never for a friend's sake do anything in violation of his country's interests or his oath or his sacred honour, not even if he sits as judge in a friend's case; for he lays aside the rôle of friend when he assumes that of judge. Only so far will he make concessions to friendship, that he will prefer his friend's side to be the juster one and that he will set the time for presenting his case, as far as the

**(3) obligations to friends and duty,**

causam esse malit, ut orandae litis tempus, quoad
44 per leges liceat, accommodet. Cum vero iurato sententia dicenda erit,[1] meminerit deum se adhibere[2] testem, id est, ut ego arbitror, mentem suam, qua nihil homini dedit deus ipse divinius. Itaque praeclarum a maioribus accepimus morem rogandi iudicis, si eum teneremus, QUAE SALVA FIDE FACERE POSSIT. Haec rogatio ad ea pertinet, quae paulo ante dixi honeste amico a iudice posse concedi; nam si omnia facienda sint, quae amici velint, non amicitiae tales,
45 sed coniurationes putandae sint. Loquor autem de communibus amicitiis; nam in sapientibus viris perfectisque nihil potest esse tale.

Damonem et Phintiam Pythagoreos ferunt hoc animo inter se fuisse, ut, cum eorum alteri Dionysius tyrannus diem necis destinavisset et is, qui morti addictus esset, paucos sibi dies commendandorum suorum causa postulavisset, vas factus sit[3] alter eius sistendi, ut, si ille non revertisset, moriendum esset ipsi. Qui cum ad diem se recepisset, admiratus eorum fidem tyrannus petivit, ut se ad amicitiam tertium ascriberent.

46 Cum igitur id, quod utile videtur in amicitia, cum eo, quod honestum est, comparatur, iaceat utilitatis

[1] *erit* Ed., Bt.[2], Heine; *sit* MSS.; *est* Bt.[1]
[2] *adhibere* B H a, Bt., Ed.; *habere* b c, Lact., Müller.
[3] *sit* Manutius, Edd.; *est* MSS., Nonius.

laws will allow, to suit his friend's convenience.
44 But when he comes to pronounce the verdict under oath, he should remember that he has God as his witness—that is, as I understand it, his own conscience, than which God himself has bestowed upon man nothing more divine. From this point of view it is a fine custom that we have inherited from our forefathers (if we were only true to it now), to appeal to the juror with this formula—" to do what he can consistently with his sacred honour." This form of appeal is in keeping with what I said a moment ago would be morally right for a judge to concede to a friend. For supposing that we were bound to do everything that our friends desired, such relations would have to be accounted not friendships but
45 conspiracies. But I am speaking here of ordinary friendships; for among men who are ideally wise and perfect such situations cannot arise.

They say that Damon and Phintias, of the Pythagorean school, enjoyed such ideally perfect friendship, that when the tyrant Dionysius had appointed a day for the execution of one of them, and the one who had been condemned to death requested a few days' respite for the purpose of putting his loved ones in the care of friends, the other became surety for his appearance, with the understanding that if his friend did not return, he himself should be put to death. And when the friend returned on the day appointed, the tyrant in admiration for their faithfulness begged that they would enrol him as a third partner in their friendship. Damon and Phintias.

46 Well then, when we are weighing what seems to be expedient in friendship against what is morally right, let apparent expediency be disregarded and Rules of precedence.

species, valeat honestas; cum autem in amicitia, quae honesta non sunt, postulabuntur, religio et fides anteponatur amicitiae. Sic habebitur is, quem exquirimus, dilectus officii.

XI. Sed utilitatis specie in re publica saepissime peccatur, ut in Corinthi disturbatione nostri; durius etiam Athenienses, qui sciverunt, ut Aeginetis, qui classe valebant, pollices praeciderentur. Hoc visum est utile; nimis enim imminebat propter propinquitatem Aegina Piraeo. Sed nihil, quod crudele, utile; est enim hominum naturae, quam sequi debemus,
47 maxime inimica crudelitas. Male etiam, qui peregrinos urbibus uti prohibent eosque exterminant, ut Pennus apud patres nostros, Papius nuper. Nam esse pro cive, qui civis non sit, rectum est non licere; quam legem tulerunt sapientissimi consules Crassus et Scaevola; usu vero urbis prohibere peregrinos sane inhumanum est.

Illa praeclara, in quibus publicae utilitatis species prae honestate contemnitur. Plena exemplorum est nostra res publica cum saepe, tum maxime bello

moral rectitude prevail; and when in friendship requests are submitted that are not morally right, let conscience and scrupulous regard for the right take precedence of the obligations of friendship. In this way we shall arrive at a proper choice between conflicting duties—the subject of this part of our investigation.

(4) apparent political expediency and duty to humanity.

XI. Through a specious appearance of expediency wrong is very often committed in transactions between state and state, as by our own country in the destruction of Corinth. A more cruel wrong was perpetrated by the Athenians in decreeing that the Aeginetans, whose strength lay in their navy, should have their thumbs cut off. This seemed to be expedient; for Aegina was too grave a menace, as it was close to the Piraeus. But no cruelty can be expedient; for cruelty is most abhorrent to human
47 nature, whose lead we ought to follow. They, too, do wrong who would debar foreigners from enjoying the advantages of their city and would exclude them from its borders, as was done by Pennus in the time of our fathers, and in recent times by Papius. It may not be right, of course, for one who is not a citizen to exercise the rights and privileges of citizenship; and the law on this point was secured by two of our wisest consuls, Crassus and Scaevola. Still, to debar foreigners from enjoying the advantages of the city is altogether contrary to the laws of humanity.

Moral right far outweighs apparent expediency.

There are splendid examples in history where the apparent expediency of the state has been set at naught out of regard for moral rectitude. Our own country has many instances to offer throughout her history, and especially in the Second Punic War,

Punico secundo; quae Cannensi calamitate accepta maiores animos habuit quam umquam rebus secundis; nulla timoris significatio, nulla mentio pacis. Tanta vis est honesti, ut speciem utilitatis obscuret.

48 Athenienses cum Persarum impetum nullo modo possent sustinere statuerentque, ut urbe relicta coniugibus et liberis Troezene depositis naves conscenderent libertatemque Graeciae classe defenderent, Cyrsilum quendam suadentem, ut in urbe manerent Xerxemque [1] reciperent, lapidibus obruerunt. Atqui [2] ille utilitatem sequi videbatur; sed ea nulla erat repugnante honestate.

49 Themistocles post victoriam eius belli, quod cum Persis fuit, dixit in contione se habere consilium rei publicae salutare, sed id sciri non opus esse; postulavit, ut aliquem populus daret, quicum communicaret; datus est Aristides; huic ille, classem Lacedaemoniorum, quae subducta esset ad Gytheum, clam incendi posse, quo facto frangi Lacedaemoniorum opes necesse esset. Quod Aristides cum audisset, in contionem magna exspectatione venit dixitque perutile esse consilium, quod Themistocles afferret, sed minime honestum. Itaque Athenienses, quod honestum non esset, id ne utile quidem putaverunt totamque eam rem, quam ne audierant quidem,

[1] *Xerxemque* B H a b, Bt., Heine; *Xersenque* c; *Xersemque* Nonius, Ed.

[2] *Atqui* Victorius, Fl., Bt.², Ed.; *Atque* MSS., Bt.¹

when news came of the disaster at Cannae, Rome displayed a loftier courage than ever she did in success; never a trace of faint-heartedness, never a mention of making terms. The influence of moral right is so potent, that it eclipses the specious appearance of expediency.

48 When the Athenians could in no way stem the tide of the Persian invasion and determined to abandon their city, bestow their wives and children in safety at Troezen, embark upon their ships, and fight on the sea for the freedom of Greece, a man named Cyrsilus proposed that they should stay at home and open the gates of their city to Xerxes. They stoned him to death for it. And yet he was working for what he thought was expediency; but it was not—not at all, for it clashed with moral rectitude.

49 After the victorious close of that war with Persia, Themistocles announced in the Assembly that he had a plan for the welfare of the state, but that it was not politic to let it be generally known. He requested the people to appoint someone with whom he might discuss it. They appointed Aristides. Themistocles confided to him that the Spartan fleet, which had been hauled up on shore at Gytheum, could be secretly set on fire; this done, the Spartan power would inevitably be crushed. When Aristides heard the plan, he came into the Assembly amid the eager expectation of all and reported that the plan proposed by Themistocles was in the highest degree expedient, but anything but morally right. The result was that the Athenians concluded that what was not morally right was likewise not expedient, and at the instance of Aristides they rejected the

auctore Aristide repudiaverunt. Melius hi quam nos, qui piratas immunes, socios vectigales habemus.

XII. Maneat ergo, quod turpe sit, id numquam esse utile, ne tum quidem, cum id, quod esse utile putes, adipiscare; hoc enim ipsum, utile putare, quod turpe
§ 40. 50 sit, calamitosum est. Sed incidunt, ut supra dixi, saepe causae, cum repugnare utilitas honestati videatur, ut animadvertendum sit, repugnetne plane an possit cum honestate coniungi. Eius generis hae sunt quaestiones: si exempli gratia vir bonus Alexandrea Rhodum magnum frumenti numerum advexerit in Rhodiorum inopia et fame summaque caritate annonae caritate, si idem sciat complures mercatores Alexandrea solvisse navesque in cursu frumento onustas petentes Rhodum viderit, dicturusne sit id Rhodiis an silentio suum quam plurimo venditurus. Sapientem et bonum virum fingimus; de eius deliberatione et consultatione quaerimus, qui celaturus Rhodios non sit, si id turpe iudicet, sed dubitet, an turpe non sit.

51 In huius modi causis aliud Diogeni Babylonio videri solet, magno et gravi Stoico, aliud Antipatro, discipulo eius, homini acutissimo. Antipatro omnia patefacienda, ut ne quid omnino, quod venditor

[a] The Cilician pirates had been crushed by Pompey and settled at Soli (Pompeiopolis). They gathered strength again during the distractions of the civil wars, and Antony is even said to have sought their aid in the war against Brutus and Cassius.

Marseilles and King Deiotarus of Armenia had supported Pompey and in consequence were made tributary by Caesar's party.

whole proposition without even listening to it. Their attitude was better than ours; for we let pirates go scot free, while we make our allies pay tribute.[a]

XII. Let it be set down as an established principle, then, that what is morally wrong can never be expedient—not even when one secures by means of it that which one thinks expedient; for the mere act of thinking a course expedient, when it is morally
50 wrong, is demoralizing. But, as I said above, cases often arise in which expediency may seem to clash with moral rectitude; and so we should examine carefully and see whether their conflict is inevitable or whether they may be reconciled. The following are problems of this sort: suppose, for example, a time of dearth and famine at Rhodes, with provisions at fabulous prices; and suppose that an honest man has imported a large cargo of grain from Alexandria and that to his certain knowledge also several other importers have set sail from Alexandria, and that on the voyage he has sighted their vessels laden with grain and bound for Rhodes; is he to report the fact to the Rhodians or is he to keep his own counsel and sell his own stock at the highest market price? I am assuming the case of a virtuous, upright man, and I am raising the question how a man would think and reason who would not conceal the facts from the Rhodians if he thought that it was immoral to do so, but who might be in doubt whether such silence would really be immoral. **Expediency *vs.* moral rectitude in business relations.**

51 In deciding cases of this kind Diogenes of Babylonia, a great and highly esteemed Stoic, consistently holds one view; his pupil Antipater, a most profound scholar, holds another. According to Antipater all the facts should be disclosed, that the buyer may **Diogenes *vs.* Antipater.**

norit, emptor ignoret, Diogeni venditorem, quatenus iure civili constitutum sit, dicere vitia oportere, cetera sine insidiis agere et, quoniam vendat, velle quam optime vendere.

"Advexi, exposui, vendo meum non pluris quam ceteri, fortasse etiam minoris, cum maior est copia. Cui fit iniuria?"

52 Exoritur Antipatri ratio ex altera parte: "Quid ais? tu cum hominibus consulere debeas et servire humanae societati eaque lege natus sis et ea habeas principia naturae, quibus parere et quae sequi debeas, ut utilitas tua communis sit utilitas vicissimque communis utilitas tua sit, celabis homines, quid iis adsit commoditatis et copiae?"

Respondebit Diogenes fortasse sic: "Aliud est celare, aliud tacere; neque ego nunc te celo, si tibi non dico, quae natura deorum sit, qui sit finis bonorum, quae tibi plus prodessent cognita quam tritici vilitas;[1] sed non, quicquid tibi audire utile est, idem[2] mihi dicere necesse est."

53 "Immo vero," inquiet ille, "necesse est,[3] siqui-

[1] *vilitas* a, Edd.; *utilitas* B H b c.
[2] *idem* B H a b; *id* c, Bt.
[3] *immo . . . est* c, Ed., Heine; *immo vero necesse est* p; *immo vero [inquiet ille] necesse est* Bt.

not be uninformed of any detail that the seller knows; according to Diogenes the seller should declare any defects in his wares, in so far as such a course is prescribed by the common law of the land; but for the rest, since he has goods to sell, he may try to sell them to the best possible advantage, provided he is guilty of no misrepresentation.

"I have imported my stock," Diogenes's merchant will say; "I have offered it for sale; I sell at a price no higher than my competitors—perhaps even lower, when the market is overstocked. Who is wronged?"

52 "What say you?" comes Antipater's argument on the other side; "it is your duty to consider the interests of your fellow-men and to serve society; you were brought into the world under these conditions and have these inborn principles which you are in duty bound to obey and follow, that your interest shall be the interest of the community and conversely that the interest of the community shall be your interest as well; will you, in view of all these facts, conceal from your fellow-men what relief in plenteous supplies is close at hand for them?"

**Is concealment of truth immoral?**

"It is one thing to conceal," Diogenes will perhaps reply; "not to reveal is quite a different thing. At this present moment I am not concealing from you, even if I am not revealing to you, the nature of the gods or the highest good; and to know these secrets would be of more advantage to you than to know that the price of wheat was down. But I am under no obligation to tell you everything that it may be to your interest to be told."

53 "Yea," Antipater will say, "but you are, as you must admit, if you will only bethink you of the

dem meministi esse inter homines natura coniunctam societatem."

"Memini," inquiet ille; "sed num ista societas talis est, ut nihil suum cuiusque sit? Quod si ita est, ne vendendum quidem quicquam est, sed donandum."

XIII. Vides in hac tota disceptatione non illud dici: "Quamvis hoc turpe sit, tamen, quoniam expedit, faciam," sed ita expedire, ut turpe non sit, ex altera autem parte, ea re, quia turpe sit, non esse faciendum.

54 Vendat aedes vir bonus propter aliqua vitia, quae ipse norit, ceteri ignorent, pestilentes sint et habeantur salubres, ignoretur in omnibus cubiculis apparere serpentes, male materiatae *sint*,[1] ruinosae, sed hoc praeter dominum nemo sciat; quaero, si haec emptoribus venditor non dixerit aedesque vendiderit pluris multo, quam se venditurum putarit, num id iniuste aut improbe fecerit.

55 "Ille vero," inquit Antipater; "quid est enim aliud erranti viam non monstrare, quod Athenis exsecrationibus publicis sanctum est, si hoc non est, emptorem pati ruere et per errorem in maximam fraudem incurrere? Plus etiam est quam viam non

[1] *sint* Bt.[1], Ed., Heine; not in MSS., Bt.[2]

bonds of fellowship forged by Nature and existing between man and man."

"I do not forget them," the other will reply; "but do you mean to say that those bonds of fellowship are such that there is no such thing as private property? If that is the case, we should not sell anything at all, but freely give everything away."

XIII. In this whole discussion, you see, no one says, "However wrong morally this or that may be, still, since it is expedient, I will do it"; but the one side asserts that a given act is expedient, without being morally wrong, while the other insists that the act should not be done, because it is morally wrong.

54 Suppose again that an honest man is offering a house for sale on account of certain undesirable features of which he himself is aware but which nobody else knows; suppose it is unsanitary, but has the reputation of being healthful; suppose it is not generally known that vermin are to be found in all the bedrooms; suppose, finally, that it is built of unsound timber and likely to collapse, but that no one knows about it except the owner; if the vendor does not tell the purchaser these facts but sells him the house for far more than he could reasonably have expected to get for it, I ask whether his transaction is unjust or dishonourable.

A vendor's duty.

55 "Yes," says Antipater, "it is; for to allow a purchaser to be hasty in closing a deal and through mistaken judgment to incur a very serious loss, if this is not refusing 'to set a man right when he has lost his way' (a crime which at Athens is prohibited on pain of public execration), what is? It is even

monstrare; nam est scientem in errorem alterum inducere."

(55) Diogenes contra: "Num te emere coëgit, qui ne hortatus quidem est? Ille, quod non placebat, proscripsit, tu, quod placebat, emisti. Quodsi, qui proscribunt villam bonam beneque aedificatam, non existimantur fefellisse, etiamsi illa nec bona est nec aedificata ratione, multo minus, qui domum non laudarunt. Ubi enim iudicium emptoris est, ibi fraus venditoris quae potest esse? Sin autem dictum non omne praestandum est, quod dictum non est, id praestandum putas? Quid vero est stultius quam venditorem eius rei, quam vendat, vitia narrare? quid autem tam absurdum, quam si domini iussu ita praeco praedicet: 'Domum pestilentem vendo'?"

56 Sic ergo in quibusdam causis dubiis ex altera parte defenditur honestas, ex altera ita de utilitate dicitur, ut id, quod utile videatur, non modo facere honestum sit, sed etiam non facere turpe. Haec est illa, quae videtur utilium fieri cum honestis saepe dissensio. Quae diiudicanda sunt;[1] non enim, ut quaereremus,
57 exposuimus, sed ut explicaremus. Non igitur videtur nec frumentarius ille Rhodios[2] nec hic aedium venditor celare emptores debuisse. Neque enim id est celare, quicquid reticeas, sed cum, quod tu scias,

[1] *sunt* MSS., Bt.[1], Heine, Ed.; *est* [dissensio] Unger, Bt.[2]
[2] *Rhodios* c, Edd.; *Rhodius* B H a b.

worse than refusing to set a man on his way: it is deliberately leading a man astray."

(55) "Can you say," answers Diogenes, "that he compelled you to purchase, when he did not even advise it? He advertised for sale what he did not like; you bought what you did like. If people are not considered guilty of swindling when they place upon their placards FOR SALE: A FINE VILLA, WELL BUILT, even when it is neither good nor properly built, still less guilty are they who say nothing in praise of their house. For where the purchaser may exercise his own judgment, what fraud can there be on the part of the vendor? But if, again, not all that is expressly stated has to be made good, do you think a man is bound to make good what has not been said? What, pray, would be more stupid than for a vendor to recount all the faults in the article he is offering for sale? And what would be so absurd as for an auctioneer to cry, at the owner's bidding, 'Here is an unsanitary house for sale'?"

56 In this way, then, in certain doubtful cases moral rectitude is defended on the one side, while on the other side the case of expediency is so presented as to make it appear not only morally right to do what seems expedient, but even morally wrong not to do it. This is the contradiction that seems often to arise between the expedient and the morally right. But I must give my decision in these two cases; for I did not propound them merely to raise the ques-

Cicero's decision in the cases.

57 tions, but to offer a solution. I think, then, that it was the duty of that grain-dealer not to keep back the facts from the Rhodians, and of this vendor of the house to deal in the same way with his purchaser. The fact is that merely holding one's peace about a

id ignorare emolumenti tui causa velis eos, quorum intersit id scire. Hoc autem celandi genus quale sit et cuius hominis, quis non videt? Certe non aperti, non simplicis, non ingenui, non iusti, non viri boni, versuti potius, obscuri, astuti, fallacis, malitiosi, callidi, veteratoris, vafri. Haec tot et alia plura nonne inutile est vitiorum subire nomina?

58 XIV. Quodsi vituperandi, qui reticuerunt, quid de iis existimandum est, qui orationis vanitatem adhibuerunt? C. Canius, eques Romanus, nec infacetus et satis litteratus, cum se Syracusas otiandi, ut ipse dicere solebat, non negotiandi causa contulisset, dictitabat [1] se hortulos aliquos emere velle, quo invitare amicos et ubi se oblectare sine interpellatoribus posset. Quod cum percrebruisset, Pythius ei quidam, qui argentariam faceret Syracusis, venales quidem se hortos non habere, sed licere uti Canio, si vellet, ut suis, et simul ad cenam hominem in hortos invitavit in posterum diem. Cum ille promisisset, tum Pythius, qui esset ut argentarius apud omnes ordines gratiosus, piscatores ad se convocavit et ab iis petivit, ut ante suos hortulos postridie piscarentur, dixitque, quid eos facere vellet. Ad cenam tempori [2] venit Canius; opipare a Pythio apparatum convivium, cumbarum ante oculos multitudo; pro se

[1] *dictitabat* c, Edd.; *dictabat* B H a b.
[2] *tempori* B H b, Bt.[1], Ed.; *tempore* a c; *temperi* Fl., Bt.[2], Heine.

thing does not constitute concealment, but concealment consists in trying for your own profit to keep others from finding out something that you know, when it is for their interest to know it. And who fails to discern what manner of concealment that is and what sort of person would be guilty of it? At all events he would be no candid or sincere or straightforward or upright or honest man, but rather one who is shifty, sly, artful, shrewd, underhand, cunning, one grown old in fraud and subtlety. Is it not inexpedient to subject oneself to all these terms of reproach and many more besides?

**Concealment of truth *vs.* misrepresentation and falsehood.**

58 XIV. If, then, they are to be blamed who suppress the truth, what are we to think of those who actually state what is false? Gaius Canius, a Roman knight, a man of considerable wit and literary culture, once went to Syracuse for a vacation, as he himself used to say, and not for business. He gave out that he had a mind to purchase a little country seat, where he could invite his friends and enjoy himself, uninterrupted by troublesome visitors. When this fact was spread abroad, one Pythius, a banker of Syracuse, informed him that he had such an estate; that it was not for sale, however, but Canius might make himself at home there, if he pleased; and at the same time he invited him to the estate to dinner next day. Canius accepted. Then Pythius, who, as might be expected of a money-lender, could command favours of all classes, called the fishermen together and asked them to do their fishing the next day out in front of his villa, and told them what he wished them to do. Canius came to dinner at the appointed hour; Pythius had a sumptuous banquet prepared; there was a whole

quisque, quod ceperat, afferebat, ante pedes Pythi pisces abiciebantur.

59 Tum Canius: "Quaeso," inquit, "quid est hoc, Pythi? tantumne piscium? tantumne cumbarum?"

Et ille: "Quid mirum?" inquit, "hoc loco est Syracusis quicquid est piscium, hic aquatio, hac villa isti carere non possunt."

Incensus Canius cupiditate contendit a Pythio, ut venderet; gravate ille primo; quid multa? impetrat. Emit homo cupidus et locuples tanti, quanti Pythius voluit, et emit instructos; nomina facit, negotium conficit. Invitat Canius postridie familiares suos, venit ipse mature; scalmum nullum videt, quaerit ex proximo vicino, num feriae quaedam piscatorum essent, quod eos nullos videret.

"Nullae, quod sciam," inquit; "sed hic piscari nulli solent; itaque heri mirabar, quid accidisset."

60 Stomachari Canius; sed quid faceret? nondum enim C. Aquilius, collega et familiaris meus, protulerat de dolo malo formulas; in quibus ipsis, cum ex eo quaereretur,[1] quid esset dolus malus, respondebat: cum esset aliud simulatum, aliud actum. Hoc quidem sane luculente ut ab homine perito definiendi. Ergo et Pythius et omnes aliud agentes, aliud simulantes

[1] *quaereretur* Edd., with authority; *quaererem* MSS.

fleet of boats before their eyes; each fisherman brought in in turn the catch that he had made; and the fishes were deposited at the feet of Pythius.

59 "Pray, Pythius," said Canius thereupon, "what does this mean?—all these fish?—all these boats?"

"No wonder," answered Pythius; "this is where all the fish in Syracuse are; here is where the fresh water comes from; the fishermen cannot get along without this estate."

Inflamed with desire for it, Canius insisted upon Pythius's selling it to him. At first he demurred. To make a long story short, Canius gained his point. The man was rich, and, in his desire to own the country seat, he paid for it all that Pythius asked; and he bought the entire equipment, too. Pythius entered the amount upon his ledger and completed the transfer. The next day Canius invited his friends; he came early himself. Not so much as a thole-pin was in sight. He asked his next-door neighbour whether it was a fishermen's holiday, for not a sign of them did he see.

"Not so far as I know," said he; "but none are in the habit of fishing here. And so I could not make out what was the matter yesterday."

60 Canius was furious; but what could he do? For not yet had my colleague and friend, Gaius Aquilius, introduced the established forms to apply to criminal fraud. When asked what he meant by "criminal fraud," as specified in these forms, he would reply: "Pretending one thing and practising another"—a very felicitous definition, as one might expect from an expert in making them. Pythius, therefore, and all others who do one thing while they pretend another are faithless, dishonest, and unprincipled

Criminal fraud.

perfidi, improbi, malitiosi. Nullum igitur eorum factum potest utile esse, cum sit tot vitiis inquinatum.

61 XV. Quodsi Aquiliana definitio vera est, ex omni vita simulatio dissimulatioque tollenda est. Ita, nec ut emat melius nec ut vendat, quicquam simulabit aut dissimulabit vir bonus. Atque [1] iste dolus malus et legibus erat vindicatus, ut tutela [2] duodecim tabulis, circumscriptio adulescentium lege Plaetoria, et sine lege iudiciis, in quibus additur EX FIDE BONA. Reliquorum autem iudiciorum haec verba maxime excellunt: in arbitrio rei uxoriae MELIUS AEQUIUS, in fiducia UT INTER BONOS BENE AGIER. Quid ergo? aut in eo, QUOD MELIUS AEQUIUS, potest ulla pars inesse fraudis? aut, cum dicitur INTER BONOS BENE AGIER, quicquam agi dolose aut malitiose potest? Dolus autem malus in simulatione, ut ait Aquilius, continetur. Tollendum est igitur ex rebus contrahendis omne mendacium; non illicitatorem [3] venditor, non, qui contra se liceatur, emptor apponet; uterque, si ad eloquendum venerit, non plus quam semel eloquetur.

62 Q. quidem Scaevola P. f., cum postulasset, ut sibi fundus, cuius emptor erat, semel indicaretur

[1] *Atque* MSS., Bt.[1], Müller, Heine; *Atqui* Manutius, Ed., Bt.[2]

[2] *ut tutela* MSS., Bt., Müller; *ut in tutela* Heine, Ed.

[3] *non illicitatorem* c (*inl.*) p, Edd.; *non licitatorem* B H a b.

---

[a] See § 70 below.

scoundrels. No act of theirs can be expedient, when what they do is tainted with so many vices.

61 XV. But if Aquilius's definition is correct, pretence and concealment should be done away with in all departments of our daily life. Then an honest man will not be guilty of either pretence or concealment in order to buy or to sell to better advantage. Besides, your "criminal fraud" had previously been prohibited by the statutes: the penalty in the matter of trusteeships, for example, is fixed by the Twelve Tables; for the defrauding of minors, by the Plaetorian law. The same prohibition is effective, without statutory enactment, in equity cases, in which it is added that the decision shall be "as good faith requires."[a] In all other cases in equity, moreover, the following phrases are most noteworthy: in a case calling for arbitration in the matter of a wife's dowry: what is "the fairer is the better"; in a suit for the restoration of a trust: "honest dealing, as between honest parties." Pray, then, can there be any element of fraud in what is adjusted for the "better and fairer"? Or can anything fraudulent or unprincipled be done, when "honest dealing between honest parties" is stipulated? But "criminal fraud," as Aquilius says, consists in false pretence. We must, therefore, keep misrepresentation entirely out of business transactions: the seller will not engage a bogus bidder to run prices up nor the buyer one to bid low against himself to keep them down; and each, if they come to naming a price, will state once for all what he will give or take.

Criminal fraud and the law.

Criminal fraud in the light of moral rectitude.

62 Why, when Quintus Scaevola, the son of Publius Scaevola, asked that the price of a farm that he desired to purchase be definitely named and the

idque venditor ita fecisset, dixit se pluris aestimare; addidit centum milia. Nemo est, qui hoc viri boni fuisse neget, sapientis negant, ut si minoris, quam potuisset, vendidisset. Haec igitur est illa pernicies, quod alios bonos, alios sapientes existimant. Ex quo Ennius "nequiquam sapere sapientem, qui ipse sibi prodesse non quiret." Vere id quidem, si, quid esset "prodesse," mihi cum Ennio conveniret.

Medea, Vahlen² 273.

63 Hecatonem quidem Rhodium, discipulum Panaeti, video in iis libris, quos de officio scripsit Q. Tuberoni, dicere "sapientis esse nihil contra mores, leges, instituta facientem habere rationem rei familiaris. Neque enim solum nobis divites esse volumus, sed liberis, propinquis, amicis maximeque rei publicae. Singulorum enim facultates et copiae divitiae sunt civitatis." Huic[1] Scaevolae factum, de quo paulo ante dixi, placere nullo modo potest; etenim omnino tantum se negat facturum compendii sui causa, quod non liceat. Huic nec laus magna tribuenda nec gratia est.

64 Sed, sive et simulatio et dissimulatio dolus malus est, perpaucae res sunt, in quibus non dolus malus

[1] *Huic* c, Edd.; *Huius* B H a b.

vendor named it, he replied that he considered it worth more, and paid him 100,000 sesterces over and above what he asked. No one could say that this was not the act of an honest man; but people do say that it was not the act of a worldly-wise man, any more than if he had sold for a smaller amount than he could have commanded. Here, then, is that mischievous idea—the world accounting some men upright, others wise; and it is this fact that gives Ennius occasion to say:

> "In vain is the wise man wise, who cannot benefit himself."

And Ennius is quite right, if only he and I were agreed upon the meaning of "benefit."

63 Now I observe that Hecaton of Rhodes, a pupil of Panaetius, says in his books on "Moral Duty" dedicated to Quintus Tubero that "it is a wise man's duty to take care of his private interests, at the same time doing nothing contrary to the civil customs, laws, and institutions. But that depends on our purpose in seeking prosperity; for we do not aim to be rich for ourselves alone but for our children, relatives, friends, and, above all, for our country. For the private fortunes of individuals are the wealth of the state." Hecaton could not for a moment approve of Scaevola's act, which I cited a moment ago; for he openly avows that he will abstain from doing for his own profit only what the law expressly forbids. Such a man deserves no great praise nor gratitude.

The standard of selfishness.

64 Be that as it may, if both pretence and concealment constitute "criminal fraud," there are very few transactions into which "criminal fraud" does

iste versetur, sive vir bonus est is, qui prodest, quibus potest, nocet nemini, certe [1] istum [2] virum bonum non facile reperimus.

Numquam igitur est utile peccare, quia semper est turpe, et, quia semper est honestum virum bonum esse, semper est utile.

65 XVI. Ac de iure quidem praediorum sanctum apud nos est iure civili, ut in iis vendendis vitia dicerentur, quae nota essent venditori. Nam, cum ex duodecim tabulis satis esset ea praestari, quae essent lingua nuncupata, quae qui infitiatus esset, dupli poenam subiret, a iuris consultis etiam reticentiae poena est constituta; quicquid enim esset [3] in praedio vitii, id statuerunt, si venditor sciret, nisi nomina-
66 tim dictum esset, praestari oportere. Ut, cum in arce augurium augures acturi essent iussissentque Ti.[4] Claudium Centumalum, qui aedes in Caelio monte habebat, demoliri ea, quorum altitudo officeret auspiciis, Claudius proscripsit insulam [vendidit],[5] emit P. Calpurnius Lanarius. Huic ab auguribus illud idem denuntiatum est. Itaque Calpurnius cum demolitus esset cognossetque Claudium aedes postea proscripsisse, quam esset ab auguribus demoliri

[1] *certe* Lamb., Edd.; *recte* MSS.
[2] *istum* p c, Edd.; *iustum* B H a b.
[3] *esset* p c, Edd.; *est* B H a b.
[4] *Ti.* Lange, Edd.; *titum* MSS.
[5] *vendidit* B H a b; *et vendidit* p c; Edd. omit.

not enter; or, if he only is a good man who helps all he can, and harms no one, it will certainly be no easy matter for us to find the good man as thus defined.

To conclude, then, it is never expedient to do wrong, because wrong is always immoral; and it is always expedient to be good, because goodness is always moral.

Concealment of truth about real estate prohibited by law.

65 XVI. In the laws pertaining to the sale of real property it is stipulated in our civil code that when a transfer of any real estate is made, all its defects shall be declared as far as they are known to the vendor. According to the laws of the Twelve Tables it used to be sufficient that such faults as had been expressly declared should be made good and that for any flaws which the vendor expressly denied, when questioned, he should be assessed double damages. A like penalty for failure to make such declaration also has now been secured by our jurisconsults: they have decided that any defect in a piece of real estate, if known to the vendor but not expressly
66 stated, must be made good by him. For example, the augurs were proposing to take observations from the citadel and they ordered Tiberius Claudius Centumalus, who owned a house upon the Caelian Hill, to pull down such parts of the building as obstructed the augurs' view by reason of their height. Claudius at once advertised his block for sale, and Publius Calpurnius Lanarius bought it. The same notice was served also upon him. And so, when Calpurnius had pulled down those parts of the building and discovered that Claudius had advertised it for sale only after the augurs had ordered them to be pulled down, he summoned the former owner before a court

iussus, arbitrum illum adegit, QUICQUID SIBI DARE FACERE OPORTERET EX FIDE BONA. M. Cato sententiam dixit, huius nostri Catonis pater (ut enim ceteri ex patribus, sic hic, qui illud lumen progenuit, ex filio est nominandus)—is igitur iudex ita pronuntiavit: "cum in vendendo rem eam scisset et non pronuntiasset, emptori damnum praestari oportere."

67 Ergo ad fidem bonam statuit pertinere notum esse emptori vitium, quod nosset venditor. Quod si recte iudicavit, non recte frumentarius ille, non recte aedium pestilentium venditor tacuit. Sed huius modi reticentiae iure civili comprehendi [1] non possunt; quae autem possunt, diligenter tenentur. M. Marius Gratidianus, propinquus noster, C. Sergio Oratae vendiderat aedes eas, quas ab eodem ipse paucis ante annis emerat. Eae serviebant,[2] sed hoc in mancipio Marius non dixerat. Adducta res in iudicium est. Oratam Crassus, Gratidianum defendebat Antonius. Ius Crassus urguebat, "quod vitii venditor non dixisset sciens, id oportere praestari," aequitatem Antonius, "quoniam id vitium

[1] *comprehendi* MSS.; *omnes comprehendi* Bt., Heine.
[2] *serviebant* Heus., Edd.; *sergio serviebant* B H a b; *sergio alii serviebant* c.

of equity to decide "what indemnity the owner was under obligation 'in good faith' to pay and deliver to him." The verdict was pronounced by Marcus Cato, the father of our Cato (for as other men receive a distinguishing name from their fathers, so he who bestowed upon the world so bright a luminary must have his distinguishing name from his son); he, as I was saying, was presiding judge and pronounced the verdict that "since the augurs' mandate was known to the vendor at the time of making the transfer and since he had not made it known, he was bound to make good the purchaser's loss."

**Scope of Cato's decision.**

67 With this verdict he established the principle that it was essential to good faith that any defect known to the vendor must be made known to the purchaser. If his decision was right, our grain-dealer and the vendor of the unsanitary house did not do right to suppress the facts in those cases. But the civil code cannot be made to include all cases where facts are thus suppressed; but those cases which it does include are summarily dealt with. Marcus Marius Gratidianus, a kinsman of ours, sold back to Gaius Sergius Orata the house which he himself had bought a few years before from that same Orata. It was subject to an encumbrance, but Marius had said nothing about this fact in stating the terms of sale. The case was carried to the courts. Crassus was counsel for Orata; Antonius was retained by Gratidianus. Crassus pleaded the letter of the law that "the vendor was bound to make good the defect, for he had not declared it, although he was aware of it"; Antonius laid stress upon the equity of the case, pleading that, "inasmuch as the defect in question had not been unknown to Sergius (for it was the

ignotum Sergio non fuisset, qui illas aedes vendidisset, nihil fuisse necesse dici, nec eum esse deceptum, qui, id, quod emerat, quo iure esset, teneret."

68 Quorsus haec? Ut illud intellegas, non placuisse maioribus nostris astutos.

XVII. Sed aliter leges, aliter philosophi tollunt astutias, leges, quatenus manu tenere possunt, philosophi, quatenus ratione et intellegentia. Ratio ergo hoc postulat, ne quid insidiose, ne quid simulate, ne quid fallaciter. Suntne igitur insidiae tendere plagas, etiamsi excitaturus non sis nec agitaturus? ipsae enim ferae nullo insequente saepe incidunt. Sic tu aedes proscribas, tabulam tamquam plagam ponas, [domum propter vitia vendas,] [1] in eam aliquis incurrat imprudens?

69 Hoc quamquam video propter depravationem consuetudinis neque more turpe haberi neque aut lege sanciri aut iure civili, tamen naturae lege sanctum est. Societas est enim (quod etsi saepe dictum est, dicendum est tamen saepius), latissime quidem quae pateat, omnium inter omnes, interior eorum, qui eiusdem gentis sint, propior eorum, qui eiusdem civitatis. Itaque maiores aliud ius gentium, aliud ius civile esse voluerunt; quod civile, non

[1] Bracketed by Unger, Edd.

same house that he had sold to Marius), no declaration of it was needed, and in purchasing it back he had not been imposed upon, for he knew to what legal liability his purchase was subject."

68 What is the purpose of these illustrations? To let you see that our forefathers did not countenance sharp practice.

**Law vs. philosophy in dealing with knavery.**

XVII. Now the law disposes of sharp practices in one way, philosophers in another: the law deals with them as far as it can lay its strong arm upon them; philosophers, as far as they can be apprehended by reason and conscience. Now reason demands that nothing be done with unfairness, with false pretence, or with misrepresentation. Is it not deception, then, to set snares, even if one does not mean to start the game or to drive it into them? Why, wild creatures often fall into snares undriven and unpursued. Could one in the same way advertise a house for sale, post up a notice "To be sold," like a snare, and have somebody run into it unsuspecting?

**Civil law vs. moral law.**

69 Owing to the low ebb of public sentiment, such a method of procedure, I find, is neither by custom accounted morally wrong nor forbidden either by statute or by civil law; nevertheless it is forbidden by the moral law. For there is a bond of fellowship—although I have often made this statement, I must still repeat it again and again—which has the very widest application, uniting all men together and each to each. This bond of union is closer between those who belong to the same nation, and more intimate still between those who are citizens of the same city-state. It is for this reason that our forefathers chose to understand one thing by the universal law and another by the civil law. The

idem continuo gentium, quod autem gentium, idem civile esse debet. Sed nos veri iuris germanaeque iustitiae solidam et expressam effigiem nullam tenemus, umbra et imaginibus utimur. Eas ipsas utinam sequeremur! feruntur enim ex optimis naturae et
70 veritatis exemplis. Nam quanti verba illa: UTI NE PROPTER TE FIDEMVE TUAM CAPTUS FRAUDATUSVE SIM! quam illa aurea: UT INTER BONOS BENE AGIER OPORTET ET SINE FRAUDATIONE! Sed, qui sint "boni," et quid sit "bene agi," magna quaestio est.

Q. quidem Scaevola, pontifex maximus, summam vim esse dicebat in omnibus iis arbitriis, in quibus adderetur EX FIDE BONA, fideique bonae nomen existimabat manare latissime, idque versari in tutelis societatibus, fiduciis mandatis, rebus emptis venditis, conductis locatis, quibus vitae societas contineretur; in iis magni esse iudicis statuere, praesertim cum in plerisque essent iudicia contraria, quid quemque cuique praestare oporteret.

71 Quocirca astutiae tollendae sunt eaque malitia, quae volt illa quidem videri se esse prudentiam, sed abest ab ea distatque plurimum. Prudentia est enim locata in dilectu bonorum et malorum, malitia, si omnia, quae turpia sunt, mala sunt, mala bonis ponit ante.

civil law is not necessarily also the universal law; but the universal law ought to be also the civil law. But we possess no substantial, life-like image of true Law and genuine Justice; a mere outline sketch is all that we enjoy. I only wish that we were true even to this; for, even as it is, it is drawn from the excellent models which Nature and Truth afford.

"Good faith" in performance of contracts.

70 For how weighty are the words: "That I be not deceived and defrauded through you and my confidence in you"! How precious are these: "As between honest people there ought to be honest dealing, and no deception"! But who are "honest people," and what is "honest dealing"—these are serious questions.

It was Quintus Scaevola, the pontifex maximus, who used to attach the greatest importance to all questions of arbitration to which the formula was appended "as good faith requires"; and he held that the expression "good faith" had a very extensive application, for it was employed in trusteeships and partnerships, in trusts and commissions, in buying and selling, in hiring and letting—in a word, in all the transactions on which the social relations of daily life depend; in these, he said, it required a judge of great ability to decide the extent of each individual's obligation to the other, especially when counter-claims were admissible in most cases.

71 Away, then, with sharp practice and trickery, which desires, of course, to pass for wisdom, but is far from it and totally unlike it. For the function of wisdom is to discriminate between good and evil; whereas, inasmuch as all things morally wrong are evil, trickery prefers the evil to the good.

Nec vero in praediis solum ius civile ductum a natura malitiam fraudemque vindicat, sed etiam in mancipiorum venditione venditoris fraus omnis excluditur. Qui enim scire debuit de sanitate, de fuga, de furtis, praestat edicto aedilium. Heredum alia causa est.

72 Ex quo intellegitur, quoniam iuris natura fons sit, hoc secundum naturam esse, neminem id agere, ut ex alterius praedetur inscitia. Nec ulla pernicies vitae maior inveniri potest quam in malitia simulatio intellegentiae; ex quo ista innumerabilia nascuntur, ut utilia cum honestis pugnare videantur. Quotus enim quisque reperietur, qui impunitate et ignoratione omnium proposita abstinere possit iniuria?

73 XVIII. Periclitemur, si placet, et in iis quidem exemplis, in quibus peccari volgus hominum fortasse non putet. Neque enim de sicariis, veneficis, testamentariis, furibus, peculatoribus hoc loco disserendum est, qui non verbis sunt et disputatione philosophorum, sed vinclis et carcere fatigandi, sed haec[1] consideremus, quae faciunt ii, qui habentur boni.

L. Minuci Basili, locupletis hominis, falsum testamentum quidam e Graecia Romam attulerunt. Quod

[1] *haec* c, Edd.; *hoc* B H a b.

It is not only in the case of real estate transfers that the civil law, based upon a natural feeling for the right, punishes trickery and deception, but also in the sale of slaves every form of deception on the vendor's part is disallowed. For by the aediles' ruling the vendor is answerable for any deficiency in the slave he sells, for he is supposed to know if his slave is sound, or if he is a runaway, or a thief. The case of those who have just come into the possession of slaves by inheritance is different.

72 From this we come to realize that since Nature is the source of right, it is not in accord with Nature that anyone should take advantage of his neighbour's ignorance. And no greater curse in life can be found than knavery that wears the mask of wisdom. Thence come those countless cases in which the expedient seems to conflict with the right. For how few will be found who can refrain from wrong-doing, if assured of the power to keep it an absolute secret and to run no risk of punishment! **Cunning is not wisdom.**

73 XVIII. Let us put our principle to the test, if you please, and see if it holds good in those instances in which, perhaps, the world in general finds no wrong; for in this connection we do not need to discuss cut-throats, poisoners, forgers of wills, thieves, and embezzlers of public moneys, who should be repressed not by lectures and discussions of philosophers, but by chains and prison walls; but let us study here the conduct of those who have the reputation of being honest men.

Certain individuals brought from Greece to Rome a forged will, purporting to be that of the wealthy

quo facilius optinerent, scripserunt heredes secum
M. Crassum et Q. Hortensium, homines eiusdem
aetatis potentissimos; qui cum illud falsum esse
suspicarentur, sibi autem nullius essent conscii
culpae, alieni facinoris munusculum non repudiaverunt. Quid ergo? satin est hoc, ut non deliquisse
videantur? Mihi quidem non videtur, quamquam
alterum vivum amavi, alterum non odi mortuum;
74 sed, cum Basilus M. Satrium, sororis filium, nomen
suum ferre voluisset eumque fecisset heredem (hunc
dico patronum agri Piceni et Sabini; o turpem
notam temporum [nomen illorum]!),[1] non erat aequum
principes civis rem habere, ad Satrium nihil praeter
nomen pervenire. Etenim, si is, qui non defendit
iniuriam neque propulsat,[2] cum potest, iniuste facit,
§ 23. ut in primo libro disserui, qualis habendus est is, qui
non modo non repellit, set etiam adiuvat iniuriam?
Mihi quidem etiam verae hereditates non honestae
videntur, si sunt malitiosis blanditiis, officiorum non
veritate, sed simulatione quaesitae.

Atqui in talibus rebus aliud utile interdum, aliud
75 honestum videri solet. Falso; nam eadem utilitatis,
(75) quae honestatis, est regula. Qui hoc non perviderit,

[1] *turpem notam temporum nomen illorum* H a (*turpe*) b, Bt.; excl. *nomen illorum* Victorius, Ed.; *turpe nomen illorum temporum* c.

[2] *propulsat* cod. Bern., O., Edd.; *propulsat a suis* Edd.

---

[a] The shame was that states enjoying the rights of Roman citizenship should need a patron to protect their interests in the Roman capital.

Lucius Minucius Basilus. The more easily to procure validity for it, they made joint-heirs with themselves two of the most influential men of the day, Marcus Crassus and Quintus Hortensius. Although these men suspected that the will was a forgery, still, as they were conscious of no personal guilt in the matter, they did not spurn the miserable boon procured through the crime of others. What shall we say, then? Is this excuse competent to acquit them of guilt? I cannot think so, although I loved the one while he lived, and do not hate the other now
74 that he is dead. Be that as it may, Basilus had in fact desired that his nephew Marcus Satrius should bear his name and inherit his property. (I refer to the Satrius who is the present patron of Picenum and the Sabine country—and oh, what a shameful stigma it is upon the times! [a]) And therefore it was not right that two of the leading citizens of Rome should take the estate and Satrius succeed to nothing except his uncle's name. For if he does wrong who does not ward off and repel injury when he can—as I explained in the course of the First Book—what is to be thought of the man who not only does not try to prevent wrong, but actually aids and abets it? For my part, I do not believe that even genuine legacies are moral, if they are sought after by designing flatteries and by attentions hypocritical rather than sincere.

**The same standard for expediency as for moral rectitude.**

And yet in such cases there are times when one course is likely to appear expedient and another
75 morally right. The appearance is deceptive; for our standard is the same for expediency and for
(75) moral rectitude. And the man who does not accept the truth of this will be capable of any sort of dis-

ab hoc nulla fraus aberit, nullum facinus. Sic enim cogitans: "Est istuc quidem honestum, verum hoc expedit," res a natura copulatas audebit errore divellere, qui fons est fraudium, maleficiorum, scelerum omnium.

XIX. Itaque, si vir bonus habeat hanc vim, ut, si digitis concrepuerit, possit in locupletium testamenta nomen eius inrepere, hac vi non utatur, ne si exploratum quidem habeat id omnino neminem umquam suspicaturum. At dares hanc vim M. Crasso, ut digitorum percussione heres posset scriptus esse, qui re vera non esset heres, in foro, mihi crede, saltaret. Homo autem iustus isque, quem sentimus virum bonum, nihil cuiquam, quod in se transferat, detrahet. Hoc qui admiratur, is se, quid sit vir bonus,
76 nescire fateatur. At vero, si qui voluerit animi sui complicatam notionem evolvere, iam se ipse doceat eum virum bonum esse, qui prosit, quibus possit, noceat nemini nisi lacessitus iniuria. Quid ergo? hic non noceat, qui quodam quasi veneno perficiat, ut veros heredes moveat, in eorum locum ipse succedat? "Non igitur faciat," dixerit quis, "quod utile sit, quod expediat?" Immo intellegat nihil nec

[a] The Platonic doctrine of ideas known in a previous existence and gradually developing into renewed consciousness. Learning is but a remembering of what the soul has known before.

honesty, any sort of crime. For if he reasons, "That is, to be sure, the right course, but this course brings advantage," he will not hesitate in his mistaken judgment to divorce two conceptions that Nature has made one; and that spirit opens the door to all sorts of dishonesty, wrong-doing, and crime.

XIX. Suppose, then, that a good man had such power that at a snap of his fingers his name could steal into rich men's wills, he would not avail himself of that power—no, not even though he could be perfectly sure that no one would ever suspect it. Suppose, on the other hand, that one were to offer a Marcus Crassus the power, by the mere snapping of his fingers, to get himself named as heir, when he was not really an heir, he would, I warrant you, dance in the forum. But the righteous man, the one whom we feel to be a good man, would never rob anyone of anything to enrich himself. If anybody is astonished at this doctrine, let him confess

The good man not tempted to unrighteous gain.

76 that he does not know what a good man is. If, on the other hand, anyone should desire to unfold the idea of a good man which lies wrapped up in his own mind,[a] he would then at once make it clear to himself that a good man is one who helps all whom he can and harms nobody, unless provoked by wrong. What shall we say, then? Would he not be doing harm who by a kind of magic spell should succeed in displacing the real heirs to an estate and pushing himself into their place? "Well," someone may say, "is he not to do what is expedient, what is advantageous to himself?" Nay, verily; he should rather be brought to realize that nothing that is unjust is either advantageous or expedient; if he does not

Who is the good man?

expedire nec utile esse, quod sit iniustum; hoc qui non didicerit, bonus vir esse non poterit.

77 *C.*[1] Fimbriam consularem audiebam de patre nostro puer iudicem M. Lutatio Pinthiae fuisse, equiti Romano sane honesto, cum is sponsionem fecisset, NI VIR BONUS ESSET. Itaque ei dixisse Fimbriam se illam rem numquam iudicaturum, ne aut spoliaret fama probatum hominem, si contra iudicavisset, aut statuisse videretur virum bonum esse aliquem, cum ea res innumerabilibus officiis et laudibus contineretur.

Huic igitur viro bono, quem Fimbria etiam, non modo Socrates noverat, nullo modo videri potest quicquam esse utile, quod non honestum sit. Itaque talis vir non modo facere, sed ne cogitare quidem quicquam audebit, quod non audeat praedicare. Haec non turpe est dubitare philosophos, quae ne rustici quidem dubitent? a quibus natum est id, quod iam contritum est vetustate, proverbium. Cum enim fidem alicuius bonitatemque laudant, dignum esse dicunt, "quicum in tenebris mices." Hoc quam habet vim nisi illam, nihil expedire, quod

[1] *C.* Bt., Ed., Heine; not in MSS.

learn this lesson, it will never be possible for him to be a "good man."

77 When I was a boy, I used to hear my father tell that Gaius Fimbria, an ex-consul, was judge in a case of Marcus Lutatius Pinthia, a Roman knight of irreproachable character. On that occasion Pinthia had laid a wager to be forfeited "if he did not prove in court that he was a good man." Fimbria declared that he would never render a decision in such a case, for fear that he might either rob a reputable man of his good name, if he decided against him, or be thought to have pronounced someone a good man, when such a character is, as he said, established by the performance of countless duties and the possession of praiseworthy qualities without number.

To this type of good man, then, known not only to a Socrates but even to a Fimbria, nothing can possibly seem expedient that is not morally right. Such a man, therefore, will never venture to think —to say nothing of doing—anything that he would not dare openly to proclaim. Is it not a shame that philosophers should be in doubt about moral questions on which even peasants have no doubts at all? For it is with peasants that the proverb, already trite with age, originated: when they praise a man's honour and honesty, they say, "He is a man with whom you can safely play at odd and even [a] in the dark." What is the point of the proverb but this—that what is not proper brings no advantage, even if you can gain your

To a good man moral wrong is never expedient.

[a] Lit. 'flash with the fingers'; shoot out some fingers, the number of which had to be guessed.

non deceat, etiamsi id possis nullo refellente optinere?

78 Videsne hoc proverbio neque Gygi illi posse veniam dari neque huic, quem paulo ante fingebam digitorum percussione hereditates omnium posse converrere? Ut enim, quod turpe est, id, quamvis occultetur, tamen honestum fieri nullo modo potest, sic, quod honestum non est, id utile ut sit, effici non potest adversante et repugnante natura.

79 XX. At enim, cum permagna praemia sunt, est causa peccandi.

C. Marius cum a spe consulatus longe abesset et iam[1] septimum annum post praeturam iaceret, neque petiturus umquam consulatum videretur, Q. Metellum, cuius legatus erat, summum virum et civem, cum ab eo, imperatore suo, Romam missus esset, apud populum Romanum criminatus est bellum illum ducere; si se consulem fecissent, brevi tempore aut vivum aut mortuum Iugurtham se in potestatem populi Romani redacturum. Itaque factus est ille quidem consul, sed a fide iustitiaque discessit, qui optimum et gravissimum civem, cuius legatus et a quo missus esset, in invidiam falso crimine adduxerit.

80 Ne noster quidem Gratidianus officio viri boni

[1] *et iam* Edd.; *etiam* MSS.

end without anyone's being able to convict you of wrong?

78 Do you not see that in the light of this proverb no excuse is available either for the Gyges of the story or for the man who I assumed a moment ago could with a snap of his fingers sweep together everybody's inheritance at once? For as the morally wrong cannot by any possibility be made morally right, however successfully it may be covered up, so what is not morally right cannot be made expedient, for Nature refuses and resists.

79 XX. "But stay," someone will object, "when the prize is very great, there is excuse for doing wrong." The moral loss that comes from wrong ambitions:

Gaius Marius had been left in obscurity for more than six whole years after his praetorship and had scarcely the remotest hope of gaining the consulship. It looked as if he would never even be a candidate for that office. He was now a lieutenant under Quintus Metellus, who sent him on a furlough to Rome. There before the Roman People he accused his own general, an eminent man and one of our first citizens, of purposely protracting the war and declared that if they would make him consul, he would within a short time deliver Jugurtha alive or dead into the hands of the Roman People. And so he was elected consul, it is true, but he was a traitor to his own good faith and to justice; for by a false charge he subjected to popular disfavour an exemplary and highly respected citizen, and that too, although he was his lieutenant and under leave of absence from him. (1) Marius,

80 Even our kinsman Gratidianus failed on one occa- (2) Gratidianus,

functus est tum, cum praetor esset collegiumque praetorium tribuni plebi adhibuissent, ut res nummaria de communi sententia constitueretur; iactabatur enim temporibus illis nummus sic, ut nemo posset scire, quid haberet. Conscripserunt communiter edictum cum poena atque iudicio constitueruntque, ut omnes simul in rostra post meridiem escenderent. Et ceteri quidem alius alio, Marius ab subselliis in rostra recta idque, quod communiter compositum fuerat, solus edixit. Et ea res, si quaeris, ei magno honori fuit; omnibus vicis statuae, ad eas tus, cerei; quid multa? nemo umquam multitudini fuit carior.

81 Haec sunt, quae conturbent in deliberatione non numquam, cum id, in quo violatur aequitas, non ita magnum, illud autem, quod ex eo paritur, permagnum videtur, ut Mario praeripere collegis et tribunis plebi popularem gratiam non ita turpe, consulem ob eam rem fieri, quod sibi tum proposuerat, valde utile videbatur. Sed omnium una regula est, quam tibi cupio esse notissimam, aut illud, quod utile videtur, turpe ne sit aut, si turpe est, ne videatur esse utile.

---

[a] Gratidianus's.

[b] Never attained, however. For his conspicuous position as a popular leader made him an early mark for Sulla's proscriptions.

sion to perform what would be a good man's duty: in his praetorship the tribunes of the people summoned the college of praetors to council, in order to adopt by joint resolution a standard of value for our currency; for at that time the value of money was so fluctuating that no one could tell how much he was worth. In joint session they drafted an ordinance, defining the penalty and the methods of procedure in cases of violation of the ordinance, and agreed that they should all appear together upon the rostra in the afternoon to publish it. And while all the rest withdrew, some in one direction, some in another, Marius (Gratidianus) went straight from the council-chamber to the rostra and published individually what had been drawn up by all together. And that coup, if you care to know, brought him vast honour; in every street statues of him were erected; before these incense and candles burned. In a word, no one ever enjoyed greater popularity with the masses.

**No material gain can compensate for moral loss.**

81 It is such cases as these that sometimes perplex us in our consideration, when the point in which justice is violated does not seem so very significant, but the consequences of such slight transgression seem exceedingly important. For example, it was not so very wrong morally, in the eyes of Marius,[a] to overreach his colleagues and the tribunes in turning to himself alone all the credit with the people; but to secure by that means his election to the consulship, which was then the goal of his ambition,[b] seemed very greatly to his interest. But for all cases we have one rule, with which I desire you to be perfectly familiar: that which seems expedient must not be morally wrong; or, if it is morally wrong, it

Quod igitur? possumusne aut illum Marium virum bonum iudicare aut hunc?[1] Explica atque excute intellegentiam tuam, ut videas, quae sit in ea [species] forma[2] et notio viri boni. Cadit ergo in virum bonum mentiri emolumenti sui causa, criminari, praeripere, fallere? Nihil profecto minus.

82 Est ergo ulla res tanti aut commodum ullum tam expetendum, ut viri boni et splendorem et nomen amittas? Quid est, quod afferre tantum utilitas ista, quae dicitur, possit, quantum auferre, si boni viri nomen eripuerit, fidem iustitiamque detraxerit? Quid enim interest, utrum ex homine se convertat quis in beluam an hominis figura immanitatem gerat beluae?

XXI. Quid? qui omnia recta et honesta neglegunt, dum modo potentiam consequantur, nonne idem faciunt, quod is, qui etiam socerum habere voluit eum, cuius ipse audacia potens esset? Utile ei videbatur plurimum posse alterius invidia; id quam iniustum in patriam et quam turpe esset, non videbat. Ipse autem socer in ore semper Graecos versus de Phoenissis habebat, quos dicam, ut potero, incondite fortasse, sed tamen, ut res possit intellegi:

[1] *aut hunc* c, Edd.; *atque hunc* B H a b.
[2] *ea species forma* B H a b; *ea specie forma* c p; *ea forma* Klotz, Heine, Ed.; *ea species* Bt.

---

[a] Pompey, who in 59 married Caesar's daughter Julia, twenty-four years his junior, and already betrothed to Caepio.

must not seem expedient. What follows? Can we account either the great Marius or our Marius Gratidianus a good man? Work out your own ideas and sift your thoughts so as to see what conception and idea of a good man they contain. Pray, tell me, does it coincide with the character of your good man to lie for his own profit, to slander, to overreach, to deceive? Nay, verily; anything but that!

82 Is there, then, any object of such value or any advantage so worth the winning that, to gain it, one should sacrifice the name of a "good man" and the lustre of his reputation? What is there that your so-called expediency can bring to you that will compensate for what it can take away, if it steals from you the name of a "good man" and causes you to lose your sense of honour and justice? For what difference does it make whether a man is actually transformed into a beast or whether, keeping the outward appearance of a man, he has the savage nature of a beast within?

XXI. Again, when people disregard everything that is morally right and true, if only they may secure power thereby, are they not pursuing the same course as he [a] who wished to have as a father-in-law the man by whose effrontery he might gain power for himself? He thought it advantageous to secure supreme power while the odium of it fell upon another; and he failed to see how unjust to his country this was, and how wrong morally. But the father-in-law himself used to have continually upon his lips the Greek verses from the Phoenissae, which I will reproduce as well as I can—awkwardly, it may be, but still so that the meaning can be understood:

(3) Pompey

(4) Caesar.

ur. Phoen. 24-625.

Nam sí violandum est iús, regnandi grátia
Violándum est; aliis rébus pietatém colas.

Capitalis [Eteocles vel potius Euripides],[1] qui id unum, quod omnium sceleratissimum fuerit, exce-
83 perit! Quid igitur minuta colligimus, hereditates, mercaturas, venditiones fraudulentas? ecce tibi, qui rex populi Romani dominusque omnium gentium esse concupiverit idque perfecerit! Hanc cupiditatem si honestam quis esse dicit, amens est; probat enim legum et libertatis interitum earumque oppressionem taetram et detestabilem gloriosam putat. Qui autem fatetur honestum non esse in ea civitate, quae libera fuerit quaeque [2] esse debeat, regnare, sed ei, qui id facere possit, esse utile, qua hunc obiurgatione aut quo potius convicio a tanto errore coner avellere? Potest enim, di immortales! cuiquam esse utile foedissimum et taeterrimum parricidium patriae, quamvis is, qui se eo obstrinxerit, ab oppressis civibus parens nominetur? Honestate igitur dirigenda [3] utilitas est, et quidem sic, ut haec duo verbo inter se discrepare, re unum sonare videantur.

84 Non habeo, ad volgi opinionem quae maior utilitas quam regnandi esse possit; nihil contra inutilius ei, qui id iniuste consecutus sit, invenio, cum ad veritatem

[1] Bracketed by Ed., Heine, et al.
[2] *fuerit quaeque* c, Edd.; *fuit* B H a b.
[3] *dirigenda* MSS., Edd. plerique; *derigenda* Ed.

---

[a] From A. S. Way's translation.
[b] The title bestowed on Cicero for saving the republic (in 63) and on Caesar for overthrowing it (after the battle of Munda, in 45).

"If wrong may e'er be right, for a throne's sake
Were wrong most right:—be God in all else
feared!"[a]

Our tyrant deserved his death for having made an exception of the one thing that was the blackest
83 crime of all. Why do we gather instances of petty crime—legacies criminally obtained and fraudulent buying and selling? Behold, here you have a man who was ambitious to be king of the Roman People and master of the whole world; and he achieved it! The man who maintains that such an ambition is morally right is a madman; for he justifies the destruction of law and liberty and thinks their hideous and detestable suppression glorious. But if anyone agrees that it is not morally right to be king in a state that once was free and that ought to be free now, and yet imagines that it is advantageous for him who can reach that position, with what remonstrance or rather with what appeal should I try to tear him away from so strange a delusion? For, oh ye immortal gods! can the most horrible and hideous of all murders—that of fatherland—bring advantage to anybody, even though he who has committed such a crime receives from his enslaved fellow-citizens the title of "Father of his Country"?[b] Expediency, therefore, must be measured by the standard of moral rectitude, and in such a way, too, that these two words shall seem in sound only to be different but in real meaning to be one and the same.

Even to gain a throne by moral wrong is not expedient.

Identity of expediency and moral rectitude.

84 What greater advantage one could have, according to the standard of popular opinion, than to be a king, I do not know; when, however, I begin to bring the question back to the standard of truth, then I find nothing more disadvantageous for one who has risen to

coepi revocare rationem. Possunt enim cuiquam esse utiles angores, sollicitudines, diurni et nocturni metus, vita insidiarum periculorumque plenissima?

*Inc. Fab.*, Ribbeck[2], 651.

Múlti iniqui atque ínfideles régno, pauci bénivoli,[1]

inquit Accius. At cui regno? Quod a Tantalo et Pelope proditum iure optinebatur. Nam quanto pluris ei regi putas, qui exercitu populi Romani populum ipsum Romanum oppressisset civitatemque non modo liberam, sed etiam gentibus imperantem servire sibi
85 coëgisset? Hunc tu quas conscientiae labes in animo censes habuisse, quae vulnera? Cuius autem vita ipsi potest utilis esse, cum eius vitae ea condicio sit, ut, qui illam eripuerit, in maxima et gratia futurus sit et gloria? Quodsi haec utilia non sunt, quae maxime videntur, quia plena sunt dedecoris ac turpitudinis, satis persuasum esse debet nihil esse utile, quod non honestum sit.

86 XXII. Quamquam id quidem cum saepe alias, tum Pyrrhi bello a C. Fabricio consule iterum et a senatu nostro iudicatum est. Cum enim rex Pyrrhus populo Romano bellum ultro intulisset, cumque de imperio certamen esset cum rege generoso ac potenti,[2] perfuga ab eo venit in castra Fabrici eique est pollicitus, si praemium sibi proposuisset, se, ut clam venisset, sic clam in Pyrrhi castra rediturum et eum veneno ne-

[1] *beni(e)voli* Stürenbg.; *benivoli sunt* c; *boni sunt* B H a b.
[2] *potenti* Nonius, Edd.; *potente* MSS.

that height by injustice. For can occasions for worry, anxiety, fear by day and by night, and a life all beset with plots and perils be of advantage to anybody?

> "Thrones have many foes and friends untrue,
> but few devoted friends,"

says Accius. But of what sort of throne was he speaking? Why, one that was held by right, handed down from Tantalus and Pelops. Aye, but how many more foes, think you, had that king who with the Roman People's army brought the Roman People themselves into subjection and compelled a state that not only had been free but had been mistress of the
85 world to be his slave? What stains do you think he had upon his conscience, what scars upon his heart? But whose life can be advantageous to himself, if that life is his on the condition that the man who takes it shall be held in undying gratitude and glory? But if these things which seem so very advantageous are not advantageous because they are full of shame and moral wrong, we ought to be quite convinced that nothing can be expedient that is not morally right.

Apparent conflicts between expediency and moral rectitude: (1) Fabricius and the deserter,

86 XXII. And yet this very question has been decided on many occasions before and since; but in the war with Pyrrhus the decision rendered by Gaius Fabricius, in his second consulship, and by our senate was particularly striking. Without provocation King Pyrrhus had declared war upon the Roman People; the struggle was against a generous and powerful prince, and the supremacy of power was the prize; a deserter came over from him to the camp of Fabricius and promised, if Fabricius would assure him of a reward, to return to the camp of Pyrrhus as secretly as he had come, administer poison to the king, and bring

caturum. Hunc Fabricius reducendum curavit ad Pyrrhum, idque eius factum laudatum a senatu est. Atqui, si speciem utilitatis opinionemque quaerimus, magnum illud bellum perfuga unus et gravem adversarium imperii sustulisset, sed magnum dedecus et flagitium, quicum laudis certamen fuisset, eum non virtute, sed scelere superatum.

87 Utrum igitur utilius vel Fabricio, qui talis in hac urbe, qualis Aristides Athenis, fuit, vel senatui nostro, qui numquam utilitatem a dignitate seiunxit, armis cum hoste certare an venenis? Si gloriae causa imperium expetendum est, scelus absit, in quo non potest esse gloria; sin ipsae opes expetuntur quoquo modo, non poterunt utiles esse cum infamia.

Non igitur utilis illa L. Philippi Q. f. sententia, quas civitates L. Sulla pecunia accepta ex senatus consulto liberavisset, ut eae rursus vectigales essent neque iis pecuniam, quam pro libertate dederant, redderemus. Ei senatus est assensus. Turpe imperio! piratarum enim melior fides quam senatus. At aucta vectigalia, utile igitur. Quousque audebunt dicere

about his death. Fabricius saw to it that this fellow was taken back to Pyrrhus; and his action was commended by the senate. And yet, if the mere show of expediency and the popular conception of it are all we want, this one deserter would have put an end to that wasting war and to a formidable foe of our supremacy; but it would have been a lasting shame and disgrace to us to have overcome not by valour but by crime the man with whom we had a contest for glory.

87 Which course, then, was more expedient for Fabricius, who was to our city what Aristides was to Athens, or for our senate, who never divorced expediency from honour—to contend against the enemy with the sword or with poison? If supremacy is to be sought for the sake of glory, crime should be excluded, for there can be no glory in crime; but if it is power for its own sake that is sought, whatever the price, it cannot be expedient if it is linked with shame.

That well-known measure, therefore, introduced by Philippus, the son of Quintus, was not expedient. With the authority of the senate, Lucius Sulla had exempted from taxation certain states upon receipt of a lump sum of money from them. Philippus proposed that they should again be reduced to the condition of tributary states, without repayment on our part of the money that they had paid for their exemption. And the senate accepted his proposal. Shame upon our government! The pirates' sense of honour is higher than the senate's. "But," someone will say, "the revenues were increased, and therefore it was expedient." How long will people venture to say that a thing that is not morally right

**(2) the senate and the tributary allies,**

88 quicquam utile, quod non honestum? potest autem ulli imperio, quod gloria debet fultum esse et benivolentia sociorum, utile esse odium et infamia?

Ego etiam cum Catone meo saepe dissensi; nimis mihi praefracte videbatur aerarium vectigaliaque defendere, omnia publicanis negare, multa sociis, cum in hos benefici esse deberemus, cum illis sic agere, ut cum colonis nostris soleremus, eoque magis, quod[1] illa ordinum coniunctio ad salutem rei publicae pertinebat. Male etiam Curio, cum causam Transpadanorum aequam esse dicebat, semper autem addebat: "Vincat utilitas!" Potius doceret non esse aequam, quia non esset utilis rei publicae, quam, cum utilem non esse diceret, esse aequam fateretur.

89 XXIII. Plenus est sextus liber de officiis Hecatonis talium quaestionum: "sitne boni viri in maxima caritate annonae familiam non alere."

In utramque partem disputat, sed tamen ad extremum utilitate, ut putat, officium dirigit[2] magis quam humanitate.

Quaerit, si in mari iactura facienda sit, equine pre-

[1] *quod* L c, Edd.; *quo* B H a b.
[2] *dirigit* MSS., Edd. plerique; *derigit* Ed.

[a] The publicans, farmers of the revenue, were the moneyed men of the times, and belonged to the equestrian order. They purchased from the senate the farming of the revenues and then sublet their contract to the collectors. Sometimes they found that they had agreed to pay too high a rate and petitioned the senate to release them from their contract or reduce their obligations, as on this occasion (B.C. 61). The opposition of Cato and others strained the relations between the senate, who had control of the business, and the equestrian order, driving many of the equites over to Caesar's side. Complete harmony between the senate and the knights, as Cicero says, was the only thing that could have saved Rome from the popular party and Caesar.

88 can be expedient? Furthermore, can hatred and shame be expedient for any government? For government ought to be founded upon fair fame and the loyalty of allies.

On this point I often disagreed even with my friend Cato; it seemed to me that he was too rigorous in his watchful care over the claims of the treasury and the revenues; he refused everything that the farmers of the revenue asked for and much that the allies desired; whereas, as I insisted, it was our duty to be generous to the allies and to treat the publicans as we were accustomed individually to treat our tenants—and all the more, because harmony between the orders was essential to the welfare of the republic.[a] Curio, too, was wrong, when he pleaded that the demands of the people beyond the Po were just, but never failed to add, "Let expediency prevail." He ought rather to have proved that the claims were not just, because they were not expedient for the republic, than to have admitted that they were just, when, as he maintained, they were not expedient.

(3) Cato and the publicans.

(4) Curio and the colonies.

89 XXIII. The sixth book of Hecaton's "Moral Duties" is full of questions like the following: "Is it consistent with a good man's duty to let his slaves go hungry when provisions are at famine prices?"

Hecaton debates the question of expediency *vs.* moral rectitude.

Hecaton gives the argument on both sides of the question; but still in the end it is by the standard of expediency, as he conceives it, rather than by one of human feeling, that he decides the question of duty.

Then he raises this question: supposing a man had to throw part of his cargo overboard in a storm, should he prefer to sacrifice a high-priced horse or a cheap and worthless slave? In this case regard for

tiosi potius iacturam faciat an servoli vilis. Hic alio res familiaris, alio ducit humanitas.

"Si tabulam de naufragio stultus arripuerit, extorquebitne eam sapiens, si potuerit?"

Negat, quia sit iniurium.

"Quid? dominus navis eripietne suum?"

"Minime, non plus quam navigantem[1] in alto eicere de navi velit, quia sua sit. Quoad enim perventum est[2] eo, quo sumpta navis est, non domini est navis, sed navigantium."

90 "Quid? si una tabula sit, duo naufragi, eique sapientes, sibine uter*que*[3] rapiat, an alter cedat alteri?"

"Cedat vero, sed ei, cuius magis intersit vel sua vel rei publicae causa vivere."

"Quid, si haec paria in utroque?"

"Nullum erit certamen, sed quasi sorte aut micando victus alteri cedet alter."

"Quid? si pater fana expilet, cuniculos agat ad aerarium, indicetne id magistratibus filius?"

"Nefas id quidem est, quin etiam defendat patrem, si arguatur."

"Non igitur patria praestat omnibus officiis?"

[1] *quam navigantem* Heus., Edd.; *quam si navigantem* MSS.
[2] *est* c, Nonius; *sit* B H a b.
[3] *sibine uterque* Victorius, Edd.; *sibi neuter* MSS.

his property interest inclines him one way, human feeling the other.

"Suppose that a foolish man has seized hold of a plank from a sinking ship, shall a wise man wrest it away from him if he can?"

"No," says Hecaton; "for that would be unjust."

"But how about the owner of the ship? Shall he take the plank away because it belongs to him?"

"Not at all; no more than he would be willing when far out at sea to throw a passenger overboard on the ground that the ship was his. For until they reach the place for which the ship is chartered, she belongs to the passengers, not to the owner."

90 "Again; suppose there were two to be saved from the sinking ship—both of them wise men—and only one small plank, should both seize it to save themselves? Or should one give place to the other?"

"Why of course, one should give place to the other, but that other must be the one whose life is more valuable either for his own sake or for that of his country."

"But what if these considerations are of equal weight in both?"

"Then there will be no contest, but one will give place to the other, as if the point were decided by lot or at a game of odd and even."

"Again, suppose a father were robbing temples or making underground passages to the treasury, should a son inform the officers of it?"

"Nay; that were a crime; rather should he defend his father, in case he were indicted."

"Well, then, are not the claims of country paramount to all other duties?"

" Immo vero, sed ipsi patriae conducit pios habere cives in parentes."

" Quid? si tyrannidem occupare, si patriam prodere conabitur pater, silebitne filius? "

" Immo vero obsecrabit patrem, ne id faciat. Si nihil proficiet, accusabit, minabitur etiam, ad extremum, si ad perniciem patriae res spectabit, patriae salutem anteponet saluti patris."

91 Quaerit etiam, si sapiens adulterinos nummos acceperit imprudens pro bonis, cum id rescierit, soluturusne sit eos, si cui [1] debeat, pro bonis. Diogenes ait, Antipater negat, cui potius assentior.

Qui vinum [2] fugiens vendat sciens, debeatne dicere. Non necesse putat Diogenes, Antipater viri boni existimat. Haec sunt quasi controversa iura Stoicorum. " In mancipio vendendo dicendane vitia, non ea, quae nisi dixeris, redhibeatur mancipium iure civili, sed haec, mendacem esse, aleatorem, furacem, ebriosum? " Alteri dicenda videntur, alteri non videntur.

92 " Si quis aurum vendens orichalcum se putet vendere, indicetne ei vir bonus aurum illud esse an emat denario, quod sit mille denarium? "

Perspicuum est iam, et quid mihi videatur, et quae sit inter eos philosophos, quos nominavi, controversia.

[1] *si cui* c, Nonius, Edd.; *sicut* B H a b.
[2] *vinum* c, Nonius, Edd.; *venenum* B H a b p.

[a] The denarius was worth at this time about ninepence.

"Aye, verily; but it is to our country's interest to have citizens who are loyal to their parents."

"But once more—if the father attempts to make himself king, or to betray his country, shall the son hold his peace?"

"Nay, verily; he will plead with his father not to do so. If that accomplishes nothing, he will take him to task; he will even threaten; and in the end, if things point to the destruction of the state, he will sacrifice his father to the safety of his country."

91 Again, he raises the question: "If a wise man should inadvertently accept counterfeit money for good, will he offer it as genuine in payment of a debt after he discovers his mistake?" Diogenes says, "Yes"; Antipater, "No," and I agree with him.

A similar debate by Diogenes *vs.* Antipater.

If a man knowingly offers for sale wine that is spoiling, ought he to tell his customers? Diogenes thinks that it is not required; Antipater holds that an honest man would do so. These are like so many points of the law disputed among the Stoics. "In selling a slave, should his faults be declared—not those only which the seller is bound by the civil law to declare or have the slave returned to him, but also the fact that he is untruthful, or disposed to gamble, or steal, or get drunk?" The one thinks such facts should be declared, the other does not.

92 "If a man thinks that he is selling brass, when he is actually selling gold, should an upright man inform him that his stuff is gold, or go on buying for one shilling [a] what is worth a thousand?"

It is clear enough by this time what my views are on these questions, and what are the grounds of dispute between the above-named philosophers.

XXIV. Pacta et promissa semperne servanda sint, QUAE NEC VI NEC DOLO MALO, ut praetores solent, FACTA SINT.

Si quis medicamentum cuipiam dederit ad aquam intercutem pepigeritque, si eo medicamento sanus factus esset, ne illo medicamento umquam postea uteretur, si eo medicamento sanus factus sit et annis aliquot post inciderit in eundem morbum nec ab eo, quicum pepigerat, impetret, ut iterum eo[1] liceat uti, quid faciendum sit. Cum sit is inhumanus, qui non concedat, nec ei quicquam fiat iniuriae, vitae et saluti consulendum.

93 Quid? si qui sapiens rogatus sit ab eo, qui eum heredem faciat, cum ei testamento sestertium milies relinquatur, ut, ante quam hereditatem adeat, luce palam in foro saltet, idque se facturum promiserit, quod aliter heredem eum scripturus ille non esset, faciat, quod promiserit, necne? Promisisse nollem et id arbitror fuisse gravitatis; quoniam promisit, si saltare in foro turpe ducet, honestius mentietur, si ex hereditate nihil ceperit, quam si ceperit, nisi forte

[1] *iterum eo* Pearce, Edd.; *item eo* B H a b; *item tum* c.

* Approximately £750,000.

Promises not binding: (1) when life or health is at stake,

XXIV. The question arises also whether agreements and promises must always be kept, "when," in the language of the praetors' edicts, "they have not been secured through force or criminal fraud."

If one man gives another a remedy for the dropsy, with the stipulation that, if he is cured by it, he shall never make use of it again; suppose the patient's health is restored by the use of it, but some years later he contracts the same disease once more; and suppose he cannot secure from the man with whom he made the agreement permission to use the remedy again, what should he do? That is the question. Since the man is unfeeling in refusing the request, and since no harm could be done to him by his friend's using the remedy, the sick man is justified in doing what he can for his own life and health.

(2) when reputation is at stake,

93 Again: suppose that a millionaire is making some wise man his heir and leaving him in his will a hundred million sesterces;[a] and suppose that he has asked the wise man, before he enters upon his inheritance, to dance publicly in broad daylight in the forum; and suppose that the wise man has given his promise to do so, because the rich man would not leave him his fortune on any other condition; should he keep his promise or not? I wish he had made no such promise; that, I think, would have been in keeping with his dignity. But, seeing that he has made it, it will be morally better for him, if he believes it morally wrong to dance in the forum, to break his promise and refuse to accept his inheritance rather than to keep his promise and accept it—unless, perhaps, he contributes the money to the state to meet some grave crisis. In that case, to

eam pecuniam in rei publicae magnum aliquod tempus contulerit, ut vel saltare, cum patriae consulturus sit, turpe non sit.

94 XXV. Ac ne illa quidem promissa servanda sunt, quae non sunt iis [1] ipsis utilia, quibus illa promiseris. Sol Phaëthonti filio, ut redeamus ad fabulas, facturum se esse dixit, quicquid optasset; optavit, ut in currum patris tolleretur; sublatus est. Atque [2] is, ante quam constitit, ictu fulminis deflagravit. Quanto melius fuerat in hoc promissum patris non esse servatum! Quid, quod Theseus exegit promissum a Neptuno? cui cum tres optationes Neptunus dedisset, optavit interitum Hippolyti filii, cum is patri suspectus esset de noverca; quo optato impe-
95 trato Theseus in maximis fuit luctibus. Quid, *quod* [3] Agamemnon cum devovisset Dianae, quod in suo regno pulcherrimum natum esset illo anno, immolavit Iphigeniam, qua nihil erat eo quidem anno natum pulchrius? Promissum potius non faciendum quam tam taetrum facinus admittendum fuit.

Ergo et promissa non facienda non numquam, neque semper deposita reddenda. Si gladium quis apud te sana mente deposuerit, repetat insaniens, reddere peccatum sit, officium non reddere. Quid? si is, qui apud te pecuniam deposuerit, bellum inferat patriae, reddasne depositum? Non credo; facias [4]

[1] *iis* Edd.; *his* B H a b; *hijs* c.
[2] *Atque* MSS., Bt.[1], Müller, Heine; *Atqui* Fl., Bt.[2], Ed.
[3] *quod* Ed.; not in MSS., Bt., et al.
[4] *facias* c, Bt., Ed., Heine; *facies* A B H a b, Müller.

promote thereby the interests of one's country, it would not be morally wrong even to dance, if you please, in the forum.

94 XXV. No more binding are those promises which are inexpedient for the persons themselves to whom they have been given. To go back to the realm of story, the sungod promised his son Phaëthon to do for him whatever he should wish. His wish was to be allowed to ride in his father's chariot. It was granted. And before he came back to the ground he was consumed by a stroke of lightning. How much better had it been, if in his case the father's promise had not been kept. And what of that promise, the fulfilment of which Theseus required from Neptune? When Neptune offered him three wishes, he wished for the death of his son Hippolytus, because the father was suspicious of the son's relations with his step-mother. And when this wish was granted, Theseus was overwhelmed with grief.

(3) when not expedient for him to whom the promise is made.

95 And once more; when Agamemnon had vowed to Diana the most beautiful creature born that year within his realm, he was brought to sacrifice Iphigenia; for in that year nothing was born more beautiful than she. He ought to have broken his vow rather than commit so horrible a crime.

Promises are, therefore, sometimes not to be kept; and trusts are not always to be restored. Suppose that a person leaves his sword with you when he is in his right mind, and demands it back in a fit of insanity; it would be criminal to restore it to him; it would be your duty not to do so. Again, suppose that a man who has entrusted money to you proposes to make war upon your common country, should you restore the trust? I believe you should not; for

Trusts not always to be restored

enim contra rem publicam, quae debet esse carissima. Sic multa, quae honesta natura videntur esse, temporibus fiunt non honesta; facere promissa, stare conventis, reddere deposita commutata utilitate fiunt non honesta.

Ac de iis quidem, quae videntur esse utilitates contra iustitiam simulatione prudentiae, satis arbitror dictum.

96 Sed quoniam a quattuor fontibus honestatis primo
§§ 15 ff. libro officia duximus, in eisdem versemur, cum doce-
§§ 40-70. §§ 71-95. bimus ea, quae videantur esse utilia neque sint, quam sint virtutis inimica. Ac de prudentia quidem, quam vult imitari malitia, itemque de iustitia, quae semper est utilis, disputatum est. Reliquae sunt duae partes honestatis, quarum altera in animi excellentis magnitudine et praestantia cernitur, altera in conformatione et moderatione continentiae et temperantiae.

97 XXVI. Utile videbatur Ulixi, ut quidem poëtae tragici prodiderunt (nam apud Homerum, optimum auctorem, talis de Ulixe nulla suspicio est), sed insimulant eum tragoediae simulatione insaniae militiam subterfugere voluisse. Non honestum consilium, at utile, ut aliquis fortasse dixerit, regnare et Ithacae vivere otiose cum parentibus, cum uxore, cum filio. Ullum tu decus in cotidianis laboribus et periculis cum hac tranquillitate conferendum putas?

you would be acting against the state, which ought to be the dearest thing in the world to you. Thus there are many things which in and of themselves seem morally right, but which under certain circumstances prove to be not morally right: to keep a promise, to abide by an agreement, to restore a trust may, with a change of expediency, cease to be morally right.

With this I think I have said enough about those actions which masquerade as expedient under the guise of prudence, while they are really contrary to justice.

96 Since, however, in Book One we derived moral duties from the four sources of moral rectitude, let us continue the same fourfold division here in pointing out how hostile to virtue are those courses of conduct which seem to be, but really are not, expedient. We have discussed wisdom, which cunning seeks to counterfeit, and likewise justice, which is always expedient. There remain for our discussion two divisions of moral rectitude, the one of which is discernible in the greatness and pre-eminence of a superior soul, the other, in the shaping and regulation of it by temperance and self-control.

**Apparent Expediency *vs.* Fortitude: (1) Ulysses's ruse,**

97 XXVI. Ulysses thought his ruse expedient, as the tragic poets, at least, have represented him. In Homer, our most reliable authority, no such suspicion is cast upon him; but the tragedies charge him with trying to escape a soldier's service by feigning madness. The trick was not morally right, but, someone may perhaps say, "It was expedient for him to keep his throne and live at ease in Ithaca with parents, wife, and son. Do you think that there is any glory in facing daily toil and danger that can be compared with a life of such tranquillity?"

Ego vero istam contemnendam et abiciendam, quoniam, quae honesta non sit, ne utilem quidem
98 esse arbitror. Quid enim auditurum putas fuisse Ulixem, si in illa simulatione perseveravisset? qui cum maximas res gesserit in bello, tamen haec audiat ab Aiace:

(Accius or Pacuvius, Judicium Armorum?) *Inc. inc. fab.*, Ribbeck[2], 55–60.

Cuius ípse princeps iúris iurandí fuit,
Quod ómnes scitis, sólus neglexít fidem;
Furere ássimulare, né coiret, ínstitit.
Quodní Palamedi pérspicax prudéntia
Istíus percepset[1] málitiosam audáciam,
Fidé sacratae[2] iús perpetuo fálleret.

99 Illi vero non modo cum hostibus, verum etiam cum fluctibus, id quod fecit, dimicare melius fuit quam deserere consentientem Graeciam ad bellum barbaris inferendum.

Sed omittamus et fabulas et externa; ad rem factam nostramque veniamus. M. Atilius Regulus cum consul iterum in Africa ex insidiis captus esset duce Xanthippo Lacedaemonio, imperatore autem patre Hannibalis Hamilcare, iuratus missus est ad senatum, ut, nisi redditi essent Poenis captivi nobiles quidam, rediret ipse Carthaginem. Is cum Romam

[1] *percepset* Bt., Ed., Heine; *percepisset* MSS.; *perspexet* Müller. [2] *sacratae* Edd.; *sacrata* B H a b; *sacratum* c.

---

[a] Cicero is careless in his dates. Regulus was consul in 267 and 256. He was defeated and taken prisoner in his second proconsulship at the battle of Tunes in 255. And the Hamilcar of 255 was not Hannibal's father, for his career does not begin until 247, when he was a mere youth, and he was still in his prime when he fell in battle in Spain, in 229.

[b] At the battle of Panormus in 250 Lucius Caecilius Metellus took among the prisoners no less than thirteen Carthaginian generals—all men of noble birth.

Nay; I think that tranquillity at such a price is to be despised and rejected; for if it is not morally
98 right, neither is it expedient. For what do you think would have been said of Ulysses, if he had persisted in that pretended madness, seeing that, notwithstanding his deeds of heroism in the war, he was nevertheless upbraided by Ajax thus:

> "'Twas he himself who first proposed the oath; ye all
> Do know; yet he alone of all his vow did break;
> He feigned persistently that he was mad, that thus
> He might not have to join the host. And had not then
> Palamedes, shrewd and wise, his tricky impudence
> Unmasked, he had evaded e'en for aye his vow."

99 Nay, for him it had been better to battle not only with the enemy but also with the waves, as he did, than to desert Greece when she was united for waging the war against the barbarians.

But let us leave illustrations both from story and from foreign lands and turn to real events in our own history. Marcus Atilius Regulus in his second consulship was taken prisoner in Africa by the stratagem of Xanthippus, a Spartan general serving under the command of Hannibal's father Hamilcar.[a] He was sent to the senate on parole, sworn to return to Carthage himself, if certain noble prisoners of war[b] were not restored to the Carthaginians. When he came to Rome, he could not fail to see the

(2) the example of Regulus.

venisset, utilitatis speciem videbat, sed eam, ut res declarat, falsam iudicavit; quae erat talis: manere in patria, esse domui suae cum uxore, cum liberis, quam calamitatem accepisset in bello, communem fortunae bellicae iudicantem tenere consularis dignitatis gradum. Quis haec negat esse utilia? quem censes?
100 Magnitudo animi et fortitudo negat. XXVII. Num[1] locupletiores quaeris auctores? Harum enim est virtutum proprium nihil extimescere, omnia humana despicere, nihil, quod homini accidere possit, intolerandum putare. Itaque quid fecit? In senatum venit, mandata exposuit, sententiam ne diceret recusavit, quam diu iure iurando hostium teneretur, non esse se senatorem. Atque illud etiam ("O stultum hominem," dixerit quispiam, "et repugnantem utilitati suae!"), reddi captivos negavit esse utile; illos enim adulescentes esse et bonos duces, se iam confectum senectute. Cuius cum valuisset auctoritas, captivi retenti sunt, ipse Carthaginem rediit, neque eum caritas patriae retinuit nec suorum. Neque vero tum ignorabat se ad crudelissimum hostem et ad exquisita supplicia proficisci, sed ius iurandum conservandum putabat. Itaque tum, cum vigilando necabatur, erat in meliore causa,

[1] *num* A L c, Edd.; *nam* B H a b.

specious appearance of expediency, but he decided that it was unreal, as the outcome proves. His apparent interest was to remain in his own country, to stay at home with his wife and children, and to retain his rank and dignity as an ex-consul, regarding the defeat which he had suffered as a misfortune that might come to anyone in the game of war. Who says that this was not expedient? Who, think you? Greatness of soul and courage say that it was
100 not. XXVII. Can you ask for more competent authorities? The denial comes from those virtues, for it is characteristic of them to await nothing with fear, to rise superior to all the vicissitudes of earthly life, and to count nothing intolerable that can befall a human being. What, then, did he do? He came into the senate and stated his mission; but he refused to give his own vote on the question; for, he held, he was not a member of the senate so long as he was bound by the oath sworn to his enemies. And more than that, he said—"What a foolish fellow," someone will say, "to oppose his own best interests"—he said that it was not expedient that the prisoners should be returned; for they were young men and gallant officers, while he was already bowed with age. And when his counsel prevailed, the prisoners were retained and he himself returned to Carthage; affection for his country and his family failed to hold him back. And even then he was not ignorant of the fact that he was going to a most cruel enemy and to exquisite torture; still, he thought his oath must be sacredly kept. And so even then, when he was being slowly put to death by enforced wakefulness, he enjoyed a happier lot than if he had remained at home an

**The violation of his oath could not have been expedient for him.**

quam si domi senex captivus, periurus consularis remansisset.

101 At stulte, qui non modo non censuerit captivos remittendos, verum etiam dissuaserit.

Quo modo stulte? etiamne, si rei publicae conducebat? potest autem, quod inutile rei publicae sit, id cuiquam civi utile esse?

XXVIII. Pervertunt homines ea, quae sunt fundamenta naturae, cum utilitatem ab honestate seiungunt. Omnes enim expetimus utilitatem ad eamque rapimur nec facere aliter ullo modo possumus. Nam quis est, qui utilia fugiat? aut quis potius, qui ea non studiosissime persequatur? Sed quia nusquam possumus nisi in laude, decore, honestate utilia reperire, propterea illa prima et summa habemus, utilitatis nomen non tam splendidum quam necessarium ducimus.

102 Quid est igitur, dixerit quis, in iure iurando? num iratum timemus Iovem? At hoc quidem commune est omnium philosophorum, non eorum modo, qui deum nihil habere ipsum negotii dicunt, nihil exhibere alteri, sed eorum etiam, qui deum semper agere aliquid et moliri volunt, numquam nec irasci deum nec nocere. Quid autem iratus Iuppiter plus

---

[a] The Epicureans.
[b] The Stoics.

aged prisoner of war, a man of consular rank forsworn.

101 "But," you will say, "it was foolish of him not only not to advocate the exchange of prisoners but even to plead against such action."

How was it foolish? Was it so, even if his policy was for the good of the state? Nay; can what is inexpedient for the state be expedient for any individual citizen?

XXVIII. People overturn the fundamental principles established by Nature, when they divorce expediency from moral rectitude. For we all seek to obtain what is to us expedient; we are irresistibly drawn toward it, and we cannot possibly be otherwise. For who is there that would turn his back upon what is to him expedient? Or rather, who is there that does not exert himself to the utmost to secure it? But because we cannot discover it anywhere except in good report, propriety, and moral rectitude, we look upon these three for that reason as the first and the highest objects of endeavour, while what we term expediency we account not so much an ornament to our dignity as a necessary incident to living. Expediency inseparable from moral rectitude.

102 "What significance, then," someone will say, "do we attach to an oath? It is not that we fear the wrath of Jove, is it? Not at all; it is the universally accepted view of all philosophers that God is never angry, never hurtful. This is the doctrine not only of those [a] who teach that God is Himself free from troubling cares and that He imposes no trouble upon others, but also of those [b] who believe that God is ever working and ever directing His world. Furthermore, suppose Jupiter had been Arguments against Regulus's fidelity to his oath: (1) he had no need to fear God's wrath,

nocere potuisset, quam nocuit sibi ipse Regulus? Nulla igitur vis fuit religionis, quae tantam utilitatem perverteret.

An ne turpiter faceret? Primum minima de malis. Num[1] igitur tantum mali turpitudo ista habebat,[2] quantum ille cruciatus? Deinde illud etiam apud Accium:

Atreus; Ribbeck[2], 227–228.

Fregistín[3] fidem?
Néque dedi neque do ínfideli cuíquam

quamquam ab impio rege dicitur, luculente tamen dicitur.

103 Addunt etiam, quem ad modum nos dicamus videri quaedam utilia, quae non sint, sic se dicere videri quaedam honesta, quae non sint, "ut hoc ipsum videtur honestum, conservandi iuris iurandi causa ad cruciatum revertisse; sed fit non honestum, quia, quod per vim hostium esset actum, ratum esse non debuit."

Addunt etiam, quicquid valde utile sit, id fieri honestum, etiamsi antea non videretur.

Haec fere contra Regulum. Sed prima *quaeque*[4] videamus.

104 XXIX. "Non fuit Iuppiter metuendus ne iratus noceret, qui neque irasci solet nec nocere."

[1] *Num* Edd.; *non* MSS.
[2] *habebat* L c, Edd.; *habebit* A B H a b.
[3] *fregistin* Edd.; *fregistine* A B H a b; *fregisti* L c.
[4] *quaeque* Forchhammer, Müller, Heine; not in MSS., Bt., Ed.

wroth, what greater injury could He have inflicted upon Regulus than Regulus brought upon himself? Religious scruple, therefore, had no such preponderance as to outweigh so great expediency."

"Or was he afraid that his act would be morally wrong? As to that, first of all, the proverb says, 'Of evils choose the least.' Did that moral wrong, then, really involve as great an evil as did that awful torture? And secondly, there are the lines of Accius: (2) "Of two evils choose the less,"

*Thyestes.* 'Hast thou broke thy faith?'
*Atreus.* 'None have I giv'n; none give I ever to the faithless.'

Although this sentiment is put into the mouth of a wicked king, still it is illuminating in its correctness."

103 Their third argument is this: just as we maintain that some things seem expedient but are not, so they maintain, some things seem morally right but are not. "For example," they contend, "in this very case it seems morally right for Regulus to have returned to torture for the sake of being true to his oath. But it proves not to be morally right, because what an enemy extorted by force ought not to have been binding." (3) oaths extorted by constraint no binding,

As their concluding argument, they add: whatever is highly expedient may prove to be morally right, even if it did not seem so in advance. (4) exceptional expediency makes right.

These are in substance the arguments raised against the conduct of Regulus. Let us consider them each in turn.

104 XXIX. "He need not have been afraid that Jupiter in anger would inflict injury upon him; he is not wont to be angry or hurtful." Rebuttal.

Haec quidem ratio non magis contra Reguli quam contra omne ius iurandum valet. Sed in iure iurando non qui metus, sed quae vis sit, debet intellegi; est enim ius iurandum affirmatio religiosa; quod autem affirmate quasi deo teste promiseris, id tenendum est. Iam enim non ad iram deorum, quae nulla est, sed ad iustitiam et ad fidem pertinet. Nam praeclare Ennius:

(Thyestes?) *Fab. inc.*, Vahlen², 403. Ó Fides alma ápta pinnis ét ius iurandúm Iovis!

Qui ius igitur iurandum violat, is Fidem violat, quam in Capitolio "vicinam Iovis optimi maximi," ut in
Unknown. Catonis oratione est, maiores nostri esse voluerunt.

105 At enim ne iratus quidem Iuppiter plus Regulo nocuisset, quam sibi nocuit ipse Regulus.

Certe, si nihil malum esset nisi dolere. Id autem non modo [non][1] summum malum, sed ne malum quidem esse maxima auctoritate philosophi affirmant. Quorum quidem testem non mediocrem, sed haud scio an gravissimum Regulum nolite, quaeso, vituperare. Quem enim locupletiorem quaerimus quam principem populi Romani, qui retinendi officii causa cruciatum subierit voluntarium?

Nam quod aiunt: "minima de malis," id est ut

[1] *non modo non* B H a; *non modo nos* c; *non modo* L c p, Edd.

(1) An oath is a covenant with Justice and Good Faith;

This argument, at all events, has no more weight against Regulus's conduct than it has against the keeping of any other oath. But in taking an oath it is our duty to consider not what one may have to fear in case of violation but wherein its obligation lies: an oath is an assurance backed by religious sanctity; and a solemn promise given, as before God as one's witness, is to be sacredly kept. For the question no longer concerns the wrath of the gods (for there is no such thing) but the obligations of justice and good faith. For, as Ennius says so admirably:

> "Gracious Good Faith, on wings upborne;
> thou oath in Jupiter's great name!"

Whoever, therefore, violates his oath violates Good Faith; and, as we find it stated in Cato's speech, our forefathers chose that she should dwell upon the Capitol "neighbour to Jupiter Supreme and Best."

105 "But," objection was further made, "even if Jupiter had been angry, he could not have inflicted greater injury upon Regulus than Regulus brought upon himself."

What is evil?

Quite true, if there is no evil except pain. But philosophers [a] of the highest authority assure us that pain is not only not the supreme evil but no evil at all. And pray do not disparage Regulus, as no unimportant witness—nay, I am rather inclined to think he was the very best witness—to the truth of their doctrine. For what more competent witness do we ask for than one of the foremost citizens of Rome, who voluntarily faced torture for the sake of being true to his moral duty?

Again, they say, "Of evils choose the least"—

turpiter potius quam calamitose, an est ullum maius malum turpitudine? quae si in deformitate corporis habet[1] aliquid offensionis, quanta illa depravatio et
106 foeditas turpificati animi debet videri! Itaque nervosius qui ista disserunt,[a] solum audent malum dicere id, quod turpe sit, qui autem remissius,[b] ii tamen non dubitant summum malum dicere.

Nam illud quidem:

> Néque dedi neque do ínfideli cuíquam

Accius, Atreus; Ribbeck[2] 228.

idcirco recte a poëta, quia, cum tractaretur Atreus, personae serviendum fuit. Sed si hoc sibi sument, nullam esse fidem, quae infideli data sit, videant, ne quaeratur latebra periurio.

107 Est autem ius etiam bellicum fidesque iuris iurandi saepe cum hoste servanda.[2] Quod enim ita iuratum est, ut mens conciperet fieri oportere, id servandum est; quod aliter, id si non fecerit, nullum est periurium. Ut, si praedonibus pactum pro capite pretium non attuleris, nulla fraus sit,[3] ne si iuratus quidem id non feceris; nam pirata non est ex perduellium numero definitus, sed communis hostis omnium; cum hoc nec fides debet nec ius iurandum esse commune.

[1] *habet* L c, Edd.; *habeat* A B H a b.
[2] *Est . . . servanda* bracketed by Unger, Bt.[2], Ed.
[3] *sit* Edd. plerique; *est* MSS., Bt.[1]

---

[a] The Stoics.
[b] The Peripatetics.

that is, shall one "choose moral wrong rather than misfortune," or is there any evil greater than moral wrong? For if physical deformity excites a certain amount of aversion, how offensive ought the deformity and hideousness of a demoralized soul to seem! (2) no evil ca be greater than moral wrong;

106 Therefore, those [a] who discuss these problems with more rigour make bold to say that moral wrong is the only evil, while those [b] who treat them with more laxity do not hesitate to call it the supreme evil.

Once more, they quote the sentiment:

> "None have I given, none give I ever to the faithless."

It was proper for the poet to say that, because, when he was working out his Atreus, he had to make the words fit the character. But if they mean to adopt it as a principle, that a pledge given to the faithless is no pledge, let them look to it that it be not a mere loophole for perjury that they seek.

107 Furthermore, we have laws regulating warfare, and fidelity to an oath must often be observed in dealings with an enemy: for an oath sworn with the clear understanding in one's own mind that it should be performed must be kept; but if there is no such understanding, it does not count as perjury if one does not perform the vow. For example, suppose that one does not deliver the amount agreed upon with pirates as the price of one's life, that would be accounted no deception—not even if one should fail to deliver the ransom after having sworn to do so; for a pirate is not included in the number of lawful enemies, but is the common foe of all the world; and with him there ought not to be any pledged What is perjury?

103 Non enim falsum iurare periurare est, sed, quod EX ANIMI TUI SENTENTIA iuraris, sicut verbis concipitur more nostro, id non facere periurium est. Scite Hippolytus 612. enim [1] Euripides:

Iurávi lingua, méntem iniuratám gero.

Regulus vero non debuit condiciones pactionesque bellicas et hostiles perturbare periurio. Cum iusto enim et legitimo hoste res gerebatur, adversus quem et totum ius fetiale et multa sunt iura communia. Quod ni ita esset, numquam claros viros senatus vinctos [2] hostibus dedidisset.

109 XXX. At vero T. Veturius et Sp. Postumius cum iterum consules essent, quia, cum male pugnatum apud Caudium esset, legionibus nostris sub iugum missis pacem cum Samnitibus fecerant, dediti sunt iis; iniussu enim populi senatusque fecerant. Eodemque tempore Ti. Numicius, Q. Maelius, qui tum tribuni pl. erant, quod eorum auctoritate pax erat facta, dediti sunt, ut pax Samnitium repudiaretur; atque huius deditionis ipse Postumius, qui dedebatur, suasor et auctor fuit.

Quod idem multis annis post C. Mancinus, qui, ut Numantinis, quibuscum sine senatus auctoritate foe-

[1] *Scite enim* A L c, Edd.; *scit enim* B H a b.
[2] *vinctos* A L c, Edd.; *victos* B H a b.

[a] See Index, s.v.
[b] 184 years, i.e., in B.C. 137.

108 word nor any oath mutually binding. For swearing to what is false is not necessarily perjury, but to take an oath "upon your conscience," as it is expressed in our legal formulas, and then fail to perform it, that is perjury. For Euripides aptly says:

> "My tongue has sworn; the mind I have has sworn no oath."

But Regulus had no right to confound by perjury the terms and covenants of war made with an enemy. For the war was being carried on with a legitimate, declared enemy; and to regulate our dealings with such an enemy, we have our whole fetial [a] code as well as many other laws that are binding in common between nations. Were this not the case, the senate would never have delivered up illustrious men of ours in chains to the enemy.

Oaths made to an enemy as binding as treaties.

109 XXX. And yet that very thing happened. Titus Veturius and Spurius Postumius in their second consulship lost the battle at the Caudine Forks, and our legions were sent under the yoke. And because they made peace with the Samnites, those generals were delivered up to them, for they had made the peace without the approval of the people and senate. And Tiberius Numicius and Quintus Maelius, tribunes of the people, were delivered up at the same time, because it was with their sanction that the peace had been concluded. This was done in order that the peace with the Samnites might be annulled. And Postumius, the very man whose delivery was in question, was the proposer and advocate of the said delivery.

Roman strictness.

Many years later,[b] Gaius Mancinus had a similar experience: he advocated the bill, introduced in

dus fecerat, dederetur, rogationem suasit eam, quam L. Furius, Sex. Atilius ex senatus consulto ferebant; qua accepta est hostibus deditus. Honestius hic quam Q. Pompeius, quo, cum in eadem causa esset, deprecante accepta lex non est. Hic ea, quae videbatur utilitas, plus valuit quam honestas, apud superiores utilitatis species falsa ab honestatis auctoritate superata est.

At non debuit ratum esse, quod erat actum per
§ 102. vim.—Quasi vero forti viro vis possit adhiberi.

Cur igitur ad senatum proficiscebatur, cum praesertim de captivis dissuasurus esset?

Quod maximum in eo est, id reprehenditis. Non enim suo iudicio stetit, sed suscepit causam, ut esset iudicium senatus; cui nisi ipse auctor fuisset, captivi profecto Poenis redditi essent; ita incolumis in patria Regulus restitisset. Quod quia patriae non utile putavit, idcirco sibi honestum et sentire illa et pati credidit.

§ 103. Nam quod aiunt, quod valde utile sit, id fieri ho-

accordance with a decree of the senate by Lucius Furius and Sextus Atilius, that he should be delivered up to the Numantines, with whom he had made a treaty without authorization from the senate; and when the bill was passed, he was delivered up to the enemy. His action was more honourable than Quintus Pompey's; Pompey's situation was identical with his, and yet at his own entreaty the bill was rejected. In this latter case, apparent expediency prevailed over moral rectitude; in the former cases, the false semblance of expediency was overbalanced by the weight of moral rectitude.

110 "But," they argued against Regulus, "an oath extorted by force ought not to have been binding." As if force could be brought to bear upon a brave man! (3) the interests of the state higher than personal advantage;

"Why, then, did he make the journey to the senate, especially when he intended to plead against the surrender of the prisoners of war?"

Therein you are criticizing what is the noblest feature of his conduct. For he was not content to stand upon his own judgment but took up the case, in order that the judgment might be that of the senate; and had it not been for the weight of his pleading, the prisoners would certainly have been restored to the Carthaginians; and in that case, Regulus would have remained safe at home in his country. But because he thought this not expedient for his country, he believed that it was therefore morally right for him to declare his conviction and to suffer for it.

When they argued also that what is highly expedient may prove to be morally right, they ought rather to say not that it "may prove to be" but that (4) nothing expedient unless morally right.

nestum, immo vero esse, non fieri. Est enim nihil utile, quod idem non honestum, nec, quia utile, honestum, sed, quia honestum, utile.

Quare ex multis mirabilibus exemplis haud facile quis dixerit hoc exemplo aut laudabilius aut praestantius.

111 XXXI. Sed ex tota hac laude Reguli unum illud est admiratione dignum, quod captivos retinendos censuit. Nam quod rediit, nobis nunc mirabile videtur, illis quidem temporibus aliter facere non potuit; itaque ista laus non est hominis, sed temporum. Nullum enim vinculum ad astringendam fidem iure iurando maiores artius esse voluerunt. Id indicant leges in duodecim tabulis, indicant sacratae, indicant foedera, quibus etiam cum hoste devincitur fides, indicant notiones animadversionesque censorum, qui nulla de re diligentius quam de iure iurando iudicabant.

112 L. Manlio A. f., cum dictator fuisset, M. Pomponius tr. pl. diem dixit, quod is paucos sibi dies ad dictaturam gerendam addidisset; criminabatur etiam, quod Titum filium, qui postea est Torquatus appellatus, ab hominibus relegasset et ruri habitare iussisset.

---

[a] "Sacred" laws, according to Festus (p. 318), were laws that placed their transgressor, together with his household and his property, under the ban of some divinity; other authorities limit the term to the laws enacted upon the Sacred Mount (B.C. 394).

it actually is morally right. For nothing can be expedient which is not at the same time morally right; neither can a thing be morally right just because it is expedient, but it is expedient because it is morally right.

From the many splendid examples in history, therefore, we could not easily point to one either more praiseworthy or more heroic than the conduct of Regulus.

111 XXXI. But of all that is thus praiseworthy in the conduct of Regulus, this one feature above all others calls for our admiration: it was he who offered the motion that the prisoners of war be retained. For the fact of his returning may seem admirable to us nowadays, but in those times he could not have done otherwise. That merit, therefore, belongs to the age, not to the man. For our ancestors were of the opinion that no bond was more effective in guaranteeing good faith than an oath. That is clearly proved by the laws of the Twelve Tables, by the "sacred" laws,[a] by the treaties in which good faith is pledged even to the enemy, by the investigations made by the censors and the penalties imposed by them; for there were no cases in which they used to render more rigorous decisions than in cases of violation of an oath.

**The most striking lesson in the story of Regulus.**

112 Marcus Pomponius, a tribune of the people, brought an indictment against Lucius Manlius, Aulus's son, for having extended the term of his dictatorship a few days beyond its expiration. He further charged him with having banished his own son Titus (afterward surnamed Torquatus) from all companionship with his fellow-men, and with requiring him to live in the country. When the son, who

**The sanctity of an oath in the old days.**

Quod cum audivisset adulescens filius, negotium exhiberi patri, accurrisse Romam et cum primo luci [1] Pomponi domum venisse dicitur. Cui cum esset nuntiatum, qui illum iratum allaturum ad se aliquid contra patrem arbitraretur, surrexit e lectulo remotisque arbitris ad se adulescentem iussit venire. At ille, ut ingressus est, confestim gladium destrinxit iuravitque se illum statim interfecturum, nisi ius iurandum sibi dedisset se patrem missum esse facturum. Iuravit hoc terrore coactus Pomponius; rem ad populum detulit, docuit, cur sibi causa desistere necesse esset, Manlium missum fecit. Tantum temporibus illis ius iurandum valebat.

Atque hic T. Manlius is est, qui ad Anienem Galli, quem ab eo provocatus occiderat, torque detracto cognomen invenit, cuius tertio consulatu Latini ad Veserim fusi et fugati, magnus vir in primis et, qui perindulgens in patrem, idem acerbe severus in filium.

113 XXXII. Sed, ut laudandus Regulus in conservando iure iurando, sic decem illi, quos post Cannensem pugnam iuratos ad senatum misit Hannibal se in castra redituros ea, quorum erant potiti Poeni, nisi de redimendis captivis impetravissent, si non redie-

[1] *Primo luci* Beier, Heine, Ed.; *primo lucis* c; *prima luci* A B H a b.

was then a young man, heard that his father was in trouble on his account, he hastened to Rome—so the story goes—and at daybreak presented himself at the house of Pomponius. The visitor was announced to Pomponius. Inasmuch as he thought that the son in his anger meant to bring him some new evidence to use against the father, he arose from his bed, asked all who were present to leave the room, and sent word to the young man to come in. Upon entering, he at once drew a sword and swore that he would kill the tribune on the spot, if he did not swear an oath to withdraw the suit against his father. Constrained by the terror of the situation, Pomponius gave his oath. He reported the matter to the people, explaining why he was obliged to drop the prosecution, and withdrew his suit against Manlius. Such was the regard for the sanctity of an oath in those days.

And that lad was the Titus Manlius who in the battle on the Anio killed the Gaul by whom he had been challenged to single combat, pulled off his torque and thus won his surname. And in his third consulship he routed the Latins and put them to flight in the battle on the Veseris. He was one of the greatest of the great, and one who, while more than generous toward his father, could yet be bitterly severe toward his son.

**Contrast between Regulus and the ten envoys from Hannibal.**

113 XXXII. Now, as Regulus deserves praise for being true to his oath, so those ten whom Hannibal sent to the senate on parole after the battle of Cannae deserve censure, if it is true that they did not return; for they were sworn to return to the camp which had fallen into the hands of the Carthaginians, if they did not succeed in negotiating an exchange

runt, vituperandi. De quibus non omnes uno modo; nam Polybius, bonus auctor in primis, ex decem nobilissimis, qui tum erant missi, novem revertisse dicit re a senatu non impetrata; unum ex decem, qui paulo post, quam erat [1] egressus e castris, redisset, quasi aliquid esset oblitus, Romae remansisse; reditu enim in castra liberatum se esse iure iurando interpretabatur, non recte; fraus enim astringit,[2] non dissolvit periurium. Fuit igitur stulta calliditas perverse imitata prudentiam. Itaque decrevit senatus, ut ille veterator et callidus vinctus ad Hannibalem duceretur.

114 [3] Sed illud maximum: octo hominum milia tenebat Hannibal, non quos in acie cepisset, aut qui periculo mortis diffugissent, sed qui relicti in castris fuissent a Paulo et a Varrone consulibus. Eos senatus non censuit redimendos, cum id parva pecunia fieri posset, ut esset insitum militibus nostris aut vincere aut emori. Qua quidem re audita fractum animum Hannibalis scribit idem, quod senatus populusque Romanus rebus afflictis tam excelso animo fuisset. Sic honestatis comparatione ea, quae videntur utilia, vincuntur.

115 *C.* [4] Acilius autem, qui Graece scripsit historiam, plures ait fuisse, qui in castra revertissent eadem

[1] *Novem . . . quam erat* c, Bt.[1], Ed.; om. A B H a b; *unum qui* Unger, Bt.[2]

[2] *astringit* c p, Ed., Heine; *distringit* A B H a b, Unger, Bt.

[3] § 114 bracketed by Heus., Bt., as un-Ciceronian.

[4] *C.* Heine, Ed.; not in MSS.

of prisoners. Historians are not in agreement in regard to the facts. Polybius, one of the very best authorities, states that of the ten eminent nobles who were sent at that time, nine returned when their mission failed at the hands of the senate. But one of the ten, who, a little while after leaving the camp, had gone back on the pretext that he had forgotten something or other, remained behind at Rome; he explained that by his return to the camp he was released from the obligation of his oath. He was wrong; for deceit does not remove the guilt of perjury—it merely aggravates it. His cunning that impudently tried to masquerade as prudence was, therefore, only folly. And so the senate ordered that the cunning scoundrel should be taken back to Hannibal in chains.

**The ancient Roman discipline.**

114 But the most significant part of the story is this: the eight thousand prisoners in Hannibal's hands were not men that he had taken in the battle or that had escaped in the peril of their lives, but men that the consuls Paulus and Varro had left behind in camp. Though these might have been ransomed by a small sum of money, the senate voted not to redeem them, in order that our soldiers might have the lesson planted in their hearts that they must either conquer or die. When Hannibal heard this news, according to that same writer, he lost heart completely, because the senate and the people of Rome displayed courage so lofty in a time of disaster. Thus apparent expediency is outweighed when placed in the balance against moral rectitude.

115 Gaius Acilius, on the other hand, the author of a history of Rome in Greek, says that there were several who played the same trick of returning to

fraude, ut iure iurando liberarentur, eosque a censoribus omnibus ignominiis notatos.

Sit iam huius loci finis. Perspicuum est enim ea, quae timido animo, humili, demisso fractoque fiant, quale fuisset Reguli factum, si aut de captivis, quod ipsi opus esse videretur, non quod rei publicae, censuisset aut domi remanere voluisset, non esse utilia, quia sint flagitiosa, foeda, turpia.

116 XXXIII. Restat quarta pars, quae decore, moderatione, modestia, continentia, temperantia continetur.

Potest igitur quicquam utile esse, quod sit huic talium virtutum choro contrarium? Atqui ab Aristippo Cyrenaici atque Annicerii philosophi nominati omne bonum in voluptate posuerunt virtutemque censuerunt ob eam rem esse laudandam, quod efficiens esset voluptatis. Quibus obsoletis floret Epicurus, eiusdem fere adiutor auctorque sententiae. Cum his "viris [1] equisque," ut dicitur, si honestatem tueri ac retinere sententia est, decertandum est.

117 Nam si non modo utilitas, sed vita omnis beata corporis firma constitutione eiusque constitutionis spe explorata, ut a Metrodoro scriptum est, continetur, certe haec utilitas, et quidem summa (sic enim

[1] *viris* c p, Edd.; *veris* A B H b.

the camp to release themselves thus from the obligation of their oath, and that they were branded by the censors with every mark of disgrace.

Let this be the conclusion of this topic. For it must be perfectly apparent that acts that are done with a cowardly, craven, abject, broken spirit, as the act of Regulus would have been if he had supported in regard to the prisoners a measure that seemed to be advantageous for him personally, but disadvantageous for the state, or if he had consented to remain at home—that such acts are not expedient, because they are shameful, dishonourable, and immoral. **Expediency and Courage identical.**

116 XXXIII. We have still left our fourth division, comprising propriety, moderation, temperance, self-restraint, self-control. **Apparent Expediency *vs.* Temperance.**

Can anything be expedient, then, which is contrary to such a chorus of virtues? And yet the Cyrenaics, adherents of the school of Aristippus, and the philosophers who bear the name of Anniceris find all good to consist in pleasure and consider virtue praiseworthy only because it is productive of pleasure. Now that these schools are out of date, Epicurus has come into vogue—an advocate and supporter of practically the same doctrine. Against such a philosophy we must fight it out "with horse and foot," as the saying is, if our purpose is to defend and maintain our standard of moral rectitude.

117 For if, as we find it in the writings of Metrodorus, not only expediency but happiness in life depends wholly upon a sound physical constitution and the reasonable expectation that it will always remain sound, then that expediency—and, what is more, the highest expediency, as they estimate it—will **The fallacy of Epicureanism.**

censent), cum honestate pugnabit. Nam ubi primum prudentiae locus dabitur? an ut conquirat undique suavitates? Quam miser virtutis famulatus servientis voluptati! Quod autem munus prudentiae? an legere intellegenter voluptates? Fac nihil isto esse iucundius, quid cogitari potest turpius?

Iam, qui dolorem summum malum dicat, apud eum quem habet locum fortitudo, quae est dolorum laborumque contemptio? Quamvis enim multis locis dicat Epicurus, sicuti [1] dicit, satis fortiter de dolore, tamen non id spectandum est, quid dicat, sed quid consentaneum sit ei dicere, qui bona voluptate terminaverit, mala dolore.

Et,[2] si illum audiam, de continentia et temperantia dicit ille quidem multa multis locis, sed aqua haeret, ut aiunt; nam qui potest temperantiam laudare is, qui ponat summum bonum in voluptate? est enim temperantia libidinum inimica, libidines autem consectatrices voluptatis.

118 Atque in his tamen tribus generibus, quoquo modo possunt, non incallide tergiversantur; prudentiam introducunt scientiam suppeditantem voluptates, depellentem dolores; fortitudinem quoque aliquo modo expediunt, cum tradunt rationem neglegendae

[1] *sicuti* L c, Edd.; *sicut id* A B H a b.
[2] *dolore. Et* Müller, Heine; *dolore: ut* MSS., Bt.; *dolore. Ut* Ed.

assuredly clash with moral rectitude. For, first of all, what position will wisdom occupy in that system? The position of collector of pleasures from every possible source? What a sorry state of servitude for a virtue—to be pandering to sensual pleasure! And what will be the function of wisdom? To make skilful choice between sensual pleasures? Granted that there may be nothing more pleasant, what can be conceived more degrading for wisdom than such a rôle?

Then again, if anyone hold that pain is the supreme evil, what place in his philosophy has fortitude, which is but indifference to toil and pain? For, however many passages there are in which Epicurus speaks right manfully of pain, we must nevertheless consider not what he says, but what it is consistent for a man to say who has defined the good in terms of pleasure and evil in terms of pain.

And further, if I should listen to him, I should find that in many passages he has a great deal to say about temperance and self-control; but "the water will not run," as they say. For how can he commend self-control and yet posit pleasure as the supreme good? For self-control is the foe of the passions, and the passions are the handmaids of pleasure.

118 And yet when it comes to these three cardinal virtues, those philosophers shift and turn as best they can, and not without cleverness. They admit wisdom into their system as the knowledge that provides pleasures and banishes pain; they clear the way for fortitude also in some way to fit in with their doctrines, when they teach that it is a rational means for looking with indifference upon death and

Epicureanism and the Cardinal Virtues.

mortis, perpetiendi doloris; etiam temperantiam inducunt non facillime illi quidem, sed tamen quoquo modo possunt; dicunt enim voluptatis magnitudinem doloris detractione finiri. Iustitia vacillat vel iacet potius omnesque eae virtutes, quae in communitate cernuntur et in societate generis humani. Neque enim bonitas nec liberalitas nec comitas esse potest, non plus quam amicitia, si haec non per se expetantur,[1] sed ad voluptatem utilitatemve referantur.

Conferamus igitur in pauca.

119 Nam ut utilitatem nullam esse docuimus, quae honestati esset contraria, sic omnem voluptatem dicimus honestati esse contrariam. Quo magis reprehendendos Calliphontem et Dinomachum iudico, qui se dirempturos controversiam putaverunt, si cum honestate voluptatem tamquam cum homine pecudem copulavissent. Non recipit istam coniunctionem honestas, aspernatur, repellit. Nec vero finis bonorum [et malorum],[2] qui simplex esse debet, ex dissimillimis rebus misceri et temperari potest. Sed de hoc (magna enim res est) alio loco pluribus; nunc ad propositum.

De Finibus, II.

120 Quem ad modum igitur, si quando ea, quae videtur[3] utilitas, honestati repugnat, diiudicanda res sit, satis est supra disputatum. Sin autem speciem utilitatis etiam voluptas habere dicetur, nulla potest esse ei cum honestate coniunctio. Nam, ut tribuamus ali-

[1] *expetantur* A, Edd.; *expectantur* B a; *exspectantur* c.
[2] Omitted by Muretus; bracketed by Heine, Ed., et al.
[3] *videtur* c, Edd.; *videretur* B H a b; *viderentur* A.

for enduring pain. They bring even temperance in—not very easily, to be sure, but still as best they can; for they hold that the height of pleasure is found in the absence of pain. Justice totters or rather, I should say, lies already prostrate; so also with all those virtues which are discernible in social life and the fellowship of human society. For neither goodness nor generosity nor courtesy can exist, any more than friendship can, if they are not sought of and for themselves, but are cultivated only for the sake of sensual pleasure or personal advantage.

Let us now recapitulate briefly.

119 As I have shown that such expediency as is opposed to moral rectitude is no expediency, so I maintain that any and all sensual pleasure is opposed to moral rectitude. And therefore Calliphon and Dinomachus, in my judgment, deserve the greater condemnation; they imagined that they should settle the controversy by coupling pleasure with moral rectitude; as well yoke a man with a beast! But moral rectitude does not accept such a union; she abhors it, spurns it. Why, the supreme good, which ought to be simple, cannot be a compound and mixture of absolutely contradictory qualities. But this theory I have discussed more fully in another connection; for the subject is a large one. Now for the matter before us.

Sensual pleasure and moral rectitude incompatible.

120 We have, then, fully discussed the problem how a question is to be decided, if ever that which seems to be expediency clashes with moral rectitude. But if, on the other hand, the assertion is made that pleasure admits of a show of expediency also, there can still be no possible union between it and moral rectitude. For, to make the most generous admission

quid voluptati, condimenti fortasse non nihil, utilitatis certe nihil habebit.

121 Habes a patre munus, Marce fili, mea quidem sententia magnum, sed perinde erit, ut acceperis. Quamquam hi tibi tres libri inter Cratippi commentarios tamquam hospites erunt recipiendi; sed, ut, si ipse venissem Athenas (quod quidem esset factum, nisi me e medio cursu clara voce patria revocasset), aliquando me quoque audires, sic, quoniam his voluminibus ad te profecta vox est mea, tribues iis [1] temporis quantum poteris, poteris autem, quantum voles. Cum vero intellexero te hoc scientiae genere gaudere, tum et praesens tecum propediem, ut spero, et, dum aberis, absens loquar.

Vale igitur, mi Cicero, tibique persuade esse te quidem mihi carissimum, sed multo fore cariorem, si talibus monitis [2] praeceptisque laetabere.

[1] *iis* Edd.; *his* A B H a b; *hijs* c.
[2] *monitis* Lambinus, Edd.; *monumentis* A B H a b; *monimentis* c.

---

[a] But Cicero never saw his son Marcus again.

we can in favour of pleasure, we will grant that it may contribute something that possibly gives some spice to life, but certainly nothing that is really expedient.

121 Herewith, my son Marcus, you have a present from your father—a generous one, in my humble opinion; but its value will depend upon the spirit in which you receive it. And yet you must welcome these three books as fellow-guests, so to speak, along with your notes on Cratippus's lectures. But as you would sometimes give ear to me also, if I had come to Athens (and I should be there now, if my country had not called me back with accents unmistakable, when I was half-way there), so you will please devote as much time as you can to these volumes, for in them my voice will travel to you; and you can devote to them as much time as you will. And when I see that you take delight in this branch of philosophy, I shall then talk further with you—at an early date,[a] I hope, face to face—but as long as you are abroad, I shall converse with you thus at a distance. Conclusion.

Farewell, my dear Cicero, and be assured that, while you are the object of my deepest affection, you will be dearer to me still, if you find pleasure in such counsel and instruction.

# INDEX

References are to Book and Section; all dates, given in parentheses (...), are B.C.

# INDEX

Agriculture, impossible without man, II, 12; man's noblest calling, I, 151.

Agrigentum, a city on the south coast of Sicily, once "the most beautiful city of mortals," ruled by Phalaris (560), II, 26.

Ajax, son of Telamon; could brook no wrong, went mad, and committed suicide when the arms of Achilles were awarded to Odysseus, I, 113; rebuked Odysseus, III, 98. Subject of a tragedy by Ennius, I, 114.

Albucius, Titus, an Epicurean; praetor in Sardinia (105); prosecuted for extortion, II, 50.

Alexander, the Great (356-323), son of Philip of Macedon, II, 16, 48; greater than his father in achievement, inferior in courtliness, I, 90; governor of Macedonia (340), II, 53; conquered Greece (338-335), subdued Asia (334-331), Egypt (331), invaded India (329-327), founded Alexandria and other cities, and died of a drunken debauch (I, 90).

Alexander, tyrant of Pherae (369); brother, son-in-law, and successor of Jason (*q.v.*), defeated and slew Pelopidas of Thebes at Cynoscephalae (364); murdered by his wife and her three brothers, II, 25, 26.

Alexandria, the metropolis of Egypt at the mouth of the Nile; founded by Alexander (332); centre of wealth (II, 82); grain market, III, 50.

Alps, the mountains between Italy and further Gaul, II, 28.

Ambition, a cause of injustice, I, 25-26, 46, 65; of moral wrong, III, 82; of treason, III, 82-83; the foe of freedom, I, 68; II, 28.

Amusements, wholesome, I, 103-104.

Anger, never excusable, I, 89.

Anio, the Sabine river, tributary to the Tiber; the battle on (340), which gave Rome supremacy over all Latium, III, 112.

Anniceris, of Cyrene (4th century), a successor of Aristippus; his school a cross between the Epicurean and the Cyrenaic: he denied that pleasure was merely absence of pain; he held that every act had its own distinct purpose and that the virtues are good in themselves; his teachings were not permanent, III, 116.

Antigonus, one of Alexander's generals, governor of Asia (323-301), king of Asia (306-301); father of Demetrius Poliorcetes and Philip, II, 48.

Antiope, mother of Amphion and Zethus, by whom she was saved from the persecutions of her former husband Lycus and his wife Dirce; her vengeance on Dirce drove her mad; subject of a tragedy of Pacuvius, I, 114.

Antipater, vice-regent of Macedon (334); father of Cassander, II, 48.

Antipater, of Tarsus (2nd century), pupil and successor of Diogenes of Babylonia; teacher of Panaetius; his ethical teachings, III, 51-55, 91.

Antipater, of Tyre (1st century), friend of Cato the younger; a Stoic, II, 86.

Antonius, Marcus, the famous orator (143-87), II, 49; advocate, III, 67; father of Cicero's colleague and grandfather of the triumvir.

Apelles, of Cos (4th century), the greatest painter of his age; court painter to Alexander the Great; his masterpiece was a Venus rising from the sea; another Venus left unfinished, III, 10.

Apollo, god of the light of day; giver of oracles at Pytho, II, 77.

Appetite, subject to Reason, I, 101-103, 132, 141.

Appius Claudius Pulcher, father of Gaius, II, 57.

Aquilius; Gaius Aquilius Gallus, famous jurist; Cicero's colleague in the praetorship; author of formulae on criminal fraud, III 60-61.

Aquilius, Manius, consul (101) with Marius; victorious in the Servile War in Sicily; prosecuted (98) but acquitted, II, 50.

Aratus, of Sicyon, soldier and statesman (271-213), removed the tyrant Nicocles (251) and averted

financial ruin, II, 81, 82; leader of the Achaean League; poisoned by order of Philip of Macedon.
Areopagites, members of the Council of Areopagus.
Areopagus, "Mars Hill," a spur of the Acropolis, seat of the highest court of Athens; the court itself, with powers of senate and supreme court, reorganized and enlarged in function by Solon, I, 75.
Arginusae, a group of islands off the coast of Asia Minor, near Lesbos, scene of the victory of the Athenian fleet (406), I, 84.
Argos, the chief city of Argolis, II, 81.
Aristides, "the Just," III, [16], 49, 87; fought at Marathon (490), Salamis (480), and commanded the Athenians at Plataea (479); exiled (483) because his policies clashed with those of Themistocles.
Aristippus, of Cyrene (flourished 370), founder of the Cyrenaic school, III, 116; disciple of Socrates, but taught that the chief end of man was to get enjoyment from everything (hedonism), to subject all things and circumstances to himself for pleasure; but pleasure must be the slave not the master; good and bad identical with pleasure and pain; I, 148.
Aristo, of Chios (3rd century), a Stoic philosopher, pupil of Zeno; he taught indifference to externals, nothing good but virtue, nothing evil but vice; his theories rejected, I, 6.
Aristotle (385-322), disciple of Plato and teacher of Alexander the Great; founder of the Peripatetic school; greatest of philosophers, master of all knowledge—physics, metaphysics, natural philosophy, ethics, politics, poetics, sociology, logic, rhetoric, etc.; II, 56; III, 35; might have been a great orator, I, 4.
Arpinates, the people of Arpinum, owners of public lands, I, 21.
Arpinum, a town in Latium, birth place of Cicero and Gaius Marius, I, 21.
Athenians, the people of Athens, I, 75, 84; their cruel subjugation of Aegina, III, 46; left their homes to fight at Salamis, III, 48; political strife, I, 86; high moral principles of, III, 49, 55.
Athens, II, 64, 83; III, 55, 87; the intellectual and artistic centre of the world; led Greece in the Persian wars (490-479); humbled by Sparta (404); the university city of the Roman world, I, 1; III, 6, 121.
Atilius; *see* Regulus.
Atilius; Sextus Atilius Serranus, consul (136), III, 109.
Atreus, son of Pelops and father of Agamemnon and Menelaus, murderer of his half-brother Chrysippus and of his brother Thyestes's children; murdered by his nephew Aegisthus; a fruitful theme for tragedy, I, 97; III, 106.
Attic, belonging to Attica, the province in which Athens is situated; Attic comedy, the comedy of Aristophanes, Eupolis, Menander, etc., I, 104.
Avarice, the great temptation, II, 38, 77; the root of evil, III, 73-75; due to delusion as to expediency, III, 36; avoided by the statesman, II, 76-77; contrary to all law, III, 21-23; *see also* Covetousness.

Babylonia, the district around Babylon at the head of the Persian Gulf, III, 51.
Bardulis, king of Illyria, conquered a large part of Macedonia from Perdiccas, the brother and predecessor of Philip; defeated and slain by Philip (358); called a "brigand," because his career did not tend to promote civilization, II, 40.
Basilus, Lucius Minucius, otherwise unknown; perhaps Sulla's lieutenant, III, 73-74.
Beauty, physical, I, 98, 126; types of, I, 130.
Beneficence; *see* Generosity.
Bribery, in Rome, II, 21-22, 75.
Brutus, Lucius Junius, led the

sor; a Stoic philosopher; orator; soldier, I, 112; defeated at Thapsus (46); judge, III, 66; stern and unyielding as his great-grandfather, I, 112; III, 88; his suicide, I, 112; close friend of Cicero (II, 2); III, 88.
Catulus, Quintus Lutatius, half-brother of Julius Caesar Strabo, I, 133; orator; scholar, I, 133; author; soldier; consul with Marius (102) in the war against the Cimbri (101); gentleman, I, 109; committed suicide to escape the proscriptions of Marius (87).
Catulus, Quintus Lutatius, son of the preceding, defeated Lepidus at the Milvian bridge; statesman, I, 76; scholar, I, 133.
Caudium, a little town in the mountains of Samnium; near it are the Caudine Forks, the scene of the disastrous battle (321); III, 109; (II, 79).
Celtiberians, a powerful people of central Spain, opposed Rome in Second Punic War, were reduced in the Numantian War (134), submitted on the death of Sertorius (72), I, 38.
Centumalus, Tiberius Claudius; unknown, III, 66.
Chicanery, I, 33.
Chremes, a character in Terence's *Heauton Timorumenus*, I, 30.
Chrysippus, of Soli (250-207), studied Stoic philosophy at Athens under Cleanthes, whom he succeeded; voluminous writer. "Had there been no Chrysippus, there had been no Stoa," III, 42.
Cicero, Marcus Tullius, the orator's father, III, 77; died (64).
Cicero, Marcus Tullius, the orator (106-43), born at Arpinum, educated at Rome under Archias, the Scaevolas, and the teachers of philosophy (*see* Introduction), at Athens, in Asia, and at Rhodes; his training was all for service, I, 155; as consul (63) he crushed the conspiracy of Catiline, I, 84; banished (58), II, 58; his enforced retirement from his profession, III, 2-4; as a philosopher and orator, I, 1-3; follower of Socrates and Plato, I, 2; of the New Academy, II, 7-8; why he wrote on philosophy, II, 2-8; III, 1-5; attitude on the downfall of the republic, II, 2.
Cicero, Marcus Tullius, the orator's only son, I, 1, 15, 78; II, 1-8, 44; III, 1, 5, 33; born in 65; served with credit under Pompey, II, 45, and Sextus Pompey; a student of Peripatetic philosophy under Cratippus in Athens (44-43), I, 1; admonished to read also his father's works, I, 3; III, 121; served under Brutus (43-42); consul with Octavian (30).
Cimbrians, a Celtic people, migrating in a vast horde toward Italy, were cut to pieces by Marius and Catulus in the Raudian Plains near Verona (101), I, 38.
Cimon, of Athens, son of the great Miltiades; victorious admiral; statesman; genial and generous, II, 64; died (449).
Circe, nymph of Aeaea, a sorceress; she kept Odysseus (Ulysses) in her halls a year, I, 113.
Civic, compared with military service, I, 74 fg.
Claudius; *see* Appius and Centumalus and Pulcher.
Cleombrotus, son of Pausanias, king of Sparta, fell at Leuctra (371), I, 84.
Cleomenes; *see* note to I, 33.
Clodius; Publius Clodius Pulcher, Cicero's inveterate enemy, one of the most turbulent and corrupt characters of Rome, guilty of mutiny in the army, bribery in the courts, profligacy in his public and private life; secured Cicero's banishment; hired gladiators to force his own election to the praetorship, but was killed in a broil with Milo's rival gang of ruffians, II, 58.
Cloelia, a Roman girl sent as a hostage to Porsena; she made her escape by swimming the Tiber, was sent back, but restored by the king with rewards for her courage, I, 61.
Clytaemnestra, daughter of Tyndareus, wife of Agamemnon,

paramour of Aegisthus, with whom she murdered her husband on his return from Troy; she was in turn slain by her son Orestes. Subject of a tragedy by Accius, I, 114.
Cocles, Horatius, the hero who with two others kept the bridge against Porsena and Tarquin, I, 61.
Collatinus, Lucius Tarquinius, husband of Lucretia, associate of Brutus in driving out the Tarquins and his colleague in the first consulship (509), III, 40.
Comedy; *see* Old Comedy.
Concealment, of guilt, III, 37-39.
Conon, famous Athenian admiral, defeated by Lysander at Aegospotami (405), victorious over Pisander of Sparta at Cnidus (394), restored the long walls, I, 116.
Considerateness, a subdivision of the virtue of Temperance, I, 99, 143.
Conversation, a division of speech, I, 132-133; II, 48; an art, I, 134-135.
Co-operation, and civilization, II, 12-16; and the virtues, II, 17-18; *vs.* Fortune, II, 19; a universal need, II, 39; how secured, II, 21 fg.
Corinth, a famous city at the Isthmus of Corinth; wealthy; next to Athens, richest in treasures of art; head of the Achaean League; sacked and utterly destroyed by the Romans under Mummius (146), I, 35; II, 76; III, 46.
Cornelius; *see* Scipio and Spinther and Sulla.
Cos, chief city of the island of Cos, one of the Sporades; famed for its silks; the birthplace of Apelles, painter of the Coan Venus, III, 10.
Cotta, Gaius Aurelius, distinguished orator; one of the speakers in Cicero's *de Oratore* and *de Natura Deorum*; consul (75); II, 59.
Courage; *see* Fortitude.
Covetousness, I, 68; III, 30; *see* Avarice.
Crassus, Lucius Licinius, the famous orator, II, 63; III, 67; at 21 (119) he won renown by his prosecution of Carbo, the one-time friend of the Gracchi, II, 47, 49; his aedileship most splendid, II, 57; as consul (95), he secured the expulsion from Rome of all who were not citizens, III, 47; this was a cause of the Social War. He was the greatest orator of Rome before Cicero, fluent, graceful, witty, I, 108, 133; Cicero's mouthpiece in the *de Oratore*.
Crassus; Marcus Licinius Crassus Dives, the triumvir; his wealth and ambition, I, 25; sided with Sulla against Marius and grew enormously rich by the proscriptions; his avarice did not shrink from any meanness or even crime, I, 109; III, 73-75. He defeated Spartacus (71); slain in Parthia (53).
Crassus; Publius Licinius Crassus Dives, II, 57; father of the triumvir, consul (97); ended his own life to escape the proscriptions of Marius (87); Cicero bought his house.
Cratippus, of Mitylene, an eminent Peripatetic, came to Athens (about 50) to lecture; foremost of contemporary philosophers and teacher of young Cicero, I, 1, 2; II, 8; III, 5, 6, 33, 121.
Cunning, not wisdom, II, 10; III, 72, 96.
Curio, Gaius Scribonius, II, 59; orator and statesman, III, 88; consul (76).
Cynics, a school of philosophy so called from the Athenian gymnasium, Cynosarges, where they met, later adapted to their snarling manner and dirty habits; its leaders were Antisthenes of Athens, a disciple of Socrates, and Diogenes of Sinope; they taught the virtue of poverty and want, indifference to all convention and decency; Cicero's contempt for them and their so-called philosophy, I, 128, 148.
Cyrenaics, the philosophic sect founded by Aristippus (*q.v.*), III, 116.
Cyrsilus, a Medizing Athenian, III, 48.
Cyrus, the Great, founder of the

Persian Empire; wonderfully gifted in winning the co-operation of men and nations, II, 16.

Damon, a Pythagorean and friend of Phintias, III, 45.

Debts, cancellation of, II, 78-79, 83-85; avoidance of, II, 84; payment enforced, II, 84.

Decius; Publius Decius Mus, father and son, I, 61; III, 16; the former, consul with Manlius Torquatus (360), devoted himself to death in the battle on the Veseris. The son did the same at the battle of Sentinum (295) and brought the Samnite wars to an end.

Demetrius of Phalerum (345–283), orator, statesman, II, 60; philosopher, poet; pupil of Theophrastus, I, 3; the only Greek who was both orator and philosopher, I, 3; he inspired the founding of the Alexandrine library.

Demetrius Poliorcetes, II, 26; son of Antigonus and king of Macedon (294–287). His life was occupied with continuous warfare against enemies in Egypt, Asia, Greece, Macedonia, Epirus.

Demosthenes, the greatest orator of Athens (385–322); pupil of Isaeus and of Plato, I, 4; might have been a great philosopher, I, 4; at 18 he prosecuted his defaulting guardian with success, II, 47; then turned to public speaking and statecraft as a profession.

Diana, goddess of the light of the night, identified with Artemis, III, 95.

Dicaearchus, of Messana (4th century), a Peripatetic philosopher, geographer, and historian, II, 16; pupil of Aristotle and friend of Theophrastus.

Dinomachus, a Greek philosopher, always named with Calliphon (*q.v.*), III, 119.

Diogenes, of Babylonia, pupil and successor of Chrysippus; best known for his part in the famous embassy with Carneades and Critolaus from Athens to Rome (156), where, on motion of Cato, they were not permitted to remain; his ethics rather loose, III, 51–55, 91.

Dion, a kinsman of the elder Dionysius and tyrant of Syracuse (356–353); a devoted disciple of Plato at Syracuse and Athens, I, 155.

Dionysius, the elder (430–367), tyrant of Syracuse (405–367), a typically cruel tyrant, suspicious and fearful, II, 25; III, 45 (?); devoted to art and literature, himself a poet crowned with a prize at Athens.

Dionysius, the younger, son of the preceding and tyrant of Syracuse (367–356, 346–343); devoted to literature; Plato, Aristippus, Archytas, and others were brought to his court. Whether the Damon and Phintias story is to be connected with him or his father is uncertain, III, 45 (?).

Drusus, Marcus Livius, son of Gaius Gracchus's colleague in the tribuneship; an eloquent orator, I, 108; as tribune (91) he attempted to renew the social and agrarian legislation of Gracchus and was assassinated.

Duty, the most important subject in philosophy, I, 4; the most fruitful field, III, 5; the philosophic sects and duty, I, 4–6; best presentation, III, 7; classification, I, 7–9; order of importance, I, 58, 152–160; III, 90; to those who have wronged us, I, 33; to an enemy, I, 35–40; III, 98–115; to a slave, I, 41; III, 89; toward the laws, I, 148; of generosity, I, 42–60; of Temperance-Propriety, I, 100–151; III, 116–121; of Fortitude, III, 97–115; to be prosperous, II, 87; duties of youth, I, 122; II, 52; of age, I 123; of magistrates, I, 124; of statesmen, I, 73–85; of private citizens, I, 124; of aliens, I, 125; *vs.* claims of friendship, III, 43–44; change of duty in change of circumstance, I, 31, 59; III, 32; "mean" and "absolute" duty, I, 8; III, 14; doubts as to, I, 147.

Eloquence, at the bar, II, 66; its decline, II, 67; *see* Oratory.

# INDEX

# INDEX

Fimbria, Gaius Flavius, colleague of Marius in his second consulship (104); orator and jurist, III, 77.
Finance, II, 87; reform of currency, III, 80–81.
Fortitude, the third Cardinal Virtue, I, 15, 61–92; its characteristics, I, 66; in the light of justice, I, 62, 157; dangers attending, I, 46, 62–63; *vs.* expediency, III, 97–115; in Epicurus's system, III, 117.
Fraud, criminal, III, 60 fg.
Friendship, motives to, I, 55–56; acquisition of friends, II, 30; ideal, I, 56; III, 45–46; *vs.* duty, III, 43–44.
Fufius, Lucius, an orator of no great ability, II, 50.
Furius; Lucius Furius Philus, consul (136), proconsul in Spain, III, 109; a learned interlocutor in Cicero's *Republic*.

Galus, Gaius Sulpicius; *see* Sulpicius.
Gaul, an inhabitant of Gaul, the land north of the Apennines, III, 112.
Generosity, divisions of, II, 52; close to Nature, III, 24; must not harm its object, I, 42–43; in proportion to one's means, I, 42–44; II, 55; to the recipient's merits, I, 45–60; motives to, I, 47–49; III, 118; means to winning popularity, II, 32; gifts of money, II, 52–60; personal service, II, 52, 53; to individuals, II, 65–71; to the state, II, 72 fg.; when most appreciated, II, 63.
Glory, a means to popularity, II, 31, 43; preferred to wealth, II, 88.
Gods, favour of, won by piety, II, 11; do no harm, II, 12; III, 102; free from care, II, 102; slow to anger. III, 102, 104, 105.
Golden Mean, I, 89; in generosity, II, 58, 59, 60; in personal adornment, I, 130.
Good, the supreme, I, 5, 7; III, 52, 119; not pleasure, I, 5; III, 116, 117, 118; but moral goodness, III, 11, 35; living in harmony with nature, III, 13; the only, moral goodness, I, 67; III, 12.
Good faith, III, 104; even to an enemy, III, 86 fg., 111, 113.
Good man, what constitutes a, III, 63, 75–77.
Gracchus, Gaius Sempronius, brother of the younger Tiberius; a more radical reformer; tribune (123 and 122); fell (121) a martyr to his reforms for the restoration of the public lands and the reduction of the cost of living, II, 72, 80; his death applauded by Cicero, II, 43.
Gracchus, Publius Sempronius, father of the elder Tiberius, II, 43.
Gracchus, Tiberius Sempronius, father of the tribunes, II, 43; in his own tribuneship he defended Scipio (187); a great soldier, II, 80; twice consul, triumphed twice; a just ruler in Spain; son-in-law of the elder, father-in-law of the younger Africanus, an ardent aristocrat; hence Cicero's praise, II, 43.
Gracchus, Tiberius Sempronius, son of the foregoing; a persuasive orator; friend of the people and helper of the poor and oppressed; murdered for attempting as tribune (133) to reform agrarian abuses and build up a class of small farmers, I, 76, 109; II, 80; his death applauded by Cicero, II, 43.
Gratidianus, Marcus Marius; *see* Marius.
Gratitude, how won, II, 63.
Greece, the land of liberty, letters, art, and civilization, II, 60; III, 48, 73, 99; cause of fall, II, 80.
Greek, belonging to or a native of Greece, I, 108, 111; II, 83; III, 82; leaders in literature, I, 3; masters of philosophy, I, 8, 51, 142, 153; II, 18; Greek and Latin studies. I, 1.
Gyges, the shepherd who dethroned Candaules and became king of Lydia (716–678), III, 38, 78.
Gytheum, the harbour-town and arsenal of Sparta, III, 49.

Hamilcar, a successful Carthaginian general in the First Punic War, defeated by Regulus at Ecnomus; opposed Regulus in Africa, III,

99; confused with Hamilcar Barca (*q.v.*), III, 99.
Hamilcar Barca, famous commander of the Carthaginian forces in Sicily (247–241); in Spain (238–229); father of Hannibal, III, 99.
Hannibal (247–183), one of the world's greatest generals, I, 108; son of Hamilcar Barca, III, 99; sacked Saguntum (219), crossed the Alps and defeated the Romans on the Trebia and Ticinus (218), at Trasimenus (217), Cannae (216), I, 40; III, 113–114; defeated at Zama (202); maligned by the Romans as treacherous and cruel, I, 38.
Harm, from gods to men, II, 12; III, 102; men to men, II, 16 fg.
Health, impossible without man's co-operation, II, 12, 15; care of, II, 86.
Hecaton, of Rhodes, a Stoic, pupil of Panaetius, III, 63, 89.
Hercules, the greatest of heroes, son of Zeus (Jupiter) and Alcmena, I, 118; his choice of his path in life, I, 118; performer of the twelve labours; benefactor of humanity, III, 25; his attainment of heaven, III, 25.
Hernicians, a tribe in the Sabine mountains, subdued by Rome (306), I, 35.
Herodotus, of Halicarnassus (5th century), lived also at Athens and Thurii; the father of history; travelled widely and wrote the history of Persia and Greece, II, 41.
Hesiod, the Boeotian didactic poet (8th century); author of the Theogony, the Works and Days, etc., I, 48.
Hippolytus, son of Theseus; his stepmother Phaedra fell in love with him; he rejected her advances but promised not to tell, III, 108; she accused him falsely; his innocence proved, Phaedra hanged herself and Theseus suffered lifelong remorse, I, 32; III, 94.
Home, of man of rank; *see* House.
Homer, the poet, author of Iliad and Odyssey, III, 97.
Honesty, the bond of human society, III, 21 fg.; the corner-stone of government, II, 78 fg.
House, suitable for a man of rank, I, 138–140.
Hortensius, Quintus (114–50), Cicero's famous rival as orator and advocate; his close friend (after 63), III, 73; enormously wealthy; lavish in his aedileship (75), II, 57; not always scrupulous, III, 73–74.
Hospitality, the duty of, II, 64.
Humility, in prosperity, I, 90–91.

Illyria, the country between Macedonia and the Adriatic, II, 40.
Ingratitude, abhorred, II, 63.
Injustice, active and passive, I, 23, 28; never expedient, III, 84; of hypocrisy, I, 41.
Instinct and Reason, difference between man and beast, I, 11.
Integrity, official, II, 75, 76, 77.
Iphigenia, daughter of Agamemnon and Clytaemnestra (*q.v.*); sacrificed at Aulis, III, 95.
Isocrates (436–338), one of the ten Attic orators, pupil of Gorgias and Socrates; a polished speaker; greater as a teacher than as an orator; might have been a great philosopher, I, 4.
Italian War (90–88), caused by Rome's injustice to the allies, provoked by the fear of prosecution on the part of the corrupt aristocrats, II, 75; resulted in Rome's granting the contentions of the allies.
Italy, in government identified with Rome, II, 76.
Ithaca, the home of Odysseus (Ulysses), an island of the Ionian group west of Greece, probably the historical Leucas, III, 97.

Janus, an old Italian sungod; a covered passage (commonly called his temple) adjoining the forum accommodated the banking houses of Rome, II, 87.
Jason, tyrant of Pherae (395–370), generalissimo of Thessaly (374–370), an able soldier and diplomat, I, 108.
Jests; *see* Wit.

# INDEX


Jove; *see* Jupiter.

Jugurtha, king of Numidia (118–106), campaigned with Scipio against Numantia; war with Rome (112–106) protracted by his bribes as much as by his arms, III, 79; executed in Rome (104).

Julius; *see* Caesar.

Junius; *see* Brutus and Pennus and Silanus.

Jupiter, the greatest of the gods of Italy, III, 102, 105; "Supreme and Best," III, 104; father of Hercules, I, 118.

Justice, the second Cardinal Virtue, I, 15, 17, 20–41; in what consisting, I, 20; not fully comprehended, III, 69; queen of all the virtues, III, 28; most important, I, 153; close to Nature, I, 153; III, 24; rule of duty, I, 29–30; in war, I, 38–40; and generosity, I, 42; *vs.* Wisdom, I, 152–157; *vs.* Fortitude, I, 157; *vs.* Temperance, I, 159–160; indispensable in business, II, 40; inspires most confidence, II, 34; the best means to popularity, II, 39; to glory, II, 43; always expedient, III, 96; in conflict with apparent expediency, III, 40, 86.

Labeo, Quintus Fabius, grandson of Fabius Maximus, consul (183); injustice of, I, 33.

Lacedaemon; *see* Sparta.

Laciads, citizens of the deme of Lacia, west of Athens, the home of Miltiades, II, 64.

Laelius, Gaius, surnamed "the Wise," III, 16; statesman; soldier under Scipio at Carthage, successful against Viriathus, II, 40; a Stoic, pupil of Diogenes and Panaetius; a man of endless charm and wit, I, 90, 108; his friendship for Africanus immortalized, II, 31; a man of letters, centre of the literary group comprising also Scipio, Panaetius, Polybius, Terence, Lucilius.

Lanarius, Gaius, Calpurnius, III, 66.

Latin, study of combined with Greek, I, 1–2.

Latins, the people of Latium, the province in which Rome is situated, the first territory added to Rome, I, 38; decisive battle on the Anio, III, 112.

Law, the origin of, II, 41–42; the majesty of, I, 148; as a profession, II, 65; its decline with the end of the republic, II, 67; III, 2.

Lentulus; Publius Cornelius Lentulus Spinther, the splendour of his aedileship (63), II, 57; as consul (57) he was largely instrumental in securing Cicero's recall from banishment.

Leuctra, a town of Boeotia, where the Spartans under Cleombrotus were disastrously defeated by Epaminondas and the Thebans (371), I, 61; II, 26.

Love, how won, II, 32; *vs.* fear, II, 23–26.

Lucullus, Lucius Licinius (110–56), surnamed Ponticus for his victories over Mithradates (84–66); famed for his wealth and magnificence, I, 140; for the splendour of his aedileship with his brother Marcus (79), II, 57; with him prosecuted Servilius to avenge their father whom he had accused of bribery and corruption, II, 50; patron of letters, especially of the poet Archias.

Lucullus, Marcus Licinius, associated with his brother Lucius (*q.v.*), II, 50, 57; soldier and orator.

Lusitania, western Spain, practically modern Portugal, II, 40.

Lutatius; *see* Catulus.

Luxury, a vice, I, 92, 106, 123.

Lycurgus (9th century), the famous lawgiver of Sparta, author (?) of the Spartan constitution, I, 76.

Lydia, the central country of western Asia Minor, III, 38.

Lysander, the Spartan admiral who defeated the Athenians at Aegospotami (405), received the capitulation of Athens (404), established the Thirty Tyrants (403), and gave Sparta her leadership, I, 76, 109.

Lysander, the ephor (241), a descendant of the admiral, a friend of King Agis (*q.v.*), sought to bring

Macedonicus, won his surname by his victories over Andriscus (148); a political rival and yet a good friend of the younger Scipio, I, 87.
Metellus; Quintus Caecilius Metellus Numidicus, nephew of the preceding, statesman and soldier; as consul (109), carried on the war with Jugurtha with distinguished success, III, 79.
Metrodorus, of Lampsacus (330–277), the most distinguished of the disciples of Epicurus; his Epicureanism was of the grossly sensual sort; his conception of happiness misunderstood by Cicero, III. 117.
Milo, Titus Annius, an unscrupulous and turbulent fellow; as tribune (57) he did much for Cicero's recall and made a sworn enemy of Clodius (*q.v.*); hired gladiators to force his own election, II, 58; defended without success by Cicero for killing Clodius.
Minerva, goddess of thought, temperament, wit, I, 97.
Minos, son of Zeus (Jupiter) and king of Crete; because of his upright life he was made judge with Aeacus (*q.v.*) in Hades, I, 97.
Moderation, defined, I, 142.
Modesty, I, 126-129.
Mucius; *see* Scaevola.
Mummius; Lucius Mummius Achaicus, as consul (146) broke up the Achaean League, razed Corinth to the ground, I, 35; II, 46; carried to Italy untold treasures of wealth and art, II, 76.

Naples, the beautiful Greek city of Campania, I, 33.
Nasica; *see* Scipio.
Neptune, god of the sea, I, 32; II, 94.
New Academy; *see* Academy.
Nicocles, tyrant of Sicyon, II, 81.
Nola, a city in Campania, loyal to Rome, I, 33.
Norbanus, Gaius, tribune (95), impeached (94) for treason, II, 49; consul (83).
Numantia, the capital of Celtiberia, razed to the ground after a long siege by the younger Scipio, I, 35, 76; treacherously treated by Rome, III, 109.
Numicius, Tiberius, colleague of Quintus Maelius (*q.v.*), III, 109.

Oath, significance of, I, 39, 40; III, 102 fg.; fidelity to, I, 39, 40; III, 99-112; violation of, III, 113 fg.; *see* Perjury.
Octavius, Gnaeus, as praetor commanded the fleet against Perseus (168) and gained a triumph; consul (165), I, 138.
Octavius, Marcus, tribune (120); had the corn law of Gaius Gracchus repealed and secured the passage of a new and more conservative one, II, 72.
Old Age, duties peculiar to, I, 123; worst vices of, I, 123.
Old Comedy, that of Aristophanes, Cratinus, Eupolis, etc., the comedy of personal abuse, I, 104.
Orata, Gaius Sergius Silus, praetor (97), III, 67.
Oratory, a division of speech, I, 132; divisions of, II, 49; a means for winning favour, II, 48; a means for service, II, 65-71; a power to save, II, 51.
Orderliness, defined, I, 142; of action, I, 142-145.
Orestes; Gnaeus Aufidius Orestes Aurelianus, consul (71), II, 58.

Palamedes, the inventor; exposed Ulysses's trick, III, 98; treacherously done to death in revenge.
Palatine, the hill above the forum on the south; east of the Capitol, I, 138.
Panaetius, of Rhodes (180-111 *ca.*), Stoic philosopher, disciple of Diogenes and Antipater (*q.v.*) at Athens, close friend of Laelius (*q.v.*) and Scipio, I, 90; II, 76; popularized philosophy, II, 35; wrote a book on moral duty, III, 7; failed to define duty, I, 7; classification of duty, I, 9; omits third division, I, 152, 161; II, 88; reasons for omission, III, 7-18, 34; how it would have been met, III, 33; other omissions, II, 86; on co-operation, II, 16; defends lawyers'

# INDEX

# INDEX

in speech, I, 132 fg.; in the home, I, 138-140.
Propylaea, the magnificent gateway to the Acropolis of Athens, built (437-431) by Pericles and Mnesicles at a cost of £500,000, II, 60.
Prosecution, II, 49; to be rarely undertaken, II, 50; a public service, II, 50.
Prudence; *see* Widsom.
Ptolemy, Philadelphus (309-247), king of Egypt, patron of art and letters, had the Bible translated; vastly rich, II, 82.
Public Lands, private occupation to be maintained, I, 21.
Public Service, as a career, I, 70 fg.; as a duty, I, 72; as an honour, I, 73; free from partisanship, I, 85-86; self-seeking, I, 87; vindictiveness, I, 88; anger, I, 89; guided by wisdom, I, 155-156.
Public shows, extravagant expenditures, II, 55-60; expected of an aedile, II, 57-60.
Pulcher, Gaius Claudius, son of Appius, aedile (99), II, 57; consul (92).
Public Wars; *see* Carthage.
Pyrrho, of Elis (fourth century), founder of the school of the Sceptics; held that virtue is the only good, that truth and knowledge are unattainable; his ethical theories rejected, I, 6.
Pyrrhus (318-272), king of Epirus, descended from Achilles and Aeacus, I, 38; a daring soldier and a gallant enemy, I, 38; a career of adventure and conquest, I, 38; III, 86; invaded Italy (280-275); the story of the poisoner, I, 40; III, 86; (*see also* Fabricius); invaded Macedonia (273) and the enemy's troops joined him, II, 26; killed in Argos (272).
Pythagorean, a follower of Pythagoras or member of his secret fraternity, I, 155; III, 45.
Pythagoras, of Samos (sixth century), studied in the Orient, great mathematician; moral and religious teacher; serious, ascetic, I, 108; taught transmigration of souls; founded a secret brotherhood of ideal friendship, I, 56; asceticism was the rule of practice, with deep meditation and lofty aspiration.
Pythian, epithet of Apollo, from Pytho, another name for Delphi, II, 77.
Pythius, of Syracuse, his dishonesty, III, 58.

Quirinus, the Sabine name for the deified Romulus, III, 41.

Recklessness, to be avoided, I, 81, 83.
Regulus, Marcus Atilius, a favourite hero of old Rome; consul (267 and 256), annihilated the Carthaginian fleet, took many towns, was finally (255) defeated and taken prisoner, I, 39; III, 99; his famous embassy and the ethics of his conduct, III, 99-115.
Remus, twin brother of Romulus, slain for leaping in derision over the new walls of Rome, III, 41.
Reproof, how administered, I, 136.
Republic, the Roman; its glory, II, 2; the protectorate of the world, II, 27; its downfall, I, 35; II, 2-5, 29, 65; III, 2, 4, 83; the tyrant's sway, II, 23-29; III, 81-85; enslaved, III, 84-85.
Retirement, the life of, I, 69-70.
Rhodes, a large island off the coast of Caria, III, 50.
Rhodian, a native of Rhodes, II, 50, 57; III, 63.
Riches, the object of acquiring, I, 25; proper use of, I, 68; compared with virtue, III, 24 (*see* Wealth).
Roman, of or belonging to Rome, III, 58; people, I, 33; III, 79, 83-86, 105, 109, 114; the people of Rome, II, 75; celebrated for courage, I, 61; champion of justice, I, 36; II, 26; hatred of tyranny and injustice, III, 19; atonement for tyranny and injustice, II, 27-29; their enslavement, III, 85-86.
Rome, the capital of the Empire and mistress of the world, I, 39, 40; III, 73, 79, 99, 112, 113.
Romulus, the mythical king, founder of Rome, III, 40; builder of its walls; not justified in slaying his brother, III, 41.

# INDEX

**Roscius**, **Sextus**, *of* **Ameria**, accused by Chrysogonus, a freedman of Sulla's, of murdering his father; bravely and successfully defended by Cicero at the age of twenty-six, II, 51.
Rupilius, an actor otherwise unknown, I, 114.
Rutilius; Publius Rutilius Rufus, a disciple of Publius Scaevola, II, 47; of Panaetius, III, 10; with Quintus Scaevola in Asia he repressed the extortion of the publicans, was banished, and devoted his life to philosophy and literature, III, 10.

Sabine, belonging to the province of central Italy, III, 74; the Sabines, unfriendly to Rome till subdued and added to the empire (290), 1, 35, 38.
Sacred Laws; the *Leges Sacratae*. laws for the violation of which the offender was nominally consecrated to some god—i.e., laden with a curse, III, 111.
Salamis, the island and straits directly in front of the Piraeus (*q.v.*), where (480) Themistocles and the allied Greeks virtually annihilated the fleets of Persia, I, 61, 75.
Sale, fraud in sale of real estate, III, 54-64; laws concerning, III, 65-71; of slaves, III, 71-72.
Salmacis, a fountain (and nymph) at Halicarnassus, whose waters made men who drank them weak and effeminate, I, 61.
Samnites, the brave, liberty-loving people of Samnium, a province of south-central Italy; after seventy-one years (343-272) of war with Rome admitted to citizenship, I, 38; famous for their victory at the Caudine Forks, III, 109; Gaius Pontius, II, 75.
Sanitation; *see* Health.
Sardinia, the large island north of Sicily, made a province (238), misgoverned, II, 50.
Satrius; Marcus Minucius Basilus Satrianus, adopted by Lucius Minucius Basilus, his inheritance, III, 74.
Scaevola, Publius Mucius, father of the pontifex maximus, consul (133) and friend of Tiberius Gracchus, an expert in the pontifical law, II, 47.
Scaevola, Quintus Mucius, the Augur, son of the preceding, son-in-law of Laelius, friend of Africanus, consul (117), preceptor to Cicero; simple in his greatness, I, 109.
Scaevola, Quintus Mucius, the Pontifex Maximus, son of Publius, preceptor of Cicero; orator, jurist; authority on the civil law, his business honour, III, 62, 70; followed his father's calling, I, 116; magnificent aedileship, II, 57; consul (95), III, 47.
Scaurus, Marcus Aemilius, consul (115); partisan rather than statesman, I, 76; ambassador to Jugurtha (112), notorious corruptionist, but loyal aristocrat; hence Cicero's praise, I, 108.
Scaurus, Marcus Aemilius, son of the preceding, stepson of Sulla, aedile (58) with extraordinary magnificence, II, 57; governor of Sardinia (56), which he plundered outrageously; successfully defended by Cicero and Hortensius; later (52) condemned and banished, I, 138; palace on the Palatine, I, 138.
Scipio, Gnaeus, Cornelius, brother of Publius (*see* following); consul (222) with Marcus Marcellus; with Publius in Spain (217-211); a gallant soldier, I, 61; III, 16.
Scipio, Publius Cornelius, brother of Gnaeus and father of the elder Africanus, I, 121; consul (218), defeated by Hannibal at the Ticinus; waged war in Spain (217-211); a gallant soldier, I, 61; III, 16.
Scipio; Publius Cornelius Scipio Africanus Major (234-183), the son of Publius, I, 121; grandfather of the Gracchi, II, 80; defeated Hannibal at Zama (202) and closed the war; never idle in his zeal for Rome, III, 1-4.
Scipio, Publius Cornelius, son of Africanus Major, adoptive father of Africanus Minor; gifted men-

tally but physically disqualified for an active career, I, 121.
Scipio; Publius Cornelius Scipio Aemilianus Africanus Minor, son of Aemilius Paulus Macedonicus, I, 116, 121; adopted son of Publius Africanus's son, I, 121; friend and pupil of Panaetius, I, 90; intimate friend of Laelius (*q.v.*) and devoted to literature; serious, earnest, I, 108; self-control, II, 76; a great soldier, I, 76, 116; at Pydna (168) with his father; captured and destroyed Carthage (146) and Numantia (133), I, 35; II, 76; a statesman of high ideals, a bitter rival and yet a friend of Quintus Metellus, I, 87.
Scipio; Publius Cornelius Scipio Nasica Serapio, known chiefly as the man who led the riot and murdered Tiberius Gracchus, I, 76, 109.
Scipio; Publius Cornelius Scipio Nasica, son of the preceding; died in his consulship (111); a charming gentleman and a brilliant speaker, I, 109.
Secret sin, II, 37 fg.
Seius, Marcus, reduced the price of corn and regained his lost popularity, II, 58.
Self-control; *see* Temperance.
Self-sacrifice, III, 25; of Regulus, III, 97-115.
Sergius, Gaius; *see* Orata.
Sicily, the great island south-west of Italy, fertile and rich, occupied along the coasts by prosperous Greek colonies, a Roman province (212 on), an easy prey for rapacious governors, as Verres whom Cicero prosecuted (70), II, 50.
Sicyon, a city near Corinth, famous as a centre of art; Aratus and the tyranny, II, 81-82.
Silanus, Decimus Junius, stepfather of Marcus Brutus, consul (62), aedile, II, 57.
Slaves, duty toward, I, 41; III, 89.
Social Instinct, man and beast, I, 12, 50; bees, I, 157; leads to justice, I, 157; weighed against justice, I, 159 fg.
Society, principles of, I, 50-57; III, 53; rights of, I, 21; service to, I, 153, 155.
Socrates (469-399), the great philosopher and teacher, II, 43; his ethics, III, 11, 77; his perfect poise, I, 90; brilliant dialectician, with a profound meaning in every word, I, 108; personal eccentricities, I, 148. "The noblest, ay, and the wisest and most righteous man that we have ever known."
Socratic, following Socrates, I, 104, 134; II, 87; most schools of philosophy are based on the teaching of Socrates—the Academy, I, 2; the Peripatetic, I, 2; III, 20; the Cynic, I, 128; the Cyrenaic, III, 116; the Stoic, I, 6; etc.
Sol, the sungod, father of Phaëthon, III, 94.
Solon, the great lawgiver of Athens (638-558 *ca.*), poet, soldier, statesman; his feigned madness and the acquisition of Salamis, I, 108; his constitution and the reorganized Areopagus, I, 75.
Sophocles, the great tragic poet (495-406), supreme on the Athenian stage (468-441); general in the war against Samos (440), I, 144.
Sparta, capital of Lacedaemon in the south-eastern part of the Peloponnesus, III, 99; constitution of Lycurgus, I, 76; national character, I, 64; position at end of Persian wars, I, 76; at end of Peloponnesian war, I, 76; her arsenal, III, 49; disasters, I, 84; despotic, II, 26; cause of her fall, II, 77, 80.
Stoics, adherents of the school founded by Zeno, an offshoot from Cynicism, I, 128; refounded by Chrysippus; philosophy with them is practical, making life accord with Nature's laws, III, 13; virtue and philosophy are identical; virtue the only good, I, 6; III, 11, 12; moral wrong the only evil, III, 106; pain no evil, III, 105; no degrees of right or wrong, I, 10; etymologists, I, 23; define fortitude, I, 62; temperance, I, 142; duties, III, 14; controversies, III, 91; their right to teach ethics, I, 6;

Cicero adopts their teaching, I, 6; III, 20; common interests, I, 22; their theology a pantheistic materialism, God working in his providence, III, 102; representative Stoics, II, 51, 86; III, 51.

Sulla; Lucius Cornelius Sulla Felix (138-78), noble, profligate, brilliant genius; would stoop to anything, I, 109; soldier against Jugurtha, Mithradates, Marius, Rome; statesman; reformed the constitution; absolute monarch of Rome (81-79); treatment of tributary allies, III, 87; confiscator, I, 43; II, 29; overturned the old morals, II, 27, Cicero opposed him, II, 51.

Sulla, Publius Cornelius, nephew of the dictator, II, 29; defended by Cicero on charge of complicity in Catiline's conspiracy.

Sulla, Cornelius, a freedman of the dictator, II, 29.

Sulpicius; Gaius Sulpicius Galus, consul (166); famous astronomer, I, 19; predicted an eclipse of the moon.

Sulpicius; Publius Sulpicius Rufus (124-88), an eminent orator of little character, II, 49.

Sungod; *see* Sol.

Superbus; *see* Tarquin.

Syracuse, a great Greek city in south-eastern Sicily, rich in art and in goods; ruled by Dion, I, 155; Dionysius, II, 25; III, 45; a popular resort, III, 58.

Tantalus, son of Zeus (Jupiter) and father of Pelops (*q.v.*), III, 84.

Tarquin; Lucius Tarquinius Superbus, the last king of Rome (535-510), a cruel tyrant, expelled by Brutus and Collatinus, III, 40.

Tarquins, the kinsmen of Tarquinius Superbus, all expelled (510), III, 40.

Taxation, levying of, II, 74.

Temperance, the fourth Cardinal Virtue, I, 93-151; definition, I, 93; the passions, I, 102; speech, I, 103; *vs.* Justice, I, 159-160; essential to success; II, 77; *vs.* apparent Expediency, III, 116 fg.

Terence; Publius Terentius Afer (195-159), a comic poet, friend of Laelius and Scipio; six plays are left; quotation from the *Heauton Timorumenus*, I, 30; the *Eunuchus*, I, 150.

Thebe, daughter of Jason and wife of Alexander of Pherae, II, 25.

Thebes, the capital of Boeotia, home of Pindar and Epaminondas, I, 155.

Themistocles, brilliant statesman of Athens, II, 16; gave Athens her fleet and saved Greece at Salamis (480), I, 75; consummate general, I, 108; not always scrupulous in his methods, III, 49; his valuation of character, II, 71.

Theophrastus, of Lesbos, favourite pupil and successor of Aristotle, a marvellous teacher, master of Demetrius of Phalerum, I, 3; a prolific author; cited, II, 56, 64.

Theopompus, of Chios (fourth century), pupil of Isocrates, orator and historian, II, 40.

Thermopylae, a narrow pass on the seashore between Thessaly and Locris, held by Leonidas and his three hundred against the hosts of Xerxes (480), I, 61.

Theseus, the great legendary hero of Athens, benefactor of the world; uniter of Athens and Attica; father of Hippolytus (*q.v.*) by Antiope; husband of Phaedra; his son's death, I, 32; III, 94.

Thrace, the vast country north of the Aegean; though the home of Orpheus, Linus, etc., it was generally considered barbarous, II, 25.

Thyestes, son of Pelops and brother of Atreus (*q.v.*), (III, 102).

Timotheus, admiral of the Athenian fleet (378-356), compared with his father Conon, I, 116.

Torquatus; *see* Manlius.

Trades; *see* Vocation.

Troezen, a city of Argolis, near the shore opposite Aegina; the asylum of the Athenians at the approach of Xerxes, III, 48.

Trusts, when not to be restored, III, 95.

Truth, the search after, I, 13.

# INDEX